D0513935

JACK STROP VD & SCAR

'Shiner' Wright RN retd

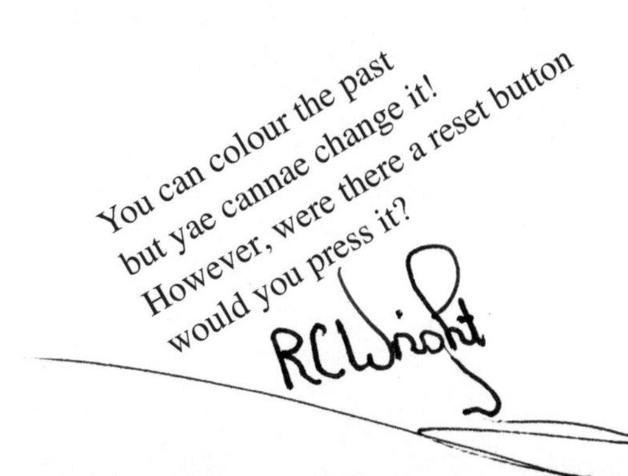

Copyright © Bob Wright 2002 Collectors' Edition - Published 2014

ISBN 978-0-9566043-0-9

Title:
JACK STROP - name traditionally attributed to a stroppy sailor
VD & SCAR - Officers were awarded a VC & bar, whereas all
lowly Jack got was VD & scar

Cowan Print, Edinburgh. email: peter@cowanprint.com
Typeset by Cowan Print and Jim Innes
Graphic design by Jim Innes. www.jiminnes.co.uk

Printed in Great Britain by Martins the Printers Ltd, Berwick-upon-Tweed

Acknowledgements

Many thanks to:

Ossie Jones

for brilliant cover artwork and caricatures of Laughing Sailor
135 Ashbourne Road, Liverpool LI7 9QQ

William Bryant Salmon

for information into the sinking of Ethel Crawford by U-218

Phil Rowe

Editor & publisher of the The Tenby Times, for his help & encouragement
email: phil.rowe7@ntlworld.com

Pusser

for all the memories

Contents

Ahoy There Matey!

It's hard-going gettin'through some books because the authors have attempted to be too clever - in reading this pungent, controversial 'near the knuckle' tale you'll find there's nothing clever about me; and conclude I'm no academic!

Told in the colourful vocabulary and perspective of 'Jolly Jack' – for all the unsung heroes of the Lower Deck past, present and future. This book is meant as a tribute to **almost** everyone in it: cheers guys, it was an education and an honour; so, keep the faith – you were all, in your own way, stars!

The language is '**choice**' for the sake of authenticity.

Radical, explicit, outspoken; yet hopefully amusing!

Swing them lamps, pull up a bollard, settle down an' make yersel comfy cos I'm gonna tell yer a story of how it was in the Royal Navy of the 'Swinging Sixties.' Days when life was simpler. Days when being gay didn't mean being a 'fairy'. 'The Glory Days', before the roof fell in, when our, *now floundering,* country was known as Great Britain, revered throughout the world; and although nothing's perfect, a nice place to live and be proud of. Yes, a time before decimalization, inflation, greed, laziness, drugs, AIDS, political correctness, racism and now, **thanks to our grinning leader**, terrorism. A time when the streets were clean and we could 'call a spade a spade'. When did **you** last hear good news? All these things don't just happen! As we know, a fair percentage of the human race are no more than self-centred mindless tosspots, with limited or no vision, many of whom have contributed to creating the paranoid stressful world we now enjoy.

After digesting the above I sincerely hope you yourself are outwith that category. So, indulge me, and read on regardless! In doing so you'll no doubt conclude that I'm opinionated, cynical, judgemental and resent authority. The latter I confess to be true, but only when I see the said authority as **not up to the job.**

Don't believe a word your husbands, partners, lovers or fathers tell you when waxing lyrical, as most were no better than me - young guys away from home get up to all kinds o' nonsense, and there's nothing to beat a laugh with the boys. These were undoubtedly the finest years of my life: consequently I'm adamant that anyone not having experienced Service life **totally missed out!**

R.C.W. April 2002

1: It's Not Down To Me Chief!

Och, it's never yersel' is it! You've just caught me, an' you'll notice ah've got ma new threads oan. Well, ah'm off tae the gospel singin' followed by a bit o' line dancin' wherra hope tae pick up an auld minger, preferably o' mixed race, take her tae Harry's Bar tae soften her up wae a wee scoop o' the bevvy. Then it's doon tae 'the Front' at Silverknowes forra bit o' doggin': well anyway, now that you've found me sit yersel doon and let me unburden masel, as there's time fir a wee story afore ah skedaddle.

This tale starts *(triggered by a family visit, a question and an old photograph album)* way back in the mists o' time, long before my enlightening journey on life's bumpy roller coaster - but, before introducin' masel, first *if I may* a brief family history to explain whair ah'm comin' frae' an' goin' to, so haud yer wheesht and bear wi' me.

My paternal great-grandfather, Robert Carnie, was a fisherman living in and sailing from Newhaven in Scotland towards the end of the nineteenth century. Newhaven was then a prosperous fishing village, situated midway between Leith and Granton on the south shore of the Firth of Forth, where they trawled for oysters and, I suppose, everything else worth harvesting which came up the Forth in the various seasons. It was a close-knit community; as fisherfolk of these times tended to be. The men caught the fish, not always in Home Waters, as they'd follow their quarry, often sailing north and round the ominous sounding Cape Wrath to the west coast of Scotland, going as far as the Irish Sea. This, in those days was a long haul in little fishing boats, which I understand had no engines, just sails that, on calm days, had to be complemented with strong arms giving it 'the old heave-ho' on big oars. Wotta game! *Let's hope the money was good!*

There was a Fishermen's Union ***(The Society of Free Fishermen)***, but the Union back then was far removed from the all too powerful bolshie Unions we know today, which have lost more jobs for the British workers than they ever won. Then, it related more to a brethren thing, ensuring no poor souls falling on hard times went hungry and suffered without help.

So much for the men of the village, as it's pretty obvious what they did

- so let's talk about the womenfolk! Yes, the womenfolk were also a hardy bunch, reputed to be the backbone of the village's economy, which without whose noble efforts would not have been so buoyant. These matriarchs certainly knew the meaning of work; and many blessed with plenty in the brains department when it came to commercial acumen. Not only did the Newhaven fishwives mend nets, gut fish, do laundry, keep hoose, look efter and feed the Newhaven bairns, they also regularly attended church and sang in the world renowned ***Newhaven Fisherlassies' Choir***.

The core of these overworked fishwives trudged to Edinburgh and beyond; weighed down from carrying their wares in heavy creels, to sell straight to the customer; *nae middlemen fir thaim*. Some of these headstrong ladies travelling far and wide daily, to places such as the Borders by way of trains from Edinburgh's Waverley Station. Crikey! Aren't you glad to be living now, and not back in "The Good Old Days"?

There is an extremely informative small museum beside Harry Ramsden's chippie at Newhaven Harbour with many interesting facts, photos, models and displays, telling this story so much better than I ever could, so don't take my word as gospel - go, see for yourself!

Anyway, getting back to my family's side of the Newhaven story - there's an excellent large oil painting, recently hung in a prominent position at the staircase in my aunt's hall. I hadn't seen this portrait before and, if the truth be known, never as much as thought of the family lineage beyond my two sets of grandparents; so asked, who was this imposing strong-featured subject encased in the heavy gilt frame, proudly displayed for all to see? Turns out to be my great-grandfather, who'd been, as already said, a Newhaven fisherman and had lived in the flat above Masons the Bakers, whose shop is on the other side of the road running past Newhaven Harbour. Crivvens! I couldn't count the number of times I've stopped the car outside this bakery and nipped in for a hot pie, or whatever took my fancy, little knowing of our family connection with the building.

My grandfather, Robert Harvey Wright, I remember very well, although he 'checked oot' way back in 1955 in Leith hospital, as the result of a broken hip and pneumonia. It was sheer bad luck that he met his end this way, as he was a great one for visiting friends and relatives, which was exactly what he was doing when he suffered a fatal accident.

One chilly Friday evening, quite early, in fact straight from work, when on his way to visit relatives, he slipped on the icy pavement, went down like a ton o' bricks and broke his hip outside Leith Academy; only yards from his destination. Because of his injury he couldn't get up - this being a Friday night in Scotland, passers-by took him to be just another drunk. Such a shame, because, although no angel, the man never touched a drop, so he lay on the cold pavement with unconcerned people stepping over him until some kind soul offered help, and called for an ambulance.

It's sad how we all get tarred with the same brush and so often the innocent suffer because of others' failings. In saying that, he deserved better, but I am not pointing the finger and condemning the passers-by, because I'm aware I would have made the same wrong judgement and walked on, looking the other way, while pretending not to notice.

So far all I've said about the old boy concerns his death, while it's his life that's more than worthy of a mention; he being quite a character and, I'm told, a brilliant craftsman-engineer. It's a pity that when youngsters we are too busy growing up and getting on with life in our own important little worlds to care, or even realize what those who have gone before us achieved in their lifetimes; *but that's just the way it is.*

Everyone of course has a story, but sadly, there's not always someone to listen and I guess a lot of interesting people think that what they did so long ago is not worth talking about now. So, to me, as a youngster, he was just my grandfather - and what could be more boring? But of course at that tender age what did I know about him? **Nothing!** I now know that this man, on finishing his engineering apprenticeship at Rosyth in the early 1900s, went off to seek his fortune in 'the good old U S of A', working there awhile before returning with 'a wedge'to Newhaven, where he made an 'honest woman' of my grandmother, who came from one of the prominent Newhaven families. Her name was Mary Carnie - Carnie incidentally being my middle name; and my younger brother's given name.

By 1920 they had two sons, David Moodie Wright aged six, and Robert Harvey Carnie Wright *known as Roy (my father-to-be)* then two. That year the family packed their belongings and sailed off to America where Grandfather got work as an engineer, landing a 'plum job' with R.C.A. Victor; one of the most successful recording companies of that time. All

this I've gleaned from Aunt Sophie, who was born there in a house that - **wait for it!** - my artisan grandfather built, in Lenola, New Jersey. This was no ramshackle affair - a proper large dwelling in the American style: you know the sort of design, high gables, big veranda with pillars; in fact, a pitch I'd be proud to own today. This was all very evident from the photos my aunt showed me while telling the story, adding she has been back to see it since, and counted herself lucky to be invited in, where she saw the bedroom she used as a child, thus stirring many nostalgic memories.

Anyway, after the family had lived in America for the required time, Grandfather obtained the forms necessary for them to become U.S. citizens. But, as luck would have it, the day he went to the office concerned, to get the federal documents processed, it was closed; and being a busy man he never found the time to go back - this may sound lazy, but it was probably a long round trip on a Greyhound bus; remember this is America and many years ago. So, when the Wall Street Crash and 'the depression' hit 'the promised land', understandably those not U.S. nationals were first in line for 'the chop'. This was obviously a bitter blow, but being a canny Scot who had been in a good job, I'm sure he'd stashed a few dollars for a rainy day. **A Rainy Day**, it must've looked like a monsoon was thunderin' o'er them thar prairies. *'Buddy, can you spare a dime'?*

David, by then twenty, volunteered to return to 'the old country' to find a job, so in the spring of 1933 he sailed back to 'Bonnie Scotland' to live with his granny, at number 8 Pitt Street, just off Newhaven Road, in the Bonnington district of Leith. He found work in, the then thriving Newhaven Fishmarket, driving one of the many lorries. There were no driving tests and licences in those days, *as he was always happy to tell us* - I guess he must have learned to drive in the States so never ever sat a test, and I must say at this point, there were occasions when this was all too evident.

Uncle David was a well-known figure, especially then, speaking as he did with his 'Noo Joisey' twang - a novelty he proudly kept all his days. He used expressions such as 'Luvva Duck' and was affectionately known as 'The Newhaven Yank'. David was a kind man, who helped many in his lifetime, liked the ladies, but *'smarter than the average bear'* managed to remain a batchelor, always paid everything 'on the nail', a church-goer who never used alcohol or tobacco and, take note all you sinners, hopheads

and druggies, lived to the ripe old age of eighty-eight.

The rest of the family returned to Scotland two years after David, in 1935, by which time my father, Roy, was a strapping eighteen-year-old and Aunt Sophie, a pretty girl of twelve, not yet completed her schooling.

Although work was hard to find my grandfather soon got employment, adding weight to the earlier statement, as to him being a skilled engineer. He worked at Rosyth Dockyard for some time, which in these days was a hive of industry, as Britain *then, a major player* had a vast navy preparing for war. When I knew him in the 1940s and 50s he was employed by Brown Brothers; a large marine engineering company, situated in the Broughton district of Edinburgh, about four miles from where the family now lived at 3 Laverockbank Crescent. This is an arts and crafts semi-detached villa sitting on a hillside overlooking Newhaven, probably less than a hundred yards *(sorry - today I must say, about ninety metres)* from the Firth of Forth's south shore, with a view 'to die for'. In the front parlour a pair of large binoculars sat on the ledge of the bay window, with which to watch all types of craft steaming by, but what happened in the late forties put paid to that and spoiled the Crescent forever.

We've all seen it: it happened then and it happens now. There was *allegedly* a bit of palm greasing at the City Planning Department; the hillside gets squared off and ***abracadabra*** a big multi-storey block of flats appear: now I ask, would you rather have the Firth of Forth or a naff apartment development to look at? **No contest!** That's blatant corruption for you; "Psst, bung me ***enough*** pal and I'll see it's rubber stamped! NEXT!" - politicians, councillors and local government officials - sleazebags, 'on the take', with their sticky fingers in the pie, couldn't give a toss! With the stroke of a pen, 25% was wiped from the value of every property in that picture book *once perfect,* crescent.

So anyway, there they were back home, living in a nice house at *the now trendy* Newhaven. Grandfather in a decent job, David driving lorries, my father-to-be, Roy, is learning his craft on the traditional fishing boats; *later graduating to steam trawlers* - and Sophie continuing her education at the nearby Trinity Academy. All that, as they say, is history and we are now coming close to my unplanned and untimely arrival.

My mother's name was Beatrice May *known as Nancy* Webber who,

before meeting and marrying my father, lived at her family home; this being 27 Restalrig Terrace - a substantial, stonebuilt, Victorian end-terraced villa on the edge of the Leith district. Her father Bickham Webber, a provision and egg merchant in Leith, was brought up in an orphanage in Wales and had married my maternal grandmother in Cardiff on 11TH February 1901. I guess they must have come to Edinburgh because of his business, which could only have been lucrative, since he managed to keep a wife and nine children *(four from a second marriage)* in relative comfort. Yes, Mother had five brothers and three sisters; par for the course, and encouraged when the Empire required 'cannon fodder'. I presume most of the siblings were educated at Leith Academy; a short distance from the family home: although Mother *(the eldest)* attended James Gillespie's School for Girls, her sisters were schooled at 'The Academy' - mentioned because years later this was where I would be incarcerated to receive my secondary education.

At the time Mother and Father met, she was a shorthand typist in Edinburgh and, like most, enjoyed going to the various dancehalls of the day. I understand they met at the Marine Gardens, which *being not far from home* was a great favourite of hers. The Marine Gardens was, seemingly, quite something with, I'm told, a dancehall, a roller-skating rink and, at the far end, a boating pond. All this was situated just a stone's throw from the then very popular Portobello, which was a great attraction with its beach, open-air swimming pool, funfair and penny-arcade.

Sadly, the stately Olympic-size pool *of art deco design* was demolished some years ago - I think that must have been in the late 1980s, consequently Portobello will never again achieve the popularity and status it once benefitted from. The Marine Gardens had vanished long before this, probably during the Second World War, in the early 1940s. On the site there has been *for as long as I can remember* a huge Council Bus Depot with to the west of that, one of our city's 'Golden Mile' car lots, and at the far end the Edinburgh Cat and Dog Home.

Here! I'm losing the plot - so let's get back to the story; my parents met, had a brief courtship and married on 13TH of November 1937; and guess who was a guest at the wedding? **Yes, it was me!** Although as yet unseen, as I was to make my, already mentioned, 'untimely arrival' on 20TH February 1938 and we hardly need a calculator to work that one out,

do we? - ***oops***, so it seems I was a mistake - a 'love child', conceived oot o' wedlock; that's a good start, **eh!** I'm told the bold pair went ahead and got hitched (*thank you God*) quietly without informing their parents and families, **then** went to 'face the music' at their respective homes. As you can imagine, in both cases this went down like a lead balloon.

I've often wondered if I was conceived on damp grass; which might go a long way to explaining the arthritis I enjoy today. Anyway, when the shock waves settled they were given help to buy a two-bedroom terraced villa - so, there was 'a new kid on the block' at 50 Logie Green Road.

Wedding photograph: Nancy and Roy, 13TH November 1937

2: Logie Green Road

Logie Green Road, lying in the Broughton district of Edinburgh, was an interesting place to grow up, surrounded by adventurous haunts for young boys. At the top of the road beside St Philip's Episcopal Church we had the cobbled entrance leading to a railway-siding incorporating the coalyard and Scottish Spade & Shovel Works. Halfway down on the other side was a sizeable piece of wasteground, known as 'the Ditch' - in the middle of the Ditch sat a huge round tank of water; there for fire engines to draw from in the event of German incendiary bombs causing fires during World War II. Further down on the same side *(right)* was the entrance to Symington's Camp Coffee Works, also giving access to the back of Duncan's Chocolate Factory; famous in their day for Hazelnut Whirls. Next was the car park and entrance to Powderhall Greyhound Racing Stadium; adjacent to Waterson's the printers and across from Symington's was a wooden Christian Mission Hut *(which, surprisingly is still there)*. Beyond 'the Mission' was another piece of wasteground, behind which there was a brace of tennis courts *(pour le Jeeves and Wooster set)* and some allotments boundaried by the railway embankment. The last buildings *bottom left* housed another printer, McGlashen & Cummings, and Lady Haig's Poppy Factory, but get this, at the foot of Logie Green Road there runs the Water of Leith - a fantastic source of fun both up and down river for hyper young scamps - and finally, on the other side of the river lies the grassy knolled Warriston Cemetery - Victorian, large and although believed to be haunted, a magnet of mystery and excitement for all who dared set foot.

Between the places mentioned, there were of course dwellings; traditional Edinburgh tenements on the right, and small two-bedroom semis to the left. Well, as you know, all streets have their characters and Logie Green was blessed with plenty; so we'll start with 'the street gossip' - Mrs Kemlie, who lived in a first floor flat opposite our house - in her 'widow's weeds' *and curlers still in* she looked like an old Pictish warrior queen from bygone times, and spent so much of the day hanging out her window

that she'd put a moth-eaten pillow on the cill, to cushion her podgy arms. We thought she was a nosey bitch, but on reflection "the auld gasbag" may have been housebound. Remember, there was no television in those days and the old wifie possibly never had a radio, so, for Mrs Kemlie, the street was a theatre and the window, her balcony.

In the adjoining tenement we had 'Biddy' Lynch, a nippy ratbag, whose man had left her, in favour of a Coldstream Guards Officer, following a chance encounter in a London air raid shelter. Now a woman scorned, she vented her anguish on the 'street singer' who, clutching his begging bowl, appeared periodically giving it big licks from Italian operas. I think he may've been an 'Eyetie' POW who'd been left behind, or maybe they didn't want'm back. Biddy would heat up pennies over her gas ring and throw them out the window to 'the wop', so when the sucker picked them up he burnt his fingers, this she thought hilarious; so there you have it, wimen kin also hae a cruel streak - *that's right; hell hath no fury!*

Then there was the 'ragman', a vulgar, lice-ridden backstreet wino, who'd exchange goldfish for rags. A right bleedin' chancer he was, no matter how many rags you gave him, you only got one goldfish and it was always 'keeled over', floating belly up in the jam jar next morning.

The 'fishman' used to pitch-up twice weekly with his little horse and nicely painted cart; which was always spick and span. His cry was "Haddies, fresh herrin", which translates to haddocks and fresh herring - true to form, we'd take the piss by shouting "hauddies ah'm fawin" which in turn means, 'hold me I'm falling'. Although he did a bit of muttering to himself, he was a mild-mannered man who never seemed to get upset, but probably took a dim view; labelling us a bunch of cheeky little tykes.

The Italian 'ice cream man'; a scruffy fellow wearing a grubby shirt worn through at the collar, under a sleeveless Fair Isle pullover *(which may well've been blagged from the 'ragman')*, he arrived when it suited him, on a sort of tricycle thing with a freezer box upfront containing his "Ice adda cream". We would continually torment the dago by asking "How much are yer threepenny cones today Tony?" and he did get 'uppa da set'.

The 'badman' had one of the aforementioned allotments, so if the divvy spied us skulking near his patch, he'd shake his fist and shout, telling us to bugger off. I can picture him yet, a lanky man with glasses, 'tache, workie's

bunnet and always wae a dreep hingin' frae his beak. Although he lived in our street we never bothered to find out his name, so whenever we saw the ogre approach we would shout to each other "Here comes the badman". *Probably enough to drive anyone crackers* - ***and maybe he was!***

The 'coalman' came twice a week with his horse and cart, later upgrading to a rather natty Albion platform lorry. He was an 'auld wido' *in his late forties*, who stayed sitting on the cart while a pair of German POWs did the lifting and shifting, I remember they wore reefer jackets with big white letters stamped on the back reading POW. I also remember the price of the coal *chalked up on a black-painted metal flag,* it was 1/8^{d} per sack, which was one shilling and eight old pence - that was for 1cwt *(hundredweight)*. The 'big boys' used to say; if the wifies had no money it was a case of "Up yer hole forra bag o'coal missus".

The Hickmans, they kept a well-stocked little shop *(which they lived behind with their daughter Shirley, who organized backgreen concerts)* halfway down the tenements - Mr Hickman, who was a bookie, had been a captain in the army; his lady wife was a very tidy blonde who, on Sunday mornings, sold home-baking. I recall her Cornish pasties being delicious: let me tell you, I've yet to taste any that come close, and believe me, it's all too evident that I've troughed more than just a few in my time.

On Wednesday and Saturday evenings, Powderhall *(known as 'The Dogs')* held their race meetings, so an enterprising tout hung about up by St Philip's side door, wearing the same shabby demob raincoat, winter and summer, selling racecards. I can hear him yet, shouting "REGELL (Regal) Race Card, three pence a Regell" repeatedly for about an hour - as if that wasn't enough, his buddy, 'Old Stumpy' - *a shifty, beyond redemption, drunkard,* stood a few paces down, playing an accordion whilst coughing his lungs up, puffing away on a Capstan Full Strength. He only knew four tunes and was crap, so twice a week year in, year out the whole street was subjected to his imagined talent: *if music be the food of love, play on!*

In those days the streets weren't like minefields, littered with dogshit, in fact there was only one dog in Logie Green, a large Alsatian called Major: maybe there had been others which had 'met their end' in helping supplement a rather Spartan 'wartime diet'. D'you ever wonder how many butchers made a bundle in the days when we had to queue for ages, then

take what we could get. Mother always sent me on Saturday mornings, as it could take up to an hour - oh, how I hated shuffling along in the queue on St. Cuthbert's sawdust covered floorboards until it was my turn to be served with some gristly scrag-ends, after which I'd rush home in order to attend the Ritz ABC Minors' Club to see 'The Lone Ranger', 'Captain Marvel' and 'Lash La Rue' with all the other little keelies. Everything seemed to be 'on the ration' except rabbit and tripe - on thinking about it, some of the local cats may well have been labelled as rabbit, but in those miserable years we were happy to believe whatever we were told; after all they were butchers and it would never occur to us *the gullible public* back then to question anyone, or imagine we were being shafted.

Mentioning Major the Alsatian reminds me of another dog I was privileged to know years later. 'Shagger' was a dug wae attitude; a magnificent short-haired reddish-brown coated Labrador - should've been a gun dog, but was a city boy. Daily he'd pass the car showroom I then had, always following the same route ambling along at a confident pace.

Recognizing a good thing, he soon became our pal, so would stop for a quick word: *uncannily always at lunchtime* - dogs are guid at givin' yae a usin' when they realize yerra a soft touch. 'Buggerlugs', our gormless valeter, christened him 'Shagger', because we couldn't count the number of times we saw him strapped on the back o' some yelpin' bitch: they didn't stand a chance against this guy, as shaggin' must've been his sole aim in life. When we 'chinned' him about it, I swear there was a sly grin on his handsome coupon when he insisted it was no big deal as they all had flat feet and he was merely pumping them up.

Our 'adopted son's' finest hour had to be when we heard high-pitched giggling screams coming from behind the showroom, so dashed round to see what the commotion was. Surprise! Surprise! There's Shagger clinging to a local tart's leg, and her off-balance hanging onto the railings as she's wearing those huge stupid platform boots, which were the height of fashion at the time. He's giving it 'nanty' and she doesn't know what to do; for that matter neither did we, in fact my glib-tongued right-hand man/ enforcer, Bernie, said later, "To get him off, we'd've had to shoot'm."

Funny how one memory can trigger another - reminiscing about the butcher, recalled this little jewel. 'Once upon a time', when we'd be about

nine, my next door neighbour, Brian Russell, and I were in Rodney Street when we met two of the 'big boys' from Logie Green, Robert Brunton and Alex Hogg. Being older, they were smarter than us and each swinging a rabbit's paw dangling from a bit of string. The chancers tricked us, saying these were lucky charms *not so lucky for el rabeet* and to get one, all we had to do was go into Munro, the butcher's shop, and ask for a rabbit's fud. So, like chumps, in we go and innocently say "Kin we huv a rabbit's fud please, mister!" Thus inciting the purveyor of fine meats to go ballistic; like shit off a chrome shovel, he belted round the counter and chased us out the door - *which seems a sight funnier today than it did then.*

Before I forget; I didn't finish telling you the Powderhall story. On race nights all the spivs and grifters *who'd made a packet during the war* would arrive in their shiny motor cars. Because Powderhall car park was small, it was soon full; so the overspill parked on our road and along Warriston Road, by the river wall. Since yobs were yet to be invented we'd look with drooling admiration at all the posh cars arriving - eventually one of the owners said "Watch my car boys and you're onna shilling when I come out". Well now, it doesn't take a gang of skint kids long to cotton on to the opportunity of earning dosh, so, thus inspired, all future arrivals were greeted with "Watch yer car mister?" Many would give us the thumbs up, so, if they'd had a lucky night, we copped a 'tanner', which made us happy and them look good in front of their mates; but of course the odd dubious character gave us a usin' and fucked off without paying, so we're learning at an early age that the real world is a cruel place.

My final memory of Powderhall takes me back to the year when the Water of Leith burst its banks; flooding the stadium and drowning a number of unfortunate greyhounds, trapped in their kennels. This must've been about 1947 - I remember the water came all the way up the road to within four doors of ours These houses had cellars - and sitting thinking about it now, I can still picture the Fire Brigade pumping out those left awash.

Isn't it always the way, you say final and then have to contradict yourself. I've just remembered the one and only time I was actually in Powderhall. It was at the end of the war, when Mother took Carnie and myself to see the Russian Cossacks put on a display. All I can tell you is that they were charging up and down on massive snorting horses and leaning away over

in the saddles picking up handkerchiefs with their teeth, quite a feat; I don't know what I expected, but was bored stiff and although it's left a lasting memory I was far from impressed by these fierce equestrian warriors.

Another snippet from around the same time was, that downriver a bit, at Warriston, was a place we called 'the Dump'; now an area of football pitches called St Mark's Park, but then it was the Dump: so named because behind a waist-high barbed wire perimeter fence were hundreds of army vehicles; Bren gun carriers, halftracks, dispatch riders' motorbikes etc., all probably brand new in that drab brown khaki colour, some with camouflage. It was amazing, what a place for 'little soldiers' to play. I guess they were stored there because of overproduction during the war, which had by then ended. There was no guard or watchman, what a marvellous attraction - however, I don't remember it being held in that capacity for long.

The banks at that part of the river are steep and tree-lined. When older, flitting around like phantoms under cover of darkness, we purloined a length of thick rope from the local sawmill *(which was within the boundaries of the railway-yard)* fixed it high up in a big old weeping-willow tree that leant halfway across the river; so making a terrific tarzan-style swing that went way out just above the water - which was deep, brown and slow-running at that point. It's fair to say, all the little urchins at sometime fell in and squelched home soaking to get a lecture; followed by a guid hidin'.

The more I think about that river the more I realize how much of our childhood was spent there and also, the amount of pleasure it afforded us. Visualize our exuberance on finding we could manhandle *long forgotten* railway sleepers down the bank and float them in the water. Then some bright spark, probably Bobby Gray, who was a bit of a 'Just William' type ringleader, got the idea to make a raft. We tied and nailed four together - great fun for a few days, but unfortunately the raft would go under if carrying more than one young 'Huckleberry Finn'. Other times, wading through 'the shallows', we'd guddle for 'tiddlers' upstream, where there was a great variety of beardies, redbreasts, minnows and brown trout, but no frogs *(we had to go to the Union Canal at Sighthill for frogs)*.

Sometimes we'd place stepping stones across the river, later filling the gaps with boulders to create a dam. George Valentine had a close one; as when warily inching his way across the stepping stones Mr Nobody heaved

a yokker to splash him - whoever the thrower, he must've been cock-eyed as it hit poor George a glancing blow on the napper, leaving him out cold - crikey, blood everywhere; we thought he was a goner. The unfortunate target was rushed to hospital in an ambulance - I tell you, it's a wonder he survived; although Georgie Boy was never quite the same.

We spent so much time down there it's a miracle no one drowned - come to think of it, one Saturday morning, when I was queuing at the butcher's, my youngest brother, Mike, who would be about two at the time, nearly 'met his Maker'; that is, **if** the kids *who couldn't wait to 'spill the beans'* were telling the truth. Carnie had been given the duty of looking after, the then, little Michael and as always they were at the river; known locally as 'Puddocky'. Mike was playing at boats, floating twigs at the water's edge and Carnie, being a bit of a free spirit *'eye off the ball' a few yards inland* is engrossed in the destructive powers of a box of Bluebell matches, completely oblivious to Mike's existence. Mike *somehow* topples into the water and, assuming the story is to be believed, only floating because of the air trapped in his coat and, **if** not total exaggeration the boys fished him out with branches. So, Mike lived to tell the tale, or rather, not tell the tale because of his young years, therefore Mother never heard what had actually happened, but probably got a long-winded story from Carnie, *cleverly concocted to save him from 'six o' the best'*.

How the gurning bairns nowadays can say they're bored, as they've nothing to do is a complete mystery to me - it rankles, when I see all the toys and gadgets the mollycoddled brats have to amuse themselves - and there's a world of entertainment outdoors. We had nothing, by comparison *'no' even a pot tae pish in'* but everyday was sheer magic, and we couldn't wait to get out to play in the mornings, rain or shine.

The gang hut - this lay hidden in the foundations under the Spade & Shovel Works' Stores, that stood on the side of the railway embankment behind Bobby Gray's back garden - he being *as said* a 'Just William' type character *he even looked the part* when exploring one evening, discovered this hideout and decided it would make a good gang hut. Bobby was a year older than me, and as the oldest in the gang his power absolute, so when Bobby got an idea in his head he had the knack of making it happen, 'off his trolley' and a manipulative little twerp he may've been, but he did make

life fun. So, with some bricks to shore up loose earth at the entrance, a sackcloth curtain-cum-draught excluder, and wooden boxes both to sit on and stash 'treasure' in, we brought another of Bobby's dreams to reality. By the time we *his loyal foot soldiers* had 'acquired' a few necessities such as paraffin lamps, candles and some silver paint it was 'just the job', and served us well for quite some time. Hidden in our subterranean den, we would plot and plan, smoke 'Wild Woodbine' cigarettes - *the now rotund* 'Spanky' Spencer said you should get a whip with them - tell jokes and ghost stories; thereby making the most of our own mysterious little world.

Once when going to our secret hideout, Bobby said there was a surprise waiting and we *(his subordinates)* would see what it was when we got there, thus keeping us in 'suspenders' until the last moment; so as to bask in the glory. Full of wonder and more than a little curious, down and in we go. Behold; there, hanging on the far wall *above our altar*, is a stag's head with this magnificent spread of antlers. He wouldn't tell us where or how he got it, but up the road there was a 'working man's pub' called the Stag's Head *(he meant well, but took a bit o' watchin', did Bobby)*.

I shall now devote some time to the young Bobby Gray; he being such a worthy and deserving case. Our revered leader resided in a semi in Logie Green Loan; this being one of two small cul-de-sacs *(the other being Logie Green Gardens)* on our side of the road. How long he had lived there I can't say, as when youngsters, we gradually become aware of each other as we spread our wings - maybe he had been there for years and kept in the house, or within the confines of the Loan. Anyway, we met Bobby *(who, by the way, had a mole the size of a half-crown on the back of his neck)*, a friendship was struck-up and a secret society born.

His mother, a tall severe woman, was at work all day; she was a manageress in a big department store uptown beside the Playhouse Theatre; which was then a cinema, where, on a 'double bill', we saw 'The Beast with Five Fingers' and 'Dead Men Walk'. The store was called Porter's, I can't remember what they sold but it was well known; anyway, Mrs Gray, I recall, always wore a dark suit and was reputed to be one of 'the high heid yins'. We were all well aware, even at that early age, that the Grays were from an advantaged background but had fallen on hard times - we never sussed whether the father had 'copped it' in the war, or 'dunna runner'; whatever,

daddy was 'in the doghouse', as his name was never mentioned.

Well now, because Mother Gray was away at work nine 'til five Bobby, when not at school, was left 'on his best behaviour' at home alone. No such thing as child minders, social workers or any such nonsense in our time, since a wee dram o' common sense an' a guid lickin' did the trick. So we *when Bobby chose to have us in* had the run of the house, and by Jove did we ever know how to amuse ourselves!

They say the Devil finds work for idle hands - *could be a shred o' truth there*, so we'd have a go at making toffee and tablet, using up the sugar ration and burning pots in the process; light the fire and roast potatoes, in their skins, on it until they were burnt black, then attempt to eat them *making us black*. He would rake through his mother's possessions, showing off her jewellery; this being quite a treasure trove, and probably expensive stuff. Before you say, or even think it: **no, we didn't dress up in her clothes!** *(That was merely a malicious rumour brought about by a misunderstanding in the ladies' toilets at the Ritz; so let's not start tongues awagging).*

Casting my mind back, I remember it as a spooky house, because the curtains were always part-drawn — *thus raising suspicions*. This day, he decides we need an assault course; so digs trenches in his back garden and rigs tightropes between the clothes poles, on which we taught ourselves to walk along using the wooden line-prop for a tightrope walker's pole.

Another classic came after we had been to see a war film at the Ritz, probably 'The Flying Leathernecks' with John Wayne or 'Objective, Burma!' starring that other screen idol, Errol Flynn. Anyway, inspired by this, our impetuous leader fancies himself as a young paratrooper, so gets his mother's umbrella from the hallstand and there he is, out on the cill of the upstairs back bedroom window. We think he's just messing about and won't do it, Oh no! This is Bobby we're talking about; he shouts "Banzai!" *or was it "Geronimo"* and jumps. The umbrella goes inside out and Bobby crashes into the flowerbed full of Mummy's lovely, all shades of blue, lupins, so that night, Bobby gets yet another 'leathering'. Mother Gray was on a loser - she couldn't handle this guy and used to whip him with the carpet beater she kept handy to punish the wayward son, but sadly for her, to no effect as the 'derring-do' lad *being crackers* was untameable.

When I was reminiscing about this and that with brother Carnie recently,

he told me Bobby wanted him to jump off the Scott Monument in Princes Street in the same manner, saying it would be OK because he was three years younger and much lighter. But Carnie, although younger, wasn't as daft as Bobby, otherwise it would have been SPLAAT! He also reminded me of the time Bobby sold his mother's jewellery for pennies to local toerags - *need I say, that night there were 'tears before bedtime'* as while being called 'the Devil's spawn', squealing like a stuck pig, the scallywag was dragged by the ear round his customers' houses by the horrified woman to retrieve her valuable hoard.

Another game we would play on the slopes of the riverbank opposite Powderhall *near the swing on the old knarled willow tree* was Firefiends and Firefighters. In late summer, when the grass was long, dry and the colour of ripe corn, two budding pyromaniacs would run amok torching the grassy slopes, while the rest of us tried to douse the flames by beating the blaze with wet sacks that we'd dipped in the river. Great fun, but all good things come to an end; and this did when one of the Warriston residents was none too pleased with the billowing clouds of grey smoke being blown towards his house, so phoned the Police and Fire Brigade, thus obliging the juvenile arsonists to 'break cover' and 'head for the hills'.

Must mention while I remember; there was a family five doors up from our house, with two pretty daughters who liked to play 'mummies and daddies' *(we would be about eleven at this time).* Janette and Margaret had a younger brother of five or six - can't remember his name, however, one of the gang discovered this kid had difficulty saying "fish and chips", so it came out as "pish and fips" naturally he was constantly asked to say "fish and chips", this of course became his party piece. It occurs to me, he may have been little more than an attention seeking rascal rakin' the pish oot o' us, and it now comes to mind that his name was 'Arfur', a happy wee guy wif sandy red hair, *and you've gethed it -* ***a lithp!***

Occasionally *ever mindful of the bogeyman* we would go timidly exploring in Warriston Cemetery as, although eerie, it was an interesting place with sombre Victorian arches, damp moss-covered stairways, family plots, and musty crypts behind padlocked rusting iron gates. A great favourite of ours we called the 'Red Lady' - this was an ornate marble tomb with Gothic windows which we'd gaze through in awe, to gape at a

life-size marble statue of a lovely young lady draped in a Grecian toga-style dress, clutching a small terrier to her breast, while resting serenely atop a substantial white marble plinth, which presumably held her coffin and mortal remains. Although not as large as some, it was a beautiful memorial; the reason we called her the Red Lady was that the roof of this monument was of red glass - casting a rosy glow inside. Freddy Martin *(a junior member of the gang, destined to become a dentist)* said the dog had been her pet, given by the love of her life, but it bit her and she died. Probably far removed from the truth, but nonetheless a romantic explanation.

Years later, I went back for a nostalgic look; when I eventually found the shrine I wished I hadn't, as the scumbags had beaten me to it. Even the plinth was desecrated, smashed to smithereens, with rotten wood to be seen sticking from its sides *(probably the coffin)*: so sad, what's wrong with those lowlife cretins, what makes them tick? **Dear diary - must remember to pray for all these underprivileged louts*. The lesson there is, you should never go back - a saying I've so often found to be true.

Oh, hang on! I'm fair burstin' to tell you about this memorable excursion into the cemetery. There we were, wending our way between the tombstones, reading their inscriptions; marvelling at how old some of the lairs were and also how young some of the graves' inhabitants, when suddenly in front of us is a **big fat hairy erse**. Crivvens; there was an old tramp squatting, troosers roond ankles, 'curlin' one doon'. Struck dumb with shock, we beat a hasty departure; none faster than the three girls (*who thought we were there to play 'kissey-chasey')* to say they ran off screaming and squealing would be putting it mildly. Giving the auld dosser his due, he never even turned his head, but there again may've been stone deaf. Well spooked, we didn't go near the graveyard for a long time after that horrific experience and were from then on wary, in case, as Spanky suggested, the tramp lived there, in the long-since abandoned 'shivers doon yer spine' lodge aside the grand *creaky-hinged* wrought-iron entrance gates.

Further downriver past Powderhall and the Dump there was a suburban railway line which had an old grey-painted iron bridge crossing the water. Beside the bridge was a telephone pole, with stout wire hawsers each side keeping it taut and upright. This day I fancy myself as a little commando and slide down a hawser from the bridge to the ground about ten feet

below. Lucky for me, I had my new leather gloves on, otherwise my hands would've been ripped to shreds; as it was, my new leather gloves were torn to ribbons instead, and so was my backside when I got home; as new leather gloves dinnae grow on trees.

'Twas close to this spot, that, one summer, there appeared a huge patch of hogweed, much taller than ourselves. We didn't know what it was - thinking it could be of the rhubarb family we started merrily chopping it down with our French sword-like brass-handled bayonets, obtained on one of our many sneaky moonlight raids to the ever-alluring scrap-metal trucks sitting in the railway siding. We were getting splashed on our bare arms and legs with the sap; little knowing it was like acid. Later that day great angry bubbles, as if from burns, erupted on our skin, so we were taken to the doctor, who didn't know what it was and supplied calamine lotion, as that's about all there was back in **'the happy days'**. Another lesson!

Beyond the old iron railway bridge, even further downriver, lay Lady Williamson's estate, which we never dared enter: it was a heavily wooded dark forbidding place, where *rumour had it* she kept a gamekeeper who carried a double-barrelled shotgun. There was a waterfall in there which we never saw, but could hear gurgling and splashing - in winter, when all the trees and bushes were bare, we could glimpse the ivy-covered mansion house *which looked dank, uninhabited and frightening* in the distance. Another reason for giving Lady Williamson's patch a wide berth was that it was outwith our territory, bordering on the Redbraes area where a fierce tribe of keelies lived; these jackals would raid our turf to steal fuel on Bonfire Night at the Ditch, thus sparking off a bitter feud, so what with one thing and another, to put it bluntly, we were sh-sh-shit-scared.

But, there was another big house and it **was** in our territory, this was lying empty and had decent-sized wooded grounds behind it on a steep slope where we built a super treetop house, under the directions of none other than 'our champion', whose idea it *obviously* was. In the late forties *or possibly early fifties* we were exasperated when a noisy team of interfering workmen arrived to renovate the sadly neglected building. So then Heriot Hill House *(which we were convinced we owned)* became the Royal Navy Association, I see it is now affiliated with the Royal Marines' Association, which seems like a case of "united we stand". It sits by the traffic lights at

the junction of Rodney Street and Broughton Road, directly across from the already mentioned Stag's Head public house.

Another thing I must tell you is how sometimes, but not so often as to spoil it, we would scurry down through Symington's entrance to where we could shout endearing remarks to butter up the ladies, dressed in white overalls and turbans, working on the first floor of Duncan's Chocolate Factory: in return for our flattery they'd chuck down a huge lump of chocolate wrapped in newspaper, causing a mad scramble amongst us insatiable sugar-starved waifs. You will realize what a treat that was when I remind you we were always skint and sweets still 'on the ration'.

Talking about rationing reminds me of the time Uncle Ray *Aunt Sophie's husband* brought us a bunch of bananas from a ship docked at Burntisland. We didn't know what they were, however I greedily wolfed down two and promptly 'spewed ma ring' on the grass in our back garden - *even now the very smell of bananas recalls the mishap*.

Just as fashions come and go, so did seasons to play with different things, such as bikes. The bicycles we had were old black pre-war wrecks, but we didn't know any better; because there was nothing else. Like all kids we'd perform tricks we thought clever, such as pedalling along without holding on to the handlebars - very smart! I remember a saying was "Look Ma, nae hands! look Ma, nae teeth!" I should've taken notice of this saying, as one day I'm showing off "look nae hands", the front wheel hits a bump, down I go and the end of the handlebar, with no rubber grip, goes right into my upper lip. It ought to have had stitches, but I made do with a plaster, consequently my 'Heidelberg duelling scar' is not quite as straight as it should be: so now you know, and all this time you've been thinking I must've been talking when I should've been listening!

Sometimes roller skates were 'the order of the day', but this was never a lasting craze, as these old skates, like the bikes, were pre-war hand-me-downs, which had buckled wobbly wheels and strapped on to your shoes. To make matters worse there weren't enough to go round, so we only had one each, meaning we would balance rolling on one foot and push with the other. Better fun were the 'guiders' *(carts)* we used to make - if we couldn't get pram wheels we would improvise with metal roller-bearings, which, like so many things, were spirited on dark nights from the scrap-metal trucks

in the railway yard. These 'guiders' were great, really noisy when hurtling along on the granite pavement up by St Philip's Church, where there is a sweeping corner with a steep incline - super for skidding round.

I forgot to say, when on about bikes, that one summer Bobby Gray had another of his great ideas. It was well known that as trains crossed the Forth Bridge, 'twas customary for well-heeled passengers to throw a silver sixpence out the carriage window *for luck* into the sea far below. So, our leader decided, he and his trusty band should pedal our old 'boneshakers' to South Queensferry, get the shoes and socks off, paddle in the shallows amongst the rocks and clean up bigtime. Well, we did get some dosh, *not a lot*, but it was a pilgrimage to get there and back, in fact we were away so long our mothers thought we'd been 'stolen by the gypsies'. It goes without saying Bobby got the blame and out came the carpet beater that night, so he ran away from home; only to be back the following morning, cold, hungry and just in time for another 'good leathering'.

Mentioning St Philip's, when on about the 'guiders', triggered this - when seven we were rounded-up and packed off to Sunday School, partly because it was the done thing, but more so to get rid of us on Sunday mornings. Now, I can't remember how or why, but Brian Russell and myself managed to get ourselves pressed into the Church Choir and, little angels we certainly were not - so, don't think for a minute, that dressing us in cassocks and surplices, then putting these bleedin' starched ruffs around our scrawny little necks changed anything. I couldn't get to grips with Jesus wantin' me forra sunbeam, but there was no option until old enough to stray from the fold. So, between that and going down the road, to the 'Band of Hope' to sing about The Old Rugged Cross and watch 'magic lantern shows' in the Mission Hut on Wednesday nights - all the kids went, as there was sod all else to do, *remember, no televisions* and anyway it was just a carry-on from beginning to end, although it stands to reason some of the Christian teachings must've got through. By the way, hast thou ever wondered - **how many pious leeches on the ecclesiastic payroll actually believe in God and all his glory?**

I would've been ten when I started keeping pigeons in an unused workshop that Father had built in our back garden, prior to attending Leith Nautical College some three years earlier. This made an ideal 'loft'

and pigeons *(never classed as pets - but recognized as a statement)* were cheap to buy from the pet shop in Cockburn Street. I wasn't the only one in the street with pigeons, Alex Hogg's older brother, Ian, had a big loft two minutes along the railway embankment from their villa in Logie Green Gardens; it must have housed thirty birds, which he raced with some success. I probably had as many as twelve at my high point but they were just 'homers' and cheap to feed, as the old Chancelot Mill *(A beautiful clock-towered architectural gem, long since demolished)* was only a couple of miles away, where the 'workies' would let us have bags of maize, *which were floor sweepings*, and I guess when the pigeons were out to play they did a bit of foraging around the neighbourhood.

When nicking along the embankment to see Ian *probably seeking advice* a movement caught my eye, so naturally I looked towards it, to be rewarded with more than a fleeting glance of a girl *said to be a ballerina* admiring her firm willowy reflection in the dressing table mirror, 'twas the teenage daughter of the Hoggs' new neighbours. Her bedroom was upstairs, but being on the embankment I was at a level height and only yards away. Ma eyes almost jumped oot thur sockets, as there she was, 'looking a dream', stripped down to her bra an' pants and luckily *saving embarrassment* didn't see me. Although transfixed, I managed to tear myself away - oh, how I've treasured that wonderful heaven-sent moment. She was older than our crowd by three or four years, so there was no point in trying to curry favour. I don't think I even knew her name, but that was a 'red-letter day' for me; this was no schoolboy crush - **I was in love!**

The next time I 'carried a torch' for one of 'the fair sex' was when I saw fifties' glamourpuss Esther Williams in 'On an Island with You'. I'd like to watch that film again someday, to see if she really looked as good as I thought at the time, because I was probably just young and impressionable - ***but maybe not***, as her lithe sun-kissed body sure looked good in the swimsuits she wore, while playing a south sea island trollop.

Now it's time to tell you about the picnics. We had the Russells on one side as neighbours and the Heriots on the other. Mother was friendly with Mrs Heriot because her husband, like my father, was at sea. He was an engineer on tankers, always away on long trips, and looked a bit like Humphrey Bogart. They had two sons; Ian being ages with me, so we were

pals, his big brother Jim was much older, so I don't really remember him, as he thought himself too big to play with us; therefore remained aloof.

Unlike some clowns who claim to remember being born, my earliest hazy memory is of when I was maybe four, which would make Carnie a mere stripling - we were going for a picnic with the Heriots to the 'Silversands' at Aberdour, a seaside town in the Kingdom of Fife; this entailed getting a train from the Waverley Station over the Forth Bridge to our destination. Talk about excitement, I had never even seen a passenger train before, let alone been on one, so could hardly contain myself *and that's the point*. Building sandcastles was good fun, but the train back again! Oh, I couldn't think what would be better and was so excited it must have triggered my 'little accident', because on the platform I had wind, farted and 'followed through', **wotta a red face!** Mother changing me in front of everyone in the carriage sort o' took the edge off the day.

Michty me that sherly reeks, ah hope ah huvnae filled ma breeks!

The next picnic with the Heriots *(who eventually went to live in Equador)* must've been two or three years on, because we were certainly older. We had gone to the Carlops, south of Edinburgh, this time by SMT bus. Before I tell you about the picnic I'll explain the name Carlops, as told many years hence by a popular and interesting car dealer friend, Ian Black. Ian, in a deal, had copped an antique pub sign depicting a grinning toothless witch flying through the air astride a broomstick; he reckoned it came from a pub at the Carlops and how this spot had been named after a crone known as 'Carlin the Hag'. Now, at the Carlops there are two huge rocks, one on each side of the road - in the olden days *when Adam was a boy* there was a toll there and the story goes that Carlin, astride her broom, would leap *(or loup)* from one boulder to the other while hurling abuse and shrieking at the infuriated toll keeper. So, the place became known as Carloups, corrupted over the years to Carlops — nice wee story, ***innit!***

Getting back to the picnic; it's a warm day and we've found a suitable dry terrace on the hillside where our mothers, having pegged out an old tablecloth on the grass, are now busy setting out the Spam sandwiches, goodies and well-diluted orange juice. We've been running around, and now I'm back helping with the spread, Carnie has already got at least one sandwich and, hands full, is getting stuck in. Ian isn't back yet; so we

wait - no sign of Ian. His mother is getting agitated and a touch annoyed, so starts shouting for him to come back. The tousle-haired young scamp suddenly appears from behind a clump of gorse and comes peltin' doon the hill shouting with glee "Mummy! Mummy! I've found a balloon!" He's waving this big white balloon - if you had seen Mrs Heriot's face, I can picture it yet. Talk about 'a face like fizz'. With the speed of light she slapped Ian's 'coupon', swiped the 'balloon' from his hand, and threw it on the jaggy whin, where it burst. This put the dampers on our picnic and of course we, the innocent wee guys that we then were, couldn't understand what had happened, so thought Mrs Heriot was a rotten old cow.

Years later, when we find out about *'buy me and stop one'* condoms or 'French letters' as they were then known, the penny drops and we realize what Ian had found at the Carlops that day was an 'F.L.' - and he'd given it a 'blow job'. Oh my! No wonder he wasn't allowed to paw the food.

I told you earlier about how we had to go to the Union Canal at Sighthill to get frogs - so here's the drill. When, in spring, the frogspawn season arrived, for a penny we would board an Edinburgh Corporation red and white double-decker bus bound for the canal and return with jam jars full of frogspawn. Some of which we would keep on our kitchen window ledges and observe growing into tadpoles, the rest we would put into pools near the weir at 'Puddocky', so as to try and colonise our river with a frog population, but we never succeeded. Maybe the fish ate them, or most likely the river was too fast-flowing, and so, carried the poor little mites down to meet their doom in the salty sea at Leith.

I captured a huge toad on one of our canal expeditions; a real beaut with nice markings and quite special; or so I thought. I took it home, called it Douglas, and imprisoned it in my pigeon loft in an old white round chipped enamel basin with some water, rocks, weed and all the other things I thought it would need to get by. Next day I go to check it and feed the pigeons, which have already been out - jings, 'my familiar' has vanished. I search the workshop high and low, as there's no way it could've got out and I very much doubt the pigeons would have eaten it. No sign of Douglas, ah'm baffled this is a mystery. Months later I'm cleaning the place out and there inside an old car tyre is the mummified toad. It had hopped in, but because of the concave curve on the tyre's inner wall, couldn't get back

out - the tyre being in an upright position under the workbench.

Crikey, it's no wonder Douglas 'croaked it' inside the tyre, do you remember how hot summers were in those days? Gee whizz, I can recall how, then, we all wore wee short grey flannel breeks and have a vivid memory of sitting atop Granny Russell's coalbox and the bitumen felt on the lid being so hot that it was burning the backs of our legs.

I'll conclude my memories of Logie Green with something that happened a few years later than the period I've been prattling on about. I was at Leith Academy by this time, just starting my secondary education - Bobby Gray was also a pupil there but, being older, in the Second Year. The Eagle comic was first published about then; what makes me sure of this, is that when it was soon to be the Second Years' Christmas Dance, Bobby said two of the dances should be 'The Dan Dare Foxtrot' and 'The Grand Old Mekon of Venus'; he was some machine, was Bobby, never without an opinion, and always knew how to milk it dry.

Many had long surmised all was not as it seemed behind the part-drawn curtains, within the confines of Logie Green Loan - and sure enough, there was a skeleton in the closet - '**Big Doris**'.

Yes, Bobby's 'long lost' sister Big Doris appeared out of thin air; *in all these years gone by we never even knew she existed.* She was in her late teens, a shapeless lump with these dreadful National Health glasses perched on her chubby face, and, oh yeah, she wore a knitted woolly bobble-hat that didnae do her any favours - not, I thought, unlike Bessie Bunter, in fact a very plain glaikit girl, whose colouring and style matched her name.

Following this revelation something untoward happened, and *I think* the police were involved; us kids were kept in the dark, but there were whispered rumours that when looking after one of the local brats, she'd tried to roll her young charge off a roof - ***goodbye little Billy.***

sung to 'Whistle While You Work'

Barrel kin ye roll?
Like a sausage roll

If ye cannae
Tell yer granny
Barrel kin ye roll?

Not long after that much speculated-about event the Grays 'took a powder' and emigrated to New Zealand; probably on an 'assisted passage', as there was a scheme on the go at this time to encourage emigrants to Australia and *if my failing memory serves me well* also New Zealand and Canada. Pay ten quid and you were wheeched off to a new life 'in the colonies'. So we lost our friend, leader and role model Bobby Gray.

Call me cynical, but thinking about it now, perhaps it would be prudent to say Big Doris, ***'The Outcast'***, who we all *including Bobby* shunned, was possibly caged in a 'special needs' establishment for many years prior to her unexpected arrival at Logie Green - at this late date it's pure conjecture that she had 'form'; but a likely explanation.

Backstreet waifs 'loosing their marbles'.

3: Wardie Primary School

This quirky little light and airy art deco-designed school in Granton Road was a modern place of learning when I enrolled, all spruced up in my new uniform. It was then fee-paying, although the amount per term modest; so I can say I spent my formative years at a 'special school'. Actually quite a few Logie Green kids went to Wardie, even though it was some four miles from home. We left together at 8.15 each morning and travelled there on a No.8 or No.9 tramcar, both of which would twang along the lines from Rodney Street down past Canonmills and Goldenacre to Granton Square, with us sitting *whenever the opportunity arose* on the upper deck in the little cabin which was situated at both the front and back of the tram.

When old enough to pay attention and understand what was going on around us life got more interesting. So, on the journey we would play 'I Spy' and games, such as guessing the different makes of saloon cars starting to reappear on the roads - during the war there were few cars around, due to both petrol rationing and requisitition. 'These were the days!'

On looking at a class photograph, taken around 1948, I've just counted forty-four heads; this wasn't considered a large class in these days; when the teachers were actually in control, due to the fact that they had **'the strap'** in their corner, and so, the respect that went with it. But there was more to it than that - they dressed the part and it worked. This certainly doesn't seem to be the case today when we hear reports of louts going through the system then leaving school functionally illiterate, which, when you think about it, is really quite a feat; this would have been considered an impossibility in my schooldays. If 'learning deficiencies' and dyslexia had been invented, we wouldn't have been allowed them - yes, the standards have rapidly gone downhill, but let's just call it progress and smirk at the numbskulls, with self-satisfied contempt.

So, back to the photograph - I see a lot of faces I recognize and can put names to, but am surprised at how many I cannot remember at all. Being me, I note we had a fair number of good-looking girls, who no doubt turned out to be real crackers in later years. In fact I can vouch for one; as when

eighteen I met Miss Dorothy Chadwick at Murrayfield Ice Rink; I hadn't seen her since leaving primary school, when twelve - my word, how she'd blossomed! She was blonde, slim and beautiful, a vision in a skating skirt short enough to be interpreted as an invitation. I never saw her again but often thought of her over the years, wondering at the same time, how many others had morphed into young goddesses during their teens.

Getting back to the story: there was a fair cross section of society in our class and although I can remember my first day at school, which confused me no end, the early days are pretty blurred. When we are, say about nine;starting to establish personalities and become truly individual, then things get interesting and friendships develop - therefore we remember certain people who, for one reason or another, became special pals.

I remember Colin Bell, *'Coco',* his father was a naval architect; Alec Young, *'The Oracle';* Charlie Bell, his dad was a trawler skipper; Kenny Turnbull, the printer's son, who lived near me in a palatial pitch, with statues in its massive marble-tiled hall, at East Claremont Street; Jimmy Hobb and his brother Eric, their father was a 'big noise' in banking. I often recall the time Charlie Bell, who'd brought in a big paper bag full of cooked crayfish as his 'play piece', offering them round to whoever wanted a taste - it goes without saying, the delicacies were scoffed with gusto by those quick enough to grab one before they disappeared.

Talking about scran reminds me - that being so far from home, we had to stomach 'school denners' which were unappetizing to *say the least;* as everyone who shared the experience will testify. What comes to mind is mince, over-cooked boiled potatoes or sloppy mash and cabbage. Cor, I can smell it yet! Pudding would be steamed something or stewed dried apple with thin watery custard, and let's not forget the 'Chinese wedding cake' and 'frogspawn' *(rice and tapioca).* There weren't many takers for 'seconds' in those days; however, in the cooks' defence, they, because of rationing, had to eke it out and make a little go a long way. On saying that, I recall a time when the Canadian Government kindly sent us paupers boxes of big rosy red apples, so each pupil got one. Yeah, that's hard to believe today, on seeing supermarkets everywhere bursting at the seams; but them were lean years!

The Headmaster had been a major in the army - he owned a Wolseley

saloon in which he transported Miss Upfirit back and forth from and to school. This was a seriously sexy blonde lady *(said to be 'cock-happy')*, who made many a young scholar's conscience waver, in looking more like a film starlet than schoolmistress; making it all seem very suspicious to us - *who wished she'd been our teacher.* On particularly foul days, at playtime, instigated by 'the Jani', us hard done by pupils would chant "we want a halfy" *(half-day)* - occasionally our wish was granted by 'the beak', because many of the kids had no trench coats and holes in their 'tackety boots'. Of course, we all knew the 'Gallopin' Major' then sneaked off 'early doors', 'happy as Larry', with 'his squeeze' - **say nae mair!**

When we were older, some of us boys would shoot-off down to the harbour at Granton to search for crabs amongst the rocks, but, as I recall, there were more 'johnnies' *(slang for condoms)*, than crabs. With all these used johnnies bobbing about in the water, we thought there must have been hundreds of people shagging down there every night - I now suppose they were being flushed into the Forth with the sewage, as the Firth, although tidal, wasn't the cleanest in these days. It was on returning from one of those lunchtime jaunts that halfway up Granton Road, when passing an old lame wifey hobbling along with a walking stick, Alec Young, ever the wit, said "That's Ballup Button Bessie!" So we, mystified, ask what he's talking about, and he tells us she's a sex maniac who uses the crook of her walking stick to rip open men's fly buttons.

Roughly a year prior to the eleven-plus exams *(the final selection tests, to establish which Secondary you would merit)* a group of 'wrist happy ham shankers' emerged from the ranks. They all sat near each other; which must have been contrived, as these obsessed scamps would blatantly whack themselves off in class, in what they thought was the privacy of their own desks, but it was more than obvious what their little game was. Talking of game reminds me that it wasn't uncommon for a race to be held to see who reached 'the funny' first - this being an abbreviation for 'the funny feeling' which was the climax, as at the tender age of eleven none of these budding undernourished studs could, as yet, 'shoot thur duff'.

There was one boy in particular who just couldn't leave himself alone; titillated by a well-thumbed copy of 'Health and Efficiency', he 'thrashed the bishop' at least once a day. I well remember his name, but for obvious

reasons we'll call him 'John Holmes'. What a tadger this boy had *(hung like a horse)*, he could've made a fortune in a travelling circus, **wotta whopper!** Alec Young reasoned its size was down to his sainted mother having used it as a grabhandle to lift him from his Pedigree pram. I mused over the chicken and egg situation - which came first? Was his cock so big because he played with it all the time? or did he play with it all the time because it was so big, *and, what did he do to deserve* **that?**

Now, the boys sat on one side of the classroom and the girls on the other, where we had one inquisitive little lady who certainly wasn't shy, and very interested in what John Holmes was up to. So myself and the guy next to me would sit right back in our seats, so she could look *wide-eyed* along the row and gasp at the answer to many a lonely maiden's prayer. Oft-times I've wondered what happened to her in later life - if she thought they were all proportioned like **that**, she was to be sadly disappointed.

God give me the strength
To take all this length
One inch at a time

Now and again I'd go to pals' houses for an hour or so after school, and recollect visiting the Hobbs, who lived in a smart Victorian villa in Trinity; a posh district close to Wardie. Their well-to-do father had a full-size Hornby train layout in the attic - it was magnificent; I'd never seen anything like it and longed for a shot, but **no chance** as only Daddy was allowed near it. Instead we went out to play in the street, where, to my utter disgust the brothers took great delight in picking up dried dog turds. I couldn't believe what I was seeing and, making some feeble excuse, horrified, went straight home; in case I was invited to stay for tea.

Another classmate I regularly visited was Brian Green, he also lived nearby, on Ferry Road, number 496, a historic turreted Scottish baronial mansion with crow-stepped gables and a garden behind that went on forever. Brian's parents were caretakers to an old lady *possibly titled* who lived upstairs. I never set eyes on her as we were kept to the kitchen, which was ginormous with a stone-flagged floor and big Aga range. The 'Lady o' the Hoose' must have been mega-rich - I now wonder who she was: certainly an animal lover, as there was a pets' cemetery with inscribed miniature headstones at the foot of the secluded walled garden.

Funny, how you recall little snippets - 'Claude' Balls used to say "I think, I think, I smell a stink, coming from Y.O.U!" The same fellow, while holding a hand to his ear, once said, on hearing *the ever flatulant* 'Stinky' Stonehouse 'let one rip', "HARK! a bugle call from tolyland, to herald the coming of the brownies!"

Granton Harbour was a busy place in those days, I can picture it packed with tall-funnelled steam trawlers, esparto grass ships and little coasters. I also recall two *or maybe three* captured German U-boats alongside a big battleship-grey Naval floating dock. Even then, to me, they looked menacing in their drab black paint, sitting low in the water and more than capable of spreading terror amongst nervous allied convoys plodding hopelessly through cold grey restless seas that showed no mercy.

A favourite topic of conversation each morning was what had happened to Dick Barton the night before. This was a serial programme on the BBC for fifteen minutes, Monday to Friday, at quarter to seven. Many will remember being thrilled by the exploits of 'Dick Barton, Special Agent' with his faithful sidekicks Snowy and Jock; *I can still hear the signature tune, 'The Devil's Gallop', in my head.* So, if you had finished your homework, and been good, you were allowed to listen to their latest adventure. They even made a film - I remember Dick making a death defying climb up the external girders on the high reaches of Blackpool Tower, in pursuit of a gang of interlopers - but their stab at the big screen was crap; much better on radio, when you pictured the scenes in your own imagination, than as a low-budget black and white film.

Dick and his subordinates had achieved cult status with the youth of our fair land, who had very little to look forward to back then - so we were vexed when, to our utter dismay, resentment and disbelief, the BBC in their infinite wisdom decided to axe our programme and replace it with 'The Archers' *(might have been 'Mrs Dale's Diary' - no matter; does anyone listen to 'the everyday story of country folk'?)*. We were dazed - at that young and impressionable age it's a shock to the system, albeit a necessary part of the learning curve to find the world doesn't actually revolve round oneself. However, even now, I can't help thinking - **tosspots!**

You'll be aware of how nowadays the 'schoolies' are taken on some amazing trips - abroad skiing, outward bounding, canoeing, it's a never-

ending list. In our schooldays it was so different; try as I may I can only recall three trips, all from Wardie Primary. The first was when the boys were taken, *(or was it sent?)* to the small swimming pool at Broughton Primary School for a swimming lesson. The P.E. teacher in charge of the pool had a long thick bamboo pole, which we were supposed to grab hold of to be pulled into the side if in trouble, however this robust clown utilized it as a cattle-prod, to assert his authority. We only ever went the once, anticipating it was to be a regular lesson *what a lovely skive that would have been,* but as luck would have it, that was, as they say, 'our lot'. I doubt if we had as long as five minutes each in the water, with the rest of the hour spent getting changed, or shivering at the side of the pool awaiting our turn, so how the heck we were supposed to have learned to swim like fish in the time allotted is beyond me. But there again, **wha'dae ah ken!**

The second outing was to the Royal Museum of Scotland in Chambers Street. This time the whole class went; 27 small boys and 17 sweet little princesses. It was an enjoyable and interesting trip, especially for those who had never been to the museum before. However, it was nothing new to me, as I had been there many times with Bobby Gray and the gang. There was no problem getting in without an accompanying adult, as the place was well supervised by uniformed attendants; so as long as youngsters behaved and were quiet, everything was fine. Because it was *(and is)* such a spellbinding place there was no reason to be boisterous.

Now then, the third treat was **the big one**, this was to Broomlee School Camp at Middleton which is about ten miles south of Edinburgh down the A7 - I think it was for ten days. Not all of the class went and those who didn't, for various reasons, had to go to school, as it was during term-time. An' hey, let me tell you before I start, there was a bit o' bleatin' done by the inmates on that little jaunt. We, of course, thought we were going on holiday; poor little buggers, we hadn't a clue - ***did we ever get a shock!***

We slept in huts, had to go to class for lessons every weekday, got our scalps raked with big sharp steel nit combs, by a hefty brassy blonde dominatrix *disguised as a nurse* in pursuit of headlice, but worst of all, God's little fan club was marched down the country roads on the Sunday to a quaint Gothic church in a tiny village. Some bleedin' holiday! Talk about captive punters - everyone had thought, surely we'd at least be left

to our own devices on the Sunday morning.

Can't remember much about the cuisine *certainly not Michelin rated* but do remember being conned the first time we went to breakfast - there we were sitting *expectantly* round a big refectory type table and this faithful old retainer bellowing "Hands up for bacon rolls". We think 'Oh yeah, brilliant', so instantly a sea of hands shoot up. Guess what we get! and it's not what you think - we each receive two slices of streaky bacon rolled up and done to a crisp. Suckered again - *there's no fool like a young fool!*

A lasting memory of school camp was; on arriving home I delighted Mother by bringing back loads of bars of soap, which was, like everything else at that time; 'on the ration'. My dozy little 'holiday' friends kept leaving their soap behind in the washrooms and I was never one for seeing things go to waste - haven't changed; if truth be told.

Think back - do you remember how long the holidays lasted in those heady childhood days, especially the seven weeks we got in summer? They seemed to go on forever, and that final one before transferring to secondary school must have been the summer all our clever little darlings grew 'titties', because by the time I went to Leith Academy most of the girls had two, bless 'em, ***in fact, you could say they were double-breasted!***

Wardie Primary School Class Photograph (late 1940s)

4: The War Years

When war was declared, Uncle David joined the RAF and Father the Royal Navy, presumably as volunteers, since the fishing industry would've exempted them from conscription. Because Father was an experienced seaman, he was rated Petty Officer and quickly promoted to Chief. Unfortunately I can't find his discharge papers and remaining family *partly because of censorship* fail to recall the names of any ships on which he served. Two aunts remember him being assigned to 'Dover Patrol' and I have a blue 'station card', from when he was a CPO on the battle cruiser HMS Hood. But that must've been in the early days of WWII as he was lucky to be elsewhere when the Bismarck tragically sealed her fate, *leaving only a handful of survivors* on 24TH May 1941.

We have four decorations *there were originally five - there being five medal ribbons;* so one has been lost. However, two of the remaining awards give clues as to where he was. One is 'The Atlantic Star' and the other 'The Africa Star', so *although we were never to hear his tales* these are two theatres where he no doubt saw some carnage, but on what ships and in what capacity is now a mystery. Towards the end of his service, in 1944, he was 'taken poorly' at Durban so sent to and hospitalized in Aden, from where he was posted back to the UK with a suspected ulcer and a shadow on one lung. He ended up at Bangour Hospital, near Edinburgh where I remember Mother taking Carnie and myself to see him. We both stood quietly at his bedside, feeling ill at ease, since we had little memory as to who he was - ***yet another absentee father; brainwashed by propaganda into believing the cause righteous and just.***

You will know how boys try to emulate their fathers - I recall Mother telling the story of a time when my globetrotting father was home on Leave, she had called him out to the back garden for some chore, on their returning through the kitchen to the sitting room all was quiet. Daddy's little soldier was nowhere to be seen, until they found me hiding in a corner behind the big old brown rexine armchair, green in the face trying to imitate him by smoking the pipe he'd left smouldering in the ashtray when called to task. I don't remember this misadventure, but it shows devious snappers must be watched, since they're quick, inquisitive and know no fear.

Father was medically discharged from the RN after his recuperation at Bangour, where he had been taught leatherwork; so this had him producing handbags, wallets, purses, belts and even mending shoes. He then attended Leith Nautical College for a period, studying to gain his 'Skipper's Ticket': after much homework and many nights 'burning the midnight oil', he achieved his goal - so it looked like 'we had it made'.

Between his stay in Bangour and being discharged from the Navy his mother died from heart failure - it would have been then because Aunt Sophie can remember that both he and David were in uniform on attending her funeral in Rosebank Cemetery - *a much favoured last 'resting place', where generations of good Newhaveners lie 'pushing up the daisies'*.

Soon after my grandmother's death, David was discharged from the RAF with pleurisy. When 'hale an' hearty' he found employment with Henry Robb, the shipbuilders in Leith whose yard, I'm told, never closed, working day and night, thus making a magnificent contribution to the war effort; reputedly, launching ships to the tune of one a month. David worked there for many years, as a driver and later a timekeeper. It goes without saying that his ex-workmates will remember and still talk of 'The Newhaven Yank'.

Petty Officer Roy Wright, 1939

As for my war - I regularly get dreamlike visions o' crouchin' in the damp, candlelit Anderson shelter, an' ma mother pushin' me *wearin' ma 'Mickey Mouse' gas mask* tae the Buttercup Dairy wi' a machine gun mounted on the front o' ma pram. Then later makin' ma way tae school, deafened by the sirens wailin' on top o' copboxes, while dodgin' bombs rainin' doon frae the gloomy grey sky.

5: Tragedy

The Spring morning in 1945 is as if yesterday, when Father and I went to visit his family and many relatives at Newhaven; but both requiring a haircut, our first 'port of call' was Wattie the barber's shop in Main Street. I suppose it must've been a Saturday otherwise I'd have been at school; Jeepers, I was scared stiff of this barber and dreading my turn because he had these newfangled electric clippers. The reason for my fear was, that up until then I'd been a victim of the local hairstylist on the corner of Beaverbank Place, just yards from the top of Logie Green Road.

Now, this was a miserable old geezer with thick glasses and an arthritic back. Due to his spondylitis ridden spine, the size of young boys and his chair not being a modern barbers' adjustable type, he would put a plank of wood between the arms for youngsters to sit on. Because he was near blind nicking ears with his fancy scissors *which he wielded like a dervish* was a regular occurrence; but the terrifying part was, when using his hand-operated clippers he would all too often pull them away before giving the handles a final squeeze to sever what hair was still between the blades. So, instead of being cut a tuft of hair was yanked out to a yell of "Oh ya!"

The old bugger must have been deaf as well as blind, because you never got a sorry, only a grunt, and your head pushed in whatever direction he required for his next error of judgement. With that explanation I'm sure you'll understand my sheer terror of what electric clippers might be capable. My fears of course were unfounded and thereafter 'The Demon Barber of Beaverbank's' torture chamber was given a body swerve.

What happened next changed my life forever. Before going to Grandfather's house at Laverockbank, we made a short detour round the corner and across the road to Newhaven Harbour, which was a five-star attraction for small and big boys alike. In those days when the fishing fleet was in there were so many boats, all nicely painted, with names such as 'Gratitude', 'The Fair Maid' and 'Fertility' so tightly packed into this neat little harbour that it was possible to get from one side of the dock to the other by scrambling from boat to boat. At such times the port was bustling with activity and, adding to this already busy scene was the fishmarket immediately beyond the slipway on the eastern boundary.

The market, like the harbour, no longer serves its original purpose and has for many years been a Harry Ramsden's chippie incorporating the Newhaven Museum, *both already mentioned* - therefore it's a foregone conclusion that the only boats to be seen in this picture postcard harbour since the 1970s, have been pleasure boats. What used to be the Bank of Scotland *no doubt a busy branch, holding the accounts of most of the Newhaven fishing fraternity and residents,* across from the harbour closed its doors years ago and was acquired in the mid 70s by the Port O'Leith Motor Boat Club - yet another sad sign of the times.

Anyway, where did I get to? - oh yeah, while I'm enjoying the scene and probably daydreaming; you know the drill, "I'd do this and I'd do that", my dad had been exchanging pleasantries with a group of fishermen he knew *having learned his profession working alongside many of them* and, I imagine, being congratulated on now having his 'Skipper's Ticket' and, if anything like 'yours truly', fair revelling in the glory.

With the gabbing at long last over, we were about to head along Starbank Road and up the hill *(Laverockbank Avenue)* to Grandfather's house, when we met a man Father obviously knew well; so *to my dismay* stopped by the sea wall for yet another blether, during which the man asks my father to stand in for him as he is due to 'shipout' but needs to stay put.

I can't, now, remember his excuse, but it was either he was going on holiday or his daughter was ill. Whichever of the two is immaterial, as he was desperate, to say the least. My dad said "No", reasoning that he did not want to sail as 'first fisherman', saying he would prefer to secure a Captain's position, having just qualified so to do. We parted company, us going towards Laverockbank and the man heading, dejected, in the opposite direction towards the harbour. When only yards apart Father turned and called the chap back - whether feeling guilty or needing 'an earner' I'll never know - anyway, whatever his reason, Father said he would do the trip. The man, looking relieved, thanked my father, shook his hand vigorously and we carried on our way to Grandad's house.

Let me tell you, there is no doubt that Grandfather Wright and Grandfather Webber were as alike as chalk and cheese; so had a totally different approach when it came to handling unruly grandchildren. Grandfather Wright was a sly old fox with a twinkle in his eyes: his method

was to tire us out, so we became quiet and subdued. His favourite ploy was allowing us into his prizeworthy back garden, but not to run amok trampling the flower beds, ***au contraire***, he had a garden roller which Carnie and myself on either side of the long wooden handle *like two harnessed oxen* would push back and forward, needless to say his lawn was as flat as a bowling green. Yeah, you'd better believe it, he was as fly as a barrel o' monkeys and sharp as a tack!

Grandfather Webber was of the old Victorian school, he remained distant - believing 'children should be seen and not heard' - *'twas probably in his house that I first heard that expression.* To this day I don't remember talking to the man other than saying please or thank you; his strict manner no doubt stemmed from his own upbringing in the said Welsh orphanage. He always sat in the parlour relaxing in **his** armchair, wearing a three-piece dark blue pinstripe suit, sporting his coveted gold watch chain on the waistcoat, listening to the BBC Home Service while smoking one of his many pipes and every so often spitting a sizzler into the open fire.

There was an impressive library of reference books in the parlour, with amongst the collection, a complete set, *volumes one to eight*, of the 'Books of Knowledge' - big well-bound tomes with blue and gold covers, full of photos, illustrations and facts covering everything from the Seven Wonders of the World to giant anaconda snakes in the Amazon. I remember a photo of this huge reptile lying coiled sunning itself on the riverbank while digesting a large animal it had swallowed **whole**, the telltale sign being a considerable lump one third of the way down the snake's body - I sure as hell didn't fancy going anywhere near the Amazon!

Well now, Carnie and I were given a book each and sent into the 'front sitting room', which was very plush, boasting a piano with silver-plated candleholders that swivelled, but we didn't dare to as much as lift the lid - what we did was what we were told and that was read the books, exchanging as and when necessary. Being young boys we found these visits boring, so hated going to Restalrig Terrace, but of course at that age there was no option. The only times we looked forward to visiting that house were Christmas Days for a cracking feed *(dig in yer at yer grannie's)* and opening lots of exciting and mysterious gift-wrapped presents from the many aunts and uncles - big families can have their merits.

So getting back to the story: with the weekend over it's time to 'earn a crust' - before leaving Father gives Mother a lingering goodbye hug, while telling me I'm the man of the house when he is away, so must look after everyone, and here's me only seven years old - I look up at him and nod in agreement saying nothing, but feeling stupid. He has to go to Ardrossan on the west coast to join his ship; in the 'dark days' no fishing was done in the North Sea - this being a tinderbox, dangerously close to Nazi Germany; instead they'd be 'working' the moderately safer waters of the Irish Sea. The steam trawler he joined was 'Ethel Crawford', registered in Granton, owned by The Ardrossan Trawling Company Ltd and managed by a Glasgow outfit trading as Walter K Paton (fish salesmen).

The vessel sailed from Ardrossan on Thursday 19th of April 1945 on what was intended to be a ten-day fishing trip. Catastrophically she and her nine crew members were blown to 'kingdom come' by a magnetic mine on Friday the 20th south east of Ailsa Craig at 55.13' N 05.14' W. All that is now left of the wreck *(WK No.43 North Channel chart)* is one main section and five smaller pieces, lying at a depth of about 160 feet, categorized as non-dangerous wreck No.3854. The mine which sank Ethel Crawford was laid by the German submarine U-218, which was operating in that area, commanded by Lt. Rupprecht Stock. Ethel Crawford's sinking was reported by the Germans as being in grid square AM65; this was the procedure used to inform 'the Fatherland'. *U-218 claimed two previous 'kills' under Lt. Stock's predecessor Captain Becker.*

DAUGHTER ILL, DID NOT SAIL

Nine trawlermen lost

Nine men, including six from Edinburgh, lost their lives when the Glasgow-owned trawler Ethel Crawford, which left a Scottish port last Thursday on a fishing trip, foundered off the coast and became a total wreck.

The missing men are:—Arthur Scales, Trinity-crescent (skipper); William Bowman, Colinton Mains-drive (mate); Roy Wright, Logie Green; Thomas Ritchie, Bonnington-road; James Geddes, Granton-terrace; Alexander Shields, Pier Place, Newhaven—all of Edinburgh; Robert Ewing, York-street, Ayr; and Thomas Drysdale, Fort Place, and John Henry, Sailors' Home, both of Leith.

The illness of his daughter saved Arthur Scales, son of the skipper. He decided to miss the trip, which was to have lasted ten days, and his place was taken by Roy Wright.

For my father, who had seen action with the Royal Navy during austere years of war and lived through the savage blitzes of the south coast ports; to then forfeit his life in this relatively safe environment, a mere 17 days before the Germans surrendered, was a travesty and what is more, the very next day would have been his twenty-seventh birthday.

On the evening of VE day the jubilant peasants were singing and dancing on the streets - we stayed, lights out, behind closed doors.

I've never found out how U-218 ended its days, but was told she surrendered to the Royal Navy at the end of the war. Of course it's fair to say, I've often wondered if she just might have been one of the U-boats referred to in chapter three as lying in Granton Harbour, after hostilities.

They go on about and glorify 'the spoils of war' - yeah, that'll be right. Father's medals arrived posthumously through the post, in a small brown cardboard box, some months after his death; uncannily on Mother's birthday - such a sad occurrance. I didn't say as much, but thought he'd managed to send her a present from wherever. That wasn't all he left us, as brother Michael was born on St Andrew's Day of that tragic year; so Mother *one of the many unsung heroines whose world fell apart,* lost her husband and was left 'boracic' with two brats and 'a bun in the oven'; which probably accounts for **her** short lifespan - ***for some, it's no bed o' roses.***

With being young, optimistic, and unable to accept reality *like many others who have lost relatives and no body recovered* the thought was always there that Father was possibly, just possibly, still alive and might, just might, turn up someday, having regained his memory, lost in the explosion, and clinging to some floating wreckage washed up days later bedraggled and dazed on a lonely beach. We all have hopes and dreams, but chance would be a fine thing - if there's such a thing as luck, there is for sure far more bad than good in my experience.

There's one thing more I must add before continuing - it came to mind earlier, but wasn't at that point appropriate to mention, because I hadn't as yet spoken of Father's premature death. On one of our lunchtime jaunts from school down to the harbour, it was a day when the seagulls seemed extremely noisy and agitated. The ever-wise Alec Young looked up and said that gulls carried the souls of drowned sailors trying to find their way home. I'd never heard that saying before and wondered if one of them could be assisting my dead father. Years later, Alec *like so many of our generation* went to sea, as an Engineer Officer in the Merchant Navy: makes me think of Auntie 'Teenie', an astute far-seeing old lady relative in Newhaven who often said "The sea's in yer blood laddie and there's nothin' ye can do aboot it!"

6: Leith Academy

That's it, the summer holidays are just a memory. I'm all of twelve years old and have a place in Leith Academy; an uninspiring brick and stone three-storey building at the foot of Easter Road. Behind, and to the east of 'The Academy' is Leith Links, in which there are two conspicuous grass-covered mounds, named in the Edinburgh A-Z street atlas as 'Giant's Brae' and 'Lady Fife's Brae'. These names I was unaware of before today; up until now they had merely been hillocks, with two interesting, but conflicting stories; probably neither of which is true. One tale tells that victims of the Black Death were buried there in mass graves. The other *sounding more feasible* was that during the siege of Leith, around 1651, Oliver Cromwell's cannons could not achieve the required elevation, so to redress the problem these mounds were built, then the artillery hauled on top, to give it greater range, and so, demolish the town's defensive walls.

It's certainly a shock to the system leaving primary school, where we get used to being 'the big boys', as when in our final year we 'rule the school'. Then we go on to secondary as new pupils and therefore the youngest, so it takes time to adjust to being 'the insignificant wee boys' again. In fact it takes until we move up to Second Year; allowing the admission of a new batch of sprogs, thus making us feel haughty and superior.

Regrettably, I don't have a class photo from Leith Academy, so can't remember classmates, other than special friends and stars. I've already exploited the fact that 'the enemy' had miraculously grown tits, consequently transforming themselves into objects of desire; so were proudly exhibiting what they had sprouted - many, as yet, untouched, but some 'hand-reared' and neatly stowed in crisp new training bras. There were more than a few 'wee smashers' in our class - yes, we'd got lucky; and just at a time when we were starting to take an interest - by now not a sissy thing to do; strange how stirring hormones can change one's opinions, ***innit!***

Being a large school it had to be strictly disciplined, unlike and in contrast to the small modern primary I'd attended for seven years. This was a total wake-up call; to me it seemed like a prison - I detested the place

from the moment I set foot in it until the day I was released.

Firstly I'll speak of a few of the teachers; there were of course many, this being a fair-sized institution. Primary schools had one teacher per class for a whole year or more. This was however a new and unnerving experience, with the day carved into segments for the different subjects - each lesson having its own teacher, requiring us to trail *in an orderly fashion* to the classroom and teacher giving us our next forty-minute lesson period; this often entailing a bit of a trek; as when changing floors from first to top or whatever. So, we could have four *plus* teachers in a single day, which is fair enough, but no joke if they all decided to give us homework, as in those days when given homework, **you did it**. Remember, we had no calculators or computers to help us, so it was an inconvenience which nonetheless resulted in us getting educated to an acceptable standard.

Well now, each class had a teacher responsible for the register - our 'reggie' - Miss McDonald - looked every bit the schoolmarm from the bun in her hair to the tweed suit and glasses. In those days teachers wore a mortar board and gown; thus proclaiming authority and, backed up with the leather strap they carried, the respect necessary to competently run a school full of what could well've been unruly teenagers. It seems cut and dried to me that if there's no respect and enforced obedience you're on a loser from day one. Look at what's happened since the sixties, when *more's the pity* sanctimonious, liberal-thinking tubes abolished punishment; teachers stopped dressing properly and pitched-up in casual gear, trying to suck up to the students; therefore lost their power, were unable to control the pupils and so, couldn't drum sense into the little imbeciles. Was that **ever** a 'no brainer' - *in essence, **you're fucked before you start!***

Getting back down off my soapbox and on with the story: here is an accurate description of our register teacher. Everyone must have seen the 'Looney Tunes' cartoon 'Tweetie Pie', so you'll be familiar with the 'lil ole lady' who owned the canary and was forever 'knockin' seven bells' oot o' that 'bad ole pussy cat' with her broom - right, you've got it! Miss McDonald was a ringer for her. She had a gift in the way she controlled her classes: this was a 'smart old gal' who had seen and heard it all; not unlike the comedian, who, on getting heckled in working men's clubs, always has an answer which puts mouthy gits in their place without actually offending

- **a professional**. There are so many things I can still hear her saying; like the time she asked an inmate whose property something he had was; his reply being "It's mines Miss" and her, wearing a shocked expression, saying "Mines boy, mines! What kind of mines? Diamond mines! Gold mines! Coal mines! **Grammar,** boy, **grammar!** It is **mine**, not mines!" That was a lesson probably well learned and remembered by him and a few other young uncouth coves whose vocabulary required a wee polish.

The prudish Miss Pope was our geography, and also our history teacher. She was, I'd guess, in her mid-to-late-twenties, pretty in a classical English-rose way, her chestnut-brown frizzy hair worn long and crimped in a style of the day. She went an'got herself married during the Easter break when we were in our second year, I remember us all scrutinizing her when she returned from her honeymoon after the hols, to see if she looked different now that she was getting the 'old meat injection'. But the delicately prim Miss Pope, by now Mrs Beaming, still looked *(and walked)* as before - *oh what innocents we were, as to life's great mysteries.*

Mr Forsyth, our science teacher, a small dapper fellow who sported a neatly-trimmed pencil moustache, in his late thirties or maybe early forties - a strict no-nonsense man. We hated his class, this may sound odd as one would imagine science to be fun with all these experiments, bunsen burners and test tubes - yeah, in yer effin dreams, pal. All I remember was him reading from textbooks and us poor little sods having to write it down page after page in our exercise books. But that's not all, when I said no nonsense I meant **no nonsense!** This man sure as hell knew how to lay it on when giving punishment. Most teachers were referred to as giving the strap, but not him, no one ever said he gave the strap, he gave **the belt** and if they came in sizes, his was extra large. Rumour had it that he soaked 'Satan' in a special solution over the weekends to keep it at peak performance level. Being 'vertically challenged' he'd stand on his platform when dishing out the strokes, with the poor scared 'never do it again' pupil quaking at floor level. This sadist really put his back into it and sometimes Satan would go further up the hand than expected, flicking the inner wrist faster than a striking snake, **"Oh ya!"**

The French teacher was a tall slim lanky man, with straight dark brylcreemed hair and a side parting. He, also, wore a 'tache'; in fact

if you ever saw 'Allo 'Allo! on telly you may remember the 'French' gendarme who said everything wrong - well, our Mr Young could've been his twin. This man had no sense of humour whatsoever, but one morning, unwittingly, had us in fits. There he was standing on his platform in front of the blackboard, chalking up sentences about the fictional French family Monsieur and Madame Lépine et leetle Toto, then using his pointer, *as was his way,* tapping it at certain words to emphasize something. ***'Zoot Alors'!*** - he didn't realize his flies were undone and shirt poking out from the the 'trouser trout's' lair. This was, as you can imagine, hilarious, especially to les Mesdemoiselles - *many close to wetting themselves.* One girl, and I do remember who, kept whispering that she was going to tell him 'the windae wus open' - she put her hand up several times saying "Please sir?" but promptly 'changed her tune' when sternly acknowledged.

Mr Lovat, this foppish young rake, was our art teacher, late twenties, quite handsome with longish light-brown wavy hair - he looked 'arty-farty'and certainly portrayed the part. His prominently checked tweed suit was fashioned from the same material as Rupert Bear's scarf; this was complimented by a spotted kipper necktie, fussy pocket handkerchief *that clashed with the tie,* and obligatory brown suede brogues.

'Twas educational, although not on the curriculum, when a girl, wrote on the blackboard "Mr Lovat is a Poof"; now, the rest of us didn't have a clue as to what this meant - we're fourteen at this time and, as said earlier, pretty innocent. So, an exasperated Maggie explains it to us 'thickoes' - luckily someone cleaned the blackboard, *thus 'saving the day'* before the art teacher arrived. The flamboyant Mr Lovat proved otherwise by marrying soon after the incident and, if other than fiction, to 'the bitch wi' the twitch' - one of his string of tidy female models.

We of course had other teachers but I can neither recall their faces nor names, although I have a fleeting image of our woodwork teacher wrapped in his brown overall; so we'll carry on to some of the more memorable pupils, starting with girls, since I've already immortalized this unforgettable bold girl. Margaret Haston was a tall, gifted but unruly, straight-limbed strawberry blonde from the Restalrig district, who no doubt would've looked rather special by her late teens. Seemingly she had three older brothers who were not to be messed with, which may well have accounted

for her wild streak and know-all brash guise. Although us boys didn't feel intimidated by, the often too lippy for her own good, Maggie, she commanded a healthy respect from all in her presence.

Norma, a fascinating female, not beautiful but extremely attractive and blessed to live in a superb body: fancying her rotten and thinking I might get lucky, I found this girl a great distraction in classes where she sat in my line of vision, I'm sure she must've been aware of this and possibly embarrassed by my very obvious attention. We bumped into each other in town a few years after leaving school, when my muse looked as alluring as ever. Her occupation escapes me, but I've a gnawing suspicion she worked in a lawyer's office; however do recall her saying she was engaged to an Officer in the Merchant Navy. I couldn't help thinking at the time, jammy git, you've got yourself a corker - ***lucky*** *golden-balled* ***bastard!***

Lorna, now here was a girl to remember, a 'stoater' - you'll have noticed I don't recollect the 'glaiks'. *Yes, it's true, I've always been good at wiping the slate and erasing memories of no interest to myself.* So, back to Lorna - an only child who lived with her mother in the fashionable New Town. No mention was made of what had become of the father; perhaps, like my own, he'd copped it in the war, but the general opinion was that he had been moneyed and 'shot through'. Lorna certainly had the airs and graces of superiority, she spoke well, was a proper little madam and, if the truth be known, a spoiled brat; said to be of French descent - ***ooh la la!*** When daydreaming, I found it so easy to conjure up an image of her dressed as a revolutionary peasant, sat on a three-legged wooden stool, caught up in the gory moment looking enthralled, and flushed with excitement, whilst feverishly knitting at the side of Madame la Guillotine's platform as startled severed heads of the French Nobility, toppled *accompanied by a drum roll* with regularity into a filthy blood-splattered straw-lined basket.

We are all aware that when fourteen, well put together girls can easily pass themselves off for eighteen plus; with the help of some 'slap', Pretty Polly seamless nylons, Maidenform bras and, as one wit said, American knickers *(one Yank and they're down)*. The story was, that this is what the precocious Lorna and 'Heather the Blether' did at the weekends, when, 'twas claimed, they flirted with gum-chewing GIs from the USAF airbase at Kirknewton - an airfield near Edinburgh, long since abandoned by the

Yanks, who were very much in evidence around Edinburgh in the fifties. They were the 'chosen ones' with plenty loot, smart uniforms and flash cars. These guys must have been anointed, and then some, what a ball they had here; I well remember them and knew a few in my later teen years - someone I worked with - *could've been 'Dirty Donald' the Polisher* said "If there's another war the Yanks won't need to send any men to help us; just uniforms, for all the bastards they left behind them!"

The boys who I remember well were - first, Willie 'Tinker' Thompson from Lochend. How he got the nickname 'Tinker' I never knew, as he was already so tagged when he arrived at 'The Academy' along with some other classmates who had attended Lochend Primary with him. He was a nice little chap; skinny, pale-skinned with glasses, a ringer for Milhouse in 'The Simpsons'; it was said from a large family - hence, wearing hand-me-down clobber, for which he took a bit o' ribbing from less than well-mannered fellow pupils. Young Tinker never got upset and took it all in his stride which said a lot for this mild-natured wee guy. The amazing thing was that I met him in Princes Street when we'd both be about eighteen and guess what? Tinker was an apprentice blacksmith, and well on his way to becoming 'one big guy' - *I recently learned that, having been a Sea Cadet privileged him to do his National Service in the Royal Navy.*

Eric Smith, he lived with his older brother and father, a professional man, in a large Georgian flat, halfway down Leith Walk. I liked Eric, he was an interesting popular lad, who *I recall* had lost his mother when he was quite young. I got out of touch with him and most others on leaving school, as one does, but think someone told me his older brother became a City Councillor - maybe not, as I've a vague notion I'm confusing him with another person, possibly Eric Eadie - well, it's been a while!

Harry Jeffreys, now here is an unforgettable young man who came from a football-mad family, another of the Lochend contingent, and so, probably a Hibs supporter. You know, two seconds ago I could see him as plain as daylight with his green and white scarf, but then imagined a maroon and white scarf, which would make him a Hearts fan. So Harry baby if you should ever read this I apologize and say in my defence "A lot o' water's passed under the bridge". Now, Harry is famous in my memory for more than just the colours on his scarf. Harry had many talents, but his claim

to fame was his impersonations of his idol Bill Haley, the creator and king of Rock and Roll. He was 'Numero Uno' in the days when Bill Haley and his Comets had teenagers rockin' in the aisles with the likes of 'See ya later Alligator'. You know, while giving it the 'old verbal' there, I could see Bill Haley's coupon in my mind's eye and realized I had made one ginormous cock-up, because something didn't look right. That face with the 'kiss curl' plastered on its forehead was wrong and slowly transformed to the face of Frankie Lane; and now the memories flood back. Whenever the teacher left the room and 'Flash' Harry got the chance, he'd be up on the platform, in his element, givin' it 'nanty' beltin' out 'Do not Forsake me Oh my Darlin' - take it from me, Harry was more than just good; he was X Factor quality; just spawned to entertain.

Alex Howden, also one of the Lochend ruffians - a likeable streetwise kid, long before being streetwise was even thought of. Alex, who wusnae fir bairns tae play wi', knew all the tricks; a born survivor. At break, or 'playtime' as it was then called, Alex, Eric Smith and myself usually teamed up and went along to the Home Bakery in Duke Street for some goodies when we were flush; and often as not when Eric and I were skint Alex would treat us, as being smart he was rarely short o' dosh. We lost our mate halfway through the Second Year, as the streetwise kid got himself expelled from 'The Academy', for what, I'm not sure since it was hushed up. Just like when someone gets their jotters at work for 'being naughty' no one in management, for some strange reason, wants to talk about it and all the troops are 'fair burstin' to know. Anyway, tittle-tattle had it that our Alex had called Mademoiselle Lorna a cow, to which she'd taken umbrage and reported him, possibly colouring the accusation, which seems a bit trivial to merit such a harsh punishment. So, one day Alex was in class as normal and the next he's history. But guys like this don't stay history for long, so being expelled from Leith Academy didn't do Alex any harm, as I will explain - **patience, pal, patience; ah'm goin' as fast as ah can!**

OK, OK, when on Leave from the Navy some years later, I met Alex outside Fairley's dancehall *(now there was a place!)*. He told me he was a bus driver with Edinburgh Corporation, but in his spare time trying to establish a career as a stand-up comedian; *which, in my opinion, he had been from day one*. I suppose that's when I should've asked him the, now

irrelevant, reason why he was 'chucked oot'. Anyway, Alex 'made the grade' and is well-known on the circuit as "Happy Howden". He has made videos, been on television on numerous occasions and appeared in major films - yes, I would say the streetwise kid achieved success.

Now then, howzabout this! One morning Sandy McSquirter *an inter-scholastic 'pocket-billiards' champion* caused considerable excitement in the ranks on claiming to be able to 'shoot his bolt', when, as far as was known, everyone was still 'firin' blanks', so we are all interested; you're right - more than just interested. But, true to form, we're needling him by calling him a liar, naturally because of our jeering, tipped over the edge, he blurts out "I'll show you, I'll fuckin' show you".

By the time we get to the music room, we've really got him wound-up and opportunity knocks when teacher gets called away on some pretext; demanding a sneak preview, everyone crowds round Sandy's desk and the chant is "Come on Sandy show us, let's see a 'nifty fifty' then". The bold lad undoes his trouser buttons, extracts the tossle, and proceeds to 'crack one off'. What a hero - **it's showtime!** It was admirable that he could 'rise to the occasion' in front of such a rowdy audience - the numbers bolstered by a group of curious giggling girls gawping in hypnotic fascination - *possibly, anxious to see what the future holds in store for them.*

As we know, some are born exhibitionists, nevertheless Sandy deserved a nomination for his performance - far from being put off 'his stroke' by his sniggering entourage the 'man of the moment' was obviously turned on, and, dedicated to his cause, giving it five, ten, double ten, five ten, a hundred hits 'the vinegar strokes' and gets a result in record time. Although other than a noble effort, the young twerp 'shot his load' and proved his point *so to speak* making him 'flavour of the month' *(it's said we all achieve fifteen minutes of fame in our lifetime - perhaps those were his).*

We, his eager audience, were anticipating much more, so pardon the pun when I say it was an anticlimax; as what we were led to expect *(from the whispered boasts of the 'big boys')* was, the grande finale being like an explosion with the 'white stuff' squirting so high it fused the lights and decorated the bedroom ceiling - ***gosh, if only!***

We had a well endowed girl in the year above us who must've been groped by every boy *and **Tut-Tut** possibly some of the girls* in 'The

Academy'. 'Twas the done thing to lunge at her tits, grab her ass or try to get your hand up her gymslip when to-ing and fro-ing changing classrooms and passing her on the stairs. Philma just giggled and said "Stoap it ya dirty buggers", but Philma Crackin must've liked it because she never grassed us up; which kept this raunchy schoolgirl right at the top of the popularity stakes 'til the day she graduated. I guess she was so delighted with the generous bounty life's lottery had bestowed on her she saw it as her calling to share her abundant charms with the rest of mankind.

Oops, I've wandered off again - where was I? Oh yeah, prattling on about classmates; so, last but not least, Arthur Copland. I recently chanced to meet 'Copey', a quiet unassuming Leith lad, and would you 'Adam 'n' Eve' it - turns out we were 'Jolly Jack Tars' at the same time in the 'Swinging Sixties'. Copey, when an innocent teenager, had 'signed on' as a 'grease monkey' and rose through the ranks to become a Leading Hand - **yes a Killick Stoker** - so, rightly or wrongly, branded an animal; as like it or not, the reputation and notoriety goes with the territory. I suppose it's a safe bet that, blissfully unaware of each other's presence, we must've crossed paths more than once when 'dahn sowf' in our heyday.

At 'Leithy' I wasn't compelled to rely upon 'school denners', as I was fed by my grandmother at Restalrig Terrace which was only five minutes walk from 'The Academy' - I counted myself fortunate, *as this was a granny who knew how to cook.* After a good tightner I would sit for twenty minutes or so, listening to the radio for an update on the Korean War, with my good friend 'Mickey the Moggy' purring while sleeping on my lap. He was called Mickey because he was tiger-striped with an 'M' mark on his forehead, and a big handsome friendly chap he was. I think Aunt Margaret had rescued him from a brewery, or some such story. It was certainly Mickey's lucky day that day, as he was well looked after and enjoyed the mollycoddled lifestyle of a favoured young prince at number 27.

One such day while sitting listening to the radio after lunch *(with Mickey sleeping and purring at the same time, while using me as a bed)*, I heard a lying twat feeding us the usual sugar-coated shite, saying we'd have to tighten our belts for a few more years, then pigs **would** fly. Well, it's not for me to cast aspersions, **but** that was more than fifty years ago and I'm still waiting: if anything this now multiracial ***overcrowded*** country is in a

worse state today than it was then. They wonder why people don't bother to vote - useless bunch of beyond reproach self-centred lily-livered trumpet-blowing sleazebags, couldnae organize a Halloween Hop! Call me a bigot if you will, but seeing the bigger picture *like many* I maintain dithering politicians and pampered religious zealots are the cancer of society.

I must give mention to 'the Impaler', I've forgotten who he was, but not his sadistic prank that backfired - I'm sure he was in our year, but certainly not our class, otherwise I'd remember. No doubt trying to impress his pals, the demon impaled a frog to a tree in the Links beside the school and to the frog's hind legs he tied 'bangers', lit the blue touch paper and hastily backed off, but his retreat wasn't quite fast enough, so got his comeuppance when one squib exploded sooner than he anticipated. This of course was quickly followed by the second banger going off; as planned, his victim *now past caring* was was blown to bits, most of which decorated the evil little rascal's blue uniform blazer and school tie. Yes, youngsters tend to be callous and attach no value to the lives of small creatures; but that was mean - ***methinks, a candidate for 'the naughty chair'.***

I travelled to Leith Academy on a No. 35 bus and returned on a 34 - *maybe it was the other way round, as one did a circular route one way and the other the opposite*. This service suited my purpose well, as it went from the top of Logie Green Road, passed Leith Docks and right to the school gates, which couldn't be better. I refer to Leith Docks, as every day when the bus passed 'The Shore' I would look at the 'Fairfree'; this was a prototype factory-trawler converted by, or I should say **for** The Christian Salvesen Shipping Co. from an old Naval wartime corvette. This innovation *(which fascinated me no end; wondering how it had looked in its prime)* was tied up there, out of commission, like a ghost ship, with only a watchman onboard for many years. The trials must have been successful, as they later designed and built the M.F.V. Fairtry, an up-to-the-minute factory-trawler on which I would, before long, get my first 'taste of the sea'; so you can anticipate that while we cover the next six years.

When fourteen I got my first job, working as a milkboy for Peter Sweeney, who had a very old-fashioned dairy shop *sorely in need of a lick of paint* in Rodney Street. Peter must have been about fifty then and had the worst hunchback I have ever seen, in fact so bad, 'Fast' Eddie was

convinced he kept a parachute under his jacket. Peter lived with his sister in a second-floor flat on the other side of Rodney Street, opposite his shop, but I'm sure he spent most of his life in the dairy, opening about four-thirty each morning, Monday 'til Saturday. We, the milkboys *I think there were five of us, one being my near neighbour Alex Hogg,* started about six forty-five and took an hour or so to do our 'runs', then rushed home to get ready for the daily dash to quench our relentless thirst for knowledge.

When I said old-fashioned, I meant it, so give me a minute to explain. Our milk wasn't in bottles, it arrived at the shop in ten-gallon churns; from these Peter would ladle out the required amount for each customer into small *lidded* receptacles, which we would then deliver to the flats on our runs, often having to pour milk into jugs left at front doors - not very hygienic, with many dingy common-stairs fair stinkin' o' cat pee - but that's the way it was. My run was mostly in Heriot Hill Terrace, a street of tenements close to the shop. On Saturdays we would start later and ring our customers' doorbells to collect the money due to Peter, who then paid us a meagre six shillings (30p) a week. Christmas was great because most customers gave us a tip, which could bolster our wage to as much as fifteen shillings (75p), this was magic, seeming like a small fortune to us back in those days, *when money wus money and worth somethin'*.

Crikey, that first winter working as a milkboy was more than just a bit parky, so one Saturday afternoon Alex and myself went up to Millets, the Army and Navy Store in Leith Street, and treated ourselves to ex-RAF pilots' soft leather flying helmets with round rubber earpieces for the planes' intercoms to plug into. Lots of boys wore them, as they were the 'in thing' and dirt cheap, so we 'style gurus' saw ourselves as 'bees' knees'.

Most of my 'hard-earned' went to Fernies of Dalry, who had a cycle shop *now a 'chinky' takeway* down by Bonnington Toll Bridge - this was me striving to become one of the elite, in buying a brand new pea-green Raleigh Lenton Racer *on 'the never-never'* - it cost about fifteen pounds and took somewhere around a year and a half to pay off - an early introduction to the rigours of a lifetime o' debt.

At the end of the Third Year, having completed my formal education, I left Leith Academy; if I had learned nothing else in my ten years of schooling, I'd discovered how to think things through and put what I

had been taught to my advantage. So, after our final exams were over I saw no beneficial reason for going to school anymore; we, who would be leaving at end of term the following month would just be marking time while waiting for the exam results to come through and hopefully gain our Scottish Schools Leaving Certificate (S.L.C.). Whatismore we were due to start learning algebra - ALGEBRA! What a complete waste of space!

Well now, having been bedevilled by acute hay fever every June and July since I was eleven *(this somewhat spoiled early summer, which should have been the nicest part of the year)* it was now time for payback. So, I decided to take advantage of my disadvantage; every week for three weeks I forged a note saying that 'yours truly' had been to the doctor who had advised that his patient should stay at home and indoors, as this season the pollen count was extremely high. These notes I posted to my register teacher, Miss McDonald: this ruse was an inspired move and I'm proud to say, never sussed out by Mother, or anyone with authority.

By the third week I was so confident that I blatantly wrote a similar note for one of my pals; and they 'bought it' - so he had a week off his school to keep me company, during which my BSA Cadet Major air rifle got a guid usin'. Better put you in the picture, in case you're thinking that I must've dropped myself in the 'tom-tit', as Grandmother would've wondered what had happened to me and informed Mother *(by now in full-time secretarial employment)*. Being a crafty little sod, I saw no point in going without; therefore, not letting good food go to waste, each day I mounted my trusty Raleigh Lenton then skited, 'hell for leather', to Restalrig Terrace for a tasty lunch; as when 'swingin' the lead', one must be devious *and then some*.

I reluctantly went back to 'The Academy' for the final term week to both bid farewell to fellow inmates and, ceremoniously, be presented with my leaving certificate. Being a logical thinker it seemed obvious to me that the S.L.C.s would be distributed on the final day, before summer break up. But no, lo and behold they are dished out on the Tuesday. Now, I ask you, were the decision-makers crackers; or what? They had played right into our hands, so like the Jew's foreskin - **we were off!** I mean to say what's the point of finishing the week, **when we have just been handed our ticket to freedom and the big outside world.**

7: The Apprentice

The big outside world - yes! Freedom? ***Ma erse!*** within days a card arrives commanding me to honour an appointment with a Careers Adviser at the Youth Employment Office in the Council Buildings on the High Street. There it is, stamped on the card, my very own National Insurance Number, you've got to hand it to this democracy, when it comes to efficiency they are on the ball. But that is only, as we all know, when the Government and Council 'freewheelers' are to benefit from their long-proven and well-oiled machinery. However, it's one-way traffic - try getting something back and nine times out of ten there are so many obstacles put in your way that, demoralized, you either give up or there's a reason to disqualify you.

So, in my quest for fame and fortune, I keep the appointment, and three further ones with this self-important charlatan, only to be offered each time van-boy jobs. But hold on, it's not as dead end as it sounds, because I have a choice, **milk or bread!** Is this slaverin' git wasting my time or wot? The useless twat's as thick as mince - it's more than likely that I'm better educated than he; and that's saying something, so, surely he jests.

All my pals who've been interviewed by Youth Employment Advisers tell the same story. Everyone knows the score, *and it's still the same today*, the incompetent mutants in cushy, well paid numbers haven't a clue, couldn't give a monkey's and don't do their jobs properly; *as was intended when the positions were created,* but 'you could bet London to an orange' they see a fat salary and index-linked pension as their divine right.

There's an old saying which springs to mind, 'too many chiefs and not enough Indians', now, come to think of it, maybe, no not maybe, that **is** what's wrong with the once ***Great*** Britain. Put it this way, the posers don't actually produce anything, so if there is no end product, where's the profit or proof of any graft at the close of day. The list is endless - what about the filthy germ-infested hospitals; firms actually get paid ***bundles*** to clean them - and we've all heard this one, "There's never a policeman around when you need one" - there's no need to expand, because everyone has a story on **that** subject. Perhaps I should stop there and get on with it, but

I've just got to include this little gem from last night's Scottish News on television. A headless torso *(nae arms an' nae legs)* had been pulled from the Clyde this week. Yesterday it was identified as a twenty-three-year-old drug addict. The closing statement was that the police were treating it as **"suspicious"** - well now; does that not make you wonder?

So anyway, fuck the Careers Officer! We realize 'we're pishin' intae the wind'; so get out there on our own initiative and soon Edinburgh is blessed with a brand new batch of spotty gangling would-be electricians, painters, coachbuilders, joiners and what have you. I've scored a job as a trainee plater in structural engineering, with Redpath Brown, a huge construction engineering firm next to the Hibs ground at Meadowbank, but quickly find it repetitive, boring and soul-destroying, so, pushin' ma luck, ask Eric, my journeyman, to put my name forward to become a welder with the company. Unfortunately, he's not buyin' it and wrongly interpreting this as an insult, pig-headedly *taking the huff* refuses.

Soon after this big disappointment, Billy Colthart, a pal from round the corner at Beaverbank Place, who is an apprentice panelbeater at a coachworks trading as Whittaker & Grant in Grindley Street Court *uptown near the Usher Hall* gives me 'the nod' that they need an apprentice electroplater. Sounds good to me, so I applied and got the job - goodbye Redpath Brown - hello Whittaker & Grant.

Being a pernickety creative fusspot, I enjoyed the work producing all sorts of finishes. Chrome on nickel plate, bronze finishing, brass polishing and lacquering on everything from car parts and letterboxes to ornate French clocks *(brought in by antique dealers from the nearby Grassmarket)*. There were three staff plus myself - I worked alongside the chargehand on the ground floor, where there were huge lead-lined electrolyte-filled baths with anodes hung on the insides, into which the articles were suspended on thin copper wires to be coated with the plating, deposited in a chemical reaction induced by a low-voltage electric current. The gaffer was a guy called Johnny; his surname escapes me - a congenial, easy to get along with chap who'd been a sergeant in the RAF during the war; a tailgunner in Bomber Command; therefore no doubt had a wealth of stories *that would bring a tear to your eye,* but like so many who'd witnessed the horrors of war, had no wish to talk, or be reminded, about it.

Once the 'jobs' had been plated they were taken upstairs to be polished on motorised buffs; this procedure being carried out by two polishers kept busy by us. One of them was a heavy-set 'Toffee Roll' who only spoke a smattering of our language, but seemed to understand it adequately - *one of the multitude who stayed after the war.* He was a quiet man but a good worker, who just plodded on regardless. I remember his face very well - he wore a brush-like moustache; his name was Joe; yeah, that's right, it was 'Joe the Pole'. I know this sounds stupid, but he looked Polish.

His opposite number was completely different - a tall short-sighted skinny character, bordering insanity. Donald was crackers, always twittering like a budgie *(when not singing 'Pale Hands I love, behind the Shalimar')* and forever telling jokes, more than often sexually orientated. The randy old goat had been in the Army and was part of the occupation forces in Berlin at the end of the war, where Donald, like many of his contemporaries, had taken a German bride with whom he now lived in Fountainbridge, I never met her, but those who had agreed she was double gorgeous. They had no children, but not for the want of trying, as every morning anyone in earshot was treated to a very explicit picture of what had happened the previous night; if even half was true, Donald was some boy. I remember the perv telling two gullible fifteen year olds *(Billy and me)* that when courting "the wife" in Berlin, on kissing her goodnight late one evening, she closed her legs and broke his glasses. We didn't know what he was on about, so it took all morning before the penny dropped and by lunchtime Donald was no longer our sexual hero, but a dirty old devil for interfering with a female's plumbing in such a fashion; which I was years later amused to hear Aberdonian messmates refer to as a 'fish supper'.

A favourite trick Billy *(who now lives in sunny Oz)* and I had was to get pennies and halfpennies on to which Billy would solder nails - then, working my magic, I'd nickel plate them, making the pennies look like half-crowns and the halfpennies appear to be shillings. We would hammer them onto wooden stairs and floors then 'end oorsels' watchin' folk trying to pick them up. Some people can be persistent, especially if of Scottish descent and money is involved, so it was amusing to anyone in on the prank; which we eagerly exploited all over town.

Under the stairs was a treasure trove of old car parts, too good to go

out with the scrap-metal. No one was interested or laid claim to what was there, so I had a wee rake around during a lunch-break and discovered some unusual car mascots, which I renovated, polished and lacquered, then had mounted on wooden plinths and since it was Christmas I gave them away as presents. It's a pity I didn't hang onto them, as pukka mascots *(now collectable)* make serious money at specialist auctions.

Mentioning Christmas reminds me of how the working hours were much longer in the fifties. It was a five-and-a-half-day week, starting at eight in the morning and finishing at five, Monday 'til Friday, then on Saturdays quitting at midday. I don't recall any Monday holidays and 'Trades Week Holiday' was one week - not a fortnight *or more* as today. We, in Scotland, worked through Xmas, however were allowed New Year's Day off. I well remember working that Christmas Day then, on finishing, going to Restalrig Terrace for my Christmas dinner which had been kept hot for me; the rest of the family having already feasted, and now relaxing in the 'front sitting room' while catching up on the gossip, with a good old natter.

As much as this interesting profession satisfied my artistic persona; 'ah wus in stook' - because *get this* the city's electroplating industry was so modest the Education Department mandarins claimed they could neither justify nor afford night school facilities to qualify the few apprentices; consequently my job was not officially a trade in Scotland, although it was down south, in England - ***quelle surprise!***

Now, you'll be forgiven for thinking 'So what? - that's no big deal!', but in those days this was serious, as back then we had mandatory 'National Service'. If your job wasn't categorized as a trade, which deferred you from conscription until your apprenticeship was completed, or, as was then said, 'yir time wus oot' which was usually by your twenty-first birthday, like it or lump it you were compelled to serve Queen and Country for a year and a half when eighteen. This controversial obligation was not something the nation's youth relished, since it generally meant getting strong-armed into being a 'squaddie' and paid a couple o' quid a week, from which the Establishment clawed back six shillings for Barrack dues and blanco money. Infringement of civil liberties! - what **are** you talking about?

D'you know, I often wonder how the country afforded all the things it did in yesteryear, when taxation was a fraction of today and there was no

VAT; which, as we know, is a 'dripping roast', bringing in billions for our *hailed as wise* Chancellor to squander. Think about it, National Service, no matter how poor the pay, must have cost fortunes *and then some* to maintain; also, back in the 'Glory Days' we had huge military bases strategically dotted round the Empire to support the Imperial War Machine; what we have now, although technically advanced, is a joke. So, what happened? How did it go stale; and, where's all the 'dosh'? This, or so we keep getting told, is a democracy. **Wotta load o' old cobblers!**

I wonder how many, given the opportunity, would vote for the return of capital punishment - *methinks it's a nap that baying lynch mobs would be draggin' gibbets oot o' storage 'quicker than that'*. The bunch of shysters who've run, or should I say stitched up, this once proud and respected Anglo-Saxon country for the last half century, wonder why a fair percentage don't bother to vote - politicos obviously don't live on the same planet as us 'serfs' who can see their none too clever track record!

Now, pay attention: try hard, real hard, to think of an industry, service or something they haven't fucked or sold off to asset-strippers - not forgetting the lies and incompetence in times of crisis; such as BSE - *believed* linked to CJD (mad cow disease). Why did so many reject the MMR vaccination for their children? Only because the public don't trust the government with their past *well-documented* deceits, when overpaid 'spin doctors' are 'greased' to make it all 'go away' and, in clutching at straws, *'the fixers'* merely dig a bigger hole for their brain-dead zombie masters, who are renowned for covering their cock-ups and inadequacies by selling the 'family silver' and moving the goalposts.

It's amazing how naive the electorate are. Think about it, we vote them in **correction, some of you misguided fools do* then pay them ten times their worth to run the country for us, which the conniving weasels carve up to their own advantage. **Talk about shittin' in yer own nest!** Crivvens, did that old soapbox sneak out again? Someone help me down!

Where was I? Oh yeah, having given a brief explanation about National Service, you'll realize that everyone in their right mind tried to avoid, or at least put it off as long as possible, since it was well-known that it was eventually to be kyboshed. **'Born free'** - who are they kiddin' - so, as far as I was concerned, due to circumstances beyond my control, there was no

option - I had to leave the electroplating business I so enjoyed.

I then became a photographic plan printer which, although sounding technical, was actually a breeze, only taking a matter of days to master. When I took the job with Aitken Dott & Son, a reputable company of fine art dealers whose main shop and gallery was in Castle Street, with workshops behind this property in Rose Street Lane, I was led to believe it was a trade, but that was pie in the sky. It was a simple operation used *before the advent of modern photocopiers* to replicate plans brought in to us by architects of the day. The process was probably archaic; that is if the machine we used was anything to go by. We fed the plans and photographic paper into rollers taking them through the contraption, which then exposed them to an arc-lamp that ran, chain-driven, clanking back and forward along a rail and out came plans and prints at the other side; to be trimmed on a hand-guillotine, with which I managed to take the tip off my right index finger *(it was a right-handed guillotine, and I, for my sins, am a 'leftie').* Crikey, blood everywhere. Health and Safety Accident Book, **what's that?** So anyway, that's more or less all there was to an important sounding job - truth being ah wus vanishin' up ma ane erse.

I worked there for a while alongside George Revolta, a quiet pleasant fellow of Italian extraction who lived with his sister somewhere in the posh Mayfield district. An odd coincidence was that Billy's younger brother Alec Colthart came to Aitken Dott, where he trained to become a picture restorer, and now with many years' experience is a well-known and respected member of his skilled profession; paid 'buckets' by Historic Scotland to return national treasures to their former glory.

Since this was neither a classified trade nor the job for me, I kept my eye on the 'situations vacant' column of the Edinburgh Evening News, in which I eventually found an advert for the position of Apprentice Chef at D.S. Crawford, a well-established firm of restaurateurs with branches throughout the city. Coincidentally 496 Ferry Road - the baronial residence I visited as a Wardie schoolboy, was now Crawford's headquarters.

Thinking, perhaps this was 'my calling' I wrote requesting an application form; then, on receipt, submitted my CV; which must have held some water since it secured me an interview with Tom Newton, the company man in charge of hiring and firing - today he would probably have the

title of Executive Chef. He was an excellent asset as far as Crawfords were concerned, a highly experienced man in the catering industry, mild-mannered and while a fatherly figure to the large staff he controlled, had an air of authority which commanded a healthy respect that we instinctively knew said, "Don't mess with me, Sunshine!".

Mr Newton explained that up for grabs was what was known as an 'Indentured Apprenticeship'; so, here's the deal; I was required to sign a contract in favour of Crawfords, which he told me was a legal document, to be witnessed and signed by my next of kin, more or less stating that, on approval, I was bound to stay with the firm for the agreed period; meaning until 'ma time wus oot'. He further accounted what would be expected of me and how I would be obliged to attend night school twice a week; also that it was down to me to provide my own uniforms, which would be laundered at the company's expense.

It sounded shit-hot. I fancied the job, which was of course a proper trade at last, deferring me from the yoke of oppression: ***'National Service'*** so, fuck'm, I'll worry about that in four-and-a-half years time when I'm twenty-one! Yes, it's in the bag, ah've 'brassed ma case' and got the job, I'm going to be a chef - unfortunately many years before being construed as 'the dug's baws'; with now, far too many self-possessed hash-slingers scratchin' each other's eyes oot for celebrity status and a prime time-slot on our 50 inch plasma screens - but who, **really**, gives a toss!

sung to the Commies' anthem - 'The Red Flag'

The working class can kiss my ass;
I've got the Chief Cook's job at last

Being a typical, eternally skint, teenager; cap in hand *pleading poverty* I approached and tapped Mother, who, glad to see 'the apple of her eye' in a decent job with a future this time, lent me enough loot to buy three sets of uniforms consisting of chefs' hats, jackets, check trousers and aprons from Clinkscales, an industrial outfitters in Leith. So, 'in for a penny, in for a pound', that was me, brimful o' enthusiasm, ready and willing to learn the culinary arts at Crawford's 'flagship' branch in the centre of Princes Street the following Monday morning, as a brand new baby chef.

8: Chef World - D. S. Crawford

Well, wha' d'you know - I'm now in the catering industry; rubbing shoulders with new workmates in the chefs' changing room at the rear of the Princes Street branch - can't remember how many chefs and apprentices were there, but certainly more than a baker's dozen; so 'twas a lively baptism. Everyone rushing to get changed from street clothes into their chefs' uniforms, hurriedly pulled from tall well-bashed grey metal lockers with their doors hanging open, some raking around, while cursing their luck, in a big brown wicker laundry basket for clean gear with their name tag. It was a hustle-bustle like that every morning, but more so on Mondays as the restaurant was closed on the Sabbath - so a fresh start at the beginning of the week with a full brigade; *all having something to say.*

I certainly found life entertaining working in the chaos of a big busy kitchen with this harmonious team. Plenty banter and rushing around, but all organized with military precision by the Head Chef, Walter McQueen, a short-sighted portly gentleman with a great sense of humour. Although forever joking and ribbing his staff; at the same time a demanding man, who, while singing 'I'm only a Rose in a Garden of Weeds', pushed the troops and kept them grafting. After all, it was his responsibility to see that the dishes on the 'table d'hôte' menu de jour were ready and all ingredients for the 'à la carte' list prepared and to hand, as required.

At first I was amazed as to how it always all gelled in time. I likened the Head Chef to a maestro, due to the capable way he could orchestrate everyone and everything to a grande finale each day - puttin' the money where the gob is, I'd say there can't be a profession where the bossman makes so much happen at the appropriate times. A very stressful position, which has me wondering how many have regular appointments with the 'shrink' or smoke the odd 'joint'. It's certainly a never-ending toil as no sooner is one meal over than it's time to prepare the next. One thing's for sure; you can never work yourself out of a job in the catering trade; so, at this point I profess to know sod all about cooking, but do know about eating; which means, this just has to be the best job I've ever had.

I started my new career in the productive larder of Mario the pastry chef - can't remember his surname and even if I could it's more than likely that I wouldn't be able to spell it. He was a big strong Polish man, with cropped spiky hair going grey; *yet another relic from World War II.* Rumour had it that our quiet solemn industrious Mario, who had a dry sense of humour when I could understand him, had at the beginning of the war been Chief of Secret Police in Warsaw, but forced to scarper when the Nazis invaded. I'm almost sure I spoke to him about this *(thinking it was a load o' old tosh)* and he confirmed the story, but it's so long ago that it is now no more than a hazy memory - so who knows? That aside, I've often wondered where and when he learned his skills as a pastry chef - this man was a wizard, conjuring up masses of pies, both savoury and sweet and all sorts of individual trifles, jellies, crème caramels etc. You name it, Mario was the man to 'pull it oot the hat' - *well, OK... oven!*

I enjoyed the work, and as you know when you like something and take an interest it quickly becomes 'a piece o' piss'. After a few weeks as 'the sorcerer's apprentice' I was moved into the main kitchen to learn the job 'across the board', so as to be of use wherever and whenever required and although we were kept hard at it there was always plenty banter, catcalling and laughs. Every department had a 'character', any bickering was light-hearted and the days, because entertaining and busy, flew in.

The only drag was when it was my turn for a 'split shift' which meant having three hours off after lunches, then coming back to do the early evening shift, as 'high teas' were served until seven-thirty. It made for a long day being on split shift; roughly thirteen hours between leaving the house in the morning and returning home in the evening. There wasn't a lot I could do in my three hours off and it was hardly worthwhile going home just to come back again, so on nice sunny days I would shoot across to Princes Street Gardens, to loiter ogling the fud or just wander round the classy emporiums in the centre of town, givin' ma mind a treat.

On dreich days, of which we in inclement Edinburgh get more than we would wish for, I'd go to The Monseigneur, this was a small but excellently appointed News Theatre in Princes Street near the West End, next door to Lillywhites, a terrific sports orientated department store which stocked up-market clothing, and sports-gear *such as diving equipment.* It was

there I first saw aqualungs and all the associated equipment; as much as I hungered to buy such objects, the meagre earnings of an apprentice chef did not extend my budget to affording scuba-diving. Instead I settled for a pair of French-made swimfins and face mask; desirable things to own in these days when everyone was enthralled by the weekly underwater adventure programmes of Jacques Cousteau and Hans & Lotte Hass on television. Thereafter I imagined myself to be a capable young 'frogman' at Glenogle Swimming Baths and occasionally Portobello open-air pool, to which we only went on hot summer days; when even then the water would *as the saying goes* 'freeze the baws off a brass monkey'.

Oh yeah, lets get back to the crap afternoons when I would go to the Monseigneur News Theatre - only a few minutes walk from the restaurant. It was a show of not much longer than an hour, during which they would run a few newsreels, not just the usual Pathé News as shown in other cinemas between the feature films; so it was interesting and informative. They also treated us to three or four 'Mickey Duck' cartoons making it a nice easy show and a good cheap way to pass an hour or more. Now, I say "or more" because it often was - let me explain by telling you that this cinema had the most comfortable seats with more legroom than any other known to man. Because of this it was so easy to nod off without realizing, and since there were no set times for the shows which ran on a continuous loop, the lights never came on. The punters came in, watched the films through until the first one they had seen was screened again and that was it; a good system, as you could pop in at any minute of the day.

Many's the time I would drop off *(for this I attach blame to the seats)* but was never unlucky enough to be late getting back to Crawfords. It was usually just forty winks, but if dead to the world, one of the usherettes, all of whom I knew, would give me a shake *(unfortunately that's not to be taken the wrong way)* in plenty time to nash along the road and get changed in readyness for my stint on the 'back-shift'.

It was company policy to move the ten apprentices, around the six branches - excellent training, as they all housed completely different kitchens; this made for a good learning curve and therefore, the apprentices adaptable. I had been at Princes Street for some six months when I got my first 'draft-chit' - to Hanover Street; a small 'one-horse outfit', which carried

a staff of just one chef, one apprentice, one kitchen porter and a couple of scullery maids. This was the branch least liked by the apprentices - the Head Chef, Joe Moss who was Swiss *or possibly Czech,* was a 'top notch' chef; in his early sixties, but such a dour man who could be a bit tetchy, and with whom it was impossible to converse. He wore a permanent frown, and only spoke to tell his staff precisely what he wanted done. Joe was the boss and while it felt uncomfortable, I did not dislike the man, although working alongside him made for a long day, come week, come month, so, understandably, seemed like a life sentence.

You'll appreciate, time dragged before again seeing me on the transfer list; more than just delighted to be moved to the Shore Leith branch; another one-horse outfit. This was a happy kitchen run by Arthur, an easy-going dapper Head Chef, I can't recall his surname, *(could've been McLeod)* but do remember his face very well, with its neatly trimmed moustache - he was a bit of a wag who knew the drill, so I got on famously with him.

For some reason when at that branch, I developed a craving for fried egg sandwiches, using triangular sweet scones in place of bread and applying a liberal dose of Heinz tomato sauce - which in these days was labelled sauce; not ketchup as today. Maybe I'm dreaming but I think that was the case, I know it certainly tasted better to me then than today; of course it could be my taste buds are now shagged oot; but let's say, over the years I've matured and developed a more delicate palate.

Following serving and enjoying my time at the Shore with Arthur who had a great sense of humour, could turn a 'banger' into a banquet and made me laugh, I was drafted to yet another small branch, in Queensferry Street, with the same complement of staff as the last two. D'you know, for the life of me I can't remember who the Head Chef was, but suspect that he was a chap with whom I'd worked in Princes Street. Now it's coming back, he was *if I've got it right* a God-fearing family man in his fifties called Bill Mc something. You will, I'm sure, forgive me for not remembering his surname, or much else about this branch, when I let you in on an unforgettable encounter I was ever so lucky to have whilst there.

The staffroom was in the basement with the chefs' and women's changing rooms running separately off the central staffroom. Amongst a clutch o' attractive waitresses, was **Katrina;** few could hold a candle to

this vivacious piece o' skirt, about twenty-five years young. 'Kat' *who lived, and breathed, only for pleasure* took fiendish delight in the telling of her exploits if she had been 'on the town' with an energetic Yank who'd given her a 'guid usin' up some dark close, the previous night; this broad got around, Katrina was quite a girl, she just oozed sex, loved kidding and provocatively flirting with myself and the Head Chef, he being strait-laced and me a relatively innocent seventeen-year-old.

Now then, are you ready for this? One never-to-be-forgotten morning at break-time she and the other serving wenches were sitting gassin' round their table in the staffroom, while I'm in our changing room with the door open, feet up, quietly reading the Head Chef's paper, but aware something's going on because of the whispering and giggles, Katrina's in a mischievous mood. I don't look up, pretending not to notice, even when I hear the other girls egging her on, and 'Thick Jenny' shrieking "I dare you".

This is all the libertine needs, she's quickly on her feet saying, "Chef, I've got a tension headache, will you massage the back of my neck?" Before I can answer she 'parks it' on the chair next to mine and says "Come on, be a pal and rub my neck, I'll keep you right, Sonny Jim"; I'm a wee bit embarrassed because everyone's watching, but what the hell, it's a golden opportunity to get my hands on the raunchy bint.

Knowing I'm at her mercy, but acting disinterested ah'm coaxed round behind her; *like a lamb led to the slaughter* - **oh yes,** this experienced sex-goddess is playing a game she knows only too well. The randy bitch knows no shame; and, **thank you God**, has half the buttons of her black uniform blouse undone exposing those fantastic tits *(that I've been allowed many a fleeting glimpse of),* cupped in a loose-fitting lacy black brassiere. To cap it all, she's made sure the skimpy black uniform pencil skirt is hitched up just far enough to expose the black stocking tops, suspenders and a tantalizing smidgen of lily white velvet soft thighs. ***Jings - does it no' make yer gums ache, jist thinkin' aboot it!***

Obviously Katrina's in charge, she's teasing me and I know it *sometimes it's wise to play 'the daft laddie'* so I'm not complaining when she gives me 'the green light'. I'm no sooner started when she says "A bit harder" and "Go lower" guiding my hands slowly down to fondle these magnificent diddies - **gulp,** they turn out to be much softer than I expected with

'jubejubes' that I couldn't've imagined. Crikey, 'the show's on the road' - they're stickin' oot like organ stops, proving the wanton waitress was enjoying her dare as much as myself. However, Katrina was in complete control of our indulgence; which all too soon came to an abrupt end - probably just as well, otherwise I'd've had 'a happening' and *to preserve the old dignity* been forced tae change ma breeks.

There you have it then, after hearing that little tale I'm sure you'll excuse me for remembering little else of Queensferry Street; even now passing the building reminds me of my encounter with the 'well worth a second look' Katrina - **guess what?** I've just had a memory jog and 'the leetle grey cells' have suddenly revealed the Head Chef's surname. It was McLean; yeah, that's right Bill McLean. It's strange and interesting how that happens - you try to remember something but no; it seems lost, so you move on thinking, 'Oh well, maybe later', and suddenly right oot the blue there it is, **the answer,** and you were unaware that your onboard computer was still searching the files - ***amazing!***

My next 'draft-chit' was a cracker, yes, I'm on the transfer list again, this time to a den of iniquity in Castle Street near the West End. This was a big busy restaurant; although not to the extent of the flagship in nearby Princes Street. We had five chefs, a lady pastry cook and two apprentices *(one of whom was me)*, backed up *as always* with a kitchen porter and a brace of kitchen maids. At Castle Street omelettes of every description were the speciality of the house; so popular that we were called upon to produce dozens every day. Naturally I, like my colleagues, became a dab hand at making them - *an art one never loses*. I still *to this day* take great pride in knocking out a mean omelette, which goes down a treat when prepared with three eggs and a good dollop of tasty filling, especially when accompanied with a ton o' crisp golden brown chips - and a can o' well-chilled Murphy's Irish Stout, to 'hit the spot'.

Well now, this was quite a place, in fact for me, a real eye opener which, if televised, would, most certainly, have put the TV soap operas of today to shame *since their storylines are pure shite* so predictably the same and far from original. You can't have failed to notice how when one of them has some dopey simpleton fall pregnant the same happens on all the others. Yeah, that's right, it goes round like a dose o''the clap'.

Here it wasn't a story, this was 'the real McCoy'; it was a loosely guarded secret that the Head Chef, a paragon of the community, "happily" married family man and bit of a toff, was 'throwin' one up' his paramour Miss Cox; *a frosty cow* - the senior of the two hoity-toity manageresses.

One of the waitresses, 'Kinky' Kate, an extremely provocative physical girl, who prowled like a panther and had a stomach as taut as a skiffler's washboard, was 'on the game', floggin' her parts to all and sundry at every opportunity and not adverse to offering her favours to male tearoom customers - *give it to me* ***large,*** *Big Boy!* So between her wages, tips and nocturnal earnings, must've been making a first rate job of 'feathering her nest'. Many's the time 'twas all too evident that Kate had performed strenuously for her rewards; that is, if her untidy appearance next day was anything to go by - conspicuously her bedraggled arrival on such mornings indicated she'd come straight from a marathon event in some rampant punter's bed. I well remember the Sous-Chef *whose approach was never subtle* remarking "Make sure you wash yer mucky hands before you start servin', hen!" earning him a sick smile from the money-mad whore.

Two of the chefs were brothers - so unlike each other it wasn't true; Duncan was 'Mr Nice Guy', not long married, didn't swear, you know the type, a solid reliable worker who went straight home every night to the wife he loved - no! no! not a bore; just a decent sort. The elder, Albert, was the Second Chef, wotta machine - hell's teeth, there was no stopping this man, he was notorious - about thirty, tall, wiry, lantern-jawed and dark-shaven with an alert mischievous gleam in his eyes. You may remember a newspaper cartoon character called Angus Ogg - maybe they'd been cloned, as Albert always reminded me of Angus. This guy was a stallion, in constant pursuit of fud; he must have shafted all the 'up for it' young available female staff of D.S. Crawford's *and then some*.

The stud made sure that he was Duty Chef on the hotplate, directly serving customers in the main restaurant at midday, so as to leer at, chat up and accost the tidy West End office girls who came in to graze at lunchtime, so God, only, knows how many assignations that ruse scored him over the years. Talk about burnin' the candle at both ends, he probably shagged himself into an early grave. What a man, didn't know the meaning of remorse, if it had a skirt, a pulse and a smile he'd be **right up it.**

Ronnie Balls was another randy sod; a short dapper man not unlike George Sanders, same 'tache, same wicked smile, same 'devil-may-care' self-confident lecherous aura that women are so attracted to - a compulsive exhibitionist, who had been a chef on the railways and ocean liners before 'dropping anchor' at Crawford's. Ronnie treated us to a voyeur's dream the day he had Mary the pastry cook *(a comely convent-educated country wench - but common as muck)* pinned against the Georgian-wired glass partition of her pastry larder. She's squealing with delight and yelling, "Stoap it, Ronnie! stoap it!" as he, tongue hingin' oot, is goin' at it hammer an' tongs, with us on the other side near pishin' oorsels laffin'.

The pastry maid ran off in fear
The villain, he pursued her
The white of an egg
Ran down her leg
The bugger, he had screwed her

Mustn't forget 'Tricky Dickie', who arrived weeks after myself, he and I became quite pally, although Dick was a loner and older than me; *still a teenager,* so we were only pals at work. There must've been a wee story behind our comrade, but he didn't volunteer; so we never asked. He was English, I don't remember from where; could've been a 'Yorkie'. Tricky had been a chef in the army, possibly National Service; demobbed up here *I presume,* and for some reason, known only to himself, never went home.

He lived in digs somewhere near me at Broughton Place *where we had moved to from Logie Green when I was sixteen,* so some mornings we would meet and walk up to Castle Street together, when he more than often had a tale to tell of some conquest from the previous night; as he was forever rakin' around town looking for a bit of the old 'rumpy pumpy'. Dick was another one with a dose o' the 'fanny rats' and it appeared that if there were any willing women missed by Albert, Tricky had plugged them.

I met the lecher four years later in Portsmouth when I was, by then, in the Royal Navy and he was 'chefing it' on a big ocean liner running from Southampton. I can't remember what ship it was or how he got in touch, however he came to 'Pompey' *(Portsmouth)* where we had a 'run ashore' together. Cor, this guy was a real piece o' work, some of his stories; bloody

hell, the things he got up to on this liner was nobody's business - it's little wonder he looked like a washed oot rag!

The best tale by far, was this little gem - he was shackin' up ashore in Southampton with this gorgeous 'Black Goddess', a stewardess, who he referred to as 'Black Velvet' and reckoned she behaved like a nymphomaniac on Death Row. Lucky old Dick, we should all be fortunate enough to encounter one of them in our 'active' lifetime. Anyway, the story goes that, she's out for some retail therapy, so seizing the moment, Tricky gets busy with a tin of wax floor polish. I'm thinking, 'What's this mad bastard yakkin' on about now?' He explains, that when she arrives home they both get stripped off for a bit action. Now, wait for this one, **you will love it!** Tricky puts four saucers on the now highly-polished floor, Black Velvet gets down on all fours placing her elbows and knees in the saucers, Tricky with a 'boner that would choke a horse', goes for 'a rearender' and steers her all round the room. Crivvens; wotta man, I can't remember his surname, but it wasn't Head! Dick certainly didn't believe in something a pal from Dalkeith, 'Big Jake' *(the expert tiler, Shakin' Stevens lookalike and well-known car boot sale predator)* recently told me, "Wimin are really aliens an' if they didnae huv 'fannies' we'd throw bricks at thum."

There was a man with a corkscrew prick
Who went by the name of One-eyed Dick
He spent his life in a fruitless hunt
To find a girl with a corkscrew cunt
But, when he found her he nearly dropped down dead
Cos her corkscrew cunt had a left-hand thread ANON

Now then, you'll recall my contract with D. S. Crawford required me to attend night school two nights a week - this was at Castlehill School *(now the Scotch Whisky Heritage Centre)* just a few yards down from the Edinburgh Castle Esplanade, So along with other apprentices from Crawford's and various hotels in the city I attended classes from six until nine on Tuesday and Thursday evenings - these were long days as it meant going there straight from work. This added up to a fourteen-hour shift having left home at seven-thirty in the morning and returning around nine-thirty at night. A rewarding sacrifice however; as we did learn about

cooking, hotel management and the many tricks o' the trade.

Our teacher was a sergeant in the Army Catering Corps doin' a bit o' 'moonlightin', so it was more like being on a Barracks Drill Square than at night school. He'd mock us with army expressions such as, "You're dancing around like pregnant nuns" or, "You're standing there like a spare prick at a wedding" - it was all light-hearted and generally a barrel o' laughs, as is the norm when a bunch of young guys get thrown together.

As usual I remember the stars and apologize to those forgotten. I know in my class there were two other Crawford's apprentices, Lachie Shearer and Robert Duff, but have a vague notion there may have been a third and if so, I'm sorry to say I forget who. No, no, watch this space, I've just remembered it was Willie Dickson, who looked like a young Tom Cruise, a quiet amiable chap from Leith who enjoyed a pint. I never actually worked alongside Willie, as he was always at a different branch from myself.

There were three apprentices from the George Hotel, two of whom I remember well. One was Malcolm Lightbody who in later years was to have *(with his brother)* Lightbody's Restaurant, a popular first-class eatery on Edinburgh's Glasgow Road. The other was nicknamed 'Scoff', which I thought must be because he ate a lot, but this wasn't the case. They called him Scoff because he had a book by a famous French Chef called Escoffier and regularly quoted from this - his Bible.

Another fellow trainee was from the iconic Caley Hotel at the West End, his name escapes me, but I will ever remember him, as he was so different. This guy was theatrical. Now! now! Don't jump to conclusions, not a poofter - a member of the magic circle and he was good; correction, very good! When we had some spare time, he'd entertain us with tricks and illusions - this in turn gave him much-needed practise as he explained that in the magic business it was definitely a case of practise makes perfect; so spent hours each week, honing his skills. He also told us he had to buy his tricks *(the best being double dear),* so his wages went in this direction, but it wasn't one-way traffic as he made 'rakes' doing shows. It's a cert that in years to come, he'd have gone professional and made the grade, but to us he was 'The Magic Chef'. There was a trick he offered to show us which involved him swallowing a long slim bandage and while still swallowing it he would be pulling the leading end from his back passage.

Maybe he was bluffing, but my colleagues and I were never to know, as we, unanimously, elected not to witness that spectacle.

We had loads of laughs at night school; but this was the most memorable. It was Pancake Tuesday, so what were we doing? Well; yes, making pancakes, so 'sarge' instructs us in the art of making the perfect batter and pancake, then opportunity presents itself when he has to go to the office to sort out some schedules, thus, leaving his disciples to it. Well now, the pancakes get bigger and bigger and are being tossed higher and higher. **It's competition time!** The pancakes are doing back-flips, somersaults, landing in the chefs' hats and on the floor; you name it. Lachie, getting carried away, has completely 'lost it', he's made this soister - it's a two-hand job. He flips it into the air at a hundred miles an hour; we watch hypnotized while it soars *as if in slow motion* over Lachie's head, travels about twelve feet behind him and splats straight into the big Expelair extractor in the window. The fan *sparks flying* blows a gasket and there's pancake everywhere. Yeah, you got it, ***the shit hit the fan!***

I must say the apprentices from the flash hotels were a different class, working as they did on dishes we'd never even heard of, but we were faster and much more versatile. At the end of the three-year course we all passed our City and Guilds exams, received diplomas, then went on to a much more intensive course at the exclusive Atholl Crescent Catering College, where sophisticated upper-crust totty were learning the noble art, but that's another story; and we're not going there - ***so dream on!***

As a further part of our training, we, in turn, spent a month at Campbells; a high-class butcher in Castle Street with the lucrative contract to supply all meat products to D. S. Crawford's Restaurants. I had a lucky break for a change as, when my month came round, I was still at our Castle Street branch; this being next door to the butcher's shop which had a small factory behind the large front sales area, unseen by 'Joe Public'.

In there we were taught to make sausages, haggis and black puddings; I well remember the sausage machines pumping 'the secret mixture' into long lengths of skin - said to be sheep or pigs' intestines. We had to link them by hand, the pork sausages were linked differently from the beef, one lot being in threes and the other in twos. I don't remember much about hacking up sides of beef, but will never forget strangling turkeys by the

dozen, *as my stint was December.* The worst job was helping the apprentice butcher peel a huge bag of onions first thing each morning, eyes streaming and being told with a snigger, "You get used to it" or to chew a piece of raw onion to counteract the reaction. Wotta load o' bollocks, these slave-drivers could fairly spout the 'porkies' to keep you graftin'.

On completion of the butchery course we apprentices were treated to an extravagant high tea and prizegiving, hosted by Tom Newton at the Shore Leith branch *where we had all worked at some time*. It's not like me to gloat, but clearly remember being 'on my high horse' after gettin' a bit o' praise from 'Uncle' Tom when presented with a large Sabatier Chefs' knife and a sharpening steel; which have, since, been all over the globe with me. On reflection I think money was involved, and have a nagging suspicion that it may just have been dosh, with which I was obliged to purchase the knife and steel from Scobie & McIntosh (Catering Equipment) Ltd.

Time for pastures new, yes once again I'm on the transfer list - this time to 'the Bridges', so called, because situated at the North Bridge just round the corner from the east end of Princes Street. It was actually part of a landmark building housing the North British Hotel, fondly known as the 'NB'; now called 'The New Balmoral'. Why do they do that - you can't change history! No, I don't agree, it's not progress, it's stupidity - **tosspots!** Anyway, this, because of its size and location, was yet another busy restaurant with three chefs *(and for some reason)* three apprentices, a kitchen porter and once again a brace of kitchen maids. I think I must've replaced Robert Duff, as somewhere around that time he married Dot, a desirable dark-haired waitress who served in the tearoom, and lived close by on the High Street; so I presume he must have met, pursued and wooed her whilst 'doing his time' there as an apprentice.

This branch was nothing like Castle Street; which was a brothel by comparison. I don't recall any 'hanky-panky', although there were plenty laughs - the Head Chef being a practical joker with a warped sense of humour who delighted in tricking us and taking the piss. His name was Ron, a heavy-set man, in his early thirties with a swarthy Mediterranean complexion; always in need of a shave. One of his favourite tricks was, when it was Lachie's turn to boil the eggs, he would distract him when they were almost ready, then take two or three from the pot, substituting

raw ones, which the old stoat had marked, so when we sat down to have breakfast in the Chefs' Restroom, all except these were cooked. Lachie, who was from Caithness, *in the 'northern reaches'* and a bit of a clown in his own right, would scratch his head looking dumbfounded while Ron *(who took great delight in calling Lachie 'Master Lachie Bates')* would ridicule him, saying he couldn't even boil an egg - for my money 'twas an even bet as to who was takin' a rise oot o' who.

Ron's 'wingman' was Paddy Gillanders, a charismatic Irishman and talented industrious worker, but sadly a jumpy nervous wreck; having endured captivity as a Japanese Prisoner of War - one of the many forced to slave on the infamous Burma Railroad. He rarely ate, due to having been starved by the Japs; swearing because of this, his stomach had shrunk. However, *to be sure* this didn't stop our Paddy putting away the pints, as the 'rubba dub-dub' was where Paddy spent his evenings. He had no family in town, and lodged with a woman who, Bessie the kitchen maid said in a knowing way with a twinkle in her eye, **"did for him!"**

When I said no 'hanky-panky', I didn't mean the place was staffed by a bunch of angels, merely that there were, to the best of my knowledge, no affairs going on, or, to be blunt, none of the chefs were shafting any female employees - while our alcoholic Teuchter kitchen porter was neither interested nor capable. But *and there's always a but* one of the waitresses was rumoured to be 'on the game'. Sounds familiar, doesn't it? I can't for the life of me remember her name *(could've been Elvira, Queen of the Night)*, however, do recall she lived near the top of Broughton Street; a slim sexual-looking lady *(not unlike Ida Lupino; a film star of the time)*.

Probably in her late twenties - you know the kind - you just look and the first thing you think is, 'I bet she'd be real dirty ***one hot mama,*** oh ya beauty just imagine that squirming and squealing in the sack' - and guess what? **I had the chance *and 'crapped it'.*** Yeah, one day after a bit of cavorting; feeling either fruity, benevolent, or possibly impressed by my magnetic personality, the harlot says on the quiet: "You could be the dish of the day, how would you like to come out with me tonight?" Well, I'll never know if I was to be on a 'freebie' that night - because, although sorely tempted, I was a tad flustered *thinking she might want to tamper with me,* so 'bottled out' mumbling the first excuse that came into my head - ***sucker!***

To further complicate matters, it dawns on me that I prefer the company of women to men; so am concerned that **I might be a lesbian.**

Can't say if I 'bottled it' through being scared of making a fool of myself, due to lack of experience - although I'd had some fumbling encounters with Shirley, a strikingly well-formed fiesty Titian-haired twenty year old sexpot with a suggestive pout, who ran the still room and whose family home was 'in the sticks' at Prestonpans; a small town just down the coast. This was a short, half-hearted, romance lasting only two or three months, as although attracted to one another we weren't compatible and what's more she nurtured a unhealthy interest in her 'patter merchant' cousin; which didn't do my ego a lot o' good. To cap it all one night I missed the last SMT bus back to Edinburgh; who'd have guessed it was at ten-thirty - so it was a 'Shanks's pony' job *(by the by - their elusive G-spot's hiding in yer wallet!)*. Anyway, it wasn't long before she left Crawford's and, as always, it petered out; we lost touch, and I was beguiled by another.

You'll recognize the coincidence I'm about to relate as it's the old cliché; like, when fair sick o' waitin' ages on a cold winter's night *in the rain* for a bus an', sure as fate, don't two come along together.

Well now, this enchanting waitress joins the team at the Bridges and I'm infatuated; Freda is one classy burd, she's a student working the summer hols and comes from a seaside town in Fife *possibly Aberdour,* but residing with her grandmother in Edinburgh somewhere around 'the Top o' the Walk'. This riveting doe-eyed filly was gorgeous with short cut rich hazel-brown hair set in light curls, an intelligent looking face and trim figure. I've been champing at the bit and flirting with her for weeks, but although she was friendly; alas, ah wus barkin' up the wrong tree.

I suppose my enthusiasm had somewhat waned when one night midweek I'm out with Joe McGlinchey. We're dawdling up Rodney Street heading for 'the chippie' when we come face to face with an attractive girl wearing this infectious smile - she's coming from where we're going, carrying a fish supper wrapped in newspaper, *to keep it hot*. Now, although by this time I'm not exactly 'God's gift', I am comfortable talking to 'the enemy' - having mixed and worked with them in the restaurants long enough to know the score, so we stop and start blethering while at the same time chattin' her up; she's easy to talk to and looks cute in her navy blazer with

Kitchen Staff at 'the Bridges':
Paddy Gillanders (2ND left), Shiner (centre),
kitchen maids Aggie (left) and Bessie (right)

its brass buttons, and I just love that mischievous cheeky grin. You know how it is; occasionally, for some reason, a spark kindles and you click with a stranger. Well, I've taken a shine to this girl, who turns out to be a laugh a minute; she tells us her name is Jude, lives in Granton and is visiting her aunt, who has a flat on the corner of Rodney Street and Eyre Place. We're getting along a treat and arrange to meet a couple of days later, to visit the fair at Pennywell Road on Saturday evening. ***Cheers, 'Big Man'!*** You've done me proud this time - have the rest o' the day off!

Well now, are you ready? - here comes, **the crunch.** The very next day the demure student I've been doing my best to impress for weeks catches me when no one else is in earshot and coyly asks if I would still like to take her out. Well, isn't that typical! I *being a novice* couldn't handle it - in later years **too right,** just watch me! - but back then I was a sensitive unsullied amateur, not yet versed in the art of deception; so told her I was now 'seeing someone'; whilst doing my utmost to let her down gently and, therefore, save face. So, who knows - I always maintain that there's a reason for whatever happens. Nonetheless, **'isn't life a bitch!'**

9: Teen Years

Just as happens in the early years when we spread our wings and venture further afield than our own front doors; thus discovering and making new friends while mixing with other kids in our street. On becoming teenagers, we boldly roam on to a bigger stomping ground and, in so doing, aquire a larger circle of pals who live in surrounding postcodes. It was quite a revelation for me at that age to meet some great guys living so close, and to forge lasting friendships with people that 'til then I had been totally unaware of - so remembered *with a smile* as exciting times.

You may have seen the comedy series 'Happy Days' on television. You know the one I mean *sure you do* starring the Fonz, his pal Ritchie with family *the Cunninghams* and supporting cast of lesser mortals. Whenever I saw that, it made me think of my teentimes - yes, the joker who thought that one up really hit the nail on the head; or could it be that my memories are clouded and I'm just romanticizing? ***No, not me!***

Tell ye what -these were relatively simple times, with so many of today's problems unheard of; look back and think about it - the list is endless. To name but a few of the trendy modern epidemics, which we, thankfully, did not have; drug addiction, muggings, car crime, AIDS, racial tension and inflation - *if things don't change they'll stay as they are!*

So, who's responsible? Well, it gives me no pleasure to once again lay it at the feet of fickle governments *past and present* for idly letting it spiral out of control, then being unable to handle the situation. I keep asking myself, are they really a bunch o' tossers? - or, too busy lining their pockets and slagging each other off to see what's happening in the ***real*** world?

Surely improvements would be achievable if a Cabinet was formed from those with insight, **the punishment made to fit the crime** and this handed out ***as a deterrent*** with equal severity throughout the land. Let's be rid of this namby-pamby approach and jobs for the boys hogwash, then get the show on the road; because if it is too late now, think about what we've got to look forward to! Yes, you all know; **don't you?** So there's no point in sweepin' it under the carpet cos "**it ain't goin' away!**"

Just realized I'm up on that ole soapbox again. Funny how this happens, and at the time I'm unaware. Could be, as suggested - I need treatment. No, no; I don't. It's not me, **it's them** ***- they're all daft except me!*** Anyway, I'm not getting down until I've said my bit about THE POOFS.

In **'the happy days'** the sexual deviants stayed in the closet - but now, God forbid, they're strutting their stuff everywhere. Perhaps it's just a fad, but turn on the telly and at least one channel will be flaunting an old queen spouting smut. In the past *when we were a real country and justice was seen to be done* the faggots, when unmasked, would've been 'put to the sword' or burned at the stake in the marketplace, not called gay, made knights of the realm and become multimillionaires. It's a joke - until you picture them hiding behind the bushes, 'nuts deep' in puny drug-crazed rent boys. As for these limp-wristed bumboys, blatantly mincing around town wearing mascara, carrying designer shoulder bags and shaking their little 'moneymakers' encased in Calvin Klein panties costing ten quid a time, of which seven quids worth is up their chuff - ***let's sacrifice them!***

Better stop raving, before being dragged off screaming to a darkened room in the Andrew Duncan Clinic; *anyway, I feel better now!* So, as I was saying, I made a lot of new friends around that time, the first being the McGlinchey brothers who lived with their widowed mother and younger sister Maureen at 9 Heriot Hill Terrace. The eldest was Arthur followed by Tam, then Joe; who was to become my lifelong pal. Joe was a bright lad; so clever that he won a bursary to George Heriot's *(one of Edinburgh's finest schools)* and got the education he so deserved. *Joe, who has now departed this world, was admired and well liked by all who knew him.*

An early memory of that friendship was when a crowd of us went to Glenogle Baths *('Glennies')*, our local swimming pool, where we always had a great time horsing about and showing off to each other with our car tyre inner tubes and suchlike. The attendant was forever blowing his whistle and scolding us, then nearly blowing the pea from the whistle and almost going crackers trying to get us out the water at the end of a session. Check this; one time when he finally got us out the pool and off to get changed, Arthur was horrified to find some rotten shitebag had stolen all his gear. It was far from funny, but of course we all laughed; except for Arthur who wasn't amused with our heartless remarks and ribbing. I don't remember

what time of the year it was, but he could hardly walk the streets in just his wet swimming trunks, so made his uncooperative siblings run home to get him some clobber. Arthur was biggest, so Arthur was bossman. Why his clothes? - well, you know wot they say, **size matters!**

I was fifteen when I had this whirlwind romance with Joyce; *my first teenage encounter with 'the opposition'*. It all began early one evening at the Ritz during the second performance; which went through from around four until seven-thirty. Anyway, I'm astonished *and flattered* when this young Amazon - take it from me, that's a well chosen description *(wotta rack!)*, sits next to me in an uncrowded cinema, indicating she contrived the meeting, and the fact that we were soon holding hands, none of this being instigated by myself, had me amazed - possibly she'd been put up to it by her friends. **Who cares - *never look a gift horse!*** It turns out Joyce lives minutes away in an apartment on the edge of the New Town, so we start seeing each other on a regular basis. Now, believe me these were *as I keep repeating* innocent times ***and just as well.*** Pay attention! Are you ready? Imagine my horror, on learning I'm a cradle-snatcher - when it comes out that **she is only twelve.** Jings, who'd've guessed - this Lolita had the looks and body of an eighteen-year-old hottie who could've rocked **your** world. Well, anyway, it didn't take long before the infatuation and novelty of *'owning'* Joyce fizzled out, as happens when you're a young blade and it's all too soon to play the doting 'sugar daddy'.

Different story nowadays when *ignoring 'the restraining order'* I'm phoning 'Rentabint' and kerb crawlin', seekin' an understanding thirty-year-old wi' the unblemished body o' a twelve-year-old tae see tae ma needs and read me bedtime stories. I keep hearing such tales, but you know the score - it always happens to the other guy; bastard, ah hate'm! That reminds me, I knew a tosser in the seventies who won a 'substantial amount' on the pools; tainted with jealousy ***we all secretly detested the jammy git.***

Now sixteen, we're hanging around the swing park and tennis courts at Eyre Place, where we show off on the 'cheesecutter' and pester the saucy pocket venuses who frequent the place. This is a good trapping ground and by now there's a fair-sized team of us, consisting of the McGlinchey brothers, myself, Billy and Alec Colthart *both mentioned earlier* and a few others from further afield, therefore not primary members of the clique - so

we are, as 'Spotty Dottie' put it, 'hunting in packs'.

Speaking of which, reminds me that it was through frequenting this park that I first met the Brattisani brothers, who lived nearby, in Henderson Row. Billy already knew 'the Brats', as they'd attended Bellevue College for Gentlefolk together. They were third-generation Italian; the grandfather having emigrated to Scotland from Parma in 1890. I suppose it's not hard to guess that the family was involved, amongst other things, in the fish and chip business, which in those days was a clean and busy shop on the corner of Brougham Place at Tollcross in the town centre, where Joe helped and later ran this shop. Our Joe was a great favourite with the girls as apart from always having a few quid 'the lucky dog' was blessed with good looks - *never a hair oot o' place, and being a snappy dresser he certainly knew how to confidently capitalize on these assets*. But, yes, he did work hard, between going to the fishmarket 'early doors', preparing for the lunchtime trade, having two or three hours off in the afternoons - *when the young rake was a 'well-kent' face around town* - then back to the shop most evenings. However, years of hard work paid off and the Brattisanis *now 'well caked up'* have two of the finest fish restaurants in the city.

Having praised Joe, I mustn't forget Charles, two years younger and also a fine-looking likeable chap who always presents himself well, a grafter who has helped Joe over the years, as well as being employed for a while in the 'Bookie's' shop owned at that time by their father. He later lived in Canada for a spell and on returning went back into the fish restaurant business; for a while owning a very successful shop in Henderson Row. Early on, Charles took an interest in antiques and has been heavily involved and well respected in the business for the better part of two decades; nevertheless still pulls his weight with Joe in the restaurants.

'How time flies', we're seventeen and imagine the streets are ours, so start heading uptown in pursuit of young fillies. Because we are nodding acquaintances of 'Charlie the Gangster', the Leith Street 'hardman', reputed to be a ruthless 'whoremaister' running a string o' prostitutes from the notorious Imperial Hotel, we think we've arrived, know it all and want to shout to the world that we've hit the bigtime, little realizing we only had the brain capacity of teenagers; *and no one had bothered to tell us*.

Up until then the population had dressed in fairly mundane clothes, as

during and for around ten years after the war there was sweet F.A. in the shops. So, in the early fifties a corduroy jerkin, a pair of jeans, turned up at the bottoms, and a cheap pair o' basketball boots from 'Woolies' was the height of fashion. However, all this changed rapidly with the arrival of shops such as the Waverley Tailoring Company in Leith Street. Believe me this was 'the business' - a regular Aladdin's cave for the trendsetters of Edinburgh. It was, for its time, a truly amazing double-windowed shop with ever-changing displays and promotions to tempt the city's style-conscious youth through its hallowed portals, to then be served, coerced and relieved of their dosh by dapper and so obviously Jewish gentlemen, looking the part in well-cut black jackets and striped trousers *as worn with morning suits*, set off by immaculate shirts and smart ties complemented with cuff links and tie pins. ***The Hebrews always end up with the money*** - so be it, these 'children of Israel' are ***born*** entrepreneurs.

What bewildered me, was how there was nothing, and then so quickly everything that we had only ever seen in American films. **We just had to have these things!** Terrific jackets and trousers of materials we had never even heard of, such as gaberdine, 'sharkskin' shirts with button-down collars, basket-weave ties, 'sloppy joes' and 'Waikiki' Hawaiian beach-shorts, talk about heaven on earth. This was dynamite - there was hardly a 'worthy' strutting along Princes Street who wasn't proudly sporting something from these shrewd cookies. They, of course, had competitors such as The Cowan Tailoring Company in Earl Grey Street and a shop called JAX up at Nicolson Street, owned by the 'live wired' Lewis Schulberg. What these magical shops did between them was a revelation, which went a long way to changing the hitherto scruffy appearance and introducing 'streetcred' to a generation of Edinburgh's male population.

There were, as you know, also the time-honoured traditional high street tailors with branches throughout the kingdom; the 'big guns' being Burton's, Claude Alexander, The Fifty Shilling Tailors, and Hector Powe. Back then, they were so cheap that most of us bought at least two 'made to measure' suits a year; sounds extravagant I know, but that's not the case, so let me tell you the drill, then the price - and I'll bet you like it.

These retailers *always on main streets* carried large stocks of ready-made clobber, as well as dozens of books full o'materials from which to choose

for your 'made to measure' suit or coat. Following a lengthy perusal, you selected a material and picked the style you wanted *again from books* adding personal touches, such as raised seams, saddle stitching, patch pockets, with or without flaps, covered buttons, lapel style and width etc. The salesman, after slyly asking if Sir might like "a wee belt up the back", would note Sir's instructions then measure his victim. These details were sent off, on paying a deposit, to the factory somewhere down in the Midlands and four to six weeks later you had a new suit, generally without a hitch - 'twas a great system, that worked well!

I know! I know! all you're really thinking is, what did this wonderful service cost? Okay, stand by for a jaw-dropper. A two-piece suit, 'made to measure', was usually around twelve pounds and a three-piece about, say fifteen pounds. I'll repeat that in case you are convinced the daft bugger's lost his marbles. A two-piece suit, to measure, around £12 and a *waistcoated* 3-piece, £15. Yeah, them were good times!

Talking of clothes and style reminds me that during this decade the 'Teddy Boy' was born. Some guys really looked the part in these 'supercool threads', which appeared pretty neat on the lucky few who were tall and slim, since the jackets, set off with velvet collars, were worn long *(similar to a frock coat)* and the trousers narrow-legged, called 'drainpipes'. This splendour was generally accessorized with a bootlace tie and clumsy-looking thick crepe-soled shoes, referred to as 'brothel creepers'.

Collectively they were frowned upon and spurned as tearaways, although most were ordinary guys, many having spent a 'king's ransom' to get 'the look', often as not making their appearance terrific. However, there were rival Teddy Boy gangs from housing schemes who, battled it out - clashing frequently, tooled up with open razors and bicycle chains. I remember the names of two as being 'the Valdor Gang' and 'the Jubilee Gang', *one of which had a radge leader called Boko.* We heard tales of blood and snot, slashings and running battles stopping the traffic when these hooligans were kickin' the shit oot o' each other in Princes Street.

As I've already told you, by this time we were prowling uptown, but that tended to be at the weekends. During the week we hovered around our own neighbourhood, often going to Sandy's Pool Hall *next to the good old Ritz* for a game of snooker; ending up at the 'Rodney' fish and

chip shop, 'sitting in' and feeding both the jukebox and our faces. I won't expand on this, which was a bit of a 'busman's holiday' for the Brattisani brothers, but will once again report the prices, as today they sound ridiculous. A fish supper was 1/1^{d} *(thirteen old pence)*, a steak pie supper was 1/- *(one shilling or twelve old pence)* and a mince *(or Scotch)* pie supper was 10^{d} *(ten old pence)*. An alternative was Lena Maran's Ice Cream Parlour, also in Rodney Street; it was in one of the booths there that we discovered ♫ "Things go better with Coca-Cola".♫ I can't remember the price per chilled bottle, it may've been 6^{d} *(a silver sixpence)*.

So, at the weekends we met and socialised uptown; and here's the drill. Saturdays were as today, mostly taken up with shopping and window-gazing; but Sunday was quite different, it was a social occasion as back in yesteryear the Sabbath was observed, so all the shops were closed. However, the cafés were open: Sunday therefore was cavalcade day when everyone 'all glammed up' in finery, strutted their stuff along Princes Street; the great meeting place for our city's young pretenders.

Now, this being Edinburgh there were plenty Sundays when it 'wus pishin' doon', so on such days the Royal Museum in Chambers Street came into its own, a big place and very interesting; but I've already plugged that one to death. So, anyway, Princes Street on a pleasant Sunday afternoon was the place to be, as half the capital's young residents would congregate there. On really hot summer days Princes Street Gardens were well appreciated by the boys, as they were always 'hoachin' wi' fresh young snatch', both home-grown and holidaymakers. I'm pleased to see it's still the same today - *so it would appear they've got something right*.

We had two favourite cafés uptown and would spend some time in one or the other halfway through the afternoon. The one we frequented most; because it was the largest - so giving us more chance of all getting seats together, was not actually on Princes Street, but a few hundred yards along past Shandwick Place on a corner by the Haymarket Clock, but like so many it is now an Indian restaurant - *a curse on our forefathers, for having had a poxy empire!* However, in **'the happy days'** it was called the Honey Dew Café owned by Rocky Martin and done out American diner style. We loved its formica-topped tables and booth-type seating, opposite the long counter with its cluttered array of shiny stainless steel coffee percolators

hissing and gurgling, and all the associated gadgetry for both the coffee and ice creams; which were the speciality of the house, from knickerbocker glories and peach melbas down to the humble vanilla with a wafer. So, if we were flush - after a mischievous waitress asking "Would anyone like crushed nuts?" a tall glass holding a knickerbocker glory was 'the order of the day' ***- and not a fat bastard amongst us.***

The other was on Princes Street near the Castle Street junction and beside the, already-mentioned, Monseigneur - the Manhattan Café, was owned by Dom Valente and obviously, with such a name, echoed 'downtown New York'. I can't remember if there was seating at street level *I think there was* but recall we preferred to go downstairs to what would, originally, have been the basement. This was well-lit and lavishly kitsch, boasting mirrored walls etched with the Manhattan skyline.

Yes, the Manhattan Café will be remembered by many as a trendy part of the Edinburgh scene in its day - those who don't but were familiar with our fair city in bygone times may recall the bright red American Studebaker with its white vinyl roof, loads of chrome and probes *(for parking)* sticking out at pavement kerb level. It was a real bit of much admired 'fifties flashbucket', always parked right in front of the café; which today sounds crazy, but back in **'the happy days'** those fortunate enough to own a car parked wherever it suited; since there were no meters or zones. Sounds like 'heaven on a stick' - and it was; so, ***up yours,*** **pal!**

We'd dash home at five for our evening meal, listen to 'Lost in Space' and be back uptown for seven-thirty; do a 'oncer' along Princes Street, stop and linger at 'Speakers Corner' *by the Art Gallery at the Mound,* listening awhile to the 'Sally Ann' Brass Band and the many clowns spouting shit from their soapboxes. This could be amusing, and often more so the hecklers, who were known to get so wound-up and out-of-hand that they had to be frogmarched away, mouthing obscenities in the true tradition of a frantic peasant under duress, by two burly polis and bundled into the copbox, *where the real pests got a 'guid kickin'.* After which, *wearing 'bracelets'* the mouthy gits were swiftly wheeched away in the waiting Black Maria and locked-up for the night, to then make a personal appearance in the Sheriff Court on the High Street the following morning; and *if unlucky* a mention in the Evening News.

We were thrilled to discover a great venue for Sunday nights: this was the ever popular West End Café in Shandwick Place. The entrance was a nondescript doorway halfway along the row of smart retail outlets on the right going towards Haymarket; close to where the two upmarket *'by royal appointment'* Rossleigh car showrooms were. Anyway, the entry fee for Edinburgh's young elite was two shillings; this got you in and provided a bottle of coke - once in, a narrow passage led through to a large shabby hall, in dire need of decoration *(shabby-chic?)* filled with an assortment of cheap tables and chairs, and over to the left a small excuse for a bandstand.

This 'bandstand' housed a 'with it' quartet; there to accompany *and bolster the courage of* those bold enough to get up and sing. Some of the would-be stars were never-to-be, but far outweighed by the good ones; many being regulars from the American airbase at Kirknewton. One big good-looking black Yankee guy, Ozzie *who Joe Brattisani knew well* was a star turn; and I've had a memory flash - the bass player, 'Stan the Man', was a pal of ours, a solemn moody type; *his ilk, the world o'er tend to adopt and sell this image*. I think you had to be over sixteen to get in; there was no alcohol, so I imagine the compulsory Coca-Cola must've been something to do with the entertainment licence - whatever, this popular weekly event was well attended, so the joint wus fair jumpin' every Sunday.

I've just remembered an afternoon when a group of us were chatting outside the Overseas Club in Princes Street as two tall strikingly handsome, well-dressed peacock males in their early twenties swaggered nonchalantly by. No one had the right to look that good; they were the sort who couldn't pass unnoticed - you know the type, ***enough tae make yae boak!*** As they passed, Tico said, "Do you know who they are?" - after a response of indifferent shrugs he told us their names. The first I immediately forgot, but the second one was called Randy something; *I've lost the surname*. It was the first time I'd heard of anyone with such a name and wondered if it was, what he was, or who he was - *probably both if looks were anything to go by.* Our informant then tells us, the word on the street is, they attend acting school and are going to be film stars; we think, **yeah, sure!** Well, you know how it is when something you didn't know existed turns up or is pointed out, you're certain to see it again very soon and that's how it was. **Coincidence** - *that's the word I was looking for.*

Back in our 'salad days', come the weekend *weather permitting* we'd take an SMT bus down the East Lothian coast to Gullane where there is a super miles-long beach with dunes and nice clean sand. **Well, wouldn't you know,** the very next time we're at Gullane there they are, the two hunky Adonises along with some poncey friends playing with a beachball and doing handstands. Billy glances at them disdainfully and with more than a hint of sarcasm, remarks, "The bodies o' Greek gods and the brains o' Greek goats!" The rest of us brand them 'a bunch o' pansies' and steer clear in case the posers kick sand in our awestruck jealous faces.

The 'green-eyed monster' episode is long forgotten, when six years down the line I go to the cinema in Elgin with my mate Jim (Scouse) O'Reilly to see 'Dr No' and guess who is playing James Bond? *Well, ah'll be fucked wi' the blunt end o' a ragman's trumpet - and I didn't even remember his name.* Well, all the world an' yer auld granny knows it now - I've often wondered what happened to the guy called Randy!

Although we went on day trips to Gullane *(pronounced Gillin by the toffs)* many times over the years *having some terrific adventures and laughs there* they sort of all blend together with no particular event associated with any individual day. However, there was the one and only time we camped there for the whole weekend with three borrowed tents.

It must have been early summer, because when we got there on the Saturday afternoon it was the town's Gala Day. We thought one of us could be 'Queen o' the May', but some local tart had already been picked and crowned - oh well, fuck yer luck somedays! But wait a minute, things are looking up; the fair is here on the village green and that should attract the hootenanny from miles around, so tonight we *the slick city kids* might score **and we've got tents**. Encouraged by this incentive we're off, with zest, down that old beach to pitch them, and establish a camp in the dunes.

That took ages, as none of us had been Boy Scouts so we hadn't a clue, and as for the tents, they were bits o' cheap crap, definitely pre-war - goodness knows where we'd mumped them; just small white ridge tents, not even canvas, the worst one having tears in it. We probably drew straws, I think there were eight of us because I'm sure two of the tents had to be shared by three and the one with the holes in it got two. So we lark about, scoff some scran, comb and tease our well-brylcreemed 'Tony Curtis'

hairstyles, then, after a bit o' preening, the young smoothies bimble, with high hopes, over the dunes heading for the magic of the fair.

It's far from the night we'd talked ourselves into expecting. Sure there's acres o' tail, but we're gettin' the old 'on yer bike, pal' - they're only interested in the fairground gypsy boys. The attraction being free rides on the dodgems, waltzers and what have you, and maybe because they had luxury caravans; whereas us chumps just had three auld paupers' tents doon on the beach. So, we were 'fartin' against thunder'. Now, that might not be 'gospel' as 'Gigolo Joe' probably 'scored' - *but what's new?*

What we hadn't taken into account was finding our way back to the campsite on a pitch-black moonless night. We are city boys, sure we have night-time like everyone else, but *with street lights* it's never a blackout. Crikey, this is something else, no stars, nothing - we can barely see each other, let alone where we're going.

Well, never say die, we know 'our pitch' is over to the right and it can't be that far, so we stumble off with bags o' confidence, in what has to be the direction for our camp. Now, this is a fair-sized beach and the dunes, of which there are many, make the task so much harder for us. Sure, it's a 'piece o' piss' in daylight, but now the place seems ten times its actual size. Of course we're going round in circles, probably visiting the same dunes more than once, and it's not funny anymore. In fact some of the happy campers are getting a touch ratty and jokes like "lucky it's not the Sahara" are wearing a bit thin. After a tête à tête we decide to use military tactics; we'll fan out army fashion and cover more ground that way; *just like we've seen in the movies*. At this point a young harbinger of doom whines, "What if some rotten twat has stolen the tents, and all our gear?" Someone else grunts "Shut up, ya fuckin' arsehole!" which may well've resulted in a punch-up - that is, if they could've seen each other.

So, the plan is to fan out, comb the area and when someone gets lucky, he has to find one of the torches, which no one thought to bring along; being too busy yakking about the fair and anticipating the snatch. He will then shine the torch, signal to the others and guide us in, ***simple!*** Well, off we go, sure of success this time. The yells and curses can be heard coming from all directions, as the gang trip over and bang into things in the dunes, with the bold ones sounding further and further away. After what seems

ages the 'chosen one' shouts **"I've found it; I'm here!"** We can detect the excitement and pride in his voice when he ***again*** shouts, **"I'm here!"** A voice bellows from the gloom "Where? ya silly fucker!", another from a different direction shouts "Well, find the fuckin' torch!" followed by the chosen one, whose tone of voice has changed from excited to harassed, hissing "I'm lookin', I'm fuckin' lookin' - **I've found it!"**

After a few minutes of hushed silence with everyone expectantly waiting, someone cracks and yells "Well, shine the fuckin' thing, ya daft bastard!" quickly followed by the chosen one's anguished cries of "I am, I fuckin' am!" Another voice snarls "Well, we can't see a fuckin' thing!" Followed by yet another bright spark, who had reasoned out the situation, saying, "We are camped in a hollow, so no one can see the torch." The chosen one, by now sounding really peeved *having suffered dog's abuse* screams "Well, what do you want me to do about it?" Abruptly a new voice enters the verbal arena, answering in an exasperated tone, **"Climb to the top of the dune, you stupid cunt!"** Problem solved!

It takes time, some having wandered far and wide, eventually the stragglers all return - all except big daft Doogie that is. Hell's teeth, he's lost again, the big soft bugger. So, in unison, we shout "Doogie where are ye?" and are relieved when Doogie shouts from somewhere in the night "Over here!" - someone replies "Come on then"; big Doogie responds "Ah cannae!" We, mystified, chorus "Why?" to which the answer is "Ah'm doon oan ma hunkers firin' one oot!" Tam mutters "Spare us the details, pal!"

The nomads hold a torchlight powwow - no one's hungry, as we've all had hot dogs and rubbish at the fair, so the best and only thing to do is turn in. Blimey! I've never spent such a cold night in my life, it was absolutely freezing in these little old tents - which, I recall; if it was raining outside and you touched the inside fabric the wet stuff would weep through: nothing like the modern beauties that will keep you snug in the worst imaginable conditions. To cap it all we, of course, had no sleeping bags *or even blankets* - so, not much sleeping, but plenty bickering and shivering was done, and with it being bitterly cold there's always someone causing ructions by having to struggle up and go for 'a slash'.

You know how it is when you're freezing; you don't want to surface, or do anything for that matter. So, come the morning we're perished and have

to force ourselves to rise bright and early *well, maybe not so bright, but certainly early* as there's no point in lying there bleating and shivering.

I've no memory of what time it would've been, but can tell you it was as soon as dawn broke, making it light enough to see what we were doing. Once organized the plan is, six will skirmish the shoreline for driftwood and sea coal while the remaining two stay put to make a field kitchen, on which to rustle up the scran. So we all set about our tasks; with me, being a chef, the obvious choice to make breakfast. Billy elects to give me a hand, he's no' daft - so sees this as a better deal than foraging for fuel on a mist-shrouded shore in the biting cold morning air.

Building the fireplace was a doddle, as all we had to do was rob the big stones from abandoned campfires - *testimonials to the toils of others*. We built a 'brammer', with the stroke of genius being; a piece of corrugated iron on top, which would get red hot and act like a stove to put the pans and dixies on. When the young hunter-gatherers returned with arms laden we 'fired up' our 'field kitchen' - which worked a treat.

With everyone's contributions divvied up we had a crackin' scran; black pudding, beans, bacon, sausages etc., a 'full English' *and then some* - a proper tightner, scoffed with gusto. We even managed to make toast by spearing bread on sharpened sticks and holding it close to the red-hot corrugated iron; with *of course* some slices falling off, causing quite a reek. It was a huge fire, which, helped by heavy timber and the sea coal, burned well into the morning. By the time we were 'fed and watered' the horrors of the night before were soon forgotten by the young and resilient team, especially towards noon when the sun condescended to shine on the righteous, allowing 'God's own' to anticipate a fun day ahead.

Being veterans with long experience of Gullane beach 'the Brotherhood' hadn't just picked the best spot to pitch the tents, but also taken into account that this was a favoured location for the sun-worshipping goddesses ritual spreading of large multicoloured beach towels upon which to display their wares. So, by midday our hopes were realized when 'the talent' began to arrive in twos and threes, settling down around our camp, at, no doubt, what they considered a safe, but not unobtainable, distance. Then came the unveiling when they would coyly *and need I say expertly* hiding behind towels, peel off and change into bikinis - *the tricks they get up to, to enslave*

us poor wretches is nobody's business. It was the anticipation of what was to come that made the excitement more than often better than actually seeing them in the bikini - I guess that's what a switched-on expensive high-class striptease artist is all about, as we tend to use our imaginations to picture our own personal perception of perfection.

Not much chance nowadays; *with bare breasts and a thong the mystery's gone*. Some of them never get it - the clever ones know it's what we can't see that turns us sex-starved suckers on. I remember watching a 'chick flick' way back in the 80s, with some colleagues in my basement office under the car showroom and when 'Chesty' Morgan *(who had a right pair o' 'thrups')* came on the screen, 'Honest Ron' remarked, "Imagine seeing them in a tight sweater" ***- too true; that says it all!***

It's a good day, there's plenty 'spare' - few we haven't chatted up, some more receptive than others, and those whom we already knew from past encounters. Six of us decide, in case we're missing out on something, to go for a dander along the beach and have a wee paddle; the sea is freezin', so, being smart, the 'pussy patrol' stick with the stretch of warm sand above the waterline; but soon bored oot our tits, do the about-turn.

Once back we discover, Tam and Doogie *left behind to guard the gear* have copped three burds. There's a bit o' frolicking going on between Tam and a gallus creature with short dark hair. They're rolling around wrestling and giggling in the sand; knowing 'Tam the ram' there's no doubt he's 'grabbin' a handful' - *perhaps tryin' tae get in touch wae her feminine side*. Doogie's all over this blonde *like the measles* while they're watchin' Tam romping wi' the blackheid, no doubt wondering how to get in on the same act themselves without being too obvious. The third young lady is sitting on her own, looking totally pissed off as she's getting no attention, but quickly perks up when the fast response squad arrive. All of a sudden she's gone from Little Miss Lonely to 'Numero Uno'.

Have her bathed and brought to my tent!
And you over there, prepare a feast!

To my mind she's the best-looking of the three and make no mistake, she knows it, so, wasn't used to playing 'gooseberry', but now fully in the limelight not going to step back out in a hurry, and so, was eager to please. She had nicely-cut auburn hair, intense brown eyes, a pretty face with cute

freckles, smooth tanned limbs and a neat figure; a bit slutty, but nice with it. The 'wee stoater's' a sitting duck after being ignored earlier, so, taking advantage of this, there's a bit of fooling around with her.

Within minutes Joe winks and says "Let's throw this mad cow in the sea" telling us to get hold of her arms and legs. We grab her, as instructed by 'the Master', and carry her down to the water's edge. She's half-heartedly resisting, probably thinking we're just larking about: then, quick as a flash, Joe *who'd been raised as a good Catholic boy* wheechs the drawers off her. Jesus Christ, that's the last thing we thought was going to happen! She shrieks; we *the dumbstruck accomplices* drop her like a hot brick and don't know where to look - *well, OK... yes we did.*

'Going bananas', she struggles to her feet, pulls up her bikini pants and, clutching her top, storms off swearing like a sailor's parrot. This puts the dampers on Tam and Doogie's fun, as their playmates dash off to console the little actress; now feigning tears and wanting sympathy.

So that's it then Baby - the game's up the pole! What the hell, the day's shagged by now anyway and angry clouds are heading our way, so, being Gullane veterans, we know it's time to 'do one'. We break camp and pack the tents, squabbling about who is to carry them while scurrying to the bus stop - because, we know when the heavens open there'll be a mass exodus and the bus queue will go on forever. What's more we've no scran left, and all our dosh vanished at the fair. However, prudently, we do have return tickets for the bus; so arrive home early, have a meal, an' after a dose o' 'Lost in Space', meet up later and once again, spruced and swathed in finery are strutting our healthy suntanned stuff uptown that evening.

Some people never learn! I know I'm forever banging on about how these were relatively innocent times - talking about the Mayday Fair reminded me that 'the Shows' came to the Waverley Market each Christmas. We, the mug punters, are there; having been enticed and eager to be fleeced, we've paid a shilling a skull to be hastily ushered through a tent flap, desperate to ogle some 'Eastern Sultan's Daughter' perform 'The Dance of the Seven Veils' *(the Scottish version being 'The Dance o' the Seven Cardigans').* Once in, we find to our utter dismay there's not enough room to swing a cat, and a net curtain screening this slapper. So, in reality we can almost see the floozie's interpretation of this classical dance

as she gracefully disposes of some coloured veils to music resonating from a well-scratched record, playing 'Everything I have is Yours', on an ancient wind-up gramophone. Then, joy at last, she whips off the bra, but before we've had time to focus our lust-filled eyes on her unleashed majestic orbs the lights go off, and she's gone 'quicker than that' - yes, the show's over and we're emptied out. ***Sod it, seen off again!***

While I remember, what's this great fascination with mammary glands then? After all, we know they are just for feedin' bairns, but 'the enemy' brazenly display them as bait to lure the unwary - knowing full well we can't keep our eyes *(or for that matter, hands)* off them. The huge ones we called paps and cute little pert jobs, titties - no doubt, you're thinking where did that spring from and why the digression? Well now, it leads me nicely to another amusing little episode, about which I can't wait to tell you.

It all starts on a Saturday, instigated by an article in the Evening News about the American singer Johnnie Ray, who, then, was at the height of his fame, so gettin' a good airing, is on his world tour and appearing in Edinburgh the following week at the Empire Theatre. However, since he had a suite in the five-star Caley Hotel at the West End, the man of the moment decided to grant his adoring fans a personal appearance on Sunday evening, from the balcony on the first floor above the hotel entrance; from where he would treat the admirers, assembled below, to a medley of his hit songs - it's a nice summer evening and 'the Brotherhood' is part of a small crowd gathered to see and hear the great American celebrity. Of course the big star keeps us waiting, we've all been there for at least half-an-hour and the 'Prima Donna' hasn't yet graced us with 'her' presence ***- bitch!***

The natives are getting restless - but not us however, as we're being entertained by Joe and Charles, who have a paper bag full of cheap Chinese firecrackers; given to them by a customer at the chippie. I'd never seen this type before *or since, come to think of it*; they were just small paper wraps that must've contained something like a cap used in 'little cowboys' toy pistols. When thrown at the pavement they went off with a sharp crack, and that's all there was to it. Nothing special, but good fun in an unsuspecting crowd ***- and here comes the icing on the cake.***

In the throng there's a big wholesome girl *(pushin' twenty, but been nice in her day)* 'tarted up' like a peasant gypsy in one of those bolero top

things - the sort that leaves the shoulders bare and displays some cleavage. It's obvious that a burd in that get up is 'fair game'. No, no - give us **some** credit, **we didn't shoot her!** She had a pair o' paps *that could've suckled a small nation* overflowing from the skimpy bolero top, so we're giving this buxom wench the treatment with the odd firecracker making her hop and jump, fair hoping that these magnificent diddies would leap free from their double D cups. We were making good progress and they were just about to pop when that prick decides to 'pitch up' and sing, putting paid to our little game just short of a well-deserved success story.

So there's Johnnie, decked out in a candy-pink tux, spouting crap to his spellbound fans below, but what the clown had forgotten was a microphone. We could hardly hear him, because, if his publicity machine was to be believed, he wasn't to know, since he wore a hearing aid; supposedly deaf as a post since thirteen - *probably a gimmick*. Deaf he may have been, but blind he certainly wasn't. Johnnie had spied the big-breasted bint's ample charms when leaning over waving to his star-struck flock, and almost fell off the balcony tryin' to tae cop a better deek, while singing 'Somebody Stole my Gal'. He treated us to a burst of the tears, which he was famous for, while singing 'The Little White Cloud that Cried', as already said, with no amplifier, so it didn't sound anything like the voice we were familiar with on radio. However, we had a bit of fun that night and although we didn't go to his concert, the 'freebie' went down a treat.

The following day, being Trades Holiday Monday, we decided on a trip to Edinburgh Zoo - few of us had been there since childhood, so thought it would make an interesting afternoon; being a big well-stocked place covering acres of hilly parkland at Corstorphine, about three miles west of the town centre. We all agreed the Aquarium was terrific and enjoyed the Aviary, as some of these cockatoos and parrots are brilliant, sporting fantastic colours. Not too keen on the Reptile House though, that lot, especially the huge snakes, gave us the creeps. The lions and tigers enclosures were honkin', but *and I bet you just knew this was leading somewhere* **the Monkey House was a hoot!** The nice little monkeys were hungry, and luckily we'd brought a supply of laxative chocolate *just for them* which they greedily fought over, making us touch seventh heaven. Good on 'em, that would stop the dirty little buggers 'beatin' their meat'

in public, thus causing embarrassment to punters who'd paid hard-earned money treating families to a day out, at the 'child-friendly' zoo.

Now, this was a move I was to remember, and put to good use, when home on Summer Leave a few years later, which coincided with our next door neighbours getting a young Shetland Collie. Everytime they let this creature out into their back garden it started yapping the second it crossed the threshold, ***and just did not stop.*** Stan 'n' Nan were a nice old couple, who I got along fine with, but unfortunately both were oblivious to the aggravation their beloved pet, with glinting evil eyes, was causing. I handled the annoying situation with surprising diplomacy, but didn't get through; we never fell out, but nothing changed - it just went on and on.

Well, I'd tried and since none of us was in control of the situation, which had wee Genghis making everyone's life a misery, barking his balls off day and night, I decided it was time for the good old laxative chocolate to be introduced. Believe me, it's so easy - and dogs love it. Half a bar a day for a week, that's all it takes. No matter how much they dote on 'Rover', if he has a dose o' the 'Tex Ritters' and is crapping on the fitted Axminster every day, **he has to go**. So, within the week our noisy little four-footed fleabag had magically disappeared, ***problem solved!*** *(everyone hates yappin' mutts - branding their inconsiderate owners **cunts!**)*

Like many, I'd been bitten by the ice-skating bug when seventeen and enjoyed going to Haymarket Ice Rink on Friday nights. This was a small select rink used by skating and curling clubs, a good place for beginners, no hassle, nice gentle people, not at all like Murrayfield which is a big rink further from the town centre; out next to the rugby ground. It's much larger, a rough all-singin'-all-dancin' place *with a cafe and bar,* favoured by the commoners, and has an ice hockey team called the Murrayfield Royals - this is where the action is; so where we want to be.

It's magic on Wednesday and Saturday evenings, as we already know a number of people who skate there and befriend many more, especially the female variety; healthy specimens - skin like porcelain and fit as fleas - love's young dream shamelessly vying for attention in these tiny pelmet-like skating-skirts revealing white knickers *usually two pairs for security* encasing pert little cheerleader-bums still in the first flush of youth and not yet affected by gravity. Such fascinating trim creatures, flaunting

themselves in tight sweaters with bumps on the front; perish the thought, but it's sad that so many would evolve into saggy-ersed moaning hags.

We wallowed in a fair bit o' nonsense whilst skating round and round to pop music of the 50s; I'm sure whoever spun the records must've had 'a thing' for the Everly Brothers, as whenever I think of Murrayfield Ice Rink I vividly remember circling endlessly to 'Wake up Little Susie'.

It sounds naff - just whizzing round for two or three hours, but that wasn't the case, since with several hundred skaters seeking prey, it constituted a huge social gathering, with heaps o' gossip, puttin' on the patter and 'tryin' the hand', a much better hunting ground than the dimly-lit dancehalls we were yet to haunt. Yes, on looking back you could see what you were chasing and it was easy to flit from one to the other; especially when you got a 'K.B.' from some snooty, toffee-nosed little madam.

One Saturday night, in fact 'twas the evening prior to Remembrance Sunday; we'd been cornered by a frail old duchess selling poppies, so were sporting them on our 'must-have' Waverley Tailor's V-neck sweaters with 'go-faster' stripes down the sleeves. During the intermission *for speed-skating and ice dancing* we, 'the young bucks', were amusing ourselves cavorting with a group of girls we'd snared, pretending we were going to jag them with the poppy pins; this caper had them jumping about and squealing with excitement. A 'rough wee tattie', christened 'Spotty Dottie' is near me, so I bend down, pin in hand and giggling insanely, say "Ah'm gonna jag you Dot"; unfortunately in the euphoria ah 'fluffed ma lines' and what ah blurted out was "Ah'm gonna shag you Dot."

Crikey, this didn't go down too well - like a bolt from the blue, I get a wallop right across the coupon, didn't even see it coming, but certainly felt it, and anyone in the vicinity who didn't witness what happened must've heard it. I never got the chance to apologize as Dottie, 'out her tree' and living up to her name, did the about-turn, waddled off *splay-footed* 'doin' her duster' and never spoke to me again, ***tough!*** That was the first of three times I copped a slap from 'the enemy', but we shall save the other two for later, when appropriate; *so, you'll just have to be patient!*

Through going to the ice rink, the team gained a few more members, who came from different districts to the 'inner circle', and so, not full members. Two of them were George Vinestock and his pal Jimmy; a big

aggressive goon, who was more like his minder than his mate. George's family had a successful business *(Craighouse Cabinet Works)* and he was first of 'the Brotherhood' to have a driving licence.

On occasion he had the use of his Mummy's MKVII Jaguar or his uncle's Daimler Majestic - both 'flash motors'. I well remember the Saturday night when he and Jimmy had the Jag; and we, the envious peasants, were outside the rink chatting to them through the car window, while they waited for the burds they'd snared. I was admiring the car, which, with its elegant lines, leather interior and walnut dash was 'the last word' in those days. As if all that wasn't enough, when George switched on the lights the panel lights glowed in an avant-garde violet. That was me hooked, I had never imagined anything so beautiful and desperately wanted one - a dream I managed to realize, on buying a pristine MK1X that 'Fat Scott' had found stored in a shed at Leith Docks some twenty years later.

I don't remember George getting called up for National Service, although he probably was *as few escaped* but Jimmy ended up in the Royal Air Force Police and so, was like an MP which suited him to a 'T'. We were once privileged to spy him uptown proudly striding around in uniform, looking the part with his peaked cap pulled well down over his eyes and head held high, like a guardsman. Yes, Jimmy looked menacing and no doubt commanded respect from the less fortunate when on duty.

Two guys who often tagged along were Billy Foggo and Sydney Drew. That summer Billy holidayed with relatives in America; when he returned, sporting a ten gallon hat and fringed waistcoat *looking every inch the cowboy* it was obvious the States had made quite an impression on him; in fact, the upshot was Billy emigrated across the 'herring pond' and joined the USAF. 'Hissing' Syd later absconded to Canada with Charles and another; who I think may've been Dale York - Dale *I'm told* became a hairstylist to Hollywood's rich and famous. Charles and Syd stayed and worked there awhile, returning to Edinburgh in the mid 60s.

The last time I saw Syd was funny and well worth a mention. A few years ago, when I had this unusual copper-roofed bungalow in the smart Craiglockhart district, Syd was working for the Gas Board, and in the area reading meters - *he didn't know I lived there*. On nipping out to post a letter and pick up a copy of the Scottish Autotrader I clocked him from the car

without him seeing me and thought, perfect, I'll give him a surprise. Yes, I'll get the kettle on and treat him to one of my *world-famous* coffees; then generosity kicks in - so I mentally add a chocolate biscuit.

Once indoors the plot thickens and the mischievous streak, we all harbour, surfaces when my eyes fall on a horrendous wig I'd bought for my daughter, Linda, to wear at a Halloween party she *with her tricky friends Bellinne, Sarah and Romana* had been invited to. This wig was hideous, I'd found it in a joke shop at the foot of Victoria Street - a mass of Shirley Temple curls; bright blonde with a spew-green hue. So I've got the wig on - a sly glance in the hall mirror inspires my theatrical temperament, so has me struggling into a check-patterned gingham smock; *used for Linda's art class at Watson's College* - then I put on a chunky pearl necklace and wait, twittering to myself in anticipation of my victim's arrival. By the time he gets to the gate, I've left the front door open and am hiding behind the fifteen-pane vestibule door with its voile privacy curtain.

When Syd rings I quickly open this inner door and standing there in all my glory say in a shy falsetto voice "Yes young man!" Syd was completely taken aback, his face a picture to behold, as he said in a deep voice "I've come to read your meter." I couldn't keep a straight face, on seeing his shock, so burst out laughing and removed the wig saying "It's me, ya dummy." A look of instant relief crossed his coupon and crackin' up, Syd confessed he didn't know what to think when confronted by such an apparition of beauty, and had hesitated about calling me Missus.

Here, this should tickle yer fancy - it was one of those balmy Saturday evenings that saw 'the Brotherhood' in a lively mood - so rather than go straight home after a session at Murrayfield we decide to get off the bus at Haymarket and stop in at the Honey Dew for a bite. After stuffing our faces, we agree to forget the bus and walk the rest of the way home; so, ice hockey skates dangling from their laces over our shoulders off we go, blethering and clowning, heading for Princes Street.

When passing Coates Crescent, with its open garden area and bench seats, we stop *for no particular reason* beside the huge statue of William Ewart Gladstone (1809-1898). He is, as befitting, on top of the monument which is adorned with smaller figures around its base; two being bare-naked cherubs holding a banner. On one of the benches a 'pished-legless'

fan has left his maroon and white Hearts Football Club scarf, so, a sharp member of our team wraps it round the neck of one of the naked boys "to keep him warm" - well, you know how one thing leads to another. Tommy Love notices that both cherubs have little sticking out cocks, so Big Doogie produces a 'packet o' three' and proceeds to put a French letter on them - to make sure they stay on, another conspirator contributes a rubber band for each of 'the twins'. Golly, these hysterical few minutes were the highlight of the evening, having us in stitches all the way home.

The following day, being a Sunday, we head for the Honey Dew *mid-afternoon as usual* therefore, once more, pass the monument, which is still as we left it the night before, but, by now some benevolent citizen had donated a workman's cap to the boy with the scarf, so, it's not hard to guess that Sunday strollers and sightseers had appreciated our humour.

It's now appropriate to introduce a madcap, yet interesting, character known to all as Benny Wilkie. I'm lost as to how and when Benny joined our merry throng, but have an inkling that we met him at Murrayfield and the more I ponder it the more I'm inclined to think he was as an electrician at the Lady Victoria Pit with Joe McGlinchey; who by now worked as a spark for the NCB. Come to think of it, the Coal Board at this time must have been getting and training the pick of the crop, because as already said, Joe was intelligent and well educated. Benny *although barking* had been Dux of his school - to bolster this view, one day in town I met a classmate from Wardie Primary, 'Basher' Stables, who was top boy in our final year. He was also employed by the NCB as an Underground Surveyor Engineer, *or some such title*. Now, surely it's more than just a coincidence that the only three guys I ever knew who worked for the Coal Board were extremely bright. Anyway, getting back to Benny; an agile lean, clean-cut guy with a crooked grin and sly look that implied he knew what you were thinking. Clever he may have been but, on the other hand, 'mad as a brush wi' nae hair'. I include his name now, as a couple of years further 'down the line' he will merit more mention.

By now we are growing up fast and on occasion swanning along tae the jiggin', dressed to kill. The first dancehall we graced was The Locarno in Slateford Road - *the last time I passed, it was a snooker hall*; however, then it was a popular dancehall, which, with its sprung floor was great for

jiving. That first time there we had our sights set on a group o' wee belters, so we're right in there 'on the pull', no Victor Sylvester dance lessons for us, just get straight in about it. We did the hokey-cokey with them and, thinkin' we were 'in wae a shout' *trying hard to impress* made a play for them, but it was obvious that we were a bunch o' amateurs oot oor depth, and although they said we were born to dance and cute, still gave us the 'bum's rush'. However, we're young guys with plenty to offer, so aren't put off by the fact that we can't score at the Locarno - they say, 'God loves a trier', so it's more than likely we're meant for bigger and better things.

There's a bigger and better hunting ground at Fountainbridge; the swanky Mecca Palais de Danse. This place is all that glitters, it's 'the dug's baws' - just like we've seen in films. It's got everything, a real flash revolving stage, two live bands, one being an orchestra with resident singer, the other, visiting musicians on tour - big names, such as Edmundo Ros.

It's an inspiring place with a balcony, on which there's a restaurant and two bars; but what impresses us no end is the 'Ladies' Lavvies' are called 'Powder Rooms'; have we ever hit the big time! Well no, not really, as although crawlin' wi' crumpet for us to leer at, we can't score here either - the fact is, we're 'blown out' for being just too young. But not too young to start suckin' on the 'cancer sticks' and this is what the stupid ones amongst us do; thinking ourselves 'well cool', since our peers and all the sophisticated screen idols 'crash the ash', so it must be the way to go. Oh yeah! It's certainly the way to go; but nobody told us in those days - an' d'you know wot: it took me twenty-five years to kick the habit - *but, we'll not go into the details of that little struggle right now.*

Anyway, we rarely favour 'the Palais', as under the initial glam there's a downside: it can be wild when the natives are on the warpath. Too often the fights are so all-encompassing and brutal that it's more like an arena than a dance floor and neds are known to launch Coca-Cola bottles from the balcony onto the gladiators below. ***Not very healthy!***

Then there's the burds - appearances can be deceptive. Yeah, these lovely girls in their 'drindle skirts' and 'beehive hairdos' are not always what they'd have us believe. Just get one up to dance and you soon find out: under a masking dose of cheap perfume is the reek of B.O. *(many houses didn't have baths back then)*, also beneath pretty outfits lurked

hefty girls held in check by whalebone corsets. By jingo! What a shock to the system that was. Aye - thanks a bunch, ah thought ah'd be holding this soft sensual feminine creature in ma arms, so how come ah've copped this plookie porker that's chuckin' up? Furthermore it was whispered that some bints paid so much for their fancy hairdos that they got their money's worth by continually scooshin' on more hairspray, thus making them as solid as plaster o' Paris an' loupin' wae lice or infested wi' beasties. With all these minus points you can understand why we gave preference to the ice rink, where you could at least scrutinize your quarry.

I've been meaning to say a bit about Portobello open-air swimming pool; a large landmark art deco building, unfortunately demolished years ago, when the visionless councils were destroying our heritage. **Shitebags!** Had it survived, today it would be 'A' listed. Anyway, this was a swish place, with considerable capacity for both swimmers and spectators; it had a splendid five-tier diving platform with boards at different heights over the deep end *(this being twelve, or maybe as deep as fifteen feet)* situated halfway down the east side of the saltwater pool. There was even a wave machine, which at timed intervals sent sizeable waves from the south end all the way down the pool to become breakers at the shallow north end. The whole concept was terrific, spoiled only by the pool temperature.

It was well-attended, not just on hot days - *a rare commodity in our inclement Edinburgh*. Even in midsummer the water wus freezin', which was the only let down to such a well-designed magnificent asset. To my way of thinking the answer stood but a few yards away, as next door was Portobello Power Station which pumped thousands of gallons of hot water from their cooling system straight into the sea. Now, this must've been piped right past the pool, which lay downhill between the power station and the seafront. Surely it's common sense that a wee bit o' recycling should've been possible in modern times, let's face it, the Romans were capable of such things some two thousand years ago.

We frequently enjoyed 'Portie' during the mid-fifties and although I often boldly dived from the lower boards, I never dared the top one which didn't look all that high when staring up at it; but drag yer erse up and look over the edge down to the water miles below, that's when the 'old ringpiece flutters'. No, not on yer nelly, **not me**. The worst thing that could happen

to the many *like me* who went up, an' knobbly knees knockin', teetered, poised on the brink with everyone watching, then 'crappin' it' and sneaking timidly down the stairs *(observed by all)* was to be followed by a young nubile girl who would perch confidently on the edge, assume the position, then, without hesitation, execute a perfect dive.

I was amazed at the suntans some of the die-hards had - generally 'auld codgers' who must've been there every day, rain or shine, making sure they got every last cent of value from their season tickets - I'd never seen people that colour. Now, now! Before you start, let me clarify; I'm talking about the days before we were invaded by millions of immigrants - as *often* said previously, **'the happy days'**. Come to think of it these tanned die-hards did have leathery wrinkled skin, but that was back then, in the 'olden times' before skin cancer was invented *(as the ingenious human race had yet to completely 'total' the Earth's ozone layer).*

Seems like I'm forever slapping wrists, but always with good intent - mark my words, one way or another nothing's more certain than, that one day arrogant mankind will be responsible for its own demise - the UK is overpopulated, yet it's criminal that immigrants still pour in, while the *near-bankrupt* State continues to dish out Child Benefits, encouraging further breeding by the mindless peasants. Man displays ingenuity in abundance when killing, thieving and seeking sexual satisfaction, but is blinkered to the main issue ***- forget 'Greenpeace', every single problem facing Planet Earth today is down to the fact that there are*** **too many people!**

The fact that we are getting older, so must accept responsibilities is sharply brought home when we lose one of our group. Yes, the harsh reality of compulsory National Service rears its ugly head. Joe Brattisani is first to be pulled from the streets; chip shop manager not being classified as a trade, so our pal is 'called up' and despatched to fight for Queen and Country in the cookhouse of some far-flung English Barracks. This wake-up call puts the fear o' death up me; as since way back 'ah've hud a bee in ma bunnet' about conscription. Bollocks to Errol Flynn; eff him an' his bleeding 'Objective, Burma!' ***- not for me, pal!*** As time passes I get more and more concerned, although I've still got a long stay of execution before my apprenticeship is complete; but one must be prepared.

Taking a leaf from Billy Foggo's book, I decide that the American Air

Force is for me - after all, just look at these guys from Kirknewton with their smart uniforms, plenty dosh, brand new Austin Healey 3000s and flash burds. Yeah, ah want some o' that *(could be I've got ideas above my station - born to be a gentleman, but not required)*. So, consumed by the thunder of youth, and trying to buck the system, I push my luck by going to the American Consulate in Regent Terrace and asking to see the Consul.

My request is granted and I'm given an audience with the man himself - nice friendly people these American officials, not like our two-faced twats. I explain my position to this important man - *who's heard it all before*. He listens, agrees with what I'm saying then politely tells me to fuck off, suggesting I come back **after** I've done my National Service, but being a diplomat puts the spiel across so well, that although spewin' lumps, I vanish bearing him no malice - *still thinking he's a decent chap, while wondering if used fivers in a brown envelope might've won the day.*

Time goes by and although I've not actually finished my apprenticeship, I've completed training and evening classes, so am, for what it's worth, qualified and doing the same work as older men being paid three times as much; which I see as a bit of a liberty. This I point out to Tom Newton, who you'll remember is my boss, but ma bum wus oot the windae as, looking after the company's interests, the skinflint bluntly declines to give me a rise. Ma feathers are ruffled - every man has his price, so *after a bout o' the sulks* out comes the good old trusty Evening News and I'm right into the situations vacant columns. My timing is perfect; there's a vacancy for a chef *with qualifications* at the Western General Hospital, which is about four miles from my home; so I decide to pitch for that.

I apply, get an appointment with Mr Airth: the catering manager and they're either desperate or I impress him as I'm offered the job on the spot, at more than triple the money I'm being paid by Crawford's. I'll even get an extra 'wee tickle' for having my City & Guilds Diploma - *sock it to me Baby; looks like 'ah'm in clover'*. This for sure beats 'chasin' rainbows', but the real bonus is that Mr Airth is more than a little confident he can swing it to have me excused National Service - hospital work being of national importance; and I *(feeling untouchable)* couldn't agree more.

Now, being indentured to Crawford's meant I was bound to stay with them until the end of my contract, unless leaving the trade - so I regretted

having to lie to 'Isaac' in order to be released. Not something I'm proud of; since he'd given me the opportunity in the first place, however, he did refuse me a rise and my attitude is; it's money we get out of bed and work for - so ah didn't exactly wrestle wi' ma conscience.

Some months prior to this I had bought a brand new motorbike *on 'the drip'* from Rossleigh, who, for many years, had a motorcycle showroom in Lothian Road which, remarkably, later became a Royal Navy Recruiting Centre. What's that word again? Oh yeah, **coincidence**. The bike was a Triumph Tiger Cub, an excellent buy, proving very useful for getting me back and forward to 'The Western', especially when on the early shift; *starting at the unholy hour of 6 a.m.*

The kitchen brigade there were fabulous, particularly Mario, 'old Harry', and Sandy - a colourful ex 'squaddie', who referred to the gaffer's 'fancy wuman' as Mrs Bigrip. I enjoyed working alongside this team and because 'ah wus rakin' it in' thought myself 'a baron'- never before having commanded so much coin of the realm in my pay packet ***- I'd arrived!***

I'd only been doin' ma thing at the Western a few months and was quite settled in when along came the glitch - Mr Airth, who'd been corresponding *on my behalf* with that bunch o' good-for-nothin' civil serpents at the Ministry of Defence, wipes the smile from my face by informing me that his pleas have fallen on deaf ears, as they've refused point-blank to excuse me from National Service; so it would be a waste of time me begging for mercy. Talk about the screamin' habdabs; ***Drat!*** *- an' ah thought ah'd found a loophole;* to say I'm vexed would be the understatement of the decade - ***foiled again;*** looks like I'm 'up shit creek without a paddle'.

Shortly after this devastating shock I tendered my notice, so as to focus my time on doing 'a runner', and it was only fair to give them the chance to find a replacement. As it happened, I contacted Arthur McLeod *(still the Head Chef for Crawfords at the Shore in Leith)* and he got my job, which was handy for him, as Arthur lived a matter of minutes from the hospital. One of my reasons for resigning was that I thought I'd got it sussed, and intending to 'ship out' with the Merchant Navy had signed on at the Seamen's Pool in Leith - back in those days it was a case of - are you available **now?** And, if the answer was **yes;** that was you an' yer holdall, off to sail the seven seas and roam the wide world in search of adventure.

10: Seatime

Unfortunately my plan was flawed; since there wasn't much doing for would-be seafarers at that time - *numerous ships being 'laid up' due to repercussions following the Suez crisis,* so, becoming more desperate by the day *leaving no stone unturned* I paid an unsuccessful visit to St Andrew's House to volunteer for work on the Fishery Protection Vessels; these being run by a government department totally unrelated to the Merchant Navy. I also did the rounds of the shipping company offices in Leith, but getting nowhere; other than close to the end of my tether, when Tam McGlinchey, *who was out of a job at the time*, gets 'the whisper' from one of his cronies that Christian Salvesen were signing up crews for their Whaling Fleet as the killing season was imminent. This major operation being based at Leith Harbour, their South Georgia Whaling Station south east of the Falkland Islands in the South Atlantic - which gets me thinking, surely the MoD wouldn't cast their net that far to catch the likes of me.

Just like migration, every year *since long before anyone can remember,* this mass exodus has taken place. With many Leith families it's a tradition; the men have always gone to South Georgia; ***they are Whalers.*** It was also instrumental in clearing out the bevvyheads who were away long enough to dry out; although I heard tell of a 'cleverly hidden' 'illicit still' pumpin' out 'moonshine' for the 'alkies'. Anyway, when these bold and hardy adventurers returned home with bulging wallets it was 'party time' until they were skint, and so; had to sign on *once again* for another spell down in the Antarctic - sure sounds familiar, don't it?

Should've mentioned earlier, there's a paradox - it seems I haven't a hope in hell of being 'shipped out' by the Merchant Navy Seamen's Pool, as they give preference to those with sea experience - *nothing's ever easy.* **So, nice one Tam**, this could be the answer! We nip down to Salvesen's Head Office in Bernard Street where we offer our services to Captain Smith, the Crew Recruiting Master, who signs up Tam *(a competent chap, never beaten)* as a deckhand for one of the whale-catchers - a wee boat with a ginormous harpoon gun up front. Tam *chuffed to haipny donuts* is grinning

from ear to ear, as this is a big deal for a young guy who has never before 'flown the nest'. Unfortunately, it looks like 'ah'm onna loser' - they don't require any cooks; however, do need a Second Cook and Baker for the factory-trawler 'Fairtry'; yes the very same one mentioned in my school days *(life, as they say, is full of coincidences).* She was due to sail from Immingham Docks on the Humber two days later. Am I interested? **Am I ever!** "Look no further Sir - **I'm your man**", and ***"Thank you God!"***

Talk about 'a pierhead jump', ten minutes ago Tam and myself were jobless wharf-bums, however the sea is now our mistress and we're sailors off to conquer the world. Well, isn't that the berries! Looking back through the years, Tam's stint at South Georgia was long in both miles and time - something like nine months *maybe even a year.* Salvesen had a huge interest down by the Antarctic, with a Base the size of a small town on the island. Don't quote me, but their whaling fleet was probably the largest in the world; consisting of about a dozen 'catchers'; of which, if my memory serves me well, Tam was on the 'Southern Jester'. These catchers supplied murdered whales to the two large factory ships, which, once again, if I remember correctly, were called 'Southern Harvester' and 'Southern Venturer' - OK, that's enough about Tam; let's get back to **moi!**

So, I've packed my grips, said my farewells and now I'm off on the overnight train racing south to join my first ship, *determined to return wae a wad o' wonga.* This is exciting, ah can hardly believe ma luck; I'm taking a giant step, as until now I've never been more than forty miles from Edinburgh and, like everyone of a similar age, think I know it all.

Yeah! **That'll be right.** In fact I'm as green as the grass - I don't even know trains have toilets. Well, guess what! I've been on this 'choo choo' since black o'clock; it's now early morning and ah'm breakin' ma neck forra slash; this is agony - what ama goin' to do? - wish I hadn't guzzled all that bleedin' 'skoosh' - **stupid Bastard!** Eventually the only remaining passenger leaves the carriage; I'm alone at last, thank fuck! Let's fill the lemonade bottle - aahhhh! Jaisus, not a minute too soon, what a relief. That was painful - d'you know, I believe I had a 'sweat on'. Minutes after 'comforting' myself, the train pulls into my destination, and it's only when I'm getting off that I see, right next door to where I've been sitting for hours, a sign saying '**toilet**'. Like I said, **green as the grass!**

I then catch an electric tramcar thing, which takes me to the docks, where I find the factory-trawler; she of course reeks o' fish. As instructed, I report to the Chief Steward, a fusspot who looks curiously like the Patriothall Laundry van driver from way back in my childhood days at Logie Green. He shows me to a cabin, which he tells me I'll share with the Second Steward - *let's hope he ain't a bender!* After dumping my holdalls, the Chief accompanies me to the Galley, where he introduces me to Eric the Chief Cook, a quiet 'born-again Christian' from the Midlands, and Jimmy, the half-baked galley-hand, who is from Leith, and has a rogueish grin. I'm told to get changed and 'turn to' right away - talk about gettin' thrown in at the deep end, don't they know I've been up all night? I'm knackered! However, if that's the way of the sea, who am I to argue.

After the evening meal I've had a snoop around, to get my bearings, and am now impressed with the size of the ship - big for a trawler. I haven't yet met the Second Steward who lives in Hull, which they call 'Ull', and will return early morning as we sail 'first light'. Vic, the Cabin Boy, a likeable lad of seventeen, who seems to think I'm his 'Ole Thrush', suggests we go to the local cinema; saying it's our last opportunity for a 'run ashore' before sailing, on what will be a long trip. I'm shagged *not literally, perhaps that was a poor choice of words - should've said 'shagged oot'* and don't feel up to it, but he talks me round and off we go all spivved up in our suits, which will hereafter be stowed in plastic *zip-up* bags in our lockers, for the duration. Don't ask me what was showing, because I haven't a clue - fell asleep during the main feature and ought to have got my money back - yeah, that's me; tight as a gnat's chuff!

Next morning with all the crew back, we cast off 'early doors' to sail 'on the tide' and the 'first tripper' is 'turned to' knockin' out gargantuan bacon wedges from the Galley. We have a nice easy two-day passage up the North Sea, then make our way through the turbulent Pentland Firth where there's always a bit of a swell, but, weatherwise, I've experienced nothing to concern masel about so far and am slowly getting my 'sea legs'; ***and so 'twas written, that I became a sailor.***

After steaming across the North Atlantic to the bountiful fishing grounds off Newfoundland, I see what this ship is capable of. She's a stern trawler - instead of the huge net being cast and hauled in over the side, as is usual,

it gets 'shot' over the arse-end, which has a steep ramp sloping down to the 'oggin' and later winched in, sliding up the ramp laden with all manner of sea creatures. Then hoisted above the fishing deck by a derrick and the 'cod end' undone, thus pouring the catch into a pound for sorting by the deckhands before being sent down the appropriate chutes to the factory below - where the fish went through state-of-the-art German filleting machines - fillets appearing from one end, and head, backbone and tail all in a oner *Korky the Cat style* from the other. Trolleyloads of tightly packed fillets were then wheeled off to huge freezer stores and the skeletons with head and tail sent down another deck level to the fishmeal processing plant to be turned into animal feed - the cod liver being rendered in large vats to produce precious medicinal oil.

Now then, that's got to be a 100% success story. No wastage whatsoever, profit all the way down the line; I love it! If only other businesses, and for that matter the country, could be run so efficiently we'd all be in clover.

M. F. V. Fairtry

Some strange old fish were pulled up from the depths - I recall a couple of sharks and loads of dogfish *(which looked like mini sharks)*, catfish with cruel eyes and rows of sharp teeth: they had to be treated with a bit of respect, as even after having been through the filleting machine were still lethal. Just a head and tail held together by the backbone, mouth always gaping, displaying an armoury of needle-sharp nashers. If you picked one

up *carefully* by the backbone and held it against a steel stanchion the jaw would snap shut, teeth locking on the upright post, where it would hang at a right angle for up to an hour; bets being taken on which would stay the longest. I remember one of the factory-hands, Mick, a young jovial type who one couldn't help but like, losing the heel from his seaboot to a catfish when working in the slimy fishpound.

Along with a number of crackpots, there were some real characters amongst what was, trawlerwise, a large crew *hazarding a guess* there would've been in excess of thirty - since there must've been at least seven in the Wardroom, catering staff amounted to six, then add on the seamen, factory-hands and stoker/greasers; so thirty-plus is a safe bet.

The Skipper was an ex-Royal Navy 'two-and-a-half ringer' *(Lt-Cdr)*, obviously good at the fishing, as he had been with the company *who didn't suffer fools gladly* many years. It was said he was absolutely 'minted', owned and lived in a huge old manor house within a large estate; which I'm sure was true, but hard to believe if looks were anything to go by. The man was like an old tramp, in his thigh-length fishermens' wellies and tatty Naval Pusser's greatcoat with half its buttons missing and tied round the waist with a length of frayed rope for a belt; looking for all the world like Captain Ahab in the film 'Moby Dick'. Who knows what he was like at home, but he was certainly the scruffiest man on the ship. He didn't mix with the crew, remaining aloof in true Royal Navy Dartmouth fashion - you know, these guys are missing out on life; but let's keep that to ourselves! I think the only time I came face to face with him was at the end of the trip, when he made out and signed my discharge certificate.

I, of course, remember all the catering staff, but am having difficulty resurrecting others; although there are always a few who stand out, making them unforgettable. For instance, the two greasers; possibly because of their easily recalled names - Peachy and Tosh. These guys had sailed together since time began, 'twas said, even on Arctic convoys *to Russia* during WWII. It's possible they lived together - I don't know, I could never quite make my mind up about that pair o' 'auld hing oots'.

Then there was the Bosun, his name escapes me, he was addicted to gambling, a gregarious well-read man, who came out with many clever and amusing things. I distinctly remember the evening when we were

dishing out a big greasy fry-up to the queuing hands and can still hear him quipping, "I thought that I would never see, two eggs upon one plate for me!" Sounds real corny now, but it was the way he said it - like the man says, "It's the way ye tell em!" Oh yeah, nearly forgot, this was his favourite tongue-twister and it certainly is that, taking a fair bit of practise to be able to say quickly - try it, you'll get there.

Old Missis Hunt
Had a cuddy bunt
Not a cuddy punt
But a hunt bunt cuddy

Mustn't forget Jim *'he of the silken tongue'* from Cleethorpes, he had some kind of title; could've been Second Mate. Anyway, Jim was a big handsome buccaneer with the chiselled features of a real hard bastard, but you can't always go by looks, because he would chat up the 'cabin boys', call them 'Flower' and flippantly offer to introduce them to 'Mr Bendy' in the ship's Paint Locker. Maybe it was all a guise to stave off the boredom, who knows and who cares these days, when 'queens' are pirouetting out of the woodwork, left, right and centre. *Could be; it's just fashionable* - in their defence, the more benders the better, as it sure cuts doon the odds when yer oot 'on the pull' - so, I suppose in that respect the 'Harry Hoofters' redeem themselves. However, burds shouldn't be allowed to be dykes, since they're in short supply as it is! - howzabout the homosexual highlander - he wus up tae his baws in peat ***(Pete - capiche?)***.

The weather had been good to us for the first three weeks, so I'm getting cocky, thinking, 'this sailor lark's a piece o' piss' - then cometh the day when it blew up a 'hooligan'. Here, wait a minute, this is **not** funny, this is **not** supposed to happen, **Help!** This is a wind that would blow a tinker off his missus, so there's no option but to stop fishing, batten down the hatches, lie head into the wind and ride it out. Well now, that means most of the crew have nothing to do but 'crash out' in their bunks, but they still have to be fed ***- looks like I drew the short straw.*** Jings, the Galley's not the place to be; getting tossed around like a cork in a bottle - cripes, it's a nightmare; but *being professionals* we struggle on.

Jimmy had hurt his hand when the hinged lid of the big soup-copper

slammed down on it as the ship rolled, so Eric asks me to ditch the gash, which I take aft, stumbling through the factory to chuck it over the stern. **Stone me**, when I get out there I can't believe the ferocity - crikey, I wanted to sail the high seas, little knowing they were anything like this high. One minute the ship rolls to starboard, which was the lee-side - so that's where I was, **terrified**, grasping the handrail and looking straight up at a heaving mountain of frothing ocean, then it rolls to port and the sea has disappeared, so now I'm looking at, and think I'm about to be launched into the sky. I'm not too happy about being a sailor today *goin' up 'n' doon like a whore's knickers* so, prompted by fear, I get my timing right and ditch the gash over the side, ***being very careful not to go with it.***

On my way back through the empty factory I feel dizzy and exhausted, so collapse on a bale of rope and conk out - I've no idea of how long I was 'dead tae the world', but when I got back to the Galley no one said a word. I hadn't been missed; so, if I'd gone over the side it would've been 'Goodnight Vienna'. Well now, maybe these guys weren't joking - between this and the ribbing I could develop a complex. I'd thought they were all just joshing when they mocked me by shouting "Who called the cook a cunt?" quickly adding "Who called the cunt a cook?"

After successfully fishing off Newfoundland for a few weeks we steamed into St John's, to refuel, store ship and take advantage of a quick run ashore. They have a big harbour there, at least that's how it seemed to me as I guess we must have been parked at the farthest point from the town. Why? I don't know, since the harbour was empty; maybe it was cheaper to berth away down there. Whatever the reason we weren't impressed as it made for a bleedin' long hike to civilization, which, when we got there, was hardly worth the effort, as it was like a ghost town. I've often wondered

where everyone was, and it came as a surprise to see the buildings were made of wood, not something I'd expected. This seemed strange to me, having lived my life in a country where the permanent buildings are of stone. What I saw reminded me of frontier towns in cowboy movies, set in the 1800s - *on referring to films yet again, I'm thinking it must seem to you that I received the better part of my education in fleapits.*

The last thing I had anticipated was a Woolworths store, but there it was, so in we went and even that was quiet. However, I spent some of the ten 'sovs' I'd 'subbed' *in Canadian dollars* on souvenirs, and so, did my first ever foreign shopping. There was nothing to do as we, being under twenty-one, were too young to have a beer, but that didn't bother us, instead we had a wander round town and stopped in at Fat Sam's Diner to polish off a few genuine American burgers, as it seemed like an opportunity not to be missed, then bored out our skulls sauntered back to the ship.

On going ashore it was made clear that we only had five hours Shore Leave and must get back within that time; which struck us as a bit mean, but as it was a non-event, we returned about two hours early - *there being more life on our old trawler.* Anyway, I was eager to see what fresh stores had been 'taken on' to supplement the fresh fish that was the mainstay of our diet - crikey, ah wus dead chuffed when ah laid eyes on the assortment o' delicacies the Canadian Ship Chandler had worked up us.

Once 'bunkered' and stored, we pulled up the gangway and steered for the fishing grounds around Greenland; being spring the ice was breaking up, allowing us to push on further north. It was spectacular ploughing through the pack ice and then fishing amongst the icebergs, especially on calm sunny days, when the azure sky was mirrored on a flat hypnotic sea and the sun glistened on giant icebergs. 'Twas colourful, not just blue and white as one might expect - those of you who've been lucky enough to have seen this will recall the glorious kaleidoscope of colours when sunlight is reflected off the icebergs and to have observed shimmering phosphoric lights churned up in the wake of the ship.

The first time I saw Greenland I could hardly believe my eyes: it was so amazing that I thought it must be a trick of the light on a cloud formation. Once again it was a beautiful clear day and there it was in the distance; *as I presume we had to fish outside their territorial waters.* What I was looking

at were Greenland's spectacular icy mountains; hundreds of white jagged peaks on the horizon, rising from the cobalt blue sea to an equally deep blue sky - with the sea being like a millpond they were clearly reflected in it giving a mirror image of the ice caps, making the whole scene appear to be floating in mid-air. It took some time to sort it all out and appreciate what I was seeing, as at first it didn't seem real, in fact totally unexpected and more like a fantasy Disney cartoon. It's a great pity I didn't own a camera, but there again I could never have done that scene justice on film, so it's probably best kept held as yet another memory in the mind's eye. *Anyway, I can't see why I should share* ***everything*** *with the likes of you!*

There could well've been a fair bit of boredom on such a long trip, as although everyone did their share of work there were many spare hours, especially in bad weather, when fishing was impossible. That was when the factory-hands and off-duty men held the 'Golden Blankets Championships', the winner being whoever could sleep for the longest period of time - believe me, some of the serious contenders, when switched into suspended animation mode, could've given 'Rip van Winkle' a run for his money.

There were many ways of passing the time, and before you even think it, I don't mean **"Aar, Jim lad, it be yoar turn in *'the Barrel'!*"** Card schools were favourite with the 'old hands', who *whilst slaggin' each other off* played like professional gamblers for cartons of duty-free ciggies

The ship had a library of sorts, so I got into serious reading - something I hadn't been arsed to do in earlier years, unless you count the Wizard and Hotspur. I was surprised at how absorbed one could become in a decent story and realized what readers meant when they said it was hard to put a good book down. I discovered a collection of Dennis Wheatley novels; thoroughly enjoying every one I could lay my hands on. Another compelling read was a trilogy by Lobsang Rampa - *some Tibetan priest, joker, who claimed to have been reincarnated many times*; the first was called 'The Third Eye' but I can't recall the titles of the sequels. They were about being reborn, the afterlife and suchlike, well-written interesting books. But, best of all were the popular American detective novels by Hank Jansen, daring for their time, and passed around until they fell to bits.

Apart from the intellectual escapism there was, as always, a bit of clowning around, like for instance our dangerous interpretation of hide-

and-seek, when 'Slippery Sam' *(the Second Steward)* and myself would squeeze through our cabin's porthole, reach up the ship's side, get hold of the deckrails and drag ourselves up to appear on the boat deck above, thus confusing whoever had come looking for us; thinking we were still in our cabin - a foolhardy caper in Arctic waters, but you know how it is; young, headstrong, invincible **and stupid!**

The 'flunkey's' favourite prank was catching the big greedy gulls that had landed on the fishing deck and hastily swallowed so many stolen fish that they were too heavy to take off again; 'Slippery' and myself would then smuggle them into crewmember's cabins, being careful not to get caught in the act, as it was a messy business for the recipients.

There were only four films onboard; the preferred one being 'The Benny Goodman Story', *'The King of Swing'* was shown more than twenty times - it was run and rerun forwards, backwards, with sound, and without sound *(when we did the voices ourselves)*. It's amazing how inventive a crowd of bored seafarers can be - the line "Don't be that way, Benny" will remain with me forever; since everyone used it as a catchphrase for weeks.

Now, here's a humdinger for you. We were obviously not the only ones fishing off Greenland - there were other British, French, Spanish and Portuguese trawlers. One morning, when close enough, we can see one of the foreign boats has a dummy hanging from the mast, rigging; or whatever sailors call these thingumajigs above the deck. We see this many times in the course of the day when our paths cross while fishing and are intrigued; thinking it must be some kind of ritual, or religious ceremony. Late afternoon our skipper finds out that during the previous night there had been a knife fight onboard 'Johnny Foreigner' so the crew had hanged the guilty attacker. ***How's that for rough justice!***

Back then *when they'd take anyone* I saw my first Royal Navy warship at sea, I can't remember which one, but it was either a destroyer or a frigate. I was, to say the least, impressed at how sleek and clean it looked, especially when compared to our, by now, dirty rust-streaked trawler. At the time I gave it a bit of thought and reasoned that this immaculate warship, unlike us, had no end product, so it went without saying that life must be good for 'Jack'; just one long cruise down 'Easy Street'.

Fat chance! How was I to know that on these beautiful grey warships

the saying 'Officer and Gentleman' means just that - these 'gentlemen' were a different breed from our 'Civvy Street' ones *who actually worked.* Royal Navy Officers *resplendent in their dapper gold trimmed uniforms* had spent years at Britannia Royal Naval College, Dartmouth, undergoing exhaustive training, teaching them how to delegate and make life hard for the lackeys - therefore a doddle for themselves. ***Oh why! Oh why! wasn't I born rich, handsome and rigged like a donkey*** *- on steroids?*

Well, at last the day dawns when the holds are full, allowing 'Captain Ahab' to 'set sail' for home with everyone looking forward to a good payoff and fat bonus within the week. A couple of days prior to docking and just before we were in sight of the north of Scotland I went 'up top' for a breather and blether with the 'deckies'. I couldn't believe the smell, **crikey, wotta stink!** They tell me that's the smell of land and how you'll always smell it before you see it. I'm convinced they're 'pullin' ma plonker', but they swear it's the smell of vegetation. Cor, it's powerful; like rotten sprouts - so how come I've never smelt it before? It's explained that we have got used to clean pure fresh air, from being weeks in the Arctic, and how people who live near the gasworks don't smell them and also, have I noticed that I don't smell the fish anymore? True - point taken!

Sure enough, the odour dissipated, and after a quiet calm uneventful run down the North Sea we are docked once again at Immingham, so everyone has secured their work stations and got themselves 'dickied up' ready to rush ashore and charge home. All we have to do now is wait our turn to be paid, then get our discharge certificates and we'll be for 'the off'.

While I'm waiting, the Chief Steward approaches in a secretive manner, slips me my pay packet and quietly asks if I'd like to come back next trip as Chief Cook, which was a compliment beyond my aspirations because of my age and with only one trip's experience under my belt; although I think the fact that he and Eric had been at loggerheads for weeks had more to do with it than my abilities. After seriously considering my position I declined, knowing it would be another dose o' the same, while 'ere's me cravin' adventure - if I was going back to sea, I wanted a look at all the exotic foreign ports dreams are made of.

At last it's my turn to go to the Captain for my discharge papers - I was well chuffed with my certificate, which would stand me in good stead for

my next ship, but scunnered with my pay which, together with bonus, barely cleared a, less than generous, hundred pounds. I've often wondered over the years if some whore's bastard 'dipped the till' because I had expected at least double in recompense for my efforts during one hundred and five days at sea - even taking into account the fact that *as pointed out* I'd had 'board and keep' for close to four months and subbed a 'ten spot' in St John's. So, although it was a compliment to be thought of as capable, I am *to this day* glad that I declined the offer of the Chief Cook's job, but have never got over the shock of being so blatantly exploited.

Along with the excited Edinburgh contingent, I hurriedly boarded the ferry which took us across the Humber to Hull then caught the first available trains north, changing at York, where we had time for a beer in a quaint medieval English pub, and then up the line to home, where when Mother answered the door, the first thing she said was "You stink of fish!"

So, I'm back in 'the Athens of the North' feeling quite flush with my recent measly pay packet added to the money I had got from selling my motorbike before going to sea and the modest amount of savings I already had. Now I could take it easy for a few weeks, catch up with all my old pals and do the rounds before shipping out to sail the seven seas and explore the rest of the world - keeping in mind that if I hung around too long, these pen-pushing pricks at the Ministry of Defence would be on ma case again, wantin' tae drag me off for an eighteen month stint as a 'squaddie'.

Not one to throw caution to the wind and be lulled into a false sense of security, after a fortnight I reported to the Leith Seamen's Pool to 'sign on' the next available ship. As luck would have it, although welcomed with open arms, now having the necessary sea experience, I was floggin' a dead horse, as the aftermath of the Suez crisis had now become critical; with more and more merchant ships being 'laid up', less and less crews were required. So, here's the deal - there are twenty-two frustrated Second Cooks registered at the Leith Office in front of me. "Ya buckin' fastard" - ah'm scuppered! What do I do now? I feel like the proverbial rat in the trap, but look on the bright side, everything happens for a reason and they say "What's meant for you won't go by you", so although the situation is desperate, let's not panic, something **will** turn up ***- always think positive.***

11: Holiday-time

That summer a couple of short well-deserved holiday opportunities arose. The first being a week at a place, with a pleasant 'oldie worldie' name - Habbie's Howe; somewhere down the A702, near Nine Mile Burn.

I thought the four of us were going to this luxury static caravan, owned by a friend of Joe McGlinchey's mother from the Old Tyme Dancing Club - should've known better, the luxury caravan turned out to be an ancient SMT single-decker bus in the middle of a field; the old chariot had been crudely fitted out as a holiday home, reminding us of 'the Broons' in the Sunday Post. Not exactly what we'd expected, but it was a 'freebie' after all and young guys can adapt to almost anything. So, we were stuck there for seven days, however, I must say, the weather 'wus braw', not something to be taken lightly or depend on in this neck o' the woods - particularly, in what we hardy Scots like to call 'summer'.

There was myself, Joe, big daft Doogie and Ronnie Taylor. Ronnie was an apprentice plumber at the time, a quiet chap with a dry sense of humour. He was a neighbour of the McGlincheys, who had grown up with them in Heriot Hill Terrace. Ronnie, was, a few years later, to become one of Sir Tom Farmer's first employees, and so a founder-member of Kwik- Fit, at what I believe was this now huge organization's original shop, on a corner at Buccleuch Place in the centre of Edinburgh near the University. I bought my first set of tyres from Ronnie who gave me a 'crackin' deal', and well remember giving him a hand to jack up my two-tone Ford Zephyr Six, one wheel at a time on the cobbled road outside the shop - things have certainly progressed since then in the modern depots of today.

Cripes, I'm off on a tangent again - let's get back to our week in the old bus. Other holiday homes were scattered around the field and on the hillside, nothing pretentious, just converted vehicles and home-made huts, none of which were occupied whilst we were there. So it was peaceful, but with, in truth, sod all to do; luckily we'd brought our air rifles, *unlucky for some* as anything that moved got blasted, generally by more than one trigger-happy youth. We 'bagged' a couple o' rabbits, which along with stolen vegetables provided the 'sons of the soil' with a tasty stew, after 'yours truly' had managed the messy job of skinning and gutting. **Yuck!**

Not a preferred undertaking; especially when there's no running water.

The day before we left, daft Doogie came back from one of his many expeditions with a fair-sized chicken he'd shot. Now wait for it - the big grinning chancer also had some eggs; he swore blind that Chicken Licken was wild, but this unprincipled reprobate could sure 'spin the shit' when required, and there was no point in trying to beat a confession out of him - so what the hell, it didn't make any difference now, the bird was dead anyway; it therefore shared the fate of the rabbits and was scoffed by the team. Big Doogie's eggs, when boiled and served up with 'little soldiers' the following morning, were probably the freshest we city slickers had ever tasted - this being the final meal before packing our gear and making for home, to then lie through our teeth about how wonderful it'd been.

The second holiday was a bit more adventurous, being further afield; in *'merry'* England, no less, at Stockton-on-Tees, and once again organized by Joe's mother, Hannah McGlinchey; a petite spritely lady, always on the go. She had even arranged a lift there and back for us with a brewery rep going to London on a business trip. He would drop us off at Stockton on his way south and pick us up again six days later on the return journey. We were 'made up' as apart from being extremely convenient it was a free run and whatismore, his 'company car' was a brand new Morris Oxford, which was pretty high on our list in these days.

There was plenty room in the Morris for three slim young guys *(barely a pick on any of us)* in the back and one, plus the driver *(who, being a 'bevvy merchant', was a heavyweight)* up front. As for luggage - we travelled light, one holdall each was more than enough for us, so no problems there.

When we arrived at our destination it turned out to be a 'semi' on the outskirts of town, owned by a widowed wifey originally from Edinburgh. She was a 'war bride'; having met and married an army major from Stockton, way back in the early forties - *when things weren't looking too clever for 'Blighty'*. Big Doogie thought she was "a guid lookin' wuman" and she obviously took a shine to him, but still a gawky teenager, he hadn't, as yet, acquired enough confidence to try his luck with mature ladies of more than twice his years. We, of course, were egging him on and a couple of times thought we'd succeeded, but he 'bottled out' at the death.

Don't remember much about Stockton - come Tuesday 'twas rainin'

cats 'n' dogs, so we went to the local cinema, where we were surprised to see the punters eating fish and chips while watching the film. I can't recall whether they actually sold them in the foyer, but reckon it's a fair bet, since so many were 'tucking in' from trays held on their laps: that was a new one to us. ***Strange yins they Sassenach tripehounds!***

Later in the week we bussed it to Redcar, thinking, that being a seaside resort, it should prove worth a look. On the day, we were all hyped up for a laugh and a bit action, but it was "nowt speshul - no' a patch oan oor Portybelly sur Mer". However, on the bus back to our free digs, daft Doogie is chatting up the 'clippie'; a crackin' bit o'gear with dark hair, Mediterranean looks; and filling out that uniform jacket a treat. The bus is near empty of passengers as it's early afternoon, so we're havin' a giggle with this lovely creature who says if we'd like to go to the Transport Club which is called the Mobile Club *(pronounced 'Mobeel')* on Friday night, she'd meet us outside and sign us in. This sounded 'pure dead brilliant', as it was to be our last night and could be the crowning glory before departing with 'Big Barry' around midday, come Saturday.

We're looking forward to this night out with the anticipation only young impressionable guys can have. The time arrives and we bimble off *lookin' cool* to find the 'Mobeel Club' casting doubts aside that the beautiful clippie was nothing, other than a cheeky cow winding up the 'thickoe Jocks', but no; there she is *true to her word* waiting at the door. There you go, I told you she wasn't a rotten cow, oh ye of little faith, and look at her posin' there in her flash gear 'wi' her Friday night face oan.' Cor, there's a sight for sore eyes, she's lovelier than ever - although, I do prefer a girl in uniform *yes, it's a fetish* **"Could ye keep the hat oan hen?"**

We pile in and sure enough, it's fab with a dance floor and small stage complemented by a tuxedo clad quartet givin' it 'big licks', and a seating area to one side, on the ground floor. Upstairs there's a big bar with a compère, looking overdressed in an ill-fitting dinner-suit, who tells the odd joke, ***neat!*** Because it's a club the prices are low, so it's fair hoachin' wi' skirt. This looks like being a good night - one problem though, we're not as yet seasoned drinkers, and the beer doon here is pish; or so we've always been told by friends who know about these things. It seems the mild's like gnat's piss and the bitter even worse. Not like 'Bonnie Scotland' where we

have heavy and export - **real men's beer.** So this is a predicament, "What in the name o' the wee man ama gonna drink?" Ronnie says, since I've been known to favour Sweetheart Stout and Mackesons why don't I try that stuff there, pointing at a row of dumpy bottles labelled 'Flowers Dragon's Blood' sittin' winkin' at us from behind the bar - "Yeah, okay, I've always had a flair for stupidity, that'll do for me, ah'll hae some o' that!"

Being new faces, and foreigners to boot, we get a fair bit attention from the girls and before long are thoroughly enjoying ourselves having a ball. But you know how it is - at such times the drink goes down quicker than you realize and that Dragon's Blood was much stronger than I thought. I can hardly tell you this for laughing while thinking about it. At the end of the evening ah fell doon the stairs and that night pished the bed, which I was sharing with Ronnie and Joe. Oh yeah! What a Friday that was!

As promised, Big Barry arrives late Saturday morning to ferry us up the road - so that's another adventure stuffed and *feeling fragile* we're off back to the promised land, *leaving the stained bed behind us.* Wouldn't you know, the first thing I see on getting home is the manila envelope with my name on it, dancing and mocking me, atop the mantelpiece. **Oh, oh, - *'trouble at mill'*** I don't want to open it, but it ain't goin' away, so I'd better see what the twats are sayin'. With trembling hands I rip it open and sure enough, ma goose is cooked - **they're on to me**, fuckin' Ministry of Defence, fuckin' National Service. No formalities, no please, no thanks, no nuthin' just report to Dean Park House, 7 Queensferry Road, Edinburgh on such and such a date and time, where I'd be given a test and medical to evaluate my suitability to serve in the Army; or maybe even the RAF, *if they could detect a glimmer of intelligence.*

Aw shite! Wha' di ah do now? Ah'm at ma wit's end, it looks like ah'm onna hidin' tae nuthin' - just haven't been smart enough tae worm ma way oot o' this crisis. Maybe I'll fail the medical; but I doubt it. I've heard of various dodges to redress the obligation, such as getting your eardrums perforated, but they're probably just stories and that's not my style - anyway, I'd be scared o' doin' masel a mischief. So, on tenterhooks *burdened with gloom* I pitch up 'early doors' on the dreaded day, thinking that if I'm late I might get put against the wall and shot.

What a beautiful building Dean Park House turns out to be, with

a splendid entrance and huge magnificent main doors - by amazing coincidence owned by the Salvesen family until the 1940s, when it was sold to the MoD for £2,750, *yes, two thousand, seven hundred and fifty pounds,* and remained their property until 1963 when acquired by 'Daniel Stewart's School' *(now Stewart's Melville College)* for an undisclosed sum.

As always, this architectural gem had been torn apart internally by the faceless bureaucrats who couldn't give a fish's tit, and more to the point haven't a brain cell between them. Period details had disappeared - *one wonders where?* Fine marble fireplaces ripped out, things bricked up, and ceilings lowered. It's enough to make you weep, sheer mindless vandalism, revealing, once again, the kind of useless wankers who've been ruining this country for as long as we can remember. There are three superb fireplaces remaining and some valuable stained glass that, thankfully, the retards had left untouched. On a happier note I'm informed that a considerable sum has been allocated for restoration work in the near future, which of course would be unnecessary if these cretins had shown some respect in the first place. *Got a bit carried away there - must try to keep control and curb my language - *perhaps I should be back on the tablets.*

Anyway, there's a resentful throng o' us *scowling* conscripts being herded around the building. We're given a written test, to determine just how dim we actually are, then seen in turn by the vets. I don't recall any rejects; so assume everyone with a full complement of limbs passed the physical, and then it was "On yer way Sunshine, you'll hear from us". "Oh yeah, will ah then - that'll be right, **pal!**" Like most I'm a bit of a dreamer, and back then fired with the rash enthusiasm of youth don't envisage this as my destiny. Nobody, but nobody wus gonna kick me in the 'hee haws' and one thing's for sure, I certainly don't see myself as a 'squaddie' up to my armpits in a mud-filled trench or yomping over Salisbury Plain with a 303 rifle and full pack at black o'clock. Ever defiant, I've made up my mind - remember that warship I saw up in the Arctic; well, so do I, and in the heat of the moment *going for broke* ***'The Renegade'*** scoots round to the Royal Navy Recruiting Office in George Street to take the plunge for a nine-year stretch, fully aware this is an OTT reaction, but what the fuck; I'm not doing National Service in their soddin' Army, no way! Now, was that a clever move or wot? ***Well, just wait and see!***

12: HMS Raleigh - New Entrant

Now too late for hedging my bets, I signed on as a radio operator; *having been impressed by the Radio Officer's job and status on the 'Fairtry'*. That was in fact my second choice - I wanted to join as a trainee pilot *(just call me Biggles)*, but the nice recruiting chief, *not recognizing officer material,* deceived me, saying I had to join the "ordinary navy" first. So there you have it, at whatever the cost, I'd escaped conscription and must admit the saying, 'bite off yer nose to spite yer face' did spring to mind. I bragged to everyone about what I'd done, everyone except the National Service twats that is. *Fuck these tosspots; let them find out for themselves.*

I must say, I was surprised that no one called me a 'cupid stunt', then the same week amazed when Joe McGlinchey and Benny Wilkie informed me that they'd followed my example and volunteered for nine years in the Royal Navy, as electrical mechanics. Now, while not wishing to be a false prophet, this, I took as a compliment to my impulsive resolution, especially since *being mineworkers* they were exempt from National Service.

Now, watch this space as the biggest surprise of all is on its way - days later at Murrayfield Ice Rink, big daft Doogie *(a rough diamond)* says "Ah've got sumthin' tae tell ye." So we chorus "Yeah, what now Doogie?" He takes a deep breath and looking a wee bit sheepish says, "Ah've joined the Navy too; as a seaman!" **Well ah'll be** - who'd have guessed; but there again that's oor Doogie alright. He must have reasoned that if we were doing it, there had to be an angle: so he's for jumpin' on the bandwagon. A few years down the line, this, as you'll find out, didn't come back to haunt me, and proved to be the smartest move Doogie ever made.

The deed now done, we're all fair burstin' to get away, but as you know, when anticipating something time seems to drag. I assumed that, being first to volunteer, it went without saying I'd be first for 'the off', but what did I know? S.F.A. - **silly me** it doesn't work like that. What happens is, when there are enough New Entrants of whatever category to make up a class, off they go to join the appropriate training establishment. So, I'm just a touch resentful, when three weeks after volunteering Joe and Benny beat me to it and blaze a trail south to join HMS Collingwood in Fareham,

Hampshire; the training establishment for the fleet's 'sparks'.

The following week Doogie and myself were instructed to report to Princes Street's Caley Station, where we were met by a dashing, uniformed Petty Officer who introduced us to three starry-eyed youths, also destined for a carefree life of fun and adventure in Her Majesty's Navy. We were put in the picture and given our travel warrants *(along with 'bagmeals')* to get to HMS Raleigh at Torpoint in Cornwall. This being the training base, Part One Basic, for seamen, communicators and possibly other branches, but I've no idea which, as my memory is blank and I need a nice cup of tea, but have no fear, I shall return refreshed and ready to start anew.

Here! That was some journey - I may be wrong, but does eighteen hours sound ridiculous? We changed trains somewhere in deepest England, after ages spent on the first one, which had stopped at every single station and halt possible on chugging its way south - that poxy train must have been the slowest old nail British Rail owned. The second one wasn't any better, - must've been the milk train or possibly 'Thomas the bleedin' Tank Engine'. We were knackered and even tried to sleep in the luggage racks, which didn't prove too comfortable. Of course the bagmeals had disappeared hours before they should've *more out of boredom than hunger* so by now we're famished and given half a chance would eat a scabby horse.

Completely shattered, we arrived at Plymouth where a dark blue Royal Navy Bedford lorry with a canvas top was waiting at the station to despatch us to our first 'ship', HMS Raleigh, which to our utter dismay was in fact a shorebase ***- ain't life just a kick in the crutch?*** Now then, have we ever got a lot to learn? Well yes, and that's just what HMS Raleigh is all about; the staff, crew, call them what you will, are real professionals - so organized it's not true. There again, 'the Andrew' have plenty experience in handling muppets; after all, they've been recruiting and training them since the beginning of time. In saying that let's try forgetting about 'press gangs', as the approach is a touch more subtle nowadays.

Wide-eyed and full o' wonder, we're driven through the Main Gate - which, like all the others I'd pass through in the following years, is proudly displaying its ship's crest, 'battle honours' and decorated lifebelt, while manned by a Regulating Petty Officer *(RPO)* and two Ratings in Number Threes with white webbing belts and gaiters - then emptied from

the Bedford and *kissing goodbye to a humdrum existence* dumped in front of our quarters. Would you believe, **it's a wooden hut;** seeing this retrieves memories of Broomlee School Camp, which, on reflection, had probably been a military camp during the war - *let's hope the nosh is better here* - thankfully it's a credit to the Duty-Watch; this we soon discover as our next stop is the Ship's Company Galley for some scran, which we are more than ready to get wired into after a journey, so long that it could've been described as a pilgrimage.

We, having travelled the farthest to get here, are the last of this 'New Entry' class to arrive; so the early birds have had 'first dibs' meaning no choice of beds and lockers for us - not that it matters, as they all look the same and, assuming we stay the course, will only be here six weeks. We claim our 'pits', park our gear, then are escorted to catch up with the rest of the class, who are already at a lecture in a large classroom. Late afternoon we are 'secured' for the rest of the day and back at the hut *which we have learned to call the Mess* are now introducing ourselves and getting to know the other greenhorns *from all walks of life,* also here to be knocked into shape before aspiring to the ranks of 'the nation's finest'.

There must have been a total of around thirty fresh-faced youths from all parts of the realm, and then some *(the significance of the comment 'and then some' will come to light shortly).* I'm surprised to find how many of them from the same cities and localities share the same name. All the guys from Wales appear to be called Taff. The Newcastle boys are all Geordie. The ones from Liverpool, Scouse, then there are two chaps from the Emerald Isle, both called Paddy; *strange indeed.* They seem to think we're all called Jock or Haggis, which I don't mind at all - ah kin live wi' that - but when they shorten it to Hag, ah'm none too pleased.

There's a squad of loud Londoners; a shower o' switched-on cowboys from 'the Big Smoke' - they **are** smart, **the wideboys;** streets ahead o' "the yokels". We, the provincials, appreciate this and over the weeks, get ourselves cool, in listening to their slick hip hop cockney street banter.

The next two days were spent mostly in classrooms having instruction and lectures on a variety of subjects from personal hygiene *(which included a film on venereal diseases, such as 'syph')* to who to salute and call "Sir" - that being just about everyone on the Base; as at that point we were brand

new, and therefore the lowest of the low - **OD's.**

There were lectures on how the Navy functioned and its traditions; we took an oath, never to reveal the secret of ***'the Barrel'*** or where to find the ***'Golden Rivet'*** and the fact that the hand that wanks the Captain runs the ship - *think about that one!* These first two days we had it easy, but stood out like a stiffy on a nudey beach, because we were still in civvies; not as yet having been issued any kit - we wanted to blend in and look like everyone else, little realizing that we were being wooed and treated well by 'Pusser' - this two-day period being the calm before the storm.

On the third day we marched to the now familiar classroom; but this time it's different. On the platform is a smooth-talking 'three ringer' *(RN Commander)* with a persuasive sincerity in his voice, who gives a quiet but stimulating talk about the Royal Navy, putting us all at ease. This guy is treacle-tongued, his timing perfect when he slips in that this is 'make or break' time. Now we must decide whether we want to sign on for a nine-year career in Her Majesty's Navy - or go home. "So, it's your prerogative boys, what do you want to do? By the way, those deciding to stay will be issued with a full kit and uniforms, into which you will change right away; your civvies will then be parcelled and sent to your respective homes."

All this was no great surprise, except the part about signing on, as we all thought we had already done so - that being, how we were here. However, that wasn't the case, probably some legal point like the cooling-off period when signing an agreement - so if you've any doubts 'me ole China', now's yer chance. Pusser knows what he's doing there; because who wants to run back to mummy, admitting he couldn't hack it after just four days away from home? That old 'three ringer' was good; closing with - it took guts to walk away, and the Navy would think no less of anyone who did, as they wouldn't be suited - therefore not Senior Service material, ***talk about gently applied reverse psychology!*** Only one guy did, which was a bit of a shock, as he seemed the least likely one to have made such a decision. There was no messing, he was shown out the room and we never saw him again. Do you suppose? - och, no, surely not! That night in the Mess the incident was of course discussed and the consensus branded him a 'wimp mummy's boy'. By the following week we had changed our opinion; *he was the smart one, and we were jumpin' through hoops.*

So, the rest of us swear allegiance, sign on the dotted line and accept the Queen's Shilling - *can't remember whether we actually got one or not.* The next step was being issued with the afore-promised kit and uniforms, of which we had to stamp every item with our names in black or white paint. One of the lads was so big that Pusser was toiling finding clothing to fit and had to have footware specially ordered, which meant him wearing his own shoes for a couple of weeks. It's a long time ago, but I'm sure the size was an amazing, sixteen - and that's what I call **big!**

I can't remember many names, which is a pity as they were a decent bunch and obviously, most, real characters; understandably so, or they wouldn't've been there in the first place. The big guy was, of course, called 'Lofty', two more names spring to mind, one for a reason and the other because anyone who ever met him will remember him and his name. The first one was a chap destined to become a seaman, his name was Pickering and because he blinked incessantly he was known as 'flickering Pickering'. The second was Lutz Andreas Fritz Linnenmoller, who for obvious reasons we called Fritz, *and on occasion* ***'the Hun'.***

Wotta ticket - a big square-jawed strong chap with a deep voice; not unlike Arnie 'The Terminator' Schwarzenegger. It seemed odd, like a joke that had backfired, that he should be in the Royal Navy - Fritz's father having, during the war, been a Luftwaffe pilot flying Stukas, but lost in action - at the end of the conflict his mother had married a member of the occupation forces, so 'the Hun' came to England as a boy with his mother and stepfather. He *like myself* had been to sea before joining 'the Andrew', in fact Fritz had been in the Merchant Marine since leaving school - so had been around, making him one worldly-wise guy who knew all the tricks, so, 'got his rocks off' entertaining us; his captive audience.

Come to think of it, Fritz was the first person to show us farts could be lit. I can picture him yet, demonstrating the phenomenon; as most of us were sceptical of the big chancer's tall stories. So there he is, modestly squatting on his Pusser's bed, big bare 'brownie' sticking up in the air, head twisted round like a contortionist, gas lighter in his right hand trying to 'blow a kiss' and light it while laughing, with us crowded round *at a safe distance* to witness the event, in fits of giggles. Because of the hilarity and his position Fritz was having difficulty and the longer it took the more he

was doubted, so for him this was approaching serious. Getting edgy, he asked if someone would do the honours with the lighter, but by now we all thought he was 'hard at it' and wild horses couldn't drag us near that hairy erse. The more we guffawed, the more challenging it became, and it's a wonder there was a fart left in him when he finally managed to 'cut one' - although a poor effort *because oot o' puff* Fritz doggedly scored his 'Brownie points'. I thought at the time,that if he'd managed to light the first 'big reeker' he'd have blown our 'home from home'apart; as it was he'd fairly singed his ringpiece ***- brek oot the vaseline!***

On the morning following kit issue day, training started in earnest; the honeymoon was over, **was it ever!** The first reality shock came early - as soon as the 'wakey wakey bugle' blared to 'call the hands', the Mess door was thrown open by our hitherto laid-back Petty Officer, who *whilst we slumbered* had been transformed into this raving maniac, bawling "Let's be 'avin' ye then." Jaisus, Gawd, talk about Jekyll & Hyde.

Well, there you go - this mild-mannered PO, whom we had known and loved as a father was now a GI *(Gunnery Instructor)*, straight as a ramrod carrying a swagger stick, wearing a black webbing belt, black gaiters and a lanyard with whistle attached, he shoots round the Mess like a madman rattling the metal bed ends with his stick. We are out like rockets to hear him shout, "**New Entry intake! New Entry intake, Ho!**" - so we smartly jump to attention as ordered. He then spouts the usual shit that anyone who has seen a film about the armed forces will be familiar with. You know the old spiel; when he says jump, 'his boys' will jump etc. etc. He is going to turn us into the finest class to pass out this establishment **EVER** and woe betide any snivelling wretch who lets him down - *and so on*.

"Now look lively me 'earties, get dressed in your nice new Number Eights and shiny boots, go for breakfast and fall in **quietly** on the Parade Ground at eight sharp, not forgetting to leave a clean Mess and neatly-made beds behind you!" - I do believe he shouted all that out in one breath. **Crikey!** What **have** we gone an' let ourselves in for???

So, it's started, we're stood ***to attention*** on the Parade Ground, it's big, it's bleak *and it's raining*. 'Daddy' informs us this is hallowed ground, which we must **never** walk across; always **'double'.** We are taught to march hour after hour over the next five weeks on this 'hallowed ground'

to the sound of "EFT! EFT! EFT! IGHT! EFT!" ringing in our ears. Most get by, but there's always 'Jimmy' wi' two left feet for the GI to rant and rave at. *(They're aw oot o' step except me, Chief.)* The Drill Instructors all have their own pet insults to belittle the poor unfortunates - our GI's two favourites being "**You've got the brains of a rockin' 'orse Laddie!**" and "**The next time you pull yourself, pull yourself together Laddie!**"

Now, although insulting and yelling at us was all part of the game, and we often deserved it in driving them to distraction, commendably, the GIs were in complete control and rarely swore, so there's something to be said for the training they themselves must have undergone at Whale Island. It was a long haul, involving plenty doubling with rifles round that Parade Ground, but we got there in the end. So, if anyone having to undergo the same is thinking, what's the point, when I'm going to be on a ship? I thoroughly agree with you, but - **up yer pipe, pal; *we had to do it!***

Getting back to that first day of the real thing. The whole morning was spent on the Parade Ground so, after the ordeal of 'square-bashing' in the fresh air, we were pretty shaken; but hungry by lunchtime. They, the instructors, are doing it continually, so it's like an assembly line for them, a strict six-week regime, well-practised and followed meticulously.

That afternoon we were marched to the Sickbay, ordered to strip to the waist and form a line to get a Tab jab in one arm and a vaccination in the other by the team of waiting SBAs *(sickbay attendants),* who probably dished out thousands of the same every year. No! no! not sadists, just totally removed from what they were doing, being long-since accustomed to stickin' their things in Jack. Back then needle sharing was the 'norm', just empty the contents into an arm fill the syringe and repeat the process: the worst that could happen was getting a blunt needle - remember these were **'the happy days'**; *AIDS hadn't been invented yet.*

Now, there's a thing! I maintain AIDS is a man-made disease that got out of control, probably first released by some twisted bastard aiming to wipe out the 'arse bandits'; forgetting many oversexed sneaky gits bat for both sides, or possibly having a go at 'Dem Black Folks' in 'Afreeka' where it is now reaching pandemic proportions. *(Everyone knows how it's transmitted; but who are we to stop them enjoying themselves?)*

Anyway, we're in line waiting to be punctured - when an elderly

overweight balding SBA steps over and whispers in my 'shell-like', "Here, 'me ole fruit', keep an eye on 'Tojo' in front of you!" Mystified, I think, 'what the fuck's baldie rabbitin' on about?' We shuffle forward; the bloke ahead of me gets jabbed, takes two unsteady steps and faints. I wasn't ready for it, but, because alerted, managed to catch him under the arms before he hit the deck. I've often wondered how the SBA had anticipated this, maybe a look on the victim's face, also why didn't the SBA catch the casualty? - could be a past experience is the answer to that one!

Over the next four weeks we're kept at it from 'call the hands' in the morning 'til 'pipe down' at night. We go to the dentist, are given further education, taught to kill with a 303 rifle, fight fires, tie knots, look after our kit, wash and iron, know what the front and back of ships are called. Yeah, we're getting there! As far as I can remember we were 'confined to barracks' for the first four or maybe even five weeks *(lest we 'shot through')*. During this period, it's the done thing to wash the Number Eights *(our working uniforms)* frequently, conspiring to give them and ourselves the worn look of an 'old hand' - no one wants to look like a brand new 'baby sailor' around the Base *or anywhere else for that matter.*

The Number Ones dress uniform also gets a bit of subtle treatment. The collar *dark when issued* is carefully bleached to a nice 'tiddly' light blue and the cap bent down each side and given a bow wave. Now all titivated and sharp as new pins we're ready to hit the town when let loose for Shore Leave. This entails clanking across the Tamar on the Torpoint Ferry, *a ramshackle chain-driven crate;* and into Plymouth, fondly known as 'Guzz' by Jack, so that's what we call it; since we're sailors now and this is our moment of glory - our very first 'run ashore'.

I don't remember who I was with, but we started with quite a crowd, which in the course of the afternoon was whittled down. Some went to the cinema, others to a Wimpy bar, a few stopping in a pub, eventually leaving three of us. We ended up finding our way to the NAAFI Club where I met, chatted up and copped off with this weird geeky burd; I'd had a couple of wets by this time, but wasn't gibbering, *at least I didn't think so*. She reckoned her name was Lucy, and what was weird was her outfit. Picture this; she wore a tailored old-fashioned coat with big velvet buttons, gloves and a tammy type hat with a pom-pom - it looked like expensive gear but

completely out of bygone times and really strange. Years later it was like déjà vu on seeing 'the Railway Children' with Jenny Agutter, as that was the way this perky nutjob was kitted out.

Anyway, 'Lucy' was easy to talk to, although she said some odd things. It's a balmy September evening, so *hand in hand* we're having a casual stroll down the Hoe. The place is deserted, things are looking good - and **yes**, we've stopped for a little necking session - having been starved of female company for weeks, I'm blowing in her ear, trying to cop a handful, and prepared to beg; but she's having none of it. Acting miffed and calling me a bad boy, she gently pushes me away, holds out her hands and thwarts me by saying "Do you like my gloves? They were a birthday present!" It's polite to say yes, so I agree they **are** nice gloves. Next, she says "Would you like to see a neat trick I can do with them?" Who am I to say no! Like yourself, after a couple o' wets I'm everyone's friend, but I'm wondering what she's on about and, is this wee cracker crackers?

She removes them slowly, one finger at a time, suggestively dragging it out, like a professional stripper tantalizing her adoring audience - *I'm mesmerized*. With both off she carefully turns them inside out, showing me the fur lining while stroking them and saying, "They are lovely." I'm coming to the conclusion that she's lost her way somewhere along the track and racking my brain for a feasible excuse, so as to take off, without hurting the soft tart's feelings; *little knowing this maiden is actually a midden*. Luckily, I kept my trap shut long enough, because I was flabbergasted when right out the blue, bold as brass, she stage whispers "Have you ever had a furry wank?" **There's only one answer to that,** so, I imagine the astonished expression on my coupon must've been prizeworthy.

By the time she had her gloves on *inside out* 'Mr Snake' was ready to, somewhat reluctantly, endure one of the best 'thrashings' imaginable *so perhaps bromide in the tea is just a myth*. This bint was a natural, appearing transfixed whilst chortling to herself - yes, 'Lucy', who majored in organ enlargement and took a dedicated pride in dishing out her favours, almost sprained her wrist putting the colour back in ma cheeks! This must've been her party piece, giving her the upper hand *so to speak* - thus diverting the danger of being podgered and 'put up the stick' by an out-of-control, uncaring accomplice - *pretty smart; but they all get 'nailed' in the end*.

Is **epiphany** the word I'm looking for? - well anyway, not quite what I had in mind, but as you know 'the flesh is weak', so I'm forever grateful to have been the 'glove puppet' 'Lucy' chose to practise her 'party piece' on, down the Hoe that evening, and swear when we passed Frankie Drake's statue his tongue wus hingin' oot - *I'm pleased to report, the rash cleared up in less than a week.*

Well, one way or another, we've been put through the mill and at last it's the final day of Part One training; the Navy having now moulded us into what they expect of seagoing killing machines. We are up and at it 'early doors', as this will be a busy day, what with final kit-muster, Mess inspection and the Passing-out Parade, to which proud families have been invited by some overzealous class members wishing to share their moment of glory. Most of us were from too far afield to consider inviting spectators and I, for one, would rather be unseen by relatives if I was going to make an arse of myself on that soul-destroying Parade Ground.

The 'Rookie' at HMS Raleigh, 1958

Need I say, everything went according to the well-rehearsed plan that has stood the test of time *year in, year out* at Raleigh where thousands of New Entrants are churned out to keep the machine running and 'Their Lordships' happy. Sounds naff, but I must admit, as much as I'm not into this Parade Ground stuff, marching to a top-notch military band makes one's chest swell with pride.

There's no hanging around at HMS Raleigh; when they've finished with you - you're history. So next day we pack our gear first light and after a hearty breakfast are handed our draft-chits and armed forces British Rail travel warrants then *minds bent, but spirit not yet broken* sent merrily on our way, kitbag on shoulder and wee broon attaché case at the short trail.

13: HMS Mercury

There's a dozen or so candidates going to HMS Mercury, near Portsmouth, for Part Two training, which will qualify us hopefuls to become the ears of the fleet - RO3s *(radio operators third class)*. We say our goodbyes to the guys who, having volunteered for other branches are being sent to different establishments for their Part Two training. For instance, my old mate Doogie is going to HMS Vernon in Pompey, as he wants to become a seaman specializing in TAS. *(Torpedo Anti-Submarine)*. That's the way it is in 'the Mob', you meet and have rakes o' great mates, but when your draft chit comes through you're off to another ship or shorebase and generally never see them again, other than maybe a chance meeting in the dockyard, a foreign port or more than likely a Pompey watering hole.

So the 'new boys' arrive at Mercury - and be told, it's a different class, no wooden 'nickel-and-dime' huts at this establishment, the Messes are in purpose-built two-storey blocks set in a tranquil hamlet of rural Hampshire. This looks good! Now, appearance, as you know, can be deceptive, but not this time - it's 'the dug's baws' and just as well, since this course is a long haul; something like nine months. We had some great and interesting gadgies in our class, with only the odd one or two full o' wind an' pish, but once again few names remain in my memory bank. One blonde-haired chap I remember was Steve Walzter - a good swimmer; having been trained relentlessly as a kid by his fanatical father - *strange how silly details stick in one's mind*. Years later someone told me he made it to PO Tel. and on leaving the Navy, like many ex-servicemen, joined the Prison Service.

Now, here's a chap, whose name I can't help but remember as it keeps popping up on television - John Howard Davies. Then, he was a National Serviceman, today he is a noteworthy comedy Producer and Director whose name I've seen in the credits after 'Monty Python' and 'The Good Life' et cetra, et cetra. I caught him recently on television tribute programmes to both Frankie Howerd and Penelope Keith; he has aged well and looks as if he himself enjoys the good life. I would, after all the years, not have recognized him, but that smooth articulate voice I did right away; making

me look up and take notice. John, when a child, had been an acclaimed actor playing the lead in two timeless classics - 'Tom Brown's Schooldays', and Oliver Twist, in the 1948 film. I think he mentioned owning a Rolls Royce and spoke of mixing with the showbiz aristocracy of the day. Yes, this young guy was in a different league, but to give him credit, displayed no airs and graces integrating avec les paysans.

John was the only one who owned a car, as few did in the 'Golden Age', however, one of my well-heeled classmates had a Vincent Black Knight motorbike which he kept at the camp. **Wotta beast** - with me clinging on behind, it was often 'wellied' down the East Meon country roads to Clanfield's 'Rising Sun', where we'd sink a much-needed pint o' Watney's Red Barrel, mingle wi' the natives and hit on the sassy barmaids.

*It saddened me to hear, John Howard Davies died age 72 *(the big C)* on 22ND August 2011 ***- we're all in the queue!***

Joe and Benny were still at Collingwood, so we arranged to meet one weekend; when *caught up in the moment* we made our first visit to the 'Hello Sailor' tattoo parlour *to feel the prick of the tattooist's needle*. I chose an eagle on an anchor *(seemed appropriate)* skillfully scribed on the top of my left arm by the big roughy-toughy artist who, because of his squint eye, lank dark hair and stubble-covered double chin, reminded me of Popeye the Sailorman's love rival for the affections of his sweetheart, Olive Oil. When the masterpiece was completed, he strapped a sheet of bog paper over it with an elastic band and sent me on my way rejoicing.

I hadn't seen Joe and Benny since leaving home - however, by now Christmas Leave was on the horizon, when we would all reunite and swap stories back in Edinburgh. This would be our first Leave, so everyone was looking forward to it with great anticipation as, although only away from home four months, we now lived in a different world.

On a prearranged Saturday we met at Aggie Weston's *(Dame Agnes Weston's Royal Sailors' Rest)* in Pompey, had some scran, which was always ace and ultracheap there, then downed a couple o' wets; but in the **'the happy days'** the pubs closed in the afternoons and we, being novices, hadn't yet learned the dodge that the old-timers used to sup all day. This was to go to and fro on-board the Isle of Wight ferry, on which the bar was open during each crossing - ***my word; talk about dedicated!***

Anyway, at a loose end on a dreich grey December afternoon, pretty stumped, we decided to go to the cinema; a small poky fleapit up the main drag. It's our lucky day, we're ushered to seats in the front stalls behind a gang o' scatty teenage girls - and believe you me, in a Naval town such as Pompey, they've got nothing to learn. While Benny, the wise guy *and ever the clown* is chatting them up he casually breaks out the 'blue liners' *(Naval issue ciggies - dirt cheap)* and tries to light up with his Ronson Varaflame gas lighter. Having no success, he pisses about with the valve which alters the flame, and tries again; **hell's bells!** it's like a flame-thrower. **Crikey!** - does he not set light to the tart upfront's hair, which must've been loupin' wi' lacquer. Fortunately it wasn't the disaster you may imagine, as she had quite a mop and a blue flame just shot up and round the frizzy extremes, so she didn't realize it had happened, but got quite a fright when we, as one, leapt up to pat it out. ***Wotta stink!***

She, and we were lucky, as that cock-up could so easily have caused a real horror story, remember Michael Jackson and the Coca-Cola *(or was it Pepsi?)* advert. Protesting innocence, we were all 'turfed oot' for creating a disturbance - poor sods have ended up in DQs *(detention quarters)* for less. Now, wouldn't that have been a 'green rub', not even had our first Leave and already 'prison bitches' getting slapped around the head whilst cowering in the corner of a dimly-lit damp cell in 'chokey'!

I shan't attempt to relate details on the subject of DQs as *luckily* I never had personal experience; not because I was 'whiter than white' for nine years, the fact is *like most* I didn't get caught. DQs is the Naval equivalent of prison *(abandon hope all ye who enter here)* and probably the worst thing that can happen to a matelot as, fortunately, QRAIs state they are not allowed to 'keel haul', lash or hang us from the yardarm these days.

Soon Christmas Leave came and went; truth is I don't remember much about it, other than it was great to get out of uniform and see the old crowd. Everyone brought a holdall stuffed with their best civvies back to camp after this first Leave, as although we were proud to be in the Royal Navy, everyone hated that horrible, antiquated, uncomfortable 'square rig' with these dreadful bell-bottoms, tight tunic with no pockets, pesky white front which was a struggle to get into and impossible to get out of without help on a hot day, that black silk ribbon thing and ridiculous white lanyard.

D'you know, the more I think about it the easier it is to realize why we didn't want to wear it - **I rant in the hope of being heard!**

Back in the days when Pusser owned us 'lock, stock and barrel' *kept on a short leash* we weren't allowed to wear civvies, so the drill was to take them ashore in a Pusser's holdall; get changed in Aggie Weston's and leave the uniform stowed in a rented locker - 'twas a hassle, but worthwhile. 'Tis said it pays to advertise; that sailor suit came into its own abroad, where we were instantly identified as out to score a 'bit o' strange' ***- the definition of a good run ashore is cheap bevvy an' a 'slice o' tail'.*** I'm sure 'the powers that be' had long known Jack would rather not ponce around in uniform, except at times of benefit such as just mentioned and for a short period in summer, when the likes of vulnerable Midland mill girls swarmed around Southsea and were 'easy meat' for Jack to exploit. C'mon now, you know we've got to go for the weak, and capitalize on what little assets we've been handed in this life.

Although 'Their Lordships' knew the score, it took them until about 1962 before issuing an AFO *(Admiralty Fleet Order)* decreeing Junior Ratings be permitted to wear civilian clothing ashore in homeports. This AFO, of course, gave a strict code of dress to be adhered to at all times, stipulating **nothing casual**; meaning jacket, shirt and tie must be worn.

I had managed to crack this, no civvies ashore, problem almost two years previously while serving on a frigate which was, at the time, on a visit to Aarhus in Denmark. It so happened that just after 'Up Spirits' I was on deck having 'a burn' when I deeked two crewmen leaving a Danish warship in tracksuits and off they trot at a leisurely pace along the jetty. Now, I'm not the brightest star in the sky, as I'm sure you've by now guessed, but there it is staring me in the face, Eureka! *The light goes on.*

That afternoon I nick ashore, on a quest to unearth a sports shop, where I buy a well-made dark blue tracksuit, a couple of nice sporty T-shirts and a pair of superb white basketball boots *(happily surprised by how little it all cost)*. I hoofed it straight back to the ship, where I changed into my natty new outfit, fair chuffed on discovering it has more pockets than the dress uniform in which to stow paybook, fags and dosh, Great! So let's give it a try - I jog back along to the Quarterdeck, hand in my station card and *unquestioned* I'm off ashore - **cracked it!**

I employed this dodge, whenever appropriate, over the years, never at any time interrogated; as Senior Rates seeing me in a boozer assumed I'd popped in for a wet on the way back from my run, and being ashore themselves couldn't give a rat's arse. An Officer might've been a different kettle o' fish, but the upper echelon didn't socialise with the riff-raff so thankfully we rarely saw them ashore. The 'Toffs' might not like that last statement, as the truth hurts - but I say it as I see it; so **tough tittie!**

OK, so we're back at Mercury after Christmas Leave and everyone has a tale to tell. Three events stick in my mind, one amusing and two not; so we'll go for the funny one first. I know I said everyone detested the 'square rig' uniform - open yer trap and you're sure to be shot down in flames. There's always the exception and here he is: Herbert *whose mother had 'squeezed oot a beauty'* loved his Number One 'dress uniform'; we were convinced he had no civvies, as he was forever ironing and pressing his prized attire - to put you in the picture and thus explain what happened and why; bell-bottom trousers are pressed inside-out with the creases going horizontally as opposed to the norm; *vertically.* These creases were measured the width of a paybook from the bottom up, making them fold like a concertina, and so, easily stowed in your small ships' locker.

Herbert is in Waterloo Station returning from Xmas Leave - he's, of course, givin' it the old yo-ho-ho, looking smooth in his cherished uniform when the funniest thing imaginable happens. One of the creases above the left knee of his bell-bottoms gives up the ghost, so the leg is dangling off his kecks in the middle of the station. He'd pressed them so much that they had either rotted or he'd possibly singed them. As you can imagine, he looked 'a bonnie laddie' with his face trippin' 'im and spittin' blood, while his 'oppos' were stiflin' fits o' the giggles. On seeing Herbert's plight, a helpful station attendant came to the rescue with some safety pins - this emergency repair getting the crestfallen dandy back to camp, tail between the legs, but in one piece - and *possibly* a sight wiser.

Right, that's it, the fun's over; we arrived back at Mercury to find the establishment engulfed in an Asian flu epidemic. More than half the camp was stricken and whole blocks in quarantine; with the 'Quacks' and SBAs stretched well beyond their limit. I was lucky, since it didn't affect me, and can only put this down to having had a serious dose of flu the previous

winter when employed at the Western General. Thoroughly convinced I was standing at death's door forced me to take three days off work - *probably copped it there anyway!* So, it's feasible that my brush with this highly contagious lurgy triggered the old immune system to kick in.

The best treatment was to sweat it out, so the poor infected unfortunates were each issued with a Jenny Wren and sent to bed. From memory, 'twas a 'three-day event' for 'them wot copped it' and soon under control.

The third thing certainly wasn't funny as far as the chap involved was concerned. Geordie was a decent normal quiet efficient chap, in fact Class Captain *and nobody's idiot* - it was pretty obvious something was seriously wrong as, for days, after returning late, he was misery personified. Eventually we coaxed him into sharing the problem - thus getting it off his chest, which visibly did him a lot of good; and with young guys being a heartless lot o' bastards we soon bucked him up.

It transpired that on the train journey back down the line from Newcastle, he had been chatting up this gronk who'd been 'up for it' and leading him on. So, seeking privacy they head for the bog, with Geordie boy thinking he's onna cert; albeit a knee-trembler, *(sounds about right, don't it?).* So, in they go, Geordie's tongue nearly getting caught in the sliding door when he pushes her in then slams it shut behind them. He's worked up and on her like a young stallion - she craps it, bottles out and screaming, pulls the communication cord. The train squeals to a halt and before you can say Jack Flash, Geordie is huckled from the carriage and locked-up in the nearest police station. **So beware, it's as easy as that.**

The outcome? - the Navy *who look after their own* successfully defend our pal in court, he's acquitted, however scores half-a-page, fingered as a "sex maniac", in that outstanding Sunday gossip sheet the 'News o' the Screws'. Due to his notoriety 'our Leader' was demoted to the ranks - after all, we can't have the likes of **that** in a position of trust!

You'll recall, we were at Mercury to be trained as telegraphists, so hours were spent in various classrooms, learning about radios, radio waves, basic electrics, navigation, Morse code and how to touch-type *(to music)*, but it wasn't all schooling; we had workstations, as everyone must 'muck in' to keep the camp 'shipshape and Bristol fashion'. While I remember, 'call the hands' each morning was the usual bugle call, immediately followed

by a spin of Duane Eddy's 'Rebel Rouser', which was topping the charts at the time - *to this day I think that was supercool.*

Well anyway, we also had to keep duty-watches; the most hated being 'North Camp Patrol': it's early February and I'm sharing the North Camp Patrol duty at black o'clock, with one of my classmates 'Rampant' Robin who hails from Hackney, or 'Ackney, as he called it, in London. It's cold, damp and miserable so we're wrapped up as best as we can, wearing our Burberrys, Number Eights, tin hats and webbing, each armed to the teeth with a standard issue wooden pick-handle to fight off intruders and Russian spies. We are totally pissed-off, as there's no sentry box or sod all to shelter in, so therefore must keep moving and patrol the perimeter fence, as intended, in order to generate warmth.

We're burbling about all sorts whilst warily picking our way along the fence, in the pitch dark, trying not to slip and go arse over tit on the wet and muddy grass underfoot. As always, the conversation inevitably gets round to fud when Robin says he joined the Navy for wine, women and song, but so far all that's been on offer is **rum, bum and baccy**.

He reminds me we have a long weekend coming up in a couple of weeks and says he's going 'up the line' as it's his birthday that weekend; then asks if I'd like to come along. He tells me there's plenty room, since his brothers have both left home, he never said as much, but I knew one had been 'sent down', and now in 'the Scrubs' gettin' raped at Her Majesty's Pleasure - *having been collared while exposing himself to a ladies' hockey team*. Well, guess what? By a truly remarkable coincidence, the Saturday of that very weekend was also my birthday and we were both to be twenty-one, so what could be better than to celebrate such a momentous occasion in 'the Big Smoke?' Making ever more outrageous plans, we carry on slowly round the perimeter doing our bit to defend the realm.

When out in the countryside in the middle o' nowhere at night: it's spooky, every sound, that wouldn't even be noticed during the day, is magnified and we'd already heard a few which gave us the jitters. All of a sudden there's a thundering drumming noise coming down the slope towards us getting nearer and nearer, and louder and louder, **what the fuck!** It happens so quickly we've hardly got time to be scared shitless: let alone guess what it might be. Then *going like the clappers* there it

is racing past on the other side of the high, barbed wire topped, military security fence. Bleedin' hell it's a horse - B'Jaisus, talk about visions o' the headless horseman, say what you like, the mind plays tricks on the 'none too bright' at such times. As it passes it slows, turns and comes over - 'Neddy' must have been wearing night-vision goggles or maybe eating all his carrots, because this 'cuddy' could certainly see in the dark, more so than us, relying on our Pusser's torches with their half-shagged batteries. Even then I wouldn't have thought it would gallop in the dark; but I guess it knew that field like the back o' its hoof. We reckoned it must've been some poncey officer's polo pony, possibly startled by a nocturnal creature, or perhaps even an adder - well, maybe not an adder so early in the year, but come the warmer weather they were plentiful at East Meon: in fact some o' the nutters used to hunt for them on the hillside.

Doesn't time fly when you're enjoying yourself? So before ah know it we are off 'up the line', flouting the rules by changing into our 'glad rags' in the Second Class carriage, heading for Robin's gaff in 'Ackney - **great!** This weekend's lookin' good because we're flush with cash, an' right now the old hormones are runnin' riot - lookout Chelsea babes, here we come, ***yeah, dem sailah boys is gonna bone some chicks!***

On the Saturday afternoon we went shopping, that's when I bought my gold St Christopher; something I'd fancied and promised myself for 'donkeys'. I coughed up so much dosh getting the one I wanted that I had to make do with a crappy cheap thin chain and was lucky not to lose the lot; when a link surrendered within a week, but that's another story which will come later, so cool it Baby, try to be patient and don't rush me!

With the way Robin had been bragging, I imagined he was up to his knees in concubines back home, so obviously ah'm thinkin', 'ah'll jemmy masel right in there an' cop one o' thaim, nae bother'. Yes, you've heard it all before and when it's your turn there's 'brussel sprout'; well, that's how it is come Saturday night. I've been imagining this 'Chas and Dave' style knees-up with wall-to-wall fud for the taking. That's the way it is for sailors on Leave in London, isn't it? ***I've seen it in the movies.***

Yeah, in yer effin' dreams, pal! Reality is some aunts and uncles come round for a wee drink and it's "Oh, how you've grown. I hear you're a sailor now", and "This is yer pal then, from where son?" "Edinburgh? Oh

yeah, that's up in Scotland, innit; we went there once, didn't we Sam?" "Oh yeah, nice place, pissed down the whole time. Wouldn't go back in a hurry!" - **bloody bollocks, this I don't need!**

So much for this amazing Saturday night I've been fantasizing about, it drags on and eventually it's too late to hit the town. The nearest we get to any hootenanny is saying hello to Robin's two dreadful *acne riddled,* schoolgirl cousins. Oh, shite... shafted again! The only highlight was when Sam and Robin's *near blotto* father rolled up their sleeves for a punch-up, but even that was nothing more than hot air - you know the scene, a Mexican stand-off - more shouting than action, each being scared of the other; making it an easy matter for their better halves to pull them apart, sort it and put the naughty boys sheepishly in their place.

Next day *a trifle vexed* I'm telling Robin, in no uncertain terms, that this isn't even close to what I had in mind for an all-singin'-all-dancin' weekend at this important time in my life - I wanted something I could remember for the rest of my natural. Robin of course can hardly disagree and I presume doesn't want me, once back in the Mess, blabbing about how we'd had a crap 'run', when everyone expected to hear some real good crack about our exploits in **'the big city'.** He suggests we head for Soho, where there should be 'an opening' for us. Turns out this is matey's game, the bold lad **doesn't have** a burd - he goes up to Soho to get his 'jollies' and knows exactly where the action is. Off we go, tongues hingin' oot, fair chokin' forra ride - now, let me tell you, having, so far, led an exemplary, beyond reproach, 'sheltered life', I'm determined tae 'pop ma cherry' - and it's about time. ***Just think of me as a late developer!***

We take in a show at the Soixante-neuf Club; one of the sleazy dives Soho is famous for, not that we needed the titillation, but because the doorman was Robin's pal, so we got in for free. Looked like my mate was on homeground, none of this buying expensive drinks for so-called hostesses. Oh no! See the action, cop whatever's goin' gratis then split.

Robin's a past master, he knows exactly where he's going, and it's close by. The lectures about 'socially transmitted diseases' at Raleigh are long forgotten when he ushers me into a phonebox and pointing to the whores' adverts, says "This one looks good, wha'd'ye think, me ole fruit?" **Think??** *Ah'm no' here tae think!* It says French model, gives a brief description

and the lie saying twenty-four - that'll be right, but who cares? He dials the number, gets the address and the "Come on up Cherie", so up we go, panting like good uns; the strumpet's had more men than the Grand Old Duke o' York and doesn't bat an eye about 'entertaining' both of us in her none too tidy 'boudoir'. Since it's a 'two's up' we negotiate a crackin' price with this average-looking "French" whore, who is probably thirty odds and from Bolton - as already said, **who cares!**

This is when I find out that pro is more likely to stand for professional than prostitute; as she does 'the business' and we're doon the stairs, oot the door and back on the cold pavement 'quicker than that'. Talk aboot "sook yae in and blaw yae oot in bubbles"; that's it then, is it? **Happy Birthday!** - we're minus a 'five-spot' and now standing bewildered on the unforgiving Soho street. Alright, before you ask; I can't remember who 'batted onna sticky wicket' - so, let's drop it! An' wha' d'you mean, 'ashamed of sinking so low' - if that was the case ah wouldnae be tellin' ye!

It's Monday night already and we are back in the Mess sitting bragging on 'Spunk Bubble's' bed surrounded by awestruck lads eagerly questioning us about our exploits in 'the Big Smoke'. Of course, Robin and myself are wallowing in the glory and fair piling it on when a voice from across the Mess bellows "**A ride's awright, but yae cannae beat a guid blaw!**" It's the class loudmouth, Jock McNutter frae Paisley, a Celtic fan renowned for his eloquence, but not the ideal emissary for Scotland - give'm a brain and he'd be dangerous. As usual he's lying on his pit, hand in boxers, trying *once again* to strangle his best and only friend. A young Scouser, intent on winding him up, retorts, "What are you on about now ya Scotch Bastard"; since most of the guys haven't understood a word he had said, partly through innocence, but more so because of Jock's 'Glesgae' Gorbals accent. At this Jock gets annoyed, waving his 'magic wand' while shouting "**A gobble ya thick cunt, a fuckin' gobble!**" In years yet to come *(one night in South America)* Jock's words were ringing in my ears - **then** he went up in my estimation for never having said a truer word.

Every class took turn at being the Guard of Honour for 'Divisions' - held bimonthly, when all the trainees, togged up in well-brushed Number One uniforms, were ordered to line up in divisions on the Parade Ground in front o' 'the Big Hoose' and execute a 'march past' for the Commanding

Officer. This pomp and ceremony stuff was never 'my thing', so I had hatched a cunning plan which I'd been saving for this very occasion.

For some time I had been quietly cultivating a growth on the heel of my left foot, and although no great problem it gave me gyp in damp weather, causing a slight, but noticeable limp and had of late been aggravated - *now was the time to make use of this asset*. So, on the week prior to our starting Guard Training, I reported to the Sickbay where on seeing the MO *(Medical Officer)* who diagnosed a verruca, I was excused boots and an appointment made for me to attend a clinic in HMS Victory *(the Naval Barracks in Portsmouth)* to have the nasty parasitic wart removed.

My timing's perfect, as I'm given a chit to produce; informing the Chief GI I'm hors de combat - now this Chief GI was an easy-ozey guy, not the quintessential anchor-faced yelling prat one expects; being 'long in the tooth' he'd been through the war and I guess Mercury may've been his last draft before being 'put out to pasture'; so he'd mellowed. However, he wasn't so stupid as to let me hang around the Mess doing nothing - each morning while my class was subjected to an hour's drill instruction, I'd slope off to clean his cabin in the Chiefs' Accommodation Block.

With him being a tidy man it was a breeze, taking no more than ten minutes; after a bit o' snoopin' I'd scrutinize the rather fetching framed nude study of a reclining Marilyn Monroe which he kept safely stowed out of sight under his bed *(Marilyn Monroe, remember her? Imagine catching the likes o' that in the middle o' a poppy field wae a Cadbury's Milk Flake)*. To while away the hour I'd sprawl on the comfy armchair, to laze reading his paper until the drilling was over and time to rejoin my class for other instruction. So, what could've been a pain in the arse - *or should I say foot?* - turned out to be a nice wee skive.

My time comes, when one day I have to report back to the Sickbay where I'm told to get changed into Number Threes *(not so good uniform; rough itchy material and red badges)* and be ready in fifteen minutes to go to Victory Barracks, where I'll wave goodbye to my verruca. I've to present myself at our Transport Section, from where I'll be given a lift in a 'Tilly' *(utility vehicle - a Bedford Minibus)* going there to pick up an Officer. Great, that makes life nice and easy; so off we go to Portsmouth.

I'd never been to Victory Barracks and expected it would be all 'hustle

bustle', real Pusser hard core *"Where are you going laddie?"* crap. But no, not at all; sure it's an enormous old Victorian barracks, but, not as anticipated - this legendary HQ is unbelievably quiet. The vast Parade Ground is empty and the few people I see are going about their business in a pretty relaxed manner. It's surreal - I had imagined bodies running all over the place *at the double* to shouted commands - this is the quietest establishment I've been to since joining, in fact it seems eerie.

I'm directed to the Sickbay, where two three-badge Leading SBAs *real 'old hands'* give me a local injection and to my astonishment get shot of my nurtured asset with a scalpel and strangely-shaped surgical scissors in a matter of minutes. There's no pain, although I don't really like watching, and it's over in the blink of an eye. No stitches, just some padding and a plaster. Then it's "That's you mate, off you go." I say "How about transport, who do I see?" , to be told "No one mate, you're on yer own now me ole fart!" Well, that's rich, surely he jests - here's me a helpless cripple an' I'm expected to get back to Mercury under my own steam; just as well I've got some loot for the bus fare, otherwise I'd be stuffed.

Off I go hobbling along the road from the Barracks, to where the bus runs up Commercial Road that will take me back to East Meon. Now, it's not all that far to walk, but with the local injection wearing off, the pain, although not excruciating, is increasing by the minute, so it takes what seems forever to get to the bus stop, and guess what? When I eventually arrive, it's Sod's Law, I've just missed one - and now doubting the wisdom of my scam. However, I get the next one; more than ready for a seat on the return trip to Mercury, where I'm still excused boots and wearing plimsolls long enough to miss the Masquerade. So the ruse worked and I'm eternally grateful to whoever passed the verruca on to me - ***which is more than I can say for the dirty bastard who gave me crabs a few years later!***

That same day I realized an interest in art, so let me gen you up. Knowing the next bus could be some time away I decided to make use of the municipal bogs next to the Guildhall, where to my utter delight I discovered a talented artist used the cubicles to exhibit his excellent and tasteful work. There, amongst the usual lewd drawings, vulgar suggestions and phone numbers were his masterpieces. Superb studies of shackled winsome scantily-clad teenage girls, their hair in ringlets and pigtails; chained-up in

dungeons, with despair, shame and rejection on angelic tear-stained faces. Here and now I would like to nominate him as the greatest erotic toilet artist of the last century, while strongly denying there is a chauvinistic thought in my head when I whisper, ***"women in chains!"***

Spring arrives and so does Easter Leave which was a bit of a drag - now, that may sound crazy, but hang about an' ah'll tell you why. After a few months the Navy 'dahn sowf' becomes your life; as all your mates and the places frequented have become more familiar than the old life at home. That said, the Navy and whatever Mess you're living in is **now** your home. Which reminds me of the OD who said "Chief, I'm homesick!" The Chief answered "This **is** yer home laddie!" The reply being "I know Chief, and I'm fuckin' sick of it!" Anyway, I've grown to prefer being domiciled on the affluent South Coast, always having plenty company and thoroughly enjoy the slick light-hearted banter and badgering that goes on endlessly in the Mess. So, whenever home, although relaxing, the solitude could be boring - this particular fortnight was a prime example of just how tedious a Leave period can seem, when used to Service life.

This Easter, company was in short supply, Joe and Benny for some reason not home, Joe Brattisani still in the Army, and by now so is Billy. Charles and Syd have fled to Canada, Carnie is God knows where at the other side of the world, employed as a seaman on the King James; a vermin-ridden tramp steamer, and brother Mike is only thirteen. However, Doogie's home and seems to have taken to the Navy like a fish to water, he's even been to sea, on a destroyer *the lucky git* and now back at Vernon. We meet up most days in town and do the rounds together; much of which seems lacking after Portsmouth and Southsea, but with winter over 'our opponents' have unwrapped, revealing what they've kept hidden away from the cold and we *being avid admirers* want some.

Come Saturday night we had a few wets around the West End and Doogie, who'd been chatting up everything in a skirt, but failing miserably, decided we should go to the Plaza; a popular dancehall up at Morningside, where it wasn't unknown to score a racy nurse while smoochin' to 'Kathy and the Kentones'. So, when the pubs close at ten *yes ten* off we go to the Plaza. As usual there's a long queue, and yards o' fud in front of us - I remember Doogie rubbing his hands together while spouting, "If ah dinnae

get ma hole tonight ah'm goin' to the Dean Bridge tae toss masel off!"

Leave is over; I'm back at Mercury where we are well into the course, but unfortunately ah'm toilin'. My theory, typing and Morse recognition are all adequate, but I'm hindered by my writing speed, being unable to jot down a signal as quickly as I could read and decipher the Morse coming through my headphones. I had always been a slow neat writer, compromised to a degree by being a 'southpaw' but hadn't foreseen this as a problem - *so much for my aspirations and pipe dreams!*

Every week the Morse got faster, but my writing didn't; so *self-esteem at an all time low* I had to admit ah 'couldnae cut the mustard' - and completely hacked off, discussed the matter with both my Instructor and Divisional Officer, who offered extra tuition. However, it was abundantly clear to me that clutching at straws would be futile. So, after giving my predicament serious consideration, I decided to 'bite the bullet' and follow a familiar path by re-categorizing to the Supply and Secretariat branch as a chef, which resulted in me being drafted to Victory Barracks in Pompey, to await the next course at the Cookery School in Chatham Barracks; HMS Pembroke.

At HMS Collingwood; Benny (left) and Joe (kneeling)

14: HMS Victory - RNB Portsmouth

I loafed for a month in Pompey Barracks; and let me tell you, this **was** the place to be - as said earlier, not as anticipated. Although *understandably* I was expecting that I would, on being ***'The Reject'***, get a proper usin' *or get thrown to the wolves* but I couldn't have been more wrong.

First I tackle my joining routine, at which I was a dab hand, having just completed my leaving routine at Mercury - this requirement is common practice, involving going to all departments marked on the card provided, when either arriving or departing any ship or establishment. So I must get this card stamped, thus informing all concerned of my existence and, more importantly, allowing me to draw bedding, be allocated a Mess, 'victualled in' for food, rum, pay *('cash in hand')* and so on.

This done, I find my Mess in one of the huge blocks, all of which have large figureheads outside and named after long dead Naval heroes. The Mess is one of four on the second floor of one of these big old Victorian buildings. It's strange, I haven't seen or heard anyone shouting **"Chop chop!"** while tackling the stairs - is this one of my weird dreams, or could ah be in the wrong place - after all this is Portsmouth Barracks; so should surely be heaving with bodies. Feeling apprehensive and dragging my kitbag, I push my way through the double swing-doors into this huge Mess with large multipaned windows and about forty beds, on which only three have bedding; two of these occupied by guys lying reading. What's goin' on 'ere then? It's the middle of the morning and they're lying reading, not a care in the world; don't even as much as glance across when I enter. So, I go over to the nearest 'non-combatant' and say, "Which bed will I take?", reluctantly the guy looked up and gestured around the Mess with an opening arm, while replying without concern, "Take yer pick mate!"

Yes, RNB was 'a different class' - when I look back it's still hard to believe, but that's the way it was *I wasn't hallucinating* nobody gave a toss, nobody bothered us, we had no duties, zilch; it appeared that all the Messes were the same, with very few beds taken. As far as I'm aware the Barracks was just a transit camp for misfits like myself and others who

for some reason were waiting for a ship, or in many cases those who had 'finished their time'; so, due for release from Her Majesty's Navy.

Even now I can't help but imagine how hectic and overcrowded this huge principal Naval bastion must have been in days gone by, when the Senior Service was a hundred times the size of today. I can easily picture how it would've been a veritable hive of activity during WWI and WWII, with sailors of all categories being drafted en masse, to commission or recommission warships of every description in ports throughout the world; not forgetting the thousands of survivors from ships now in Davy Jones's locker who passed through these Barracks to be rekitted then ordered to other vessels to put their lives on the line for King and Country yet again.

It occurs to me that my father, during his wartime Naval Service, was probably no stranger to Pompey Barracks and may well've been billeted in that very Mess a few years before me. *One couldn't help but sense, HMS Victory just reeked of history and ghosts from the past!*

We, being 'Blue Card men', could go ashore at any time we pleased, which was, of course, never before 'Up Spirits' and lunch. Yes indeed life was a peach, no one ever, as far as I remember, questioned us, but don't forget Jack isn't daft, and always knows how to keep a good thing going, so we very quietly went about whatever we were not doing. The Barracks seemed to be staffed mainly by RAs *(married men living ashore, and on ration allowance)* so these guys obviously had a 'good number' and no one, but no one, was rocking the boat. In fact, when the RAs all steamed off home at four in the afternoon it looked like the place was closed.

It was there in 'Vicky' Barracks that I met and befriended Jim Shannon, a two-badge Killick Seaman. The basis of this old mates thing was, he also came from Edinburgh, which was a turn-up, as although I met plenty Jocks in the Navy, relatively few, for some strange and obscure reason, came from the Capital. Jim was in a different Mess from myself - his was within the next block to the one I was billeted in. We had met by chance when queueing for lunch *after 'tot-time'* in the main Junior Ratings dining hall. On immediately recognizing each other's refined Edinburgh accents we shared a table, and while troughing through the scran, had a blether about 'Auld Reekie', discussing the merits of our fair city loudly for all to hear, as 'townies' tend to do when away from home.

As it was early summer and the weather perfect, we'd often swan down to The Seahorse at Southsea; guaranteed good for a laugh, and a generous helping of entertainment from that celebrated old poofter, Reg - *always at his best on the Hammond organ, when there was a new man in his life.*

So anyway, how's this for strange? - one night midweek Jim had arranged to meet a couple of mates from Vernon at The Seahorse, and I tag along. When we get there, I'm impressed by his mates who turn out to be Clearance Divers - *highly specialized guys,* but I can't believe my eyes, as guess who's with them? None other than big Doogie who has decided that's what he's going to become; and be told, something he later excelled at.

Here now, wot's not to like in this place - it has be the best kept secret in the Royal Navy. They feed me, ply me with strong drink, and pay me, asking nothing in return - so I'm beginning to think *and hope* I've been forgotten, when I'm rumbled and my draft chit comes through ordering me to report to Chatham Barracks Cookery School. So, next morning, with little or no enthusiasm I do my leaving routine, collect my papers and travel warrant: *this is the life* - once again I'm off to the unknown wondering what to expect, as I've not yet met anyone who has been to Chatham and therefore able to 'mark ma card'. One thing's for certain, it's not going to be anything like the cushy heaven on earth draft I'm leaving behind.

HMS Victory - Royal Naval Barracks, Portsmouth

15: HMS Pembroke - RNB Chatham

Well, that's it - 'vacation' over; I've arrived at Pembroke and am struggling with my kitbag, Pusser's holdall and wee broon attaché case through the small arch to the left of the Main Gate, which houses the office containing the Officer of the Watch, guarded by an RPO and entourage of sailors in Number Threes and white webbing, when I hear someone shouting **"Gangway! Gangway for a Naval Officer!"** On looking up, there's this bespectacled nutter arriving from somewhere up the main road inside the Barracks. He's dressed in Number Threes, wearing cycle clips and riding a strange looking three-wheeled bike, left hand steering the contraption and his right holding a tray, covered by a red chequered teacloth, above his head. Turns out to be the Officer of the Watch's lunch being delivered from the Wardroom Galley by Officers' Steward Darryl F. Bailey, the cleverest and craziest character imaginable. Darryl, another wideboy Londoner, got up to no end o' calculated tomfoolery and became a legend before finally getting himself booted out 'the Mob'.

Once again I do my joining routine and find a billet in a Mess one floor up in a typical Victorian Barracks block. I'm the 'new boy' joining a class just completed Part One training - I've no idea where, but presume in Pembroke; although I'm the new boy I'm an 'old hand' compared to these guys who've only been in 'the Andrew' a few weeks.

Now, because I've been a chef for years, the course is a walk in the park; in fact the PO Cook in charge has me tagged as flavour of the month and being a wily bird makes use of my abilities, so I'm his second-in-command, helping to instruct. The course passes quickly and as an accolade for my efforts and culinary skills I'm declared 'a special case' and rated Officers' Cook *(Cook (O))* rather than Assistant Officers' Cook.

Since this was a short course, lasting only twelve weeks, I'm at a loss when it comes to memories or tales to tell; but I'll dredge up something.

I didn't have many runs ashore in Chatham, which may have been due to accessibility, I don't remember, so other than having a narrow busy high street I can't picture the town at all - in saying that, I recall being scared

shitless by that street, as that's where I had my first driving lesson.

Midterm, *on a Bank Holiday weekend* 'Tiger' Timmins and myself took ourselves on a trip to Margate, where I entered him in a pie-eating contest - a bit of a laugh and a nice wee break well away from the Barracks. On our return, being thirsty, I put a tanner in the milk dispensing machine on the ground floor of our accommodation block; nothing happens, it's on the blink - **sod it!** Annoyed, I kick the twattin' thing and am amazed when the front swings open revealing the inside, stacked full o' cow juice. Tiger and myself take two or three cartons apiece and nash up to our Mess where, glowing with pride, we report "Free milk downstairs boys." Needless to say, that money-grabbin' cabinet was emptied 'quicker that that'.

Oh yeah, cop this; one night after 'pipe down' the Mess was a bit rowdy, nothing dramatic, just capering; so anyway, this duty PO *(probably an RA, choked because he's not at home tucked up with the wife and possibly worried that some tartar from the starboard watch might be)* doing his rounds comes into our Mess. Pished wi' power, he decides we, like naughty schoolboys, need punished, so gets us all out of our beds, into plimsolls and has us running round the Parade Ground **twenty times** - *in our striped Pusser's issue pyjamas*. Ah'm gutted - as it's the old story, thirty of us being chastised, like children, for the stupidity of a few tubes.

It's dark on the Parade Ground and the all powerful PO is exercising his lungs at the far end. There are buildings round the perimeter, one of which is the Gymnasium, so on the second lap I'm thinking, 'fuck this' and duck into the shadow of a doorway, where I stay until the final lap which I know is coming, as the retard is shouting the numbers, amongst other things, while the now pissed-off knackered Junior Ratings 'double' round the Parade Ground. The 'sprogs' thought this pretty smart, but I was so annoyed that it gave me little satisfaction to get one over on that contemptible prat who possibly had problems stemming from childhood.

We would often hear little stories of the incorrigible Darryl, who wasn't a trainee, but proper Ship's Company, therefore Wardroom Staff. The two I recall, which we thought highly amusing, were, one, when *it was said* Darryl danced all the way down the Wardroom table in his hob-nailed boots. Oh, how I wished I could have seen him doing his 'Fred Astaire', it must have been hilarious; but I can't see how he got away with it. The other

was, during an important Mess Dinner a rather harassed Chief Steward told Darryl "Drop everything and come with me." Unfortunately for the Chief, Darryl was carrying a huge silver tureen of consommé, which he promptly dropped - when later told he would have to pull his socks up, that's exactly what he did; Darryl obeyed orders to the letter.

The course is over, so draft chits are being dished out to the newly qualified - being a star, I'm wondering what kind of ship I'll be joining. A big cruiser? A destroyer? Who cares, as long as it's going abroad - I've served in the 'Wavy Navy' a year already and never even been in a dockyard; let alone on a ship. Most have scored crackers and are over the moon; so what about me? I get sent for; exuding confidence I *blissfully unaware* rush round to the D.O's office. anticipating something rather special, in keeping with my sound catering experience.

Dream on - I'm mortified when told I have the honour of being chosen as the Captain's chef. Now, wait for this one, because it's a poisoned chalice - yes, a drop kick in the goolies. Not the Captain of a warship - **oh no;** the Captain of the Barracks; an' cop this - not in the Barracks, but at his 'grace and favour' residence, *a modest squat outside Pembroke*. What's more, I'll be on ration allowance *(cheerio Tot)* and have to take a room in the NAAFI Club in town - as if that's not enough, there's no one else, only me. I'm supposed to be chuffed *and then some*. Wha'd' ye mean miffed? - ***Ah'm spewin' lumps,*** this is punishment; *lucky white heather!*

This sucks!!! They say, if you can't take a joke, you shouldn't've joined, but this'ere's a liberty, it's beyond the call o' duty, talk about upstairs and downstairs! I never see the Captain, but the 'missus'; the snobby bitch is never off ma back. It's "Chef this and Chef that!" - an' talk about mutton dressed as mutton; *an apt description*. She who rules, expects me to dance the hornpipe, sing sea shanties and produce dishes I've never heard of when throwin' her la-di-da dinner parties, and there's a further demeaning twist, she seems to think I'm also going to be her waiter, so, you'll appreciate - because of her attitude, I despised the woman.

What Madame failed to 'get' was, if she'd dropped 'the attitude' and treated me with just a smidgen of respect I'd've been eager to please. And, oh yeah, she had this randy little dog that was forever humpin' ma leg an' yapping roond ma ankles. Well now, guess what it got? Yes, you're spot

on - a king-sized bar of laxative chocolate from the local chemist; yes, ah'm a creature o' habit an' dem ole habits die hard; so some of my ration allowance went to 'mummy's little treasure'. ***Take that Sister!***

That draft would've suited some old lag three-badge RA a treat - why couldn't someone see this? I was lonelier than a castaway - working there all day then going back *feeling sorry for myself, wondering where it all went wrong* to languish fretting in my tiny room, which didn't even have a black and white telly. The only compensation was not being required until ten each morning; possibly because the 'old crow' hit the gin so hard in the evenings, that by the time she got up and 'put her face on', any earlier would've been a problem. There was no way I could bond with this woman and often on the verge of saying something was forced to bite my tongue - **I had to get out**: after all, let's face it, me; the firstborn, who'd been groomed for stardom since day one, didn't join the Queen's Navy to end up in a two-bit job like this. So, on a particularly shitty day when totally pissed off, I went to the Barracks to request a transfer.

After that, as is so often the case, everything seemed to happen at once. My only friend at this miserable time was a scraggy dark brown gelding, 'doin' solitary' in the paddock I passed in despair each day, when traversing my boulevard of broken dreams to and from the Captain's squat. Being a decent sort, whenever the chance arose I filched a carrot or a bun for him, so on clockin' me he'd canter over for a wee blether.

Anyway, that same week after yet another of 'Lady Muck's' dinner parties I'd had a couple o' wets *(one of the few perks of the job)*, and on the way back to the 'Ranch House' my pal came over as usual, but tonight was different. Chester said "You've always been kind to me, so now it's payback time, jump aboard and I'll give you a oncer round the field!" Sounds good to me, I climb onto the fence and grab hold of his mane just as he moves away, so I do a header off the fence into the field and sprain my wrist. Next morning it's so painful and swollen that I have to phone the 'old burd' telling her I'm off to Sickbay, where, when I get there, they strap me up and dish out the compulsory aspirins. I can't remember how it happened, but Madame must've got a replacement for me toute suite, because I never went back to 'the Big Hoose'. Now, that's power for you!

**yes indeed, the hand that wanks the Captain runs the ship.*

Instead, I was seconded for a short spell to a Naval hospital somewhere near the NAAFI, *where I was still billeted.* I must've been at the top of the transfer list when, being short staffed,they requested a hand, or possibly my records showed I had experience of hospital kitchens. Anyway, the work was a doddle and the cooks *(all ex-RN)* gave me an easy run - everyday was a two o'clock finish, which would've been great if I'd had something to do - also, if there were any nurses, of the female variety, they were invisible.

The fact is, skirt was in short supply; which was of course down to me, because I didn't motivate myself to go 'ashore' on the pull often enough; you know the old proverb 'seek and ye shall find'. There were, of course, always Wrens hanging around the NAAFI Club, but these saucy trollops weren't remotely interested in big screamin' ODs like me, they were into the 'old hands' - *or dare I say; the 'old hands' were into them.*

I often reflected on that first run ashore in 'Guzz' and how I'd scored so easily with the wee loony doon the Hoe; thinking at the time it was a cinch and would always be 'nae bother at all'. ***If only!*** Looking back, it must've been beginner's luck; there again, maybe she was just 'pullin' ma pisser'. Anyway, my services are no longer required at the hospital; so, after vacating my 5-star NAAFI accommodation and arriving back at Barracks there's a draft chit waiting for my good self. ***"Thank you God!"*** I've to report to HMS Bellerophon in Chatham Dockyard. Brilliant, that's for me, I'm ecstatic, a ship at last. I wonder what it is and where it's going? As it transpires - not a sleek warship, an' would you believe - **nowhere!** The scales are falling from my eyes, ***bigtime*** **- just what am I doing in this man's Navy?**

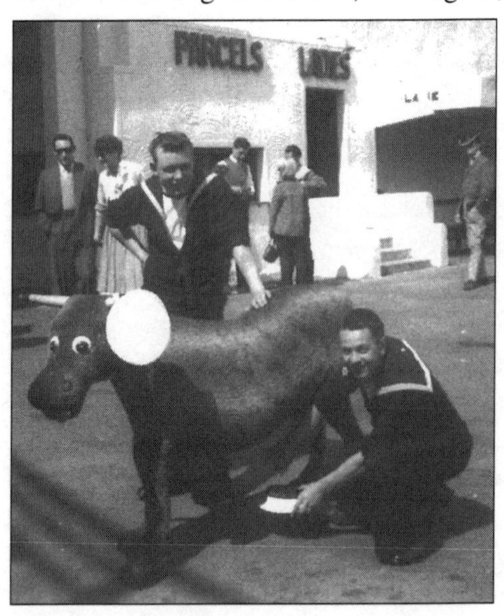

Milking it for all it's worth with 'Tiger' Timmins, Margate 1959

16: HMS Bellerophon/HMS Neptune

To my dismay, HMS Bellerophon turns out to be two old wartime 'Liberty ships' called Duncansby Head and Mull of Galloway, each about eight and a half thousand tons displacement, built in Canada around 1944 to be used as maintenance and repair depot ships; now berthed alongside each other assigned as accommodation ships with the joint name of Bellerophon. While I was serving there the 'Siamese twins' were separated and shunted into dry dock for scheduled scraping and painting. When there they were renamed, I can't recall which was which, but believe I remained on Mull of Galloway, which was renamed HMS Neptune and stayed put in Chatham Dockyard as a floating barracks. Ah'm in the dark about Duncansby Head - however, suspect she was either 'mothballed' or sent as a fleet depot ship to Faslane; the submarine base in Scotland; then in its infancy - *that last sentence may be a right load o' bollocks; so don't quote me.*

Although I thought I'd had yet another 'green rub' in finding that when I had at last got a ship, it wasn't the sleek warship of my dreams, and didn't even 'leave the wall', let alone sail the high seas, so wasn't exactly singing

Mull of Galloway going into dry dock

to me, I nonetheless lapped up being with the slovenly laugh-a-minute team I worked alongside, for the four months I was part of the crew. It was a revelation to again be bandying insults with an amusing gang o' chancers, as opposed to doin' ma head in, cooped up brooding in the 'ranch house' *dignity and self-respect in tatters* while tasked as bitch woman's slave - so my tumble from Chester's fence was a small price to pay.

There was the inevitable friendly rivalry in the Galley, as to who could make the best this and who could make the best that. One lunchtime I knocked out a curry that must've been a winner, since it received compliments no end. Obviously I'm flattered and I guess this time I'd excelled myself, since my curries are a hit or a miss and never the same twice - ah just lob in any dodgy leftovers wot need usin' up. The following day my 'Killick of the Watch' Leading Cook Sarson *who thinks I'm stealing his thunder* sees this as a challenge, so throwing down the gauntlet, gives us the "I'll show the mothers what a real curry's all about" - **did he ever!** It was so hot that the stewards told us the soft gits in the Wardroom were toiling to 'down it', sweat running from foreheads and eyes streaming while guzzling pitchers of iced water, not wanting to admit defeat - giving it the old "When I was in India" routine. A few reckless serfs with a spirit for adventure tried some, and later *unimpressed* reported that when they went forra 'pony' their ringpieces were on fire. The saying that springs to mind is **"arseholes like poppies on Remembrance Sunday!"**

Yeah, this is more like the Navy I thought I was joining: I'm not at sea but at least I'm on a ship in the dockyard and take delight in being surrounded by every type of warship imaginable, albeit most of which are 'mothballed', including the record-breaking high-speed minelayer HMS Manxman, berthed close by. So anyway, when I go up on deck for a 'shufti', I feel I'm getting closer to what I had in mind when I volunteered.

Here, brace yersel for two amusing funnies I associate with that time. One being the young Scouser who wrote home saying "Dear Mother, it's a bastard"; the reply - "Dear Son, so are you!" And the other; the 'Three-Badger' who said his missus would only 'do it' with the lights out; because she hated to see him enjoying himself *(sounds vaguely familiar)*.

Hay fever was still a problem each June and July, so that summer one of the 'Quacks' in Pembroke Barracks had conducted a series of tests to

establish just **what** I was allergic to. An antidote was then ordered from Duncan, Flockhart & Co. *a large pharmaceutical supplier* with which to inject and hopefully desensitise me. I was told that this would be spread over a period of time starting off with a minimal dose, building up to max out over a course of twelve injections. I'd forgotten all about it when one morning months later while still on, the by now, HMS Neptune I'm called to the Sickbay onboard; where this poncey Surgeon Commander gives me my first 'shot', then sends me on my way telling me my Tot will be stopped - so no rum for me today. After lunch I'm 'off watch' and as usual get my head down in the old 'mick' for a couple o' hours kip.

On surfacing, I feel grotty - big Moyesie glances at me, then, gaping,

says "Cor blimey Shiner, what's up wi' you mate?" So I say "Wha' di ya mean?" He replies "Cop a squint in the mirror an' see for yersel!" I think it can't be that bad, he must be takin' the piss, but when I look I don't even recognize myself. My coupon's so puffed up and distorted that I look like a pig; so, on everyone's recommendation I hasten back to the Sickbay, where, when the duty L/SBA sees me he panics, gets me to lie down then he's off like a whippet, heading for the Wardroom Bar to fetch Dr Dolittle, who *plastered on arrival* prances around the bed in a flap; as by this time I'm probably a lot worse than when I'd looked in the mirror earlier. He checks my pulse, which is going like an express, and injects me with something then gives me the old nod and wink, while saying "Lie there quietly for an hour and keep this to yourself!" *(no, brain damage wasn't mentioned - but maybe that clown's cock-up explains everything).*

What had happened was, the gin-soaked buffoon hadn't read the instructions properly and given me an overdose many times the amount specified. "Close one, wot!" - I can't help wondering if this did any lasting damage, as these days I have the heart of a much older man.

We, the lesser mortals, slept in hammocks on this big old ship. I don't know about now, but it was still quite the norm back then. They were the place to be, once you got the hang of them *(pun not intended)* and had given 'Norrie the Nose' *the Buffer's Mate* a wet of your Tot in exchange for a pair of hammock stretchers - these necessities were fashioned from a broomstick cut in half with a notch in each end. I can't be bothered

HMS Manxman. Fast Minelayer (40 knots max)

explaining how they worked and what they did; so you can find out for yersel' - **and, who knows?** Possibly even **you** can figure it out, because I've taught you everything **I know;** *and **you** still know fuck all!*

Anyway, ours was a big Mess 'tween decks taking about fifty guys. It had long lengths of rail attached to the deckhead *(OK... ceiling)* from which to hang the 'micks', so when a weary 'Tar' jumped up to grab the bars and swing, in an agile well-practised fashion, into his mick a tremor would run through all the other hammocks sharing the same rail.

Now, the same can be said of another activity; as the bars and likewise the hammocks would vibrate if some randy sailor was pleasuring himself by 'polishing his helmet' after reading a 'Port Said Bible' - *oh yes, 'twas a dead giveaway.* So, although you couldn't see the culprit suspended in the privacy of his cocoon, it was obvious what was going on: his patience tried, some irritated soul sharing the rail would shout **"Who's wanking?"** and it would stop for a few minutes, but always started again; ***Tut-Tut***, talk about shameless - *strange indeed are the ways of man!*

On returning from weekend Leave, Nick, a popular, career-conscious Wardroom Steward from Harrow *(one of London's posher districts)*, announced he was getting engaged at the end of the month and asked three of us if we would like to come up to 'the big city' to attend the engagement celebration party, and stay the weekend. This sounded shit-hot to us; so, on the day, Leading Officers' Cook Larry Debona hired a car and off we went for a belter of a weekend 'up The Smoke'. When introduced to 'the intended' it was more than obvious why the lucky sod wasn't letting this lovely creature slip through his fingers, ***what A cracker!***

At the party ah got masel hooked-up to a terrific girl, the 'well-to-do' best friend and future 'maid of honour' for the bride-to-be; it goes without saying that I was really attracted to this serene interesting girl, who was Jewish - I'm a sucker for them, as they always seem rather special. Anyway, after the shaloms *and 'alreadys'* we paired up - I must've made an impression - as the following week Rachael surprised me with a nice long letter and a little package containing a pair of pink woollen bedsocks, "to keep my toes warm in my hammock at night." Needless to say, I didn't dare to wear them. However, wasn't that a novel pressie? I did say she was interesting - didn't I? Nick reckoned she was ready to 'swallow me

whole', so it appeared I was 'well in there', and furthermore he said her 'old boy' was the Chairman of a large insurance company - **jackpot!**

We, it seemed, shared a mutual attraction and given half a chance I would definitely have taken things further *(so who's to know)* but regret it fizzled out when Dame Fortune smiled and I was unexpectedly drafted to HMS Tenby, which was *as luck would have it* lying close by Neptune, on the same jetty in the dockyard, so 'doin' a moonlight' to my 'new home' was a doddle - things were looking up.

Crikey! *Wonders'll never cease;* a warship, an' here's me only been in 'the Andrew' nineteen months. Probably not a record, but nonetheless not anticipated when I signed on - crosses my mind, I've been like a dog chasin' his tail an' goin' nowhere; it's ironic, if I had knuckled under, in respect of my mandatory National Service it would've been 'done and dusted' last month. Aah, but I'm much too clever for that; too right I am Squire - because then lil ole me wouldn't be joining HMS Tenby and I'm dead chuffed. ***Yes, this is for real - at last ah've 'nailed it'!***

'The Six-Five Special'

HMS Tenby - Whitby Class anti-submarine frigate

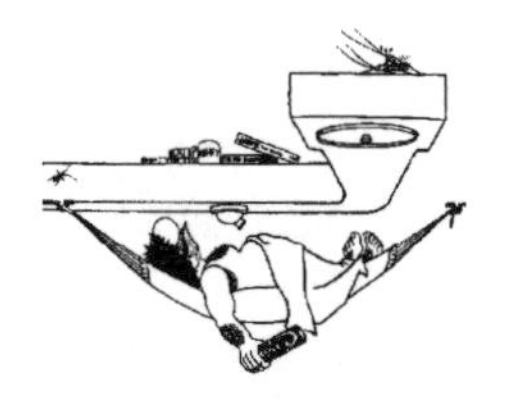

17: HMS Tenby

HMS Tenby is a Whitby Class anti-submarine frigate, the latest type launched in 1955 - only done one previous commission, which started in December '57. This, her second 'commish'; began some five months ago, so ain't I lucky as they've done the 'work up' and all the shitty jobs - **kushti!** We will leave Chatham next week, steam round to Pompey, where Tenby will join Scarborough, Torquay and Salisbury to form the Fifth Frigate Squadron, and then sail on 4TH March for deployment in the Far East - ya beauty, ah'm 'made up', ah've scored ***- wotta stonker!***

So, after pinnin' ma colours tae the mast, I tackle my joining routine and meet the guys I'm going to live and cavort with for the next year and a half. Being a Chatham ship most of the crew come from the south east, so there are plenty loud London 'widos' - always good for a laugh!

The tiny Wardroom Galley is staffed by three Officers' Cooks *(one of whom is me)*; my boss, a placid PO called Len Costen - I should mention, most Chiefs and POs had been through WWII, so deserved more respect than they got - **but that's life!** The other Wardroom cook was Raymond Sole, a two-badge Killick; mid thirties, sallow complexioned and going thin on top, nicknamed 'The Mole' as he never went on deck, or out in the sun - *maybe he knew something, way back then, that we didn't.*

The remaining Wardroom staff consisted of six stewards - one PO, two Killicks and three ODs; *like myself.* I divulge the numbers to show how well the 'chosen few' are looked after in the Royal Navy - there we have nine staff to see to the needs of fourteen Officers. Whereas the Lower Deck, totalling some two hundred Senior and Junior Ratings, was attended by only four Ships Cooks - one PO Wintie, one Killick, L/CK Bage and two ODs, 'Parky' Hannant and George Chapman. Parky was very popular with the crew; forever spouting quips, such as, when asked what the scran was, his answer was always "**Your favourite!**"

So, if you're thinking of a career in the RN, stick in at school and make sure you go to Dartmouth with the 'Toffs'; they say we're all born equal - *but some are more equal than others.* I continually marvelled at how the

'Pigs' remained slim and trim; when they got real shepherds in their pies, lived like kings and rarely as much as lifted a finger. No doubt the 'blue-bloods' put it down to good breeding - **jammy bastards!** Should any of them ever get lucky and be drafted to heaven on Judgement Day, they'll be sadly disappointed on completion of their joining routine.

And here's how the 'other half' lived: No. 8 Mess was the Officers' Cooks and Stewards' Quarters - a tiny rathole just for'ard of the bridge on the starboard side - the serfs merited 'steerage class'; down below near the waterline with no portholes. It was about eight feet by fourteen, a tight squeeze, where seven of us had to live, eat and sleep. Primitive, to say the least *by today's standards,* as there was nowhere else to go when off-duty at sea except up on deck: this explains why, when the opportunity arose, the 'bilge rats' went ashore so often - yes, the living conditions endured by those 'below decks' on warships in the 'Good Old Days' were atrocious, with asbestos everywhere,which *it now comes to light* caused many deaths on the Lower Deck, from both TB and asbestosis.

I suffered the creature comforts of this cramped compartment with L/CK(O) Sole, L/Std Packer, L/Std Lewis and the three OD stewards - Taff Hitchin, Taff Pritchard and our youngest steward Dave McAllister, christened 'Scats' by 'Lew'; our wideboy Londoner - since I'm to share such a small space with this motley crew *(who, I had wrongly thought would be a coven of old tarts)*, for the next eighteen months, I'll do a quick rundown on them in my usual fashion; hoping not to get it too wrong in the process, before continuing my meandering down memory lane.

L/Std Brian Packer; our 'sea daddy', an old hand three-badgeman, and fountain of knowledge who'd seen it all, done it all and knew how to keep the ODs in their place. Rumoured to have been a PO, but busted down to Killick due to a drink-related misdemeanour, not an uncommon occurrence in 'the Mob'; putting paid to many a promising career.

Enter L/Std Lewis; he's the type that makes you sick, a tall lean dark handsome unprincipled 'shaggin' machine' from Hampstead; all in all one slick guy with five years service under his belt, and already been to many foreign ports - a real old hand for his young years; hated the Navy, hated the 'Pigs', hated 'the Mole' *(they had fallen out before my arrival, in fact, on Christmas Day when, in a tussle for supremacy, Lew gubbed the Mole).*

The two Taffs; I can't remember where Taff Hitchin was from in Welsh Wales *(could've been Swansea),* he was a trifle swarthy, as if of Romany blood; a good worker who quietly got on with it. The other was Taff Pritchard - I apologize to both, for not remembering their Christian names, but that is usually the case with guys who get called Taff, Scouse or some such collective handle. Where was I? Oh yeah, Taff Pritchard was a soft-spoken sturdy blonde-haired chap who religiously did weight-training with the barbell and weights that he kept and 'pumped' in the Mess. I remember where he came from, because I had never heard of it before and thought Mountain Ash was such a charming name, conjuring up an image of a quaint little village nestling on a sheltered Welsh hillside.

Dave McAllister, the youngest in the Mess - at the time an Assistant Steward and therefore the Mess 'whipping boy'. Now now, don't jump to conclusions, he got plenty ribbing and was worked hard, as is the norm, but never bullied - and anyway, big enough to look after himself.

A quick note about bullying since I've used the word. We hear that it's commonplace in today's modern Army, and this could well be true. I must say there was never, in my experience, any such malarky in the Senior Service; *although stupidity was not tolerated.* Nonetheless, we revelled in continual good old-fashioned verbal-humiliation, sarcastic ribbing and banter - all part of the fun; nine times out of ten given and taken as such, but bullying I repeat **never**, and after nine years service in many places I think I qualify as credible. The nickname 'Scats', attributed to young McAllister by Lew was short for scatterbrain; something he was not - being at the foot of the pecking-order, he had so many bosses that he was forever running around, as if demented ***- good training for a lad, Wot!***

The night before we left Chatham it was decided that a wee run ashore to *my recent digs* the NAAFI Club, for a few wets would be a good idea, since it might be a while before the next opportunity arose. So, those off duty went on ahead, followed about an hour and a half later by myself and the stewards who had to provide the Wardroom evening meal.

By the time we arrived at the 'Ranch house' the party was in full swing round a big table commandeered by my new crewmates, accompanied by a sprinkling of Jenny Wrens in uniform, one of whom is a real brammer and has been trapped by L/CK(O) R. Sole, who is beaming from ear to

ear and all over her like a rash on a sick child. Having 'pulled', therefore feeling benevolent the 'smoothie' asks us newcomers what we're havin', and enthusiastically leaps up to get them in; meanwhile the 'Jenny' switches her attentions to me - I can't believe this, *ama loozin' it* - what in the name o' fuck's goin' on? Now, while I'm honoured with this transfer of affection I'm mystified, because this isn't just any old Wren, the floozy's a two-badge Killick and I'm just an OD. Normally this one wouldnae 'pish on me if ah was on fire'; so what's the score? Do 'cap tallies' of real ships make that much difference? Here, keep it up hen, dinnae stop, ah'm gettin' delusions o' grandeur, an' happy to be your plaything.

No such luck, I'm no more than a patsy - all the shrew's doing is givin' me a usin' to get shot o' Ray, who, on returning with the bevvy, takes the hump and gives me a look that could kill; wrongly concluding I've been sneaky and copped the burd that he thought he was going to charm out her knickers. Venting his anger, he slams the tray on the table wasting half its contents in the resulting splashes, then with a monstrous 'cob on', does the about-turn and seething with rage, storms off back to the ship. But, this was no storm in a teacup, 'the Mole' who clearly had issues but seemed friendly up until then, now slighted and showing his true colours, obviously despises me, and although it beggars belief, doesn't talk to me, other than professionally, for the rest of the commission. Yes, I do mean for the next eighteen months, talk about 'sour grapes', wotta bitch 'she' turned out to be, continually endeavouring to make life difficult for me the lowly OD - *even I couldn't hold a grudge that long!*

There's always a nigger in the woodpile; if anything spoiled this once in a lifetime cruise 'twas that devious cow of a Killick Wren - *and she didn't even know.* Talk about unrequited love - if she'd only stayed on track; even just letting him into her Pusser's blouse forra wee tweak at the nipples he **might** have been a different bloke, making life better for both of us.

Well, we've formed the Fifth Frigate Squadron, Pompey is history and we're now on passage to 'Gib', not looking forward to the notorious Bay of Biscay, since it's March; but it must've been the 'Bay of Tranquillity' that day - otherwise I would *'sure as eggs is eggs'* remember.

Here we are, at Gibraltar, my first foreign port - St John's, Newfoundland some two years previous didn't seem like being abroad, 'twas more like

some Scottish Highland town, but built from wood. So I'm in a real foreign port at last; L/Std Packer, who has been here 'more times than that' *and whose cat is blacker than mine* has already told me that 'he was in Baghdad before I was in dad's bag'. First chance I get I'm ashore on a mission - having been told how cheap everything is; this being a duty-free port.

Now, you'll recall how I bought that cheap crappy gold chain for my St Christopher medallion in London, well, this is what I've been waiting for, I've rifled my piggy bank, so now I'm going to splash out on a 'corker' - just watch me, ah'll show them how it's done. Ignoring all the distractions a foreign port has to offer, I spend a bit o' time 'sussing the place'; not wanting to be taken to the cleaners in some wog rip-off shop. After casing the joint, I choose a big reputable jewellers on the main drag and pay twelve 'huckle' for a well-crafted solid gold chain *(a steal, which I'd be pushed to afford here today)*. ***Mission accomplished!***

Other than a bit shopping, couple o' wets and a bacon roll in 'The Greasy Spoon' there wasn't much to do. I couldn't be arsed seeing the Barbary apes, so returned to the ship fairly early with some other ODs; who'd obviously never been abroad before - very apparent, when the plonkers ended up in the harbour, fully-dressed because "the water is warm" - **they make you proud!** I certainly didn't go up the gangway with that bunch o' eejits, as it's easy enough to tempt providence without trying.

So that was Gibraltar, not much of a place, in fact, I was discussing Gib recently with my good friend Rod McLaren, as the question of ownership had reared its ugly head yet again. He, having lived and worked there, is of the opinion that "It is nothing but a shithole, and we should let the Spaniards have it." My personal views are purely financial, if it's making money keep it; if it's costing, get shot of it! Or howzabout this! We turn the whole shebang into a mini Vegas, then sit back and 'coin it in'. Now there's a plan, but unfortunately the twats ***without vision*** running our country wouldn't wear it - being far too busy blowing the folding stuff *(think Millennium Dome; then think again)*. Whatismore, they rely on taxation to fill the *now empty* coffers; a ploy at which the 'inner circle' excel beyond comparison. ***Don't complain, you voted for the worse than useless conniving parasites!***

Next stop Malta, where we are 'anchored off' in Sliema Creek near

the destroyer HMS Dainty, and guess who's on her? Yes, it's my 'old mucker' Joe McGlinchey, who knows I'm on Tenby, so nips over at the appropriate time and mooches half my Tot; after which we have a quick run ashore down 'the Gut', but Joe has to return early, so we call it a day and, unimpressed with the place, I'm back on my ship before supper. I don't bother going ashore again in Malta, as we are only there two days - and anyway, I've been advised by Lew *a sound judge* to save my loot, as we're 'under starter's orders' and thar be good pickin's ahead.

Malta and 'the Med' are long forgotten as here we are at Port Said, lying 'anchored off', sitting in the queue wishing to take 'safe passage' through the Suez Canal, while plagued by wogs in 'bum boats' - don't remember buying any tat from Ali Baba or his persistent annoying wallah mates, who chose to ignore 'the infidels' courteous requests to "Bog off".

Our turn to 'make way' through the Canal came at six the following morning, - shan't bother describing this, as every time I went 'up top' for a dekko; *apart from the odd friendly Arab chappie hoisting the robes to moon the sailor boys,* 'twas the same old same old. We cleared Suez at midnight, then embarked the Chinese Laundry Crew and Tailor from the Squadron being relieved by us on the Far East Station. ***Wotta gift*** - recently I'd been fretting, as to how we were meant to keep these white tropical uniforms clean, while enjoying the perks o' the job ravishing coloured chicks in the Eastern boozers and brothels we were duty-bound to patronize.

These Chinese guys were ace, their charges unbelievably cheap in return for their keep and whatever food PO Wintie allocated them. I don't know if the saying widely used can be attributed to him or some wit from years past, but everyone knew the phrase "fuck'm give'm rice", commonly bandied, with no malice intended - merely yet another example of Jack's humour. There's no stopping us now, we're haring down the Red Sea bound for Aden; gateway to the promises of the mysterious Orient.

But, trouble was brewing in paradise, as the misanthropic 'Mole' *a prisoner in his own private hell* was becoming increasingly bitchy. The buzz was there'd been a 'Dear John' from 'her indoors' telling him not to even think about coming home next Leave - I would've felt sorry for him, if he hadn't been such an awkward 'opposite number' - *sod'm, ah wus overjoyed at seein' the cantankerous twat in the doldrums.*

I've already described the Wardroom Galley as small; all too evident when the three of us were jammed in preparing the Officers' lunch; so it was essential to respect each other's space. I know I shouldn't constantly berate the shitebag, but this was when Mole regularly took the opportunity to display bad manners *probably playing the intimidation card* by nudging or barging in front of me ***'The Underdog'*** without as much as a 'by your leave'. Now, I'm mild-tempered, but even the meek get riled, so occasionally was guilty of rattling his cage - I just couldn't help myself, so, getting my timing right, would give the prat a hard elbow in the ribs, then instantly apologize. Ever aware of my predicament, I had to be extremely careful - he being of higher Rate could easily have given me the old 'get your cap' routine and had me in front of the Officer of the Watch on a trumped up charge. Len knew what was going on, but he was an old pussycat who'd seen it all before, he'd spoken to Mole, who was a crafty crow; definitely a veteran of many past hate campaigns. So it was a nap that a showdown was on the cards - in essence we were all biding our time - they say 'absence makes the heart grow fonder' - *given half a chance I'd've happily helped the vindictive cunt over the side.*

We are steaming down the Red Sea; WOW! it's hot and this ship isn't air-conditioned; not something I'd taken into consideration, or even thought about until now. The deck-swabbers are consequently 'swanking it' in their Pusser's issue shorts and sandals and fair lappin' it up; but for those who work below decks especially in the engine room and galleys it's stifling. When 'off watch' most of the crew are working on their tans by getting in as much 'bronzy time' as possible, including Lew and myself who, perhaps because we both detest the Mole, have become great buddies. We, like many others, had taken to 'crashing out' under the stars on our camp beds - No.8 Mess, 'down below' being like a Swedish sauna.

Let me wise you up about the camp beds. Just as on Neptune we have hammocks which are excellent in cool climates and great in 'roughers', but cocooned in one in the tropics is murder as you and your bedding are soaked with sweat long before you get to sleep. We must therefore bless some bright spark from the past, who came up with the idea and devised a metal frame which fits into loops on the heavy canvas hammock, thus turning it into a very comfortable camp bed.

We slept on the boat deck *under a star-filled sky, that can only be described as amazing* other than when exercises didn't permit or we hit a rain squall, which would all too often sweep across the upper decks in the middle of the night, making it a case of 'lift thy bed and run'; quite funny really, bodies scurrying everywhere and jostling for a good spot in the passage *('The Burma Way')* down below. I got to be a dab hand at this, having noticed that always in advance of a squall, there was a cool breeze, so being a light sleeper, had tuned myself in to wake up when this tickled ma coupon. Eventually wideboy Lewis, using the promise of Pusser's 'jungle juice' as his lure, blagged a sheet of tarpaulin from 'Stripey' *the three-badge Buffer's Mate,* so at such times we just pulled that over the top of our comfort zone, said "Fuck it!", and drifted back into a dream-filled sleep in the arms of Morpheus; *aah, the Beverley Sisters.*

While on passage steaming down the Red Sea, Leading Seaman Findlay *'Slick'* Carr, the Duty QM, made the funniest 'pipe' I've ever heard rasping from a ship's Tannoy system. It went like this. "**Jay hey there!** There will be no moon for Junior Rates tonight. However, there will be a small moon for Chiefs and POs 'twixt the hours of 2200 and 2359; thereafter there will be a full moon for Commissioned Officers!"

We arrive and tie up alongside at Aden - Christ, it's roastin'! But I'm delighted when, my *by now* best mate, Lew tells me the score; it seems that now, being 'east of Suez', we are on 'Tropical Pay Routine'. This means we don't actually get paid, because money is of no use at sea - instead, when in port, two big barrels will be placed on the Quarterdeck, one full of rum and the other of money, to which off-dutymen going ashore help themselves to however much their needs require. Some unfortunates never made it passed the first barrel and had to be tucked up in bed by the nice Officer of the Watch. After the run ashore, if there was any dross left in your pocket, you threw it into the baying throng of guttersnipes, causing a mad scramble; just like a 'poor-oot' at a Scottish wedding. Needless to say, all the little 'cocopops' loved Jack ***- well, it sounds good to me!***

Can't remember buying any iffy merchandise while perusing the market stalls, although we did some haggling with the unscrupulous shifty-eyed street traders; just to get our hand in. But being a tight Scot, I'd long since taken the Eleventh Commandment - ***"Thou shalt not part!"*** After

the novelty of this wore thin, we found a rather exclusive Beach Club, enhanced by a bevy of tanned hootenanny sprawled out in the sun; but, unfortunately, no spare, just families. They must've belonged to 'pongoes' based in Aden; and on a cushy number by the looks of things.

Full o' the joys, we raced each other to the sea for a swim - sheer luxury, but I was none too happy on finding shark-nets securing the area. "Bollocks to that!" No way ama goin' back in the water; *maybe that's how 'Old Stumpy' had a peg leg*. I couldn't believe how hot the sand was - actually uncomfortable to walk on barefoot *(and I thought Gullane was hot on a sunny summer's day!)* So, seeing the need, we sort that one out on the spot by purchasing flip-flops - a 'must-have' in the Far East.

The Squadron had rendezvoused at Aden along with the aircraft carrier HMS Albion, and guess who was on her? None other than the man himself - Darryl F. Bailey. Wotta turn up and wotta a laugh, you'll love this - now, abroad there are, as we are all aware, plenty shopping bargains to take advantage of, so Jack is well-known for buying presents for loved ones back home, which helps salve his conscience; ***what conscience?***

I never thought to find out why, but presents bought abroad are known in the Navy as 'rabbits' so to go shopping overseas is to go on a 'rabbit run'. Well, by now, it's evening and all the young sea dogs are returning to their ships laden down with swag, including Darryl who is kicking up merry hell at the foot of Albion's gangway, because the Officer of the Watch has refused the errant Steward permission to bring his 'rabbits' on the ship. Why? you may ask. Why indeed! - well, Darryl is at it again, he's bought a real camel and a real snake - *his was a hard act to follow!*

Howzabout this for misconstruing an order! The 'buzz' was; when steaming down the Red Sea, his Divisional Officer, realizing Darryl was hard to beat, had had enough, so wanting rid of him, decided the problem was Darryl resented being a steward. His solution was to have the rebel recycled to perform seamen's duties; at which he excelled, until the day the Buffer told our erstwhile flunkey to paint the Admiral's Barge, then left him to it on the quiet boat deck. Darryl, in his usual interpretation of an order, took the Buffer at his word. He painted the Admiral's Barge; making a good job of it, in

fact he made a super job of it. He painted the ornamental brass dolphins, he painted the windows, he painted the screws, **he painted everything** - well, that's what he was told to do! When we arrive at Singapore, Darryl *(who, you'll have guessed by now, is intent on 'working his ticket')* is sent to the Base Psychiatrist, but, rest assured, we **will** come to that later.

That night we decided on a cheap run ashore, to see a movie; with Taff Davies and 'Rosie' Lee - Aden, in those days being better known for tacky souvenirs than its nightlife, so the plan was to save dosh for better times elsewhere. We went to a cinema showing an English *(or more likely American)* film, I forget what, but well remember that cinema, because, during the movie, on looking up I was surprised to see the most amazing ceiling, which reminded me of the Odeon back home with all its twinkling lights. I nudged Lew saying "Cop a look at the ceiling!"; he glanced up, then turned to me, nonchalantly replying "It's the sky ya thick cunt!" C'est moi Monsieur - it's not often I'm right, but I'm wrong again. ***Yeah, that's me, the ship's idiot!*** *So, how much are the magic beans then?*

Aden is but a distant memory as we sail some two thousand nautical miles across the Indian Ocean, bound for Colombo in Ceylon. Yeah! Yeah! I know it's called something else now - what's that all about then? It's still the same place; so what's the point? I'll give you a pound to a pinch o' shit that there's a dose o' punters who'd go to Ceylon for a holiday. Remember it? - the place where that nice tea came from; but Sri Lanka? Where the bleedin' hell's that? Oh yeah, that's the joint where these crazy Tamil Tigers are blowin' people to bits, isn't it? ***Fuck goin' there!*** Anyway, back in **'the happy days'** - remember them - *when Andy Pandy got chucked off TV for Muffin the Mule* it was called Ceylon.

To me it was a miniature India, with its people looking the same as those of its near neighbour; to which the island was obviously joined at the beginning of time. So, that's it! As far as I'm concerned, they're all descended from the same primitive tribe - wha'diya mean, 'tunnel vision'?

In many foreign ports the Navy visit trips are organized for Jack; so I took the opportunity to go with a coachload of young eager beavers to a sun-drenched fairytale beach; just like I'd seen on travel posters. Golden sand, blue sea, palm trees - *the whole bit!* But, you know wot; in all the years since, I've thought and told people it was called Kandy. Well, I guess

I must've had more than my fair share out of that big barrel o' rum I told you about, because I've just consulted my atlas and see Kandy is slap bang in the middle of the island - mmm, so whae kens whair we went!

So what! It was as nice a beach as I've ever set eyes on, with the added bonus being, a fat old 'Indian' wifey in flowing regalia and colourful headscarf, selling us juicy pineapples for 'washers'. She chopped them into generous slices with fast precise sweeping strokes from the well-honed flashing silver blade of her razor-sharp machete. This, to me, looked like a dangerous occupation, but she must've had a good eye and steady hand; because all the fingers were still there.

Now then, thinking about that has reminded me that my old mate from Victory Barracks, Jim Shannon, had been drafted *or so I was told* to HMS Scarborough; so I was hoping to meet up with him in one of the ports 'out East'. But, on making enquiries, was informed by one of his crewmates that he had been the ship's butcher and *'somehow'* managed to chop off one of his thumbs with a meat cleaver when 'shiters' after a lively session at 'tot time', so because of this *'accident'* had been invalided back home forra bit o' major surgery in Haslar Naval Hospital. How much truth that story held, I never found out, but heard sometime later he had been medically discharged from 'the Andrew' and working as a postie in Edinburgh. I tried to contact him when, next, home on Leave, but never managed; although I knew he and his wife, Jean, lived in Grove Street, ah wus onna loser, because ah couldnae remember the number or location of their flat.

On leaving Ceylon, the flotilla steamed further across the Indian Ocean and down the Malacca Straits to Singapore - **'Singers'**, this is what it's all about; now we really are in the Far East. It's a month since we left Pompey, so them wot got in some bronzy time are lookin' fit, tanned an' 'ealthy. But - *and there's always a but,* not everyone is glowing as **one of the crew has already 'copped a dose'** and would you believe, he's a pillar of the Establishment - yes, the buzz is one of the *Officers* is 'pishin' broken bottles'. Now, although it's a safe bet that the Captain was far from amused, the Lower Deck thought this epiphany **"pure dead brilliant!"**

There are no secrets on small ships, especially when the Medic is an old tart of a three-badge Killick SBA. Yep, the bender was a gossip; bless 'her'. No matter what the affliction, if you went to see 'Doc' the first thing

'she' would say was "Drop your trousers sweetie!" Yeah - *he was an old poof, but he was our poof.*

There 'she' goes, on 'her' toes
Chasing arseholes I suppose

Life's full of coincidences - *there's no doubt about that.* We've just tied up 'alongside' in the huge strategic Naval dockyard at Singapore, I've popped along the jetty to ditch the gash and the very first person I meet is Benny Wilkie; well 'bugger me sideways', you go to the other side of the world and there, standing in front of you is an old pal from home. He was an EM on the ocean-going fleet tug HMS Warden berthed in front of us; due to sail later that day. On saying that, I have a nagging suspicion that it may've been HMS Reward - no matter which, knowing Benny, he would've invited himself round to scrounge a generous wet *(gulpers)* of my 'bubbly'; *how come it's never the other way round?*

Now then, where was I? Oh yeah Singapore! 'Singers' this is the place to be, I've never experienced anything like it; this is the original Sin City; Jack's playground - it's cheap, it's dirty, it's all here and **everything** is negotiable. **I love it!** - now hold on, in case you're thinking 'what's this soft git on?' Let me explain. This was back in 'nineteen oatcake' before sweeping changes were made and, I hasten to add, many for the better.

Way back in 1963 an honourable farsighted chappie known as Mr Lee Kwan Yew took the helm, forming a dictatorship which has the people's blessing. He then transformed the island into the enviable modern well-heeled State it is today - ***while Britain frittered away the Great!***

Some may think the laws draconian, but they work; with fines dished out for anything considered a wrong doing; such as spitting, littering, chewing gum, public nudity - *so beware all you exhibitionists;* and as for drugs - **well! How does the death penalty sound?** They call it 'Fine City' and it is a fine city so take note all you weak-willed kowtowing politicians and politically correct self-righteous clowns with lunatic ideas, who between you have ruined our **once great** country. My point being - are you scared to do what you were elected for **and what the people want?** OK; enough o' that! ***- Ah'm just another voice in the sodding wilderness.***

Let's go ashore; yes sir that's where I'm going with my mate and mentor Lew, who has been here before. He was on HMS Warrior when she was

on the first mission to take part in experiments involving the H-bomb detonated at Christmas Island - *apparently,* the crew were lined up on deck to witness the event; which for sure sounds foolhardy and irresponsible to me. However that's another story, the protocols of which we will all hear more in the future. *I'm informed a web page and an association are being put together as I pen this account *(it'll be amusing to see how the MoD, in their usual fashion, wriggle out of this one).*

So, pockets jinglin' we're ashore on a quest in Singers, thinking we cut a dash all togged up in our crisp 'tropical whites' - Lew telling me in no uncertain terms how he's going to "bury the Vomiting Cobra". By jingo! This guy was like the Pied Piper, and I, the impressionable young green OD, encouraged by 'Shagnasty's' enthusiasm *and eager to participate* am gaily skipping along in his wake, hungry for experience. ***Game on!***

At first the place doesn't do it for me - busy roads, shoddy buildings - plenty stalls selling everything imaginable, at prices you'd love. Not the cleanest and a trifle whiffy, especially near what I thought to be a river somewhere around the city centre, but, judging by the foul stench wafting from it, may well've been a typhoid riddled open-sewer.

I'm beginning to think this guy's got it wrong and lose faith in his abilities when Lew takes me to 'The Happy World' - it's a fairground, but nothing like back home. I'm not a exactly jumpin' wi' joy and to make matters worse, need a 'pony an' trap' and can't see anything vaguely like a toilet. After a bit o' huntin' we find what we are told is a 'khazi', so in I go to wave goodbye to an old friend, and, **blimey!** - there it is - **a hole in the ground**; the place is tiny, unlit and grotty, I'm scared to touch anything and you know what I'm going to say - don't you? **there's no paper!** This is gruesome - I'd rather not use the place, but have no choice, when you gotta go, you gotta go! So I rush to a stall, with that look o' desperation on ma coupon and buy a copy of - now wait for it; this is sheer class, **'The Beano'.** So, there I am in the middle o' Singapore wipin' ma erse on Biffo the Bear, wi'oot a shred o' dignity ***- shit happens!***

When I catch up with the hunk, ah'm well impressed as he's targeted and propositioned two enchanting Malayan girls 'suitable for purpose', who take us to their hovel in a warren nearby ***- and so it begins!!!*** There was no privacy while we had our wicked way with them, but at least they had

separate beds. With the deed done and the baws emptied, my accomplice says "Can I have a shot of yours?" Crivvens! now yer talkin' Baby - 'twould seem our suave Leading Steward is no more than an animal; this greedy git wants two for the price o' one. So, with the girls giggling while pointing at Lew and saying "Yoa is buttafly" the 'jockeys' swap mounts, grab the reins and again sprint to a photo finish - after our 'standing ovation' I conclude, it's Jack's birthright to fraternize with 'the enemy'.

Following our midday workout, we're swaggering down the road *whistling merrily* with a newly-found spring in our step, proud to have served our country, doing what sailors are expected to do and rejoicing in the knowledge that we have nine months of this cruise in front of us. Before you ask; yes, we did practise safe sex - back in **'the happy days'** *before AIDS*, safe sex meant giving your best pal's name and address!

Well, **dipsy-doo,** all that under the belt and it's not even teatime. My knight in shining armour says "Come on, I'll show you the Brit Club" - *the Britannia Club;* this was a Services Club, scrupulously clean, cheap and well run. Across the road is the Raffles Hotel; even I had heard of that legendary elitist establishment. It looked 'oldie worldie' conjuring up visions of films seen in a previous life at the Ritz cinema - I could easily picture the likes of Oscar Wilde and Noël Coward elegantly draped around shining smoked glass tables in a lavish art deco-style room with ceiling fans whispering sedately overhead; gentlemen in tropical Savile Row tailored suits, sucking on fat Cuban cigars *handrolled on the inner thighs of fit young virgins* while sipping cocktails from tall dew-frosted crystal glasses - this ambience complemented by several beautiful slender ladies, clad in long fashionable silk evening gowns of the period, perched chatting gaily on tall bamboo stools, their elbows on a gleaming mirror-topped kidney-shaped bar tended by an immaculate barman, 'decked out' in pinstriped waistcoat, bow tie and slicked-down brylcreemed hair.

I just had to see this opulent reserve of the aristocracy for myself; if only to be able to say in the future "I've been there!" - after all, this has to be everyone's dream of gracious living. So, dodging trishaws, over the road and in we go - and yes, it's more or less how I imagined, minus *of course* Oscar and his suave elite clan. The impressive entrance and foyer were cool, quiet and minimalist with several smart showcases displaying expensive

goods to tempt 'well-to-do' guests into parting with fistfuls of 'Dollahs'. Strangely I can't remember the bar we graced, the possible reason being that it was, as expected. However, I do know that we were recommended *and had* the speciality of the house; a 'Singapore Sling', then headed for the Brit Club, before our wallet alarms were triggered.

The Brit Club; nice place built around a good-sized swimming pool rather than a courtyard; *as would be in cooler climes*. It wasn't somewhere we frequented, except for 'nosh'; and, with the architecture being utilitarian I won't attempt to describe it in any great detail. Being late afternoon and having enjoyed a bit action *which stimulates one's appetite* we were feeling the pangs of hunger, so the Club's praiseworthy restaurant was 'the order of the day', where we chose and got wired into a tasty scran of 'flied lice', 'flied plawns' and nasi goreing, which we divvied up between us and washed down with some thirst-slaking icecold Tiger Gold Medal Beer.

Before continuing, I'll explain that Tiger and San Miguel were the popular beers 'out East' at that time, so there was no question, you either drank one or the other, and often both, ***well aware of the consequences.***

Now then, we've been fed and watered and it's still 'early-doors', far too soon to even contemplate returning to the ship - the night *like us* is young - so off we trot for a wee rake around; that's when we bump into Johnny Gamble and two of his 'oppos'. Johnny is a stoker who lives in the MEs' Mess back aft, but often frequents our cave, strangely, always at 'tot time', with his guitar, when the convivial young troubadour sings a few songs in exchange for a couple o' 'wets'. We rarely return the visit, as it's pointless since his Mess has more than its quota of 'Three-Badge rumrats'; so we'd be busy getting a sniff o' their 'gibber-juice', never mind anywhere near the highly-prized and jealously guarded 'rum-fanny'.

We follow each other into the nearest trendy bar forra 'wee livener'; being 'early doors' it's empty, so we're sussing out the bar staff as to what might be the best place to spend the evening, when *grinning slyly* the 'Pied Piper' says "Let's go to Bugis Street." Well, I don't know about the stokers, but I've never heard of Bugis Street *now Bugis Village* and think the worldly-wise Leading Steward has said Boogie Street, so this sounds good to me, as once again my mind is working overtime - I must be one of life's romantics, because I'm mentally picturing a street full o' swingin'

Piano Bars and Jazz Joints - you know; New Orleans style.

I couldn't be more wrong, **it's the red-light district** - so the stokers are happier than pensioners in a charity shop. This Lewis is some machine; *when it comes to women he's like a jet propelled rat up a drainpipe.*

Bugis Street is jumpin'; it's like a set in a movie, stalls selling everything from Chinese food *the pungent aromas are delightful,* to cheap tourist junk and paper dragons. Furthering this colourful scene hawkers are pushing fake Zippo lighters and trinkets galore, whilst circling the beer stalls; so the team settle amidst this wonderful chaos to sink a few 'Tigers'. I said it was the red-light district; and it could hardly be that without the girls.

The girls indeed! It was heavin' wi' droves o' saucy little honey-coloured Susie Wongs provocatively posing in doorways and parading, 'ten a penny', around the street in slinky silk cheongsams with demure high collars and splits 'up to there' displaying the wares - ***Oh, be joyful!***

Talk about magic - these 'street girls' are young and getting lovelier with every gulp of Tiger. There's nothing seedy, and no stigma attached to this licentious behaviour; out here it's a way of life - they've got to eat and young guys need to get their 'Nat 'King' Cole'. After all, we're only passing through; long courtships paving a path to the inevitable end result are impossible for us. So, it's a case of "wham bam thank you Mam of course I love you, no shit Baby; the money's on the table!"

Hey, I didn't make the rules and there's no disguising the fact that this lot are 'floggin' their mutton', even an idiot would get the message on hearing such an upfront sales pitch as, "Yoa cum wiff me sailah boy, foh a few dollahs I giff yoa sumfing yoa nevah haff befoe." At the next table, a Jock with a heavy Glaswegian accent, retorts "Aye, whit's that then hen, **leprosy?**" There's plenty banter and everyone's having a ball, including the slutz who every so often can be seen taking an intoxicated matelot in hand and leading him off for who knows what purpose; and those trying to get their hole "foh flee" being told "Nevah appin sailah boy!"

Needless to say 'old hand' Lew *a stickler for tradition* feels obliged to display his leadership qualities and show the naive ODs what it's all about; so within minutes he's on his feet slinking off with one of the girls while glancing back over his shoulder grinning at his protégés and shouting "Look after the gear boys, I'll be back" - one by one my shipmates are

disappearing. Now, **really**, I had no such intentions; but you know how it is - emboldened by the lager I've downed and not wanting to lose face, I seek solace in the arms of a cute little, almond-eyed Eastern princess. I could get used to this - three different burds on one run ashore. ***And, so it came to pass, that I was proclaimed an 'old hand'!***

That night, while negotiating our way up the gangway to our sleek warship in the wee small hours, Lew - a professor in the 'University of Life' furthers my education in telling me "A slut is something you find in the gutter and drag down to your own level."

With Singapore being the main British Naval Base for the Far East Station we always return for maintenance and Shore Leave after deployment; so in our ten months 'out East' we spent in excess of eleven weeks there, and although every night wasn't a 'nookie run', most were. Therefore suffice to say, many were repeat performances of my debut, but never again a 'hat-trick', so I won't keep banging on about the obvious, but must mention Bugis Street one more time before moving on.

Sung to 'La donna è mobile'
Arseholes are cheap today
Cheaper than yesterday
Standing up or lying down
They'll cost you half a crown

Now, cop this, when *once again* in Bugis Street, who should we see but Doc, lurching towards us - I recall 'Cock' Roach saying "It's a blank week, he'll be after pressin' the flesh of a 'smally boy' at half price." - we got paid fortnightly, so everything was cheaper on a blank week to entice us ashore; *that's enterprise for you!* Anyway, LSBA R.Spandit is blitzed, and, looking like a walking scranbag the old 'sweetie-wife' staggers past without as much as a "Yoo-hoo Boyz!" quick as a flash Johnny Gamble came out with a classic, on saying "A drunken arse carries no steaming lights." This had us all ending ourselves - maybe I shouldn't have joined in, because the very next day I had toothache compelling me *as nervous as an 'altar boy' summoned to the vestry* to visit 'Betty's Boudoir'.

After the old dame's "Drop your trousers and assume the position" routine in 'her' affected falsetto voice, and my "For fuck's sake Doc, it's toothache", 'she' makes out a chit and sends me to the 'tooth fairy' in

HMS Terror - *the RN Barracks next to the dockyard.* I'm aghast when Dr Pullem, a big rough Scotch rugby-type 'two-ringer', yanks the culprit out in two minutes flat, and before I know it I'm back through the dockyard, in shock, spitting blood, but luckily in nice time to be sedated by my rum ration at 'Up Spirits', which helps me forget the sorry episode.

Mentioning HMS Terror has jogged my memory - you'll no doubt recall me reporting Officers' Steward Bailey's update in Aden; well *as promised* when Albion docked at Singapore, he was sent to be assessed by the Psychiatrist in Terror - after studying Darryl for a week the 'trick-cyclist' agreed with the earlier diagnosis, in recommending our hero should remain *well supervised* on seamen's duties - problem solved. ***We'll see!***

Another snippet relating to Terror has surfaced - hidden within the grounds there was a beautifully built swimming pool with its tower of four diving platforms and a springboard, this ideal hangout was complemented by tiled changing-rooms with showers. 'Twas a credit to the man responsible for its existence and also to those for its upkeep; at all times immaculate. We were well impressed with this retreat, and amused by the faithful old retainer always 'on watch' with his refrigerated barrow, from which he sold ice cream, frozen Mars bars and chilled drinks. We made good use of this excellent facility, spending off-duty afternoons lazing there in the tropical sunshine. **Yeah, them were good times!**

Once, through nothing more than sheer bad luck, we spent the night there - an' this 'ere's how it came about. We frequently graced the Imperial Dockyard; however, this time not 'against the wall', but 'fastened to' Hartland Point, a fleet maintenance ship, stuffed to the gunnels with machine shops swarmin' wae 'tiffies' *(artificers)* in sweat-stained blue 'ovies'. This large vessel *(similar to Mull of Galloway)* was moored to a buoy in the dockyard and we were attached to her for a 'self-maintenance period' prior to an exercise; so this meant using Liberty Boats to get ashore and back, *always an inconvenience, but never a deal breaker!*

The last returning Liberty Boat each evening was at 23.59 and our giddy gang of high rollers had missed it by a 'baw hair'; even though the native taxi driver *encouraged by us* had his foot to the boards, caning it all the way back. Rather than hang around the jetty until morning waiting for the first Liberty Boat, we decided to make for the nearby Terror swimming

pool, where we could have a kip on the chairs round the pool.

On arrival the plan gets shot to ribbons, as there are no chairs *(seems, the ever-efficient staff stow them away each night)*. We think about 'crashing out' on the deck until Taff Davies - a plucky young seaman with dark curly hair, a winning smile and a big gold earring, says "What about snakes?", so right enough; fuck that for a game o' soldiers. Next suggestion - we could doss down on the diving boards, which are covered in coconut matting. So, some of us clamber up the ladders for a 'butchers' but agree that could be dangerous, as we might roll off in our sleep. That's when our 'sea lawyer' 'Foxy' Fowler shouts "Get yer arses down 'ere, we're in luck, one of the changing-rooms is open."

The entrance is a full height turnstile and Foxy's spot on, it's not locked, so, dead chuffed, in we go to get our weary heads down for a bit o' zonking time on the slatted benches, using our caps as pillows - knowing we'll easily make it to the jetty for the Liberty Boat, come morning.

Next morning it's all happenin', as we now have daylight - it was pitch dark when we entered. We make use of the ablutions, to perform our morning ritual and are ready to go, when it transpires we can't get out as the turnstile *of course* only goes one way and the other, for getting out, is locked. **Oh, shite!** There are no windows to climb through just horizontal slits near ceiling height, for ventilation and light; assuming we could get up there they are too narrow, even for lean fighting machines to squeeze through, sod it, we're trapped! Panic stations - we'll be posted missing! We're adrift! No two ways about it, **heads *will* roll!**

But, ***hallelujah!*** God smiles on his faithful servants. The pool staff 'turn to' early doors, setting us free in time to get back to Tenby on the Liberty Boat and pick up our station cards from 'big 'Arry 'Arris', the Duty QM, before being classed 'adrift'. *(In later years the 'well 'ard' Harry Harris, I'm told, made a name for himself on the wrestling circuit).*

While docked in Singers for maintenance periods stretching as long as eighteen days, various events were organized to keep Jack happy - *and out of trouble,* such as canoe trips down mosquito-infested jungle rivers, coach trips inland to places of interest, a Swimming Gala, a visit to Slim Barracks *(a Gurkha Camp near Singapore)* and 'Banyans' - the Naval name for a glorified picnic. This 'Jolly' entails going off in an 'MFV'

Shiner and Lew, Singapore 1960

(Motor Fishing Vessel) to a deserted island with loads o' grub and copious amounts of bevvy for a glorified piss-up. I remember going on many a Banyan, although returning was often hazy - anyway, the first one sticks in my mind *(everyone remembers their first time!* **don't they?**), because on this little jaunt we took the NAAFI Canteen Manager's Assistant, Kevin Dobie, a scrawny, confirmed airhead, no' long oot o' nappies.

Before continuing, I'd better tell you that onboard Tenby we had a small NAAFI shop; which was no more than a little caboose with a narrow hinged-counter at the door, this godsend was situated halfway down the main passage, where we could buy all sorts of necessities and goodies - just like a very small corner shop. This tiny store was run by two civilian NAAFI staff for the commission - I regretted not buying one of their 'specials' early in the trip, when they had a few Omega watches which were, I'm sure, less than ten quid a piece; but when Lew explained how many runs ashore I could have for the price *being 'strapped' at the time* I swithered and they were quickly gone: ***yes, he who hesitates is lost!***

It's our first Banyan, the half-sozzled pissheads are swinging from trees, jumping in the 'oggin' or just lying 'flaked out' on the beach. ♫ "Mad Dog of an Englishman goes out in the Midday Sun". ♫ Them wot 'aven't

been ‘catchin’ rays’ are looking a touch red; particularly so, the peely-wally Canteen Assistant, ‘crashed out’ on the sand - *probably ‘tanked up’*. Eventually ‘Pricky’ Price notices how red the lad’s back is and wakes him; **oh yes** - Kevin was in pain and by the time we returned to Tenby his back was one huge blister with Kev in agony, fighting back the tears. This put him in Sickbay, where he had to suffer the old knobhound prancing around fussing over him for a week, poor chap. “Hey Doc, this medicine don’t arf give yer a sore arse!” “Quiet now young man, you’re delirious!”

I’ve mentioned one of the ‘Jollies’ was to the Gurkha HQ at Slim Barracks, where those wishing to chill out would be honoured guests in the Sergeants’ Mess. A football match had been scheduled - apart from that, it was ‘our call’; this sounded like a good skive, so the freeloaders quickly swamped the list, newly pinned on the main noticeboard outside Coxswain Bunting’s office. I know both Lew and Johnny Gamble took advantage of that weekend, and have a notion that the contingent included our stroppy OD ‘Jack Dusty’ ‘Jesse’ James - a loose cannon, said to have supped with the Devil and no stranger to a bit o’ ‘bovver’; due to many minor skirmishes after differences of opinion with those higher up the food chain. Anyway, that Easter *treated like visiting royalty* we lazed round the pool guzzling Gurkha Rum; and managed to consume their duty-free beer ration for the month. As to the football match; ***je ne sais quoi!***

Although the world was our oyster, we often got no further than the rowdy Fleet Canteen where the problems of the world would be put to rights by the hopheads; when not partaking in the ‘Dance of the Flaming Arseholes’or trading yarns while downing foaming pints of ‘Tiger’ on a Sunday ‘lunchtime sesh’. Following many a heated altercation it wasn’t unknown for a punch-up to erupt; with the Brits and Aussies *pished as handcarts* setting about each other like rabid dogs. That dockyard canteen will have seen some action over the years - aye; “if walls could talk”.

Filled with the spirit of adventure one afternoon, I went to Gillman Army Barracks near Singapore with the usual team and two Yank sailors *(Butch and Davis)* a pair o’ ‘no good hoss thiefs’ we’d met when exercising with their ship - the old two-stack destroyer USS Gurke.

How we knew about it, or why we went there eludes me, but we must’ve known it had a pool, as I have photos of us there in our ‘cossies’ clutching

'fresh young snatch'. We were all pleasantly surprised with this beautifully landscaped equatorial haven, which could've passed for an exclusive country club - *the 'cannon fodder' lived well.* The most amazing thing was, that when casting an eye over the hootenanny *as one does* I recognized a girl, lounging on a deckchair by the pool. **Surprise! Surprise**! - it was Shirley Hickman; her parents, you'll remember, owned the shop at Logie Green Road *(memories of super-duper Cornish 'nasties').* I hadn't seen Shirley for about six years; so, after her explaining that she was married to a soldier stationed there, we renewed our acquaintanceship with a good old chinwag. Well now, if they ever got a better posting than that, they were indeed lucky, since this idyllic place was Shangri-La.

I didn't intend to mention Bugis Street again, but this 'little beaut' is a must. It was a 'blank week', so we were 'boracic' and shouldn't have been out to play, but you know how it is, sometimes you yearn for freedom; *don't forget, we were travelling 'steerage' below decks.* Nevertheless Bugis Street was the last place we should've been when 'the well wus dry', but Lewis *(who could be described as a wrong 'un)* had nagged me into going there with him, an' champin' at the bit forra ride, cops this essence burd *that he can't afford,* and guess what? She gives **him** money - for services rendered - and, screamin' for more, pays our taxi fare back to the dockyard on the understanding that he'll return at the weekend.

Few have left Bugis Street better off than on entering, so he must've given'r 'a guid seein' tae' - this womaniser was totally dedicated to his chosen contact sport, and should've had a loyalty card. Now, don't misinterpret events; although dishevelled and the worse for wear, 'Hampstead's finest' was walking normally after the encounter, and I'm prepared to testify *on oath* that it was a burd, not a big 'Bootneck' sergeant in drag.

C'mon, lets have another shot at Singapore before moving on - looking for something different, we had been taken by a taxi driver to the Rodeo Club; a nightclub on the top floor of a newish high-rise building - a real smart gaff, with plenty hookers, a mini dance-floor, a 'chinky' rock 'n' roll tribute band and a huge bar. The downside was the 'khazi' being far from adequate, so there's a queue waiting to 'point Percy at the porcelain' and we're in it, Gamble, ever the clown *(madder than a March hare)*, says "Fuck it", opens a tilting window, unleashes the dick and he's pishin' oot

the windae. Remember we are about a hundred feet up, so the 'fountain of youth' has a long way to go and gather momentum. I guess, there must have been a thin corrugated tin roof at ground level in the backyard, as, crikey, you should've heard the noise this gusher was making, on hitting it. This of course caused fits of laughter, and with half-cut matelots being big daft laddies others followed suit increasing the crescendo.

I don't remember if anyone scored or how the evening ended, but who can blame me, since that memory wipes the slate of all else. Who ama kiddin' - **even I don't believe that!** We scored every night, as long as we had 'Dollahs' to spend. You didn't need to be a good-looking stallion in those days; just willing to 'part'. Yeah, that's right, it was all too easy to fall by the wayside on hearing invitations, such as "Yoa wan' jig-a-jig sailah boy?" from these petite lithe winsome smooth-limbed beauties.

Okay, so we've been in Singers for three weeks, and by now well ahead o' the game - but duty calls, so it's time for pastures new when we *reluctantly* put to sea to join the Yanks and Aussies in the South China Sea and Pacific Ocean, for a ginormous multi-national SEATO exercise code-named 'Sealion' *(contrary to opinion, it wasn't all play).*

Now, let me tell you that Jack and the Wardroom see exercises and warships through totally different eyes. There's nothing gung-ho about Jack, he sees exercises as a 'loada clap' and warships as things to live on while travelling the world in search of a good time, and **that's it.** The Officers regard exercises as war games *(Lew referred to the 'Pigs' as "war-mongering bastards")* and think warships are toys, with which to play their games. The Toffs are well aware of the Lower Deck's attitude to both them and their indulgences, but tolerate the situation because without the trained monkeys, their toys wouldn't work; putting paid to the war games - consequently they'd be out of a job; and a very cushy number, if the truth be told. That said, it's obvious that I'll have little more opinion on the subject - and we mustn't let them get ideas beyond their station! By the way, that reminds me, I never told you my 'action station' was in the Magazine, way down in the bowels of Tenby below the twin 4.5 cannons up for'ard; hot, sweaty and not a nice place to be - **oh how I suffered!** all that training, only to end up as no more than a 'powder monkey'!

Well now! Do you remember Darryl? Yes, of course you do, he's that

'seaman' chappie on HMS Albion, isn't he? Well, guess what? Albion is with the British Task Force on 'Sealion', in fact she's the 'Command-Ship', and no doubt full to the gunnels with 'top brass' - *Pip, Pip, jolly good show!* It's the middle of the Pacific at black o'clock and the young varlet is duty 'lifebuoy ghost'; this is the Rating on watch at the 'blunt end' whose task is to throw a lifebelt to anyone unlucky enough to fall over the side, and then make the Bridge aware of the situation.

The ever vigilant Darryl is bored out his tits, so overcome by temptation, clicks on the ship's Tannoy and pipes **"Man overboard!"**. This brings the exercise to a grinding halt and, causing havoc, has ships of all the Navies taking part, frantically searching the Pacific Ocean until sunrise for this non-existent man. Needless to say, that was the last we heard of Darryl F. Bailey for quite sometime; but, be told, he **will** be back.

Our next 'port of call' is Manila in the Philippines for a couple of days. Blimey, this place is 'high-octane', the dockyard just reeks o' dosh, and is jam-packed wi' warships; these Yanks sure know how to make their presence felt. Everything seems so efficient, it's streamlined, modern and looks just like a mini, *but still big* San Diego type USN dockyard - *as I've seen in 'the thrupny scratchers'* so I guess all the American Naval dockyards are architecturally similar. A strong contrast to our own, which muddle along, looking so archaic and rundown that I doubt they've been modernised since before the First World War; it really is a wonder that we get by. Talk about underinvested; but yes, it's the same old story no matter what. Industry, railways, roads, NHS, police, everything falling to pieces about us, through lack of investment **and bad management**. The only thing we excel at is taxation, so, tell me - where does all the money go? ***Seems we get shafted frae arsehole tae breakfast time!***

Maybe I'm biased and peering through rose-tinted glasses, but listen - them thar varmints get paid packets, everything in the States is cheaper - which points to a better lifestyle; *'Buddy, can you spare a dime?'*. In saying that, nothing's perfect - there's always the flip side. What if, on going to the American Consulate - when trying to dodge National Service, I'd been spirited into the USAF? Look at it this way - I might well've been sent to Vietnam, got my legs blown off and ended up as a paperweight on some Five Star General's desk in the Pentagon!

Yahoo! This is Manila, Lew and myself have heard all about it and, rarin' to go, leap ashore to see for ourselves. The first thing we notice is the security; this is tight, there are chain-link fences, compounds, gates and guards galore - every fucker has a gun, except us. We finally get let out the dockyard through a heavy wire-mesh gate - OK; hazard a guess, as to what we're looking for! That's it; got it in one - **the 'Tufty Club!'**

Let the good times roll; wotta place this is, talk about hustle bustle, with the emphasis on hustle - it's like coming from a quiet Middle England garden fête straight into a New Year's party in a lunatic asylum. There are crazy native taxi drivers clamouring to take us to "Yallabah foh flee", which translates to "the Yellow Bar for free" - so they're on 'commish', meaning it'll be an expensive joint full o' slappers. Well, dipsy-doo, that's a good start, just what we had in mind; so we're off smartish to pay our respects - **aye, you've got tae get yer priorities right!**

Cor, if you'd seen the taxis - ex-Yank WWII Willys jeeps, dickied up to the hilt, all chrome and bright colours and believe me, much brighter when in front of you under a seering tropical sun. That's not all, they're driven by maniacs; I thought the Singapore taxi drivers were pretty hairy the way they threw their diesel Mercs around, but they were placid, if compared to these 'cowboys'. It was like little America, the streets loupin' wi' Plymouths, Chryslers and 'Caddys', huge neon signs, night clubs and bars with inviting names like the Miami Club, The Loaded Dice and Sunset Strip. This was a real servicemen's run ashore, geared up in pursuit of the 'Almighty Yankee Dollah' catering for all their needs, while *quickly* 'trousering' the 'Greenbacks'; ***wot an atmosphere!***

We arrive at the 'Yallabah', and yes, it's Jack's natural habitat - **a minge minefield,** hoachin' wi' early revellers, noisy servicemen in uniforms of every description drinking and dancing with local fud to a blaring jukebox that has Connie Francis beltin' out 'Lipstick on your Collar' *which Jack had long since reworded to 'Lipstick on your Chopper'*. It's heavin' wi 'spare' offering their bodies - some poised with legs akimbo, coyly fanning themselves by flicking their dresses up and down, and in so doing, 'flashin' the dish' while waiting to be picked up, propositioned and shafted by the as yet unattached punters. On seeing this Leading Steward Lewis is in his element an' ah'm well pleased, as genetic selection is unimportant, and,

yes, this just has to be 'snatch heaven' ***in glorious technicolour.***

Now, the original plan was to have a sniff around Manila first off; then pull some skirt in the evening and be back onboard before curfew, which was set at 01.00. Well, it goes without saying that the plan was 'arsed' the second we stepped into that taxi, and now with us in the 'Yallabah' Lew's got a sniff o' fanny, so that's it, we're goin' for an 'empty oot' and we are goin' now by the looks o' things. Because in a jiffy two chicks have latched on to us; they're not exactly oot the cast o' 'South Pacific' but yiv got tae take whit ye kin get - *'any port in a storm'*. It only takes one dance with the Jezebels rubbing their pert bodies encouragingly against us; we're hooked - after explaining we don't want to buy it - only rent it, a price is hastily negotiated and *like the Jew's foreskin* we're off.

Behind this gaudy American facade is 'shanty town' - grinning like imbeciles *while pawing the goods* we're led by the toggle into this rickety hut on stilts. Lavish, it isn't, a couple o' cheap beds seperated by a tattered 'mozzie' curtain, a plywood table, two chairs and that's yer lot. These prostitutes are destitute! Now, I realize that men of our position shouldn't be seen in such a place - but you're not going to tell anyone; **are you?**

On leaving, 'wrecked' after doing 'the business' for buttons *(afternoon rates, a lotta bang for yer bucks)* I remarked "That must've been the worst jump I've ever had", Shagger's instant reply being "I've never had a bad ride in my life; it's just some are better than others." Ah like the way this guy thinks, and admire his philosophy - talk about blasé. OK, we've started the day with a 'bang', now we'll go sightseeing; should've been the other way round, but it's evident we're a pair o' weak-willed pushovers. However, that was then and this is now, and I, being a shallow creature, am glad I got 'some' when ah had a 'full hoose'.

We get to what I'll describe as 'Manila proper'; since I've no idea of district names and believe that there are even other cities which link-up to make Manila as a whole. I think one was named Pasay City, but won't put money on that statement. Manila 'proper' is some place with big handsome buildings on either side of a long sweeping bridge spanning a wide stretch of water. Plenty 'top dollar' shops displaying expensive goods, way above our budget. There was also the fact to take into account that we would soon be visiting Hong Kong, the, then, shoppers' paradise of this world, so yes,

we've been saving for that golden opportunity.

Later that afternoon we chanced upon a set-up that impressed me no end, I've a vague notion that it was called the USO; a prestigious shopping mall, with high ceilings an' yards o' marble; quiet, cool and gleaming. I think it was Yank-owned, housing offices as well as shops and possibly even the American Consulate, whatever, there was certainly an official atmosphere about the place. The shop window I particularly remember displayed amazing paintings, some appearing iridescent; unfortunately they were beyond my means, but I nearly talked myself into buying one.

I've often since thought about these exquisite works of art, never having again witnessed the likes, and wondered whether I would see them through the same eyes today; probably not, as sadly although our bodies don't, our tastes become more sophisticated with age. *Get me, in ma 'kiss me quick' baseball cap an' Ray Ban shades* ***- guid taste costs nuthin'!***

Manila, although brilliant, being an American Base was too expensive for us, so; *havin' had oor nookie,* we headed back to Tenby in time forra free scran. We didn't venture ashore that night, or the next *when we were 'duty-watch'*; this was no great loss as the entertainment in harbour was 'the dug's baws', in fact, bordering the ridiculous - dozens of warships were tied up alongside the quays, at some places five deep, each screening a different movie on the upper deck, so we were spoilt for choice. That's the Yanks for you, everything extreme - ***pure magic!*** Oh yeah, there was, of course, the local radio station whose signature was 'Dee Zee Double X', playing non-stop music 24/7 with a time check between spins.

Now, it goes without saying that Manila is a wild place to be at after dark, so on reflection Lew and I had probably done the right thing, as there was more than just a fair bit trouble while there. In most cases this was caused by confusion with the curfew - our American cousins only got Shore Leave until midnight, but Jack generally had all-night, so, although the curfew was set at 01.00 the bars didn't shut until the last customer left; *just like South America.* Adding to this problem, the beer was 'big bucks'; so Jack, being an adaptable creature, was downing cheap, but potent, Manila Rum resulting in many getting 'rat arsed', consequenting in lashings of punishment being dished out after leaving the Philippines.

Daily flogging will continue until the crew's morale improves.

Loads of stories were told after this visit, the top two being; a Junior Seaman from Albion getting knifed and 'Jock' Strapp, one of our very own stokers waking 'early doors' horrified to then realize, the previous evening *when 'off his face'* he'd married this 'twenty dollar whore' curled-up to him snoring peacefully on a grotty spunk-stained bed. We had to leave the reprobate behind in hope that the Authorities could undo his folly, as there was an in-house procedure for panic-sticken American servicemen in the same predicament. Jock was flown back to join us at a later date, I don't recall at what cost to him in the form of punishment and stoppage of pay, but rest assured it would've been considerable ***- ought to have been 'drummed out', as his type are a disgrace to the Service: WOT!***

We were scheduled to be in Manila for two days, no doubt for debriefing on how the exercise was going, so off we go to sea again, only to return the following day wae a fucked boiler, which kept us in harbour for a further three days. When we finally sailed, the Yanks had dug up a piper who stood in full Highland regalia atop the Bridge of the destroyer we were berthed alongside, playing us out of harbour to a wailing Scottish lament; these guys never miss an opportunity to put on the old razzamatazz.

We then completed Phase II of 'Sealion' and returned to Singapore to prepare for a visit, to South Korea. However, we never pitched-up, because, when on passage the good ship Tenby developed a boiler-blower defect and the steering-motor sounded like a bag o' nails, leaving Captain Parker no choice, other than divert to Hong Kong for repairs.

Wotta result! An unexpected week in 'Honkers! Blimey, this **is** the place to be *even the name sounds magical*, it's Aladdin's Cave and then some; the shops are incredible, fair burstin' at the seams with swag I've never even seen before - all 'the toys' up to the minute and so cheap that you spend more here than anywhere else on the planet. The city is awesome, simply teemin' wi' life and awash with distractions - I'm dumbfounded, there's nothing you can't do, buy or enjoy. I'm so glad I heeded sound advice and squirreled a wedge for this unmatchable experience; now I'm going to 'tan'the lot, no ifs, buts or maybes.

I've already had three pairs of polished cotton trousers made by 'Sew Sew' the chinky tailor, whose tiny workshop is down in the bowels, next to our Mess. Oh yeah, and a new Number One uniform top with red silk

lining and big coloured Chinese dragons embroidered inside the cuffs, that will show nicely 'Jack the Lad style' when unbuttoned and turned up ***- the things we ODs have to do to look the part!***

Lew and I rush ashore to hit the shops at the first opportunity, where, in a bout of uncharacteristic madness, we indulged in a frenzied shopping spree. The tailors' shops were amazing, air-conditioned, quiet, relaxed and so professional, providing glasses of cold San Mig while eagerly measuring you up for some 'proper-cool' threads - obviously dirt cheap, and wait for this one; **ready to collect next day.** Same goes for the shoe shops, boots and shoes made to measure, pick the style and the leather, then get told, with a toothy grin, "Yoa cum back tomollow suh!"

I've died and been beamed-up to heaven - so, order a camel suede jerkin with black woollen collar and cuffs and two pairs of moccasin-style shoes. Then in a mad rampage, treat masel to the latest SLR camera and a guitar; because Johnny and Lew promise to teach me the chords, a radio/record player *(it's Japanese; as is the camera)*, doses of LPs and a delicate Chinese tea set - crated up there and then, and sent by seamail to reward my very deserving grandmother for providing all these special lunches in my Leith Academy days. The package took six months to arrive in the UK, in fact, I was home before it was; but no breakages. Sure, it goes without saying that I also bought some crap, since we all stray from the masterplan when splashin' the cash around Hong Kong.

Feeling peckish after our bout of madness, we bimbled round to the China Fleet Club late afternoon for a nosh-up; **jings!** - that was some place, run by Ratings for Ratings; nothing to do with the NAAFI or any of the other organizations. The service second to none, and probably the cheapest in the world. While relating this I wonder what's become of that wonderful haven now the 'tiddly winks' have the island back, most likely been blootered to oblivion and completely redeveloped.

So anyway, the China Fleet Club was the place to go in for 'big eats' at prices one could generally only dream about. Within minutes of ordering from an impressive menu, the attentive chinky waiter conjured up a brace of entrecôte steaks with the full tootie, and a pair o' huge glasses of iced tomato juice, the idea being to gird our loins in preparation for a serious night 'on the lash' in as many as possible of the exciting, neon-signed,

American-style bars, crawlin' wae spritely Asian chicks.

With this in mind, we're out to create a good impression and cement international relations - after all, His Eminence is forever 'clearing the Lower Deck' to hammer home that we are ambassadors for our country, and woe betide anyone forgetting to act accordingly - so, heeding his every word, we see ourselves as bold young emissaries of the Queen.

The first 'run' in a new port is always a hit or a miss cos you're really just 'sussing it out' to find the best places for which to make a beeline next time. Although 'The Messiah' had been there on Warrior a couple of years previously, it had changed so much that other than landmarks such as the 'Fleet Club' and Kowloon Ferry, he was as much a stranger as myself. We head for 'the street of a thousand arseholes' *as we used to call it.* This was a street in Wanchai, heavin' wae risqué neon-signed bars whose names probably changed with the seasons - no matter; we are all drawn like moths by the temptation of bright lights and names such as the 'Original Suzy Wong Bar'. These Chinese entrepreneurs have life's weaknesses well sussed - yeah, here ***'cash is king',*** so these crafty 'Charlie Chans' know how to tease every last red cent oot o' Jack's moneybelt ***- ker-ching!***

Since we were in Hong Kong for a week that first time, followed by two or three later visits; this probably amounted to a glorious month overall, in which to savour the delights of this Oriental Utopia. As with Singapore it is hard to distinguish individual runs ashore, so, it's best I just describe that moment in my life as a never to be forgotten experience.

The Yanks, as always, were a major presence, their Armed Forces being so colossal that the Brits were heavily outnumbered. We were doing well if Pusser had three warships in port, and by that I mean a couple of frigates and a destroyer. At least our ships were alongside, whereas the Yanks would be 'anchored off' - but there could be a flotilla of destroyers, a couple of submarines and maybe an aircraft carrier at any given time, equating to hordes of randy, thrill-seeking American sailors. 'Our cousins' were great fun to mingle with; so we enjoyed many a wild night in their company - yeah, these guys knew how to party, which they *of course* could so easily afford. We thought ourselves flush 'out East', but next to those minted dudes, we were no more than down an' out bums.

I well remember their shore-patrols as being ultra strict; tolerating no

nonsense whatsoever. For instance; one night we were in a flashy nightspot, having a rootin'-tootin' hooley - the Yank Shore-Patrol had come in, and having words with this, 'pished as a fart', guy, who looked like an 'old hand' with many a 'drunken run' under his belt. He hadn't been causing trouble, just a bit loud - you know how it is; *the bevvy was doing all the talking and he was merely its puppet.* Left alone he'd've been OK, but since they'd rubbed 'Old Salty' up the wrong way, what he was going to do to their "cotton-pickin' asses" was nobody's business. Now, this Shore-Patrol was the type we've all seen in films, three gorillas; a grizzly old Chief and his two black henchmen, one of whom was gi-fuckin' huge - he obviously doesn't take too kindly to being prodded and called 'boy'. So, gracefully removes the grimacing sailor's white pork-pie hat and is stroking the guy's napper with this formidable nightstick - *and it goes like this* "Yo" thud "ain't" thud "goin" thud "nowhere" thud ***"boy!"*** thud. After which, a starry-eyed 'Salty' *held upright by Chiefy* quietly buckled at the knees. The big black enforcers then take an arm each, and in a slick military two-step, he's dragged from 'the Last Chance Saloon' and thrown in the 'Paddy wagon'. It appeared they had this routine well-rehearsed and I can't help but wonder how many encores they did that night.

It's common knowledge that the USN punishments are severe, with in extreme cases a letter sent home to the family telling of the man's misdemeanour and how 'Li'l Elmer' has disgraced the flag. Now, that's serious stuff if you think how patriotic the Yanks are. However, such an approach would be pointless with our lot *(who march to a different drum)*, since Jack would see this as a 'badge of honour' and imagine himself a hero in the same circumstance; strange indeed how attitudes can differ so!

You'll recall how our American cousins only had midnight-leave while we had all-night - it was the only thing we had that was better than they. This, of course, because it cost sweet F.A. - that's the Brits for you every time; **second class** - *och, dinnae get me started again!*

Well anyway, this was magic, since the Yanks would lash-up the hostesses to drinks, affording them a hefty kickback and these bar girls knew just how to play it, with little hands wandering under the table, having a wee stroke here and a wee fumble there - some o' the whores nippin' out with horny 'Leroy' or 'Virgil' for a 'short-time'. Meanwhile, Jack lurked

patiently *like a praying mantis,* watchin' like a hawk, while letting them get on with it and come twelve o'clock when the Yankee Doodles had toddled back to their ships, at the drop of a hat, the snakes would slither in, buy the burds one or two wets, then slope off for a cheap 'all night inners'. I felt sorry for these critters, but that's life - we didnae make the rules an' you know what they say, **"A hard-oan disnae hae a conscience!"**

We made some good friends amongst the Yanks and one night had a great run with three guys from a USN submarine who invited us onboard for a shufti the following day. For a while I'd had a fixation about 'subs', so jumped at this opportunity. It was an old 'boat', probably WWII design, but very impressive - I'm known to be prone to exaggeration, but believe me, she was **gleaming**, every pipe, nut and bolt polished *they must have carried more Brasso than fuel.* These bullshittin' bastards sure know how to put on a show - the world's a stage, and it works for them.

The sub was berthed alongside a Fleet Support Ship, on which her pampered crew was victualled when in 'harbour routine', so our new best pals treated us to lunch onboard her. ***Well, howdee-doodee!*** - this put us to shame; 'Uncle Sam' certainly looked after his boys. Unlike us they had a proper dining hall and self-service hotplate, stainless steel trays with compartments which you just slide along the counter, helping yourself to whatever and as much as you want from a tempting selection, obviously including steaks *(any bigger an' ye could've milked 'em).* There was fresh milk, ***yeah fresh milk,*** different flavours of ice cream and chromed soda fountains just like in their drugstores back home - get right in about it, an' help yersel', sailor. What an eye-opener; maybe I should've taken the risk of becoming a paperweight in the Pentagon after all.

I'd noted the smart, but inexpensive jewellers' shops in 'Honkers' and now wish I'd bought some jade or amber objects d'art, but back then I was an OD, so thought and acted the part. Well anyway, one night I was admiring the glittering trinkets in the basement shop of the Fleet Club; far from surprised to see the baubles were even cheaper there. So, in a moment of weakness, succumbed to temptation and bought a gold signet ring, set with a star sapphire, which I was extremely proud of - but, being a useless twat, managed to, crack the, stone before getting home; that reminds me - *I must order a new bahookie, as this one's got a crack in it.*

Jings! - nearly forgot I have something else to remind me of Hong Kong - no, not 'a dose' ya tube, **a tattoo!** - well, actually two tattoos, and here's how they came to be. Whilst larkin' about with some mates in the swimming pool of a Services Club, I spied this 'Pongo' with a superb tattoo of a scorpion on his shoulder blade. Being as I am, I thought it was out of balance, why, oh why hadn't he got a matching one on the other side? This must've touched a nerve, because the thought persists and stays with me for the rest of the day. That evening, after a few San Migs are down the neck, I find myself in Pinky's Tattoo Parlour scanning the hundreds of designs around the walls, '***voila !***' there it is, **the scorpion**. Well, you know what's coming - don't you? I can't help myself, I just have to put to rights the discrepancy that's been niggling me all day, and so have Pinky tattoo a 'breeding pair' on my shoulder blades.

What ama like? I sometimes wonder about the extremes I'll go to, in order to get my own way and prove a point. However *although goin' thru a phase* it's fair to say, I don't end up a few years down the line looking like a Maori warrior. These were the last I had done *each of the four discreetly placed* having taken notice of the sound advice a Senior Rate imparted in the early days - "You never know where your career might take you in the future and having tattoos that are seen, like on your hands, may well lose, or cost you a job." *Words of wisdom from the gob of a wise man!* Well now, there you go Baby - contrary to what you have may've heard, sometimes I do listen, so 'play the white man' an' cut me a bit o' slack!

That's the broken bits fixed, so we're back in the game and racing 'full steam ahead' to join our Squadron and the cruiser HMS Belfast; yes the very one now lying decommissioned and on show in London. I always thought it to be an ugly top-heavy tub: it's a pity, no, not a pity, a crying shame that they didn't keep the battleship HMS Vanguard, the finest ship I ever saw; so sleek - looking as a warship should, with its eight *'big fuck off'* 15-inch guns. Now, that would've made a statement worthy and symbolic of a once revered and proud nation - the tight-fisted Brits got it wrong again *(nae class)* - Nelson would slit his throat!

We had missed out on South Korea. Were we concerned? Not us, we'd have happily stayed in Hong Kong for the rest of the commission, only a bipolar manic depressive could get pissed off with that place. Well

anyway, as said, we're off to rendezvous with the other ships and proceed in 'line-ahead convoy' through the Formosa Straits to Kobe in Japan - and thankfully the 'golden eagle' shits before we dock.

The Formosa Straits; 'the powers that be' were a wee bit edgy about going through there - because the Maoist 'Commie' chinks on the Mainland were embroiled in a conflict with Chiang Kai-shek's Nationalist chinks on Taiwan, so, not content with merely sabre-rattling, had resorted to shelling each other; and we have to steam straight through the middle - **stuff that!** 'Joe' King remarked, "Thank Christ the ship is on the Skipper's slop chit, not mine!" On the day *obviously concerned* we are taking no chances of being misidentified and bombed by chinky warplanes - the ship's name is painted in large letters on top of the Bridge accompanied by the biggest Union Jack you've ever seen ***- nothing reckless or heroic about us!***

Well, here we are at Kobe in 'Jaypan'; regarded as the 'jewel in the crown' of our Far East Tour, but it didn't do it for me, well, I mean, what could possibly match Hong Kong? - which has it all at half the price. Now, don't get me wrong, Kobe was great and I'd sure like to be there right now - especially right now, because on looking from the picture windows of my ivory tower I see a familiar grey sky; yes, it's fair chuckin' doon, and guess what - the Edinburgh International Festival kicks off today; ***is that no' jist like the thing!*** Anyway, nice place Kobe, but Lew and I only went ashore twice while there *(that's the routine; when you go anywhere with him, you have to go back next day, cap in hand, to apologize).*

Gluttons for punishment, we were always amongst the first batch to nick ashore, forra 'butchers' in a fresh port, and this was no exception; although, that afternoon we both felt knackered; possibly because we had been 'closed up' at 'action stations' during the night. Whatever, I remember trudging along the road outside the docks feeling cacked and agreeing that we should've got in some 'kippo time' before coming out to play, when we see this big sign 'Kobe Turkish Baths' *(yes, in English)*; a quick discussion and, **yeah!** Why not? It's worth a try - of course our minds are working overtime, so 'the jockeys', spurred by lust and psyched up, trot through the door at a rate o' knots thinking Geisha! Geisha! Geisha!

No such luck! this place was what the sign said and nothing more. Well, we're here, so may as well chance our hand; the draw being the staff - cute

little Japanese gals full of Eastern promise in enticing skimpy sports bras and short shorts, but they were in charge *no messing* yes, our hopes were dashed; not even a little tease. These girls knew their job, giving us 'the works' - the finishing touch being, a walk down our backs, toes digging into places that must've mattered, because we went in feeling 'shagged-oot' and reappeared bouncing like spring lambs ***- money well spent!***

Reinvigorated, we stroll around the city centre, impressed by the big shopping malls - yes, they had them way back then, years ahead of us; and *hard to miss,* were the noisy amusement arcades everywhere, to which the 'little Tojos' seemed addicted. There was no point in buying anything, since there was nothing we couldn't get in Honkers for 'washers', so not fancying raw fish and rice for big eats, nipped back to our floating hotel for a freebie and didn't rush ashore that evening. **Hold on!** Ah wusnae 'past it' - only twenty-two, sound of wind and limb, an' fair burstin' wi' vitality. ***Crikey, wish I could go back.*** Recently 'Binky' Brown told me "We should be born old and grow young." - *now, there's a thought!*

We had another 'kick at the ball' before leaving 'the land of the rising sun', and, believe me, it's well worth crowing about. This was an evening run to the bright lights; as by now we'd heard all the stories from those who'd already sampled the goods. The taxis on the jetty touting for our business were free - their, 'hard at the lash' drivers who *goin' like the clappers* ferried us around, were inscrutable bar owners after captive punters *you've got to hand it to these 'wee yellah con artists'* so that's how we got to where it was all happening. It has to be said, the Japanese hostess girls were superior to any others we encountered, polite, better-looking, brighter, well-groomed, scrupulously clean - **and great fun!**

Keeping our options open, we visited a few taverns, flitting from one to another *as always* looking for something where the grass was greener. Can't tell you how or why we ended up in this backwater upmarket hotel; a complete contrast to the throbbing dockland pleasure palaces we'd visited earlier. We were the only punters in the place and I was for moving on, but as luck would have it, Lew *(in a story as old as time itself)* struck by Cupid's arrow, has fallen in love with this waitress who's givin' him the old "I could be yours, Big Boy", so refuses to move, coaxing me to stay for "just one more drink", yeah that'll be right; we've all heard that one,

but who can blame the randy sod; she's a topper - statuesque for a Jap, a high-cheekboned classical beauty if ever you saw one.

Lew's besotted *having sniffed the barmaid's apron* so he's layin' it on with the expertise of a ballroom gigolo and Yoko *who knows what buttons to press* is fair lappin' it up: Luvver Boy says he's as horny as a toad, an' gonna to slip this one a length tonight. Well, as ever he's spot on, but what he didn't know was "**it's gonna cost ya sailah boy**" because this sensational piece o' skirt, with remarkable bone structure, was 'on the game' *and just happened to have the tools of her trade with her,* so without further ado she's put her victim in the picture and propositioned him.

Yoko's scored; he's chokin' and got a 'yen' for her; *well actually, a good few Yen,* so no matter how much she'd asked, it would've been a case of "drop yer drawers, the money's yoars". That's it, the 'serial shagger's' on his feet, saying "Sorry pal, you're on yer tod." Oh well, that's mates for you, but givin' him credit, he slipped me a drink before leaving. Wha'diya think; guilty conscience, or has he got a heart after all? Naa - just keeping me sweet for next time; or some such ulterior motive.

So I'm left sittin' on my jaxie whistlin' dixie, thinking I'll finish this drink and piss off back to the ship. The chatty serving wenches who speak halting, not bad English are talking friendly nonsense to me; and *sensing I'm 'an easy touch',* giving it the "You no go way yet." I think they must feel "solly foh" me sitting here, like 'little boy lost', until I get told coyly, in a very long and roundabout declaration, that the petite barmaid *whose attentions I'd been conscious of* fancies me, making me think - wait a minute; the whole bleedin' team are 'at it' - **not at all!** What's this then? My suspicions are aroused, there's got to be an angle. *I trust no one* - what **have** I become? But no, she's kosher and what's more if I want to go with her she can finish work early - in fact, right now.

Jings, talk about luck; who am I to argue! - she's not a star, like wot Lew's copped, but still a wee belter with a lovely timid smile - **well; what would you do?** Ah'm for some o' this - ***banzai... here comes daddy!***

They must've wangled it somehow, as we scored a sumptuous room on the top deck of the hotel - let me tell you, there was no contest between this and my hammock in No.8 Mess and I certainly never paid; *although did my best to earn my keep*. The room even had a sunken bath, which

I well remember as when I kneeled to check the temperature the playful little minx nudged me in with her foot and, oh yes, it was HOT!

"Fuck me!" said the Duchess, more in hope than anger
And the Duke, who was slowly masturbating in the corner
Pulled her on like a well-worn seaboot

Cor! Did I say timid? Julia Roberts could've modelled herself on this athletic creature when portraying the ultimate whore. Wotta sesh - *pray tell, are they* ***all*** *double -jointed?* My flexible friend and I pleasured each other, indulging in unbridled passion on a hot Japanese bed of sin 'til 'early doors', thus making the liaison a memorable ego booster - *lets face it, ah'm no George Clooney.* Now, I'm only telling you this snippet on the understanding that it'll go no further - *forever the pessimist,* years later when watching a TV documentary about 'The Ladyboys of Bangkok' I thought of my 'freebie' in Kobe *(och, no, surely not)*, but you know what they say - **"Scared to try it, in case you like it!"**

Kobe's hospitable ambience was enjoyed by most, apparently impressing one of our crew so much that, in a token gesture, he decided to 'jump ship' and stay. I can't recall seeing him again and at this late date it slips my mind as to who he was - probably just another hairy-ersed stoker.

Well, goodbye Kobe, hello again Hong Kong - longer would've been trumps, but this time we only had two or three days actually in Honkers. The best part of a fortnight was spent patrolling the South China Sea and around the New Territories; very picturesque, with its atolls, volcanic islands, junks and sampans - *no doubt smuggling good-style right under our noses*. Who knows what we were supposed to be doing there; most of us were rarely privy to what was going on and cared even less; after all we were just cooks, stewards, stokers and whatever, whose job was just the same no matter what games the dandies on the Bridge were playing. One thing's for sure, regardless of how well the ship performed in the 'war games' the 'bilge rats' were never likely to be mentioned in dispatches.

During this patrol Lew and I took part in a training manoeuvre - there's no danger that we volunteered, so must've been detailed off to be involved *("Volunteer for nothing" was our motto)*. We and other misfits were formed into what was loosely termed a platoon, then one pitch-black moonless night, were landed on an uninhabited island somewhere near

Hong Kong; the plot being that we were terrorists, who overnight must establish ourselves, secure the area, and come first light landing parties will storm the island - *'send in the clowns'*. Then in the course of the morning the goodies would flush out, round-up and capture the baddies - *talk about original, I wonder who dreamt that one up -* ***sheer genius!***

Well, it got off to a good start; with not a star in the sky we're ferried ashore in inflatables all tooled up like commandos. "**Here you, that man, quiet there - coxswain, take that man's name!**" The seamen in charge of the Geminis are scared to go in close in case they get a puncture and rewarded with a bollocking, so we have to jump over the side, fully booted and spurred *with packs* yards from the beach. Jaisus H. Christ it's deep - *should've used ma 'stunt double'*. None too soon my boots touch and I'm struggling spluttering to the shore - just a few feet to go now and the briny's only up to my waist when, **bloody bollocks!** - the Pusser's torch, which is *somehow* switched on, jumps off my webbing belt and there it is *still working* shining on the bottom at my feet. **Wonderful!** ***- trust ma rotten luck;*** it's an offence to lose equipment, so I've no option other than duck under the water to retrieve it, wotta game! - whae'd be a sojur?

Some lark this - the bedraggled 'terrorists' are all ashore, their spirit already broken, and the exercise yet hours away. We regroup on the beach and after wringing out our clothes, fire-up the 'field kitchen' to cook a 'potmess'. Some potmess that was, we just raided the ration packs and threw anything that was edible into the cauldron - d'you know wot, I think there was tinned fruit in that stew, and some yoyo had contributed a packet of Rowntrees gums. Yeah, **there's always one!**

After the the commotion had calmed down, the Chief GI ordered us to form groups, conceal ourselves in good hiding places round the island and get some rest before the exercise commenced at dawn. On hearing this, Lew said "Stuff this! Sod them, and their bleeding exercise, let's split!" So we craftily sloped off in the dark, thinking it would be a good idea to go up the way to a position where we could skive and get a good view of the loonies at daybreak. We weren't dry, but certainly warm after scrambling as high as we deemed necessary - by this time it was getting a touch blustery, so we, luckily, stumbled upon a sheltered spot that looked like a cave entrance. However, on shining our Pusser's torches into the

'Albion' Rating, Lofty, Shiner and 'Blondie' Brookes downing 'Tigers' in the Britannia Club, Singapore - prior to taking 'the pledge'

gloom, it proved nothing so pretentious, only going in about four feet, but the way it was hollowed out and facing was at least sheltered from the wind. We endured a dismal night ensconced there, but had at least got away from their 'Boy's Own' war games and felt quite smug, knowing nothing much could be said as we had been told to keep ourselves well out of sight by **thee** Senior Rating.

Next morning the assault had hardly got underway when whistles start blowing and adversaries can be seen scurrying around like blue-arsed flies below us - not at all what we'd anticipated. What the fuck's goin' on? - they've got one of these battery-operated bullhorn things that the 'big cheeses' just love shouting through. We make out that the exercise is cancelled - "Everyone muster on the beach". We suspect it's a trick - but, so what, we don't mind being captured and sent back to the ship, where we can get a shower and into some clean clobber. This isn't the most comfortable of places to spend the day anyway - *and what are all these holes in the hillside?* So, down we go thinking 'couldn't organize a piss-up in a brewery'. It transpires that typhoon 'Olive' is heading our way, so it's time to scarper, and howzabout this, imagine our horror when 'Tug'

Wilson informs us that the holes we'd seen in the hillside were snake holes. **Woops!** ***No one mentioned poisonous snakes at the briefing.***

Following that 'damp squib', we copped a couple o' days in Hong Kong; to recover from 'battle fatigue' before returning to Singapore for a planned maintenance period, prior to yet another exercise code-named 'Fotex' to be supervised by Rear Admiral Michael Le Fanu. **Yes you're right**, one of 'the hierarchy' forever remembered by Jack and associated with July 31ST 1970 when grog was stopped and the last tot of Pusser's rum was issued in the Royal Navy. *Someone's head had to go on the block, so why not an Admiral!* Although I'd bailed out of the fraternity prior to the ending of this hallowed tradition, my heart bleeds - pity aside, I'm convinced the responsible 'Tars' left clinging to the wreckage were ecstatic not to have been plied with a daily ration of 'the Devil's Nectar'.

This cartoon was published in the aircraft carrier Eagle's magazine 'The Eagle Express' when grog was stopped. Going by the look on 'Jolly Jack's' coupon, the Lower Deck were none too chuffed.

That spell in The Imperial Dockyard lasted twenty-four days, during which we had countless runs ashore in Singers; *now very familiar to us*, so we had by this time established a neat routine. Instead of rushing to town at the first opportunity, we'd grace Terror's swimming pool in the afternoons for a couple of hours, which were spent lazing around under the hot tropical sun - when necessary diving into the water to cool off, then have a shower before heading to Singapore, where our first stop would be the Brit club to 'go through the 'big eats' card' and sink a pair o' 'Tiger tops' - *pints of cold Tiger beer topped with lemonade*, **deeelightful!**

Need I *again* say; how time flies when you're enjoying yourself. It's the end of July already, seeing Tenby back in the South China Sea, this time on a Fleet Weapon Training Exercise - yeah, you're 'on the ball', 'Fotex' with Rear Admiral Le Fanu. I won't bore the arse off you by going into detail since basically all these 'war games' are much the same load o' old cobblers designed to keep Jack on his toes, while working his nuts off:

what's more, the truth is I can't remember a thing about it!

However, this wee associated bit I do; and worth a mention. We had stopped for a breather at the weekend, so the Squadron was anchored off an island called Pulau Tioman, near the east coast of Malaya. This exotic south sea island was probably inhabited, but I can't be sure, never having got further than the beach, where we had a Banyan, but that's not the way I want to go - *you know how it is; nae wimen, nae shaggin', nae story.* But, howzabout this? On the Sunday morning 'the Guv'nor' decides to hold a service on the Quarterdeck, in praise of his God, so at his behest all the heathens are flushed from their Messes and detailed off to attend; so as to have their souls cleansed, no matter where their faith or beliefs *if any* lie.

Shades of being marched to church years earlier at school camp - that's right, I don't forget and am known to hold a grudge. You know, that could well be why church attendance levels are so low today - force people to do something and when they later have a choice it's "Go fuck yourself!" *(I suppose for that remark I'll return as a dung beetle).*

So, the Ship's Company are mustered on the Quarterdeck, then distributed in an orderly fashion round our esteemed Captain and his pandering servile entourage, while he is spoutin' from 'the book o' words' cradled on the majestic ships' lectern. Unknown to him and the inner circle, those on the perimeter of his flock were paying no attention whatsoever; many actually facing the other way watching two large sharks idly circling the stern *to a rapturous rendition of 'Abide with Me',* no doubt attracted by delicacies, as the Ship's Cooks had not long since ditched the gash - *or just possibly the Skipper's sermon was a winner.*

Which hymn diyi want? - **Him wi' the big drum!**

With the exercise over, we hastened back to Singapore for what was ***supposedly*** our swansong. Weeks later, when casting off from the Queen's Dockyard, it was the 'full tootie': 'Big Brass' perched proudly on their rostrum saluting the gallant ship 'fare thee well' with heads held high and tears in their eyes; we've even got a Royal Marine band striking up a rousing version of Colonel Bogey to play us out of harbour, an' guess what? **We broke down!** *Wotta fuckin' red neck!* After the grease monkeys had sweated blood, we quietly sneaked out of harbour and headed once

again for Hong Kong to join Albion and Scarborough in a 'shop-window' exercise - this being a demonstration of our capabilities for the Governor and his 'bigwig oppos'. 'Twas said that we enjoyed Albion's flying displays as much as anyone; however, I distinctly remember one of our crew *(and I'm not saying who)* standing on deck for hours on end with his fancy new SLR camera, muttering to himself "Crash, ya bastard, crash!"

This was our final visit to Hong Kong, lasting, from 23RD August until 2ND September. I remember it well, as apart from some great runs ashore and last minute shopping, that's when my problems with the dysfunctional 'Mole' came to a head; now, let me say, I had done extremely well to tolerate his numerous snidey moves and provocation for so long.

We did 'watch-about'; meaning that whoever had the duty-watch was responsible for the Wardroom evening meal and breakfast the following morning; with Len and the other cook 'turning to' around eight-thirty - *breakfast now over and the Galley 'squared-up'*. So, all hands mucked in preparing lunch, which, when ready, then let the Duty Cook from the night before 'knock off' at tot time leaving the Galley clean, tidy and set up for his relief. A good routine which worked well, except that Mole, still pursuing his vendetta, consistently did his best to leave something *that he should've done* for 'yours truly' - so as to have a little dig and, as he thought, prove his seniority. It was generally so trivial that *although he was 'doin' ma head in'* I played the fool and rarely bothered to mention it; which hopefully needled the schmuck more than it did me.

Showdown - this day; at 'change of watch' in Hong Kong he attempted to slide off and leave the full gash bin, for me to take ashore and empty. Since it had been filled on his watch he was well aware it was his responsibility to ditch it, so I said as much to Len, who *while sucking his teeth* told Mole to get rid of it before going 'off-watch'. But our 'leading lady', who was in one of 'her' real bitchy moods *possibly PMT* stood 'her' ground, claiming it was "too heavy". So, to keep the peace, Len told me to give 'her' a hand, which I *being in no position to refuse* was obliged to do.

Mole was really pissed at having to help **me**, so, throwing a tantrum grabs one handle, leaving me to take the other. With an exasperated sigh 'she' drags the bin *and me* out the Galley, rushing off down the 'Burma Way' towards the Quarterdeck at a great rate o' knots. Now, the bin is full

size, but, although metal, not heavy. Mole is in front and because 'she' is going so fast my shins are hitting the bottom of the bin, and, yes, it's painful. Grudgingly I say so and ask 'her' to slow down; true to form, the prune goes even faster. That's it, ah've lost ma cool - I've had enough o' this cretin, I crack, and have no option but to retaliate by stubbornly digging my heels in and so jerk to a halt, pulling the bin and the Mole back.

My timing, although spontaneous, was impeccable. 'She' goes flat on 'her' arse, and there 'she' is sprawled on the deck 'tits up' with a look of utter astonishment on 'her' coupon, right in front of a surly-faced 'Tiffy' PO who was coming from aft and hasn't a clue as to what has happened. The 'drama queen' quick as a flash *(you've got to hand it to the cunt, talk about playing to the galleries, this twat was good)* screeches to the thick Tiff *now helping him up* "Did you see that?" The sneering pillock says "Yes", then, after telling me *the lackey* to "Shit 'n it" barks "Get your cap" and that's it, I'm in the 'tom tit', which really got to me, since I'd tried to explain the error of my ways, but to no avail as the crass git didn't want to know - so I hoped his next shite was a hedgehog, **backwards!**

We think the drones so far removed, they're ignorant as to what's going on with the riff-raff below decks, so I'm expecting the worst as I'm on Captain's Report for the skirmish *(while acting unconcerned - nails bitten to the quick, I was secretly quaking in my galley boots)*. So, here's me, thinkin' I've picked the wrong week to quit smokin'; as 'Piggy' Malone had said I'd probably get charged with assault and banged up in DQs, which at Hong Kong means **Stonecutters Island**. Jings! - the very name says it all! However, the outcome is not at all what I dread, as good old Len must've briefed my Divisional Officer who, in turn, had the Captain's ear, so when hauled in front of him as ***'The Accused'***, I'm rewarded with a lecture, three Hail Marys and seven days stoppage of Leave, *which is a breeze* - I'm amazed to have got off so lightly, since life is rarely fair.

Let me tell you that I had, in truth, got off scot-free, as we were sailing next morning and I, being duty-watch, had no intention of going ashore that night. But, now comes the good bit - we would be at sea for at least a week - meaning I couldn't go ashore anyway, so by the time we hit our next 'port of call' my punishment would be history - **but, that's not the best bit**: Mole was also on Captain's Report for the incident. I can't recall

the charge, but he didn't fare so well, since the *good* Captain had been extensively briefed on the situation. I take no pleasure, in reporting that my foe copped his just deserts when his Leading Rate was revoked, thus making the weed a 'two-badge fuck-all' therefore, the same rate as myself; possibly with less seniority - so, **who d'man!**

Well, rinky dinky doo; it's said every cloud has a silver lining *but let's not gloat!* For 'her' pains and to avoid conflict, auld 'nae mates', who'd been as popular as a pork pie at a bar mitzvah in No. 8 Mess since long before my arrival, rued the day when foisted on No. 2 Mess up for'ard, where 'Jesse' James and his nest o' vipers had the privilege of 'her' company in their den of iniquity for the remainder of the 'commish'.

Please excuse me, I need a little moment to compose myself!

Although good triumphing over evil gave me exquisite pleasure I rarely took advantage of the twat's humiliation and tried to appear indifferent; *whilst grinning like a Cheshire cat.* Kiss and make up - **that'll be right**, we just kept on looking daggers at, and blanking each other for the next eleven months, not a preferred situation when living and working so close - **almost** as bad as being married to a sour-faced sarcastic shrew, and I'm sure you can understand that one - ***tell the truth, ya fuckin' liar!***

Tenby 'upped anchor' from Hong Kong for the last time, as scheduled, on 2ND September, exercising with other 'men o' war' including Albion and tubs from the Aussie and Kiwi navies while on passage, once again, to Singapore. On the way we detached for a quick visit to Labuan in North Borneo - known in bygone times for its missionary-eating headhunters; so, taking no chances, we didn't venture inland. As a safe option, a group of us went to a nifty little palm-fringed beach in a nearby bay for a swim and scout around - just so as to get off the ship and stretch our legs.

Not far from the beach there was a pontoon anchored in the bay, so we swam out to it and *topping up the bronzy* basked in the sun for a while. When swimming back to shore we heard a slapping plop in the water, close by; wondering what it could be we stopped and while treading water were looking around us. When it happens again we see, leaping out the oggin, something that looks like a Manta ray - because we were at sea-level it probably appeared bigger than it actually was, but that's enough for us; and don't they have a sting in their tails? Panic stations, we're oot o' the

briny and safely back on the beach double fast, ***and then some.***

Later, when paddling in the shallows *(we're no heroes - stuff goin' out there again)*, we spy shoals o' jellyfish - that settles it, as they sting too, don't they? So we're just lazing around on the sand, gassin' about runs ashore when Lew asks in a matter-of-fact tone, "Do you remember that Jap burd I had in Kobe?" Grudgingly, I say, "Yeah, so what?" thinking 'here it comes, something juicy!' "Her dad had a dose o' the shitz!" Like a muppet, I then say, "Wha'diya mean?" "She was a slap-happy Jappy with a crap-happy Pappy!" Drat, fell right in - should've seen it coming!

We are back at Singapore, this time for our annual inspection by the Commander-in-Chief who, on the day, came aboard with his minions for a 'walk round' the ship. When he reached the Galley, I shared my Tot and burnt a couple of 'duty-frees' with him; in return he did his best to give me a wee hand with the lunch while we extolled the virtues of 'the good old days'. Nice guy! It's just an observation, but have you noticed that the higher up the tree, the easier they are to talk to - *almost human!*

On leaving Singapore Tenby sailed up the west coast of Malaya bound for Penang to visit Port Swettenham. While there I had to get a trim; the irony being I was the only one in our clique who had to have his hair cut ashore; as I had long owned a pair of clippers and, while not exactly the ship's barber, tidied up many of the lads' heads for a few shekels, while jokingly posing the question "Something for the weekend, Sir?". It was amusing when this shoreside barber, whose name was Abdul Kaleem, asked, on finishing the job, if I wanted "Blill Kaleem" *(Brylcreem)*. It'th twue, I'm not taking the pith out of the bwown gentleman. **Honitht**!

This was another place that, for reasons long forgotten, we were 'anchored off', therefore not so easy to step ashore and get back. So, like many, Lew and I resolved to stay onboard that night. However, the lure of twinkling lights from waterfront bars on a balmy evening can be very enticing *as many a poor sailor will tell you,* so once more the willpower faded and the wallet took a hiding. I guess he must've led me astray again, as I can't think of any other way we would have missed the last Liberty Boat. That night I slept on a bale of rope on the jetty waking stiff and filthy - *thank Christ for the chinky laundry* - not like the gap year student who, when hitch-hiking in Israel, woke to find a heavy dew *(Jew)* on him.

Need I say we returned to Singapore, but **this time** for our last stay and Captain F's quarterly inspection - to us a mere bagatelle; *you'll be familiar with the old saying 'bullshit baffles brains'*. This behind us we had yet another maintenance period alongside the good old Hartland Point, **finally** leaving Singers on 12TH October and steaming back across the Indian Ocean to Trincomalee in Ceylon arriving there on the 17TH - *I can't remember Shore Leave, so perhaps there was none*. Whilst there our ship took on fuel from the RFA *(Royal Fleet Auxiliary)* tanker 'Tideflow' before sailing up the Arabian Sea, bound for Karachi to participate in a significant showcase of maritime might, code-named 'Midlink'. This must have been a large exercise, going by the serious extravaganza of warships from Britain, the US, Iran, Pakistan *and countless other allies*, assembled off Karachi; looking, for all the world, like the Spithead Review.

Tenby was lying offshore, where it was a bit cooler - we were, of course, still kippin' on the upper deck; where one morning at 'call the hands', the still fast asleep, Taff Pritchard had this creepy-crawly locust thing on the corner of his gob - *no doubt attracted by Taff's saliva*. I, being ***'Mr Nice Guy'***, knocked it off, which roused a bleary-eyed Taff - wondering what was going on. Let me tell you, that beastie took a bit o' a thrashin' wi' ma flip-flop before givin' up the ghost - it was a tough little bleeder whatever it was. I should've mentioned the good ship Tenby, like most crates in those days, was infested with cockroaches *(cockies)*, an unpreferred situation one has to accept, as there's no getting rid of the little bastards. At least there weren't *to the best of our knowledge* weevils in the ship's biscuits.

We must have gone 'alongside' after the exercise, because I remember the 'Professional Boil Sucker' *who turned out to be no more than Gunga Din with a drinking straw* came aboard. I thought the 'old hands' were takin' the piss, but no - that's **exactly** what he was.

Can't speak for others, but I only ventured ashore once - as, lacking pizzazz, there was nowt to coax us, especially after what we *having been spoilt rotten in the Far East* had come to expect. Karachi was, then, a busy place throbbin' wi' sullen-faced geezers - probably as quiet as the grave now, since everyone and their uncle are here in the UK raping the Benefit System! ***(verily, I say unto you; this is the tip of the iceberg).***

When the British Task Force, consisting of Albion, Tenby, Torquay,

Salisbury, Scarborough and the two RFAs, Tideflow and Resurgent, left Karachi the flotilla headed for East Africa; Albion, Torquay and the two RFAs going to Mombasa, Salisbury and Scarborough to Dar es Salaam and ourselves to Mtwara, a small Port in Tanganyika which didn't have much to offer as far as Jack was concerned, but showed us the most amazing hospitality, well appreciated by our fun-loving crew.

We hit Mtwara ahead of schedule; as the grease monkeys had been issued bigger shovels and the Engineer Officer had found a "genuine" slave-masters' whip in a Karachi market; so to kill time the Captain *a keen angler* decided to catch our dinner *using the traditional poachers' method*.

We steamed into a quiet bay and lobbed off a couple of anti-submarine mortars, which exploded beneath the oggin creating a series of shock waves followed by a spectacular foaming eruption. When the sea settled, dead fish of all colours floated belly up on the surface, so it was **"away sea boat's crew"** to retrieve the bonanza. This novel approach produced a wealth of fish suppers - swiftly demolished by the delighted ship's company.

Tenby only stayed at Mtwara for two days; allowing the chance of one run ashore for each watch. On our night off we went to the expats' Mtwara Club; as the choice was either go there or to the one and only hotel, for a few wets. The clubhouse was in the middle of nowhere, so when returning in single file down a narrow track through the undergrowth in the dark, 'the nation's finest' were none too happy with the jungle-type noises around us. The thought of snack-seeking lions, and the likes, pouncing, quickened the pace and heightened our nervous drunken giggles, as *without as much as a cudgel to defend ourselves* we stumbled willy-nilly back to the ship.

A few days later our magical cruise came to an end at Mombasa, where we were berthed alongside a clapped-out dusty jetty at the far end of the harbour - nae sweat, as the beat up taxis, always lined up and waiting, are ultra cheap in such places. This visit was to be for five days and since we would soon be back in the UK looking at Christmas Leave *(it by now being 20TH November)* Lew, once more voicing the accumulated wisdom of a Leading Hand, suggested we clean up our act and 'keep it in our trousers', well away from the readily available Kenyan ladies; having so far been extremely lucky paying homage to the time honoured pursuits - *'never even caught a cold'* - so no point in 'sailing close to the wind' at this late date.

sung to 'These Foolish Things'

A pair of knickers, and a worn French letter
A patch of syphilis that won't get better
Oh, how my foreskin stings
These foolish things remind me of you

That agreed, erring on the side of caution, we seek out the highly recommended Nyali Beach Hotel, where we take advantage of the excellent facilities and enjoy an idyllic afternoon swimming in the fabulous Indian Ocean and lazing in the dappled shade of graceful palm trees under the hot African sun; returning to the ship early as planned. So, the first run, that's what happened - it was ace, the hotel first class, the beach clean, deserted and five star, with thousands of tiny soldier crabs, much too quick for us to catch, vanishing into holes in the wet sand in a flash. The sea was beautiful with breakers of a very acceptable size rolling on to the shore. A magic afternoon, in fact so good that the next time we're off-watch two days later, with no hesitation whatsoever, we're back for a second helping.

Same again - sheer bliss, but this time two snazzy English chicks appear from thin air. Oh, oh! Lew's leaps to his feet and launches himself at them so fast it's a blur, the silk-tongued Lothario is on form. He steers them over to sit with us and while flirting bigtime, makes a great show of photographing them with his fancy new Japanese SLR camera. This guy *who knows every trick in the book* takes a bit o' watchin' and, penetration being the name of his game is layin' it on full blast, as this is the first 'hot white snatch' we've chatted up in donkeys, but often's the case that flattery gets you nowhere - **they ain't buyin'!**

No chance! Turns out, their fathers mastermind the Kenyan National Railway - and no doubt top bananas, as this plummy-voiced pair are a class act. They're good company and it's refreshing to have some intelligent conversation after the pidgin English banter we've become so familiar with. However, they, all too soon, to our utter disbelief, have to leave, so it's on wi' the sunhats an' off they go, with the intrepid duo's doting lovestruck eyes following them 'til they're out of sight ***- you can't win em all!***

That's it, the show's over, but the damage is done and I can see what's coming - it's on the cards, Lucifer's had a sniff, he's got the fanny-rats again and straining at the leash, sweet-talks me into going to town, "just for an

hour or so, a couple of drinks, a laugh and back onboard". Oh yeah? I'm dead easy and he knows it - that's why he's a Killick and I'm an OD - so Big Boy wins again and off we go carrying our towels and 'cossies'.

Before ah kin change ma mind, a 'fast black' *(taxi)* whisks us to the Star Bar and we're sittin' slurpin' down Elephant Ale surrounded by a drunken rabble of gibbering wasters and promiscuous 'plunge'. Well, they're a few shades darker than those we've been interfering with of late, but so what? They're all the same when dem lights is out - "**smile, so ah can see where you is**". Anyway, this isn't a 'sexpedition', we're just havin' wee gargle an' a laugh wi' the 'black ham' - then, it's back to the ship.

Well, so much for denial - it came to pass that this healthy creature wedged on Shagger's lap began plying her trade, by wriggling around *(lay it on me, White Boy!)*. Picture it, we've had a few, the world's our friend and there she is - a young Nubian seductress; obviously of noble blood - scantily-clad, glistening silky-smooth firm body, ready, willing and cheap. He *half-heartedly* tries to shoo her away, but *blessed are the weak,* so she's 'hit pay dirt' - all good intentions are swiftly blanked and the animal instincts about to take over; going by the twisted *lust-filled* grin on his flushed coupon - ***is you is, or is you ain't ma Baby?***

I chirp "Lew, remember what **you** said", but I'm wasting my breath, and I know it, as the brain's in neutral and the 'dick's' in charge. Never the soul of discretion, he resorts to taunting me, saying "You can take the towels and cossies back, flunkey!" On hearing his jibe I'm thinking, 'ah'm not yer bleedin' servant', I know he's only pullin' ma chain but can't help myself and rise to the bait saying "Fuck you, pal, take your own things back, ah'm havin' a wee dabble at this", and cop hold of her mate *who'd been teasing me* - yes, another flawless black beauty. She tells us they call her 'Snowdrop'; which is fine by me - ***good breeding stock, wot!***

They didn't have bones through their noses and protruding erses, so who knows what tribe or ancestry they were from; *and who cares!* It seemed to us they weren't long out the jungle, what with their age and innocent novice-like approach. This pair o' whores may well've been friends, but didn't live together, so when the time came the bwanas went separate paths to mate with the savages. I don't know about Lew; but I was led by the codpiece to a seedy backstreet squat somewhere in downtown Mombasa.

They say when you've had 'jiggy jig' with a 'darkie' you'll never again want a piece o' 'white trash' - that may well be true of the men but most certainly not the females. We did 'the business' on a none too clean bed in her squalid room, but it was nothing special; she may have looked a perky specimen, but this 'jungle bunny' knew no tricks and I was in too much of a hurry, ***as usual,*** to teach her - *must learn tae pace masel!*

After the union, I was more than happy to pay the agreed price, but a problem arose when about to perform the old disappearing act. Now ah'm getting the "I like you! You come back tomorrow," as I'm trying to back out into the street - ***aw, shite, this is all ah need!*** First she wants my St Christopher, to make sure I'll return - **no chance!** Then it's my towel and trunks; I should've just let her have them an' made masel scarce, but *obstinately* didn't. Snowdrop follows me out giving it big licks, creating a scene hanging onto ma arm, crying and wailing noisily. A crowd of dem black folks surround me, thinking I'm trying to 'shoot through' without paying, but, shedding crocodile tears, she assures them that's not the case; so some big Zulu geezer, sportin' a shark's tooth necklace, pacifies then leads the whore back to her hovel, and I'm sent on my way rejoicing while breathing a huge sigh of relief and hearing taunts of **white honky bastard** echoing off the walls and following me down the litter-strewn alley.

That was in the Sixties, before we were 'sold down the river'; still afforded respect abroad and, before *absurd as it may sound* **we** were the Third World country: today in the same situation it would be curtains. Thank fuck for **'the happy days'** - else I'd've had a burnin' tyre roond ma neck *(a beacon to all)* and telling you this story through a medium. Well, there you have it, luv clouded our judgement, and we fell by the wayside so near to home, when full of such good intentions; this lapse resulting in an anxious couple of weeks, doubting the wisdom of our ways; sure that we were going to regret the deed and get more than we'd bargained for. I remember Lew singing "A blob on your knob, will delay your demob!" I also remember 'Bumper' Green saying "What is African Roulette?" - "It's when six 'sooties' are chewing each other and one's a cannibal!"

Well, that's it, once more unto the fray, and although still a long haul we're homeward bound, so Tenby's navigating her way up the Indian Ocean making for Aden. Just as when coming down it's bloody roastin' crossin'

the Equator an' stuck here slavin' over a hot stove ah'm 'sweatin' neaters', but this time the NAAFI is out of soft drinks and the chinky laundry has run oot o' 'goffers'. What a bastard, I've got a ragin' thirst, *ah'm gaspin'* and the only thing I can see to make a fizzy drink is Alka Seltzer; sod it, I'm 'as dry as a stick', that'll have to do! Here, this isn't bad! - in fact, pretty good, I'll have another - and, fuck the expense, just one more.

B'gorra an' B'Jaisus - *does that stuff ever work!* My stomach's bubblin' an' squealin' in next to no time. Talk about 'Montezuma's revenge', I must have been in the 'kludgie' for hours. Every time I thought 'that's it this time' and went out the door I had to rush back in *cheeks clenched* squat on and 'pebble-dash' the aptly named 'thunderbox', thus making the scowling 'Captain of the Heads' even more chokka, and it was sweltering in there. Ye wouldnae chuckle mate, that was a real clean oot - they say "there's none so pure as the purified", which reminds me; the 'Honky Boys' weren't 'squeezin' up', everything tickety-boo in the plumbing department ***- not a drip.*** So it would seem there could be more than an ounce o' truth in the saying, 'God and the Devil look efter their ane'.

I earlier confessed to having more than just a passing interest in submarines and meant to expand on this, but it slipped my mind - during one of the many exercises 'out East', I was sent a sign when one *(referred to at the time, as a 'tin of people')* surfaced close by: it looked sinister and mysterious, I was totally captivated and intrigued knowing this was for me; yes, definitely a career option worth exploring. After serious thought I decided to 'go for broke' and 'follow the money', so *enthusiastically* requested to volunteer for the Submarine Service and anxiously awaited the decision, *confident that I'd be recommended.* The reply saw me as sick as a parrot; I'd been declined on two counts - they didn't entertain them wot cooks for the gentry, and because of my hay fever; saying they wouldn't want some spastic sneezing and spluttering in a submarine.

Yeah, that's what we're up against; did they have anything at all in the brains department? At least some indifferent twat **had** looked at my papers, but that same thick tosspot obviously didn't know there are no pollens at sea, so to get hay fever in a submarine would be nothing short of a miracle - are you ready? Here comes the tantrum - **fuck fuck fuckity fuck!**

When we arrived in Aden *(this time anticipating home)*, those feeling guilty

rushed ashore to buy cheap Christmas pressies for their nearest and dearest, gutted to find the prices sky-high compared to all those wonderful bargains we'd nabbed in Hong Kong. It didn't help that both the Yanks and a big P&O cruise liner were in Port; when this is the case it's common knowledge that the snidey Arabs *being switched-on businessmen* give it **'right up the Khyber'** to the unwary. Luckily, I wasn't in need of any more swag, but did go ashore; a haircut, once more being 'the order of the day' - since it was early December I wouldn't need to visit a barber again before Xmas Leave; therefore, not be arriving home with a 'baldie'.

It was a fine plan, but the barber I chose was a bad move although the haircut was as good as I've ever had; this wog guy had style, open razor-work on the top, flames in the ears - the whole bit - but, there's always a downside. 'Dan Druff' was 'chuckin' up' and here's me a prisoner in his chair; he must've been chewing garlic, or something equally foul and was breathing it right into ma coupon; I'm squeamish at the best of times, but this was something else. Phew, ah thought ah was goin' tae puke, so it was a case of "that's great, that's fine pal, just what I wanted", then wing'm **a handsome tip**, an' leap swiftly out the door gaspin' for fresh air.

After Aden it was back through the Suez to the Med - can't remember a thing about that return trip through the Canal, so perhaps it was a case of "been there, done that!" I'm not best pleased to be heading back to 'the sceptered isle'; having revelled in all the 'dime a dozen' carnal pursuits 'out East'. Going back puts the dampers on these little games as I'm not returning to a steady girlfriend, and although it's the Sixties it's not yet the 'Swinging Sixties' - that came nearer to the Seventies, so it's nae nookie fir me; *let's hope ah dinnae get withdrawal symptoms*. However, let's not brood, because as we know, hope springs eternal.

Tenby coordinated exercise 'Decex', which, along with 'damage control' routines and war games, involved getting through the, abnormally choppy, Mediterranean Sea as quickly as possible. As we push our way further west the weather worsens and by the 11TH are being battered head on by a full gale, making life more than just a touch uncomfortable for the sailor boys *(the Med is always flat calm - **oh yeah, that'll be right!**)*. I often think about *and can picture* Billy the 'chippy' passing the Galley, fingering his worry beads while muttering **"It's murder, fuckin' murder!"**

During this howling storm tragedy struck when one of Tideflow's AB's lost his life whilst working on the upper deck, a very sad end and quick startle back to reality after an amazing trip. When the weather abated, we refuelled once more from Tideflow, then parted company, she heading for Newcastle and us to Chatham. But, the Queen's men ain't home yet and run into more 'roughers' *(take that, ya bastards)* off Portugal before returning safe 'n' sound to our homeport, and a heroes' welcome, after 'clocking-up' sixty thousand miles in forty one weeks and three days. ***Game over!***

Remember my homeward-bound misgivings - we've only been docked a matter of hours when I get a jaw-dropper, in losing my best mate. Yeah, that's right, Lew's for 'the off'. The 'wide boy' gets confirmation that his compassionate discharge - *something he'd never mentioned - known as 'Discharge by Purchase'* has been granted, meaning with 'services no longer required' he can buy his freedom for a paltry sum, after which he intends returning to Peru - to marry his heart's desire (**marry** - *the very idea - who'd've guessed);* but therein lies another story; although *perhaps under a deportation order* he did go to Peru *where he resides to this day* - over the years we've kept in touch; from his comments he remains a bit of a lad. There again, it's hard to supress the habits of a lifetime - need I tell you, he ends his letters with ***"Keep it up, and keep it clean!"***

Bet you thought I'd forgotten - allow me to reintroduce **Darryl,** *Naval steward and seaman extraordinaire* so as to make his curtain call. 'Twas our first weekend back in Chatham Dockyard; those not on First Leave Party are huddled in the Mess, wrapped up against the cold, whilst reading the Sunday papers. Would you believe it? There he is in the 'News of the World' Darryl F. Bailey telling his story; ***he's done it*** - yes, Darryl's been discharged on medical grounds. He'd played his cards so well, convincing 'them wot be' he was a basket case; clever guy *(many try this ploy; only to end up twiddling their thumbs in Netley nuthouse)*, so there he is selling his story. The guy must've been 'well caked up' to afford all the things he'd got up to - he certainly had style, as there was the man himself, looking the part wearing a blazer sporting his self-designed family-crest. I think he said he was opening a restaurant, which I can only assume *knowing his abilities* would be rather special - so exit Darryl.

It's the middle of December; as said, First Leave Party has gone and

Wave Prince about to refuel Tenby (R.A.S.) whilst on 'Iceland Patrol'.

now the ship has been moved into dry dock, meaning we are on shoreside power, which for some unexplained reason means short power supplies. Amongst other hardships we have no heating in the Mess and 'JC', it's 'taters' - ah've hud tae brek oot ma thermal kilt; and as if that isn't enough, we've been told that after the Leave period, Tenby has been earmarked for 'Iceland Patrol' to guard our trawlers in the godforsaken fishing grounds up there - we, the Brits, were involved in a dispute with the Vikings at that time; christened the 'Cod Wars'. Yes, 'the powers that be' had got it right again - just back from the sweltering tropics and straight up to the Arctic!! Talk about out of the frying pan and into the fridge!

Brother Carnie *being made of 'stern stuff'* had been Merchant Seaman for many years, so our paths hadn't crossed in a while, but as luck would have it, he was serving on the RFA 'oiler' Wave Prince which refuelled us at sea on that patrol and whilst not exactly a family reunion, we managed to ridicule one another as our ships ploughed along, 'joined at the hip' by a big black umbilical cord pumping f.f.o. into our tanks way down below. As Wave Prince was now returning to Rosyth I took advantage of this by

sending some belongings, including my Hong Kong-bought guitar, over to him by 'jackstay transfer' - this little move was to save me lugging it all the way up from Chatham come next Leave. Being tone-deaf, I couldn't play the bleedin' thing anyway, and eventually gifted it to someone who could - that's me 'Big Herted Boaby'.

I'm at a loss, as to any other highlights during that miserable and rarely calm patrol. We were really on the rundown towards the end of the 'commish' by then, and, as always, involved in various exercises. One taking us to Londonderry - *which was a stonkin' good run ashore before becoming the ultimate training ground for the British Army* and I'm sure we must have gone to Portland since nobody escapes that dismal place.

We proudly 'showed the flag' to Brest in 'La Belle France' - *far from impressed with our reception, talk about gettin' the 'cold shoulder'*. On returning from a run ashore the ever-wise *but unbalanced* Jock McSporran remarked, "That lot wouldnae gie ye a nod in the desert!" Yes, one couldn't help but get the message that we were being tolerated and nothing more - wouldn't go back in a hurry! After saying that, they can poke thur effin' Euros - we all know the prices will be 'up oor erses' again, just like wot 'appened with decimalisation, ***sacré bluey mon ami mate; wotta con that was!***

The next 'Jolly' was a trip through the Kiel Canal to reach Aarhus in Denmark; a charming town with medieval shops and quaint dwellings, *where, you'll remember, I got the tracksuit idea* - there's a park called The Tivoli Gardens, which our 'sea daddy' L/Std Packer said was hoachin' wi' 'bum bandits' at night, and well known for its 'whispering bushes' where 'the benders' lurked under a cloak of darkness, calling out **"Psst Jack! Psst Jack!"** - it may well've been one from his treasure trove of wind-ups: I recall the sarky git saying in an off-hand fashion "Shiner, when is your time up?" Caught on the hop, I answered innocently "67" to which he replied "Have a look in the bottom of my locker and you'll find a big old key, lock the dockyard when you've finished!" - **Shitehouse!**

That summer Tenby was 'Guardship' for the Cowes Annual Regatta, which really just involved us lying at-anchor offshore looking the part and creating a nautical backdrop for the filthy rich ponces in their yachts and dinghies. It was of no interest to Jack, but I daresay this gathering of the 'smart set' went down big bundles with the Wardroom bunch, as hobnobbin'

it at the many "simply spiffing" cocktail parties must have resulted in some of the 'Hooray Henrys' gettin' 'a bit oot o' watch'.

Here's a little beaut from our Regatta detail. 'Twas was a pleasant Saturday afternoon; those with nothing better to do were on the Quarterdeck taking the air, and goofing around while idly scanning all manner o' craft sailing by, when 'Nobby' Clark, who is over on the port side, shouts "Hey cop a load o' this!" We gather round him, jostling to grab a squint at this clinker-built dinghy, aptly named 'Saucy Sue', stuffed to the gunnels wae healthy young snatch, scantily clad in bikinis and shorts, drifting slowly past; the brazen hussies circle our stern to make sure we get an eyeful.

So there we are ogling, waving and calling when a voice behind us yells "Get out of the way so they can see **me!**" It was like the parting of the Red Sea in the Bible and there's this grotty little stoker posing against a broom in his dirty 'ovies', 'steaming boots' and sweatrag, looking the very image of Doberman in the 'Phil Silvers Show' - I tell you; precious memories such as that, are treasured in the recesses of my mind forever.

Our last visit before the paying-off pennant got hoisted was to our 'name town' Tenby in the Principality of Wales, I guess this was supposed to be the grand finale; so mustn't let the side down and happily there is *as always* a tale 'waiting in the wings'.

Tenby's a seaside town with a picturesque harbour, not deep or large enough to accommodate a frigate of the line, so we are 'anchored off' in Carmarthen Bay - therefore it's a Liberty Boat shuttle service. Tough, but that's not going to deter us stalwarts from leaping ashore in a blaze o' glory, to sniff around; intent on ferreting out some 'Welsh rough'.

Being back in the UK and without my nemesis to light the way, whilst flitting down his well-trodden track I'm struggling and if truth be told, getting S.F.A - but they say 'God loves a trier', so it's early afternoon and I'm ashore on a quest with the team. We're down at the beach, and have trapped two chirpy Welsh rarebits; they're in their early twenties and *if to be believed* school teachers. We've been chattin' them up for about thirty minutes; everyone's having a laugh and getting on famously.

Now, you know how sayings come and go with the times. Well, then, a popular one with us was "**you've no scruples at all**". 'Dai' Laffin *(I assume)* had picked this up wrong and during the conversation smiles

one of his best at the girls and slips it in at what he sees as an appropriate moment, saying "**The trouble with you girls, is you've no scrotums at all**!" Silence, followed by sniggers, and Taffy, with an inscrutable grin on his coupon, saying "**What?**" *seemingly* unaware of the fact that the once interesting and entertaining sailor boys were suddenly scuppered and completely blown-out - ***you can't beat an unconscious comedian!***

Later I dropped into a snack bar for a quick scran, rather than return to the ship and then come back - that's fine when alongside, but stuff the Liberty Boat nonsense. That must've been when I got in tow with three raunchy bints, on holiday from somewhere in the Home Counties. We were getting on a treat, so I spent the evening entertaining my new friends; during which we consumed strong drink and had a sparkling time *(get them laffin' an' yer halfway there)*. Well, you know how it is when you're enjoying yourself in good company - the night was gone; and so was the last Liberty Boat. **Bollocks**! However my, by now, best friends came to my rescue, inviting me to get my head down in their static caravan. I'd love to say otherwise, but I *of course* got 'the baldy heid' - I'm so glad I made a pig o' masel in the Far East - talk about feast and famine!

Next morning the Dawn Patrol of knackered party animals are traipsing back to the quayside through the still-asleep town, as it's 'early doors', and if we don't get on the Liberty Boat we're adrift and 'in the rattle'. Understandably most of last night's revellers have a raging thirst, acquired from a hard night trying to drink the pubs dry, so are forced to swipe pints of milk from doorsteps; ***and it never tasted better!***

On the jetty, stories of last night's escapades are being swapped and, as ever, blown out of proportion. My mates, knowing where I'd been and wrongly assuming ah'd 'got ma end away', jealously called me 'trailer trash' with 'Wiggy' Bennet saying "You must've slept like a rabbit, Shiner!" When I gave him an enquiring look, he said "You know, out one hole and in the other!" As already admitted I'd got 'brussel sprout', but smiled and discreetly said nothing; happy to let their minds work overtime.

That's it folks, the commission is 'done and dusted' and the draft chits have arrived. Wow! this is exciting, yet sad at the same time, as everyone; ***well, almost everyone,*** has established valued friendships with some terrific and amazing characters, most of whom we'll never see again - but, that's

just the way it is in 'the Mob'. That said, there are always the few we're glad to see the back of, praying they get a real sickener and we never ever again set eyes on them. I could think of two or three obnoxious gits who well deserved the old 'Brothel Bred Fuckpig' title.

So, it's over, and we're all being sent off to new homes - sort of like *or so I imagined at the time* leaving Barnardo's and being fostered out. Well, come on! come on! my hands are shaking with excitement. It's got to be a ship, I wonder what kind, let's hope its going to exotic foreign shores teemin' wae dusky maidens *who'll pander to my every whim* - that'd be ace, just like the Far East all over again - yes, let's keep it real!

Aw fuck! ***A shore Base!*** A bleedin' air-station! HMS Fulmar - RNAS Lossiemouth *(now RAF Lossiemouth)*. **Bollocks!** - ah'm gonna hate it!

This is my story - this is my song
I've been in 'the Andrew' too fuckin' long

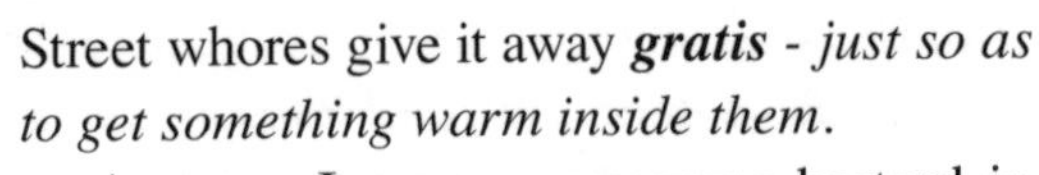

So dry the tears, it won't be forever. I disguise my devastation with a forced smile and say "Just the ticket!", pack my gear, collect my travel warrant from the 'Swain', dear old Bertie Bunting, at the Coxswain's Office and I'm off, kitbag on shoulder and wee broon attaché case in free hand *once again* to a brand new life and more adventures. But, I know I'm going to a place where the sun don't shine - as a couple of guys, who'd been stationed at the northern outpost, took delight in telling me me how far above the snowline it is, and so brutal in winter that Aberdeen's Union Street whores give it away ***gratis*** *- just so as to get something warm inside them.*

Anyway, I guess some smug bastard in the Haslemere Drafting Office thought, 'he's a Jock - he must want to be up there with the Picts'. So it looks like ah'd better haul ma' sorry ass up the road; after all, ah've been wi' thae English twats *(who eat their young)* long enough and without realizing, have lapsed into their ways. Now aware of this, it occurs to me I'd better brush up my hoots maun och aye the noo native tongue, so as to make masel' understood whair ah'm goin'.

HMS Fulmar's crest

18: HMS Fulmar RNAS - Lossiemouth

I've arrived, shattered *after changing trains in Aberdeen,* yes, I'm here standing at the gates o' Hell, and **yes**, this **is** a long way up the road. Remember, we're talking about a time before motorways and the Forth Road Bridge; d'you know what ah'm sayin'? It was ferries wi' paddles over the Forth back then, *and no mobile phones; ya spoilt gits*. Never mind, look on the bright side - I've sold my inflatable sheep, because they've got the real thing up here and ***ah ha!*** I've got a brand new pair o' wellies - oh yeah, a wee bit o'sheep shaggin' is the done thing in these parts, an' you've got to go wi' the flow *(ah'm savin' the last dance for ewe).*

So, I'm at the Main Gate looking down into Fulmar, seeing rows of Nissen huts - it's amazing what can go through one's head, because, stood there daydreaming, I imagine it's a WWII airfield; *since that's what it resembles*. It's easy to picture in my mind's eye, pilots in heavy well-worn brown leather flying-jackets with big fur collars sitting on upturned Sunlite soapboxes beside Spitfires and Hurricanes, playin' cards, smokin' Wild Woodbines and listening to Dame Wots'rface singin' about bluebirds wingin' it over the white cliffs o' Dover, on an old wind-up gramophone while waiting to catch **"Scramble"** squawk from a tinny Tannoy.

On hearing this they'd leap up and race to the camouflaged fighters, decorated with swastikas painted on the sides of their cockpits, indicating kills by young indoctrinated aces who have shot down Messerschmitts, Fockewulfs and Stukas, while defending the Realm - the lucky ones becoming Group Captains, and the chosen few surviving to reach the dizzy heights, proudly sportin' chests plastered wi' medals.

I'm snapped out of it when the Duty RPO enlightens me by snarling "Bloody General Servicemen, you'd better shape up if you want to get by up here, Sunshine." *(traditionally there was friction between the General Service types and Fleet Air Arm bods)*. Och, do me a favour; loosen up toots, I know it's a first date, but don't be afraid to put some feeling into it, I've just travelled four hundred sodding miles to get here.

Anyway, the mouthy git's probably never even seen a ship, let alone

gone to sea, so who the fuck does this jumped-up oik think he's talking to? Yes Siree, I'm an old hand now; a real 'Jack me tickler tin'.

The sneering moron points me in the required direction, while warning me the first three huts on the right are Wrens' Quarters and the **next one down** belongs to the Officers' Cooks and Stewards - mmm, now there's a challenge, *velly intelesting!* To the left are tennis courts with beyond them the Wardroom and Wardroom Galley, and at the foot of the road a huge modern accommodation block incorporating Ship's Company Galley and dining hall with the large NAAFI canteen above. Behind this is the airfield with its hangars and all the gubbins associated with an air-station.

So I park my gear beside an empty bed and locker in my new Mess, which is only yards from the Main Gate. It's just the usual - no more than a big hut; not unlike the first billet I was cooped up in, when a rookie at Raleigh. It has about thirty beds, some doubled-up; *no, ya stupid prick, not that way - one on top of the other*. There's a pot-bellied stove at each end and the deck is shining; so it's hunky-dory.

D'you know what I do now? Yes, you're way ahead of me - my joining routine. It takes a while, as this is a big sprawling place with the stores *(bedding etc)* and offices tucked away higgledy-piggledy in nooks and crannies. There are at least a dozen spaces to be stamped on the joining card - Pusser likes everything 'cut and dried'; so there are no short cuts.

That done I report to my new D.O. across at the Wardroom - he's a Supply Officer, a dapper wee 'Subby' called Foreskin *or something like that* an arrogant twat, you know the type *(like us to be 'umble)*. I'm sure we'll get along just fine, that is, if I can keep out of his way. Anyway, I'm stood *to attention* in front of this pompous tosser, who, with large horn-rimmed spectacles covering half his supercilious coupon, reminds me of Ronnie Corbett, while he pontificates then gestures dismissal whilst ordering me to report *at the double* to the Chief Cook.

Funny - ever noticed how, no matter what day you join you're duty-watch - as if to prove a point, I'm told "Get into your whites and turn to in the Wardroom Galley". "Right away Chief, yoa d'man!" As you know, I've had reservations about this place - but, this 'ere's a bit of alright! There's a big brigade of cooks and it's a laugh a minute with this band of seasoned brigands, who couldn't give a fish's tit about authority, so it's not beyond

the realms of possibility that I'm going to enjoy working alongside this shower o' knaves - *mostly from Aberdeen and Glasgow.*

The Chief and his POs really can't handle them, so discipline is lax, but because the work gets done they tolerate the situation; so there's a certain harmony that's respected by all. It's much the same story with the stewards; an alliance o' philistines - everything gets done the way **we** want, but since it goes like clockwork those further up the ladder turn a blind eye. None of the Regulating Branch *or others of that ilk* ever come near our 'drum', it's as if the sanctum is out of bounds - this is like Pompey Barracks all over again, so it seems that we shouldn't pass judgement before the event - *but that trait is predetermined; human nature being what it is.*

Our shift's over and we're back in the Mess with heaps o' 'sarnies' an' kettles o' tea - duty-watch coming off always bring stacks of scran over from the Wardroom Galley; *crumbs from the rich man's table - why starve in the land of plenty!* Just goes to show, you shouldn't listen to unfounded gossip, I could get used to this place in a big way. It's not the same where the 'hairy-fairies' live; it's 'Pusser' down there; with even the shitehawks *(mafia of the skies)* patrolling in formation, but what do we care? **Not a jot**, shacked-up here in our bolt hole, a law unto ourselves.

Well, I'm now one of the merry gang - which feels good; but there's always an other side to the coin. My new 'shipmates' are telling me how it is up here in the 'northern wastes' - and while speaking highly of the rutting season, not exactly painting a rosy picture. The first kick in the nuts is the taverns close at nine-thirty, *yeah, nine-thirty*, and don't open on Sundays - ***but; aar, we be smart - we be 'avin' the NAAFI canteen!***

I've already met some of the civilian staff, who are locals employed to work in the Wardroom and elsewhere around the Base; a battalion o' loveable rogues, who've been here forever and have it all sussed out to their advantage. In their ranks they even have a gang o' poachers lead by Big Jim *the brains of the outfit* who has it so well organized that the Wardroom is their best customer for salmon and venison. Nae wonder they're called the canny Scots, it's cannae dae this and cannae dae that, when asked to do something they don't consider is in their job description. Yeah, you've got it, they're the real old hands around here, **all clued up.**

There were so many characters in that Mess who, for their antics,

deserve a mention, but that would take forever, so I'll concentrate on the 'big noises'. Starting with the 'in yoar face' 'Ben' Gunn, as it's impossible for me to think of Fulmar without remembering Ben; a wit, hailin' frae the fair city o' "Aeburdeen". This comic, who took delight in referring to the padre as ***'the Munching Monk'***, entertained us from the minute he woke - even when moaning his ugly face off about some injustice he imagined only he suffered he nevertheless had the knack, expression and tone of voice to make us laugh. Officers' Steward Gunn occupied a top-bunk and had the top-locker beside his pit, so everything was to hand when 'turned in'.

Ben wore thick heavy-framed glasses and liked a fag, so every morning, on waking, followed a well-rehearsed routine. His left hand would grope around the locker-top to find his glasses and tabs, then he'd fire up a 'blue liner' and have a guid cough, often in a foul mood, which may well've been an act to make us laugh, especially when his regular tormentor, a gobby Glasgwegian steward, took the piss, but the novice was no match for 'Mr Lightning' who retaliated instantly, rippin' him up for arsepaper. He'd missed his vocation and should've been 'treading the boards', many of his 'one liners' being as much for his own amusement as ours.

'Twas after a rather harassing Wardroom Mess Dinner in honour of some historic sea battle; this had been a trying day for the skivvies; *most, now justifiably a bit niggled,* so taunts and venomous insults were hurtling - talk about 'The Clash of the Titans' - Ben's 'tormentor' is having a pop, pointing and commenting, with a sly smile on his face, that Ben has a little pot belly. 'The Lossie Lip' immediately shoots him down in flames, responding loudly for all to hear, "Just made tae fit the small o' yer back, **pal!**"

Later, when gathered round our glowing cast iron stove, all was forgotten and Ben *now in fine fettle* had us in stitches. The jokes and wit just kept coming and the more we laughed, the more wound-up he got, everyone *including him* had tears in their eyes - I remember he kept taking his 'Gregorys' off to wipe them and his eyes, without missing a beat. Our sides were aching, making us beg him to "Gies a brek!" - thus merely encouraging him into 'rapid fire mode' - nobody could 'pull his plug' that night - pure vaudeville Baby; no' a dry eye in the hoose!

Now, here's a classic for you, back in **'the happy days'** before discos and AIDS were invented, I've already crowed of how we went to real

dancehalls with live bands, groups and singers. Thursday nights we frequented The Two Red Shoes in Elgin; always a good night dancing to Alex Sutherland's Sextet, or top groups, touring. We copped all the big names such as The Swinging Blue Jeans, Emile Ford and the Checkmates, and a host of others, in fact few didn't make it to Elgin. Well, anyway, this time it was a young Lulu and the Luvvers; so picture this - Ben, who doesn't dance, is with us flash gits *'flauntin' it' in civvies* we've had a wee bevvy to liven things up, so are 'on the pull'. Lulu's on the stage, in a very short skirt, looking brilliant and giving it 'laldy' behind the footlights: there's our Ben lurkin' in front of the stage in a world of his very own, still wearing his Naval Burberry hands in pockets and fag in mouth leering up at her firm body through the bottle-top glasses. That image will stay with me until my dying day; which I fear may not be far off. - did I tell you? Last funeral I was at; guess who caught the wreath?

Ben was adamant that there was a poofters' hotel in Elgin; swearing, a sign hanging in one of its windows read **'Fred and Breakfast 5/-'**.

Now it's 'Perry' Mason's turn - another Aberdonian; he, like me, was a 'slosh' in the Wardroom Galley. Perry had a flair for getting in trouble - correction, getting caught; probably just unlucky, as he was no worse than most, but spent more time than anyone I can remember in the brig, or on 'Number Nines'. His accent was very broad - the cause of great amusement when he reported sick and had to see a rather dishy Wren Lieutenant Medical Officer who, when she asked Perry what ailed him, her smiling patient smartly replied "Piesantaes, Mam!" The lady was completely bewildered; she'd never heard of that one before, and sure as hell wouldn't be mentioned in her medical books - no most certainly not, but if she'd had wee peek under POISONED TOES all would've been revealed.

I'd only been there a matter of weeks when Perry's younger brother, Brian *also an Officers' Cook* arrived; they were two of a kind, both popular good-looking hunks with dark-brown mischievous eyes and buckets o' panache. The amusing thing was, they shared a family trait which was hard to miss, because their white cooks' aprons were always grubby in the middle *(they couldnae keep thir hauns oaf thimsells)*. I've just remembered a story of how Perry had escaped from one of his many stays in the brig and was chased by a helicopter, while going pell-mell over rough country.

That tale may well've been blown way out of proportion, but reminds me of a cracker, so if you think you've heard it all - get this.

'Twas Yuletide at Fulmar, and the day of the RAs' sprogs' Christmas party. 'Banjo' West *a PO 'hairy-fairy'* had been detailed off to be Santa Claus - *remember him from the days when you were a greedy little Me! Me! Me! bastard?* Well now, Banjo was far from chuffed; it was just after 'Up Spirits', so he'd probably sunk more than his fair share of Pusser's 'bubbly'; 'forced' upon him by mates who felt sorry for the poor cunt. 'Three sheets to the wind', he's got all the Santa gear on, shouldering a sack full o' pressies and, amid jeers, being slowly winched down from this big red Wessex rescue-chopper to the wide-eyed open-mouthed pointing snot-nosed snappers, when he shouts "Ho! Ho! **Fuckin'** Ho!" Needless to say, Banjo was bang in trouble, and *as they say* 'his feet didn't touch'. However, *most* of us knew Santa wasn't for real and curled up laffin', while thinking it well worth whatever festive punishment the Jimmy dished out to the half-pished bellend ***- oh yes, for him, it was 'a rum do'!***

Just delved into the grey matter and dredged up yet another two of Ben's sardonic jibes, casually flung to belittle his arch-enemy - "Hey pal, why don't ye graft a pair o' tits on yer back, so we kin aw feel at hame!" **and** "If it wisnae fir the Navy ye'd be lyin' in the gutter wi' yer baws hingin' oot!" *(When the gloves were off, Ben had a way with words).*

'Big' Don, also from 'the granite city' - if you saw him in the showers you'd know why he was called **Big** Don. He was a real happy chappie *it's not hard to guess why* another one with an all consuming interest in gynaecology, always sniffing around the Wrens with a knowing grin on his coupon. He and I pulled a few strokes, as Don was a big twisted chancer always game for a laugh. On thinking back I remember Ben saying "It'd make yer eyes water" and christened him 'Jock the Cock'.

One episode worth relating was the time we conned our wee Divisional Officer into letting us go on an 'outward bound expedition' to Loch Lomond. He sanctioned our request on the understanding that we take the two Junior Cooks, as it would be "character building". **Was it ever!** We got them 'well guttered', then had them looking for the Loch Ness Monster and their tent blew off, leaving them soaked two nights in a row - *'twas more than just sheer luck our young charges didn't cop pneumonia.*

Where was I? Oh yeah, we drew tents, sleeping bags, provisions and transport, then off we went on our expedition *unsupervised* to Loch Lomond; where none of us had been before. We camped there for two days but the weather was grim and there was no action, so on the third day we moved on to Oban, where, when mixing with the common people in a popular little lounge bar called The Lobster Pot, Don and myself trapped a couple of hospitable bits o' fanny "frae Glesgae". They were sisters and a pretty game pair who seemed 'up fir it' so we told the laddies to fuck off, find a chippie, feed their faces and go back to camp. They knew the drill, so made themselves scarce, leaving us in the boozer with the two slappers.

Following traditional foreplay procedure we got them 'tanked up', telling each other what we were going to do to them each time we were up at the bar or they were in the 'lavvy'. By closing time we've got them well bevvied, an' it wisnae cheap - it's cold outside and the four of us are heading unsteadily for the campsite; *Don and me smirking and telling them we'll soon get them warm.* We're nearly back when the older sister, **mine**, says she's "fair burstin' furra 'single fish' an' cannae wait". Ah can hardly believe ma eyes when she squats down right there in front of us and 'lets go' on the pavement - as if that's not enough the daft bitch is so drunk, she forgets to pull her jeans down. Excuse the pun, but that puts the dampers on it for me; Don, wearing a lop-sided grin, is pleading with me, and for that matter so is her sister, but they're on a loser, I can't, I just can't. Hell's bells, ah wus traumatized, *I didn't even know they pished.* So it wasn't a case of 'spread 'em and brace yersel Baby' - 'twas 'no way José!'

It was a nap - Big Don's weapon eventually got him into 'bovver' when he gave the Captain's secretary a bellyful o' arms 'n' legs. Wotta shame, lovely girl; she had long dark hair - looked like the singer Sandie Shaw. We all worshipped her from afar, *all except Don that is,* **crikey!** we didn't realize he even knew 'Sandie' and there he was slippin'r a length, the big crafty bugger - *Ben was all for havin'm neutered.* She got twins and he got a draft chit - aye; they guid lookin' wimen kin git a laddie intae trouble!

Well, spank my ass and call me daddy!

Oh yeah, we mustn't forget the Killick of the Mess, 'Matt' Dillon was an amusing little bog-trotter, who 'ruled the roost', so, had his own room over to the right just inside the entrance of our hut, this was a blessing, as

in there he used to murder his clarinet, which *to be sure - to be sure* only he thought he could play. I well remember his coupon, with its beaming smile and jutty-out chin - *like the joker in a pack of cards*. Whenever I see a picture of the man in the moon in children's books it reminds me of Matt; who had a warped sense of humour. Two things which Matt thought funny spring to mind. One was, he bought a brand new grey minivan when they first came out and were ultracheap *(about £350),* and whenever driving back from Elgin to Lossie if he passed any Ratings thumbing a lift he wouldn't stop, just wave and give them a big silly grin. The other was when our confused cat, Rover *(also named Jynxie),* surprised us by having four super little kittens with lovely markings; the stupid Irish git, in his infinite wisdom, drowned them in the Mess fire bucket - in the ensuing rumpus, Paddy came close to 'swinging from the rafters'.

'Ere's a diamond geezer, wae a roving eye, who never missed a trick and became a really good mate - in many ways a seasoned old hand, as before joining 'the Andrew' he'd been in 'the Paras', but discharged on medical grounds - *the ole 'dukes' didn't take too kindly, on landing from great heights with a thump*. His name? Oh yeah! Jim 'Scouse' O'Reilly - another wisecrackin' 'wacker', from 'the Pool' and yes, the same guy already mentioned as being at the cinema in Elgin with me when we saw 'Dr No'; starring the 'hunky young god' from the 'Teen Years' sighting in Princes Street - Sean 'Canary'. Scouse, like myself, was an Officers' Cook; when out gallivanting, we had some hilarious times, so it was a loss when he was drafted *I've forgotten where,* but I'm delighted to say we were destined to meet again and again in the following years.

I remember going to Liverpool on the second half of my Christmas Leave that year and being treated like visiting gentry at the O'Reilly family home. Scouse showed me some magic nights in his favourite alehouses and I recall being 'made up' when introduced to 'the grape' in those wicked wine lodges; also a mental trip to the Liverpool/Everton football derby on the back of a coal lorry. *(Grandfather Webber cashed in his chips when I was down in Scouseland but, not having left a contact number, the first I knew of this was after our return to Lossie).*

I doubt if we ever missed the Thursday night jiggin' at The Two Red Shoes - a good trapping ground for local talent; the first lassie I copped

there wasn't the object of my desires for long; *her name was Aileen.* On the night I met her *to me* she looked terrific when peering through my beer window in the dimly lit romantic dancehall - she was an Elgin girl, so seeing her home was no problem; as by this time I owned a set o' wheels *better tell you that next.* Anyway, we made a date for the following Saturday - on seeing her again, I was confused, as in the cold light of day she looked so different that I wasn't sure if it was the same girl - and strangely, nothing resembling Miss World; which had me, once more, doubting the wisdom of my ways. The next time, I picked Aileen up at her home, where, on clockin' the mother *a bruiser, who reminded me of an Eastern European shot-putter* my enthusiasm vanished in a trice - yes, the magic was gone. Shortly after that the fire went oot an' ah bolted the course.

One's first car *being a milestone in a young man's life* should've been bragged about earlier, so I'll fix that now. I had been taking driving lessons from an instructor in Lossiemouth *(the town, not the Base)*, and, just to rain on your parade, yet again, they only set me back seven shillings and sixpence per hour - that works out in today's loot at thirty-seven and a half pence; ***pray tell, have I already mentioned* 'the happy days'**?

I can't remember how I found out, so assume one of my pals back home phoned or wrote telling me that an Edinburgh lawyer was about to sell his car *said to be "in good nick"* so I went back home on a 'long weekend' and bought my first motor for the princely sum of 180 sheets. It was a powder blue Standard Vanguard *(Phase II)* with radio, heater and overdrive - *all extras at the time;* and, from memory, about five years old.

Now then, not as yet having sat the test I was still a Provisional Driver; so needed a qualified driver at my side to get the car back to Fulmar - no sweat, I had that sorted with one of the cooks in our Mess. Bill, a 'Fly Fifer' from St. Monance, had volunteered; saying, since he was taking the same weekend he'd get the early train over to Edinburgh on the Monday morning, then we could go up the road together, doing me a favour and letting him cadge a run back; like I said, sorted - ***aar, I be smart, I be!***

Everything goes to plan, so there we are 'cruisin' kool' up the A90 with stacks o' time in hand, Perth's well behind us when I ask Bill if he wants a 'shot'; ***that's when he tells me he can't drive.*** **The stupid git**! I think I had just cause to be annoyed and, on reflection, ought to have emptied

him out there and then. Well, I had no option other than *fingers crossed* to press on regardless - luckily making it back to Lossiemouth without gettin' 'a pull'; no thanks to Bill - *about as much use as a nun's tits.* **Do I find them, or do they find me?**

Apart from the lessons I got in plenty practise driving round the Base; *this being private property and a fair size.* So when I took my driving test it seemed a piece o' piss, as being up north the Elgin roads were very quiet back then - and listen to this; the nearest traffic lights were in Inverness. I thought I'd got a 'green rub', as my test fell on Market Day - slightly busier than the norm. Piece o' piss or not, it's still a great feeling to have a full licence; this was something I had long yearned for - now, when out on the prowl, I possessed the key to wider horizons. ***Sweeet!!!***

Owning a set o' wheels certainly helped weeds *like me* cop the bints - definitely, instrumental in opening up a whole feast of opportunity, but for six months or so I was 'going steady' and taking delight in 'doing things' down many a quiet country lane with Jodie: so was 'off the circuit'.

The lively Jodie was an affectionate *but somewhat disturbed* girl who scrubbed up incredibly well, but I always thought there was a mean streak that showed in her eyes paired with a wee chip on her shoulder. This affliction may well've been down to the fact that her mother *(who turned out to be a two-faced insincere cow with a nippy tongue)* was a single parent - *well frowned upon back then.* Also mummy liked a bevvy and as if that wasn't enough, had a barmpot boyfriend who 'took a bucket', so all that possibly made Jodie a touch insecure. Oh! did I say, she was only seventeen; it's best to catch 'm fresh an' groom'm tae suit yer needs!

We saw a lot of each other in the early days; when I was welcome at their house in the Bishopmill estate on the outskirts of Elgin. Jodie and I did the rounds together; I well remember this night in the hotel bar down by Lossiemouth Harbour when the landlord refused to serve me, thinking I was underage. I, affronted, showed him my Naval ID which doesn't say much for his judgement, since he wasn't questioning Jodie's age - there's her sweet seventeen, and me twenty-three. I guess I must've been a right 'piece o' skin' in these days; I wonder what's happened, as it seems like yesterday ***- oh, how cruel the years can be!***

I'm thinking of the time we went to a Dusty Springfield concert in Elgin

Town Hall - this was in the early days of Dusty's career, so she was still with her brothers and billed as 'The Springfields'. We must have arrived 'early doors', since we scored front row seats - for me the show was a brammer, because, unbeknown to Jodie, the diva kept giving the glad eye to 'yours truly'. Now, I twigged it was all part of the act, for her to home in on one of the audience, but nothing matches a smile from a pretty girl to give the old morale a major boost. Although Jodie was none the wiser, ah wus 'chuffed tae fuck'; at that time little realizing 'Lusty Coalfield' *as the boys called her* had leanings towards the other persuasion. Maybe she recognized something about me that I was unaware of; like I said, 'a nice piece o' skin' - ***oh well, I suppose it's a bit late now!***

Suddenly Jodie's 'old wife' went right off me, not only was I treated like a bad smell - the auld has-been *(who, by the way, was in her mid thirties and had been a fair bit o' gear in her day)* told Jodie to stop seeing me - **ouch!** I can't recall her reasoning; it may well've been down to their own relationship - volatile, to say the least. There always seemed to be resentment on both sides, with an undercurrent feud on a smouldering fuse. The mother's attitude merely fuelled our relationship which was by then dying the usual death, as at that age we're all playing the field and move on frequently, thus keeping life interesting - *probably a primal urge inbuilt from the dawn of civilization; the thrill of the hunt and all that.*

I told you Jodie had a mean streak - to my eternal delight she proved me right by being a spiteful little bitch shortly before we called it quits. **Get this**, one weekend the lush and her overripe toy boy went to a wedding on Mull; *'when the cat's away, the mice will play'*. Seizing the moment we partook in a Friday 'til Sunday 'sleepover'. These rewarding nights were spent in the Rottweiler's *just-delivered* new double bed, so, breaking all the rules, we 'christened it' - **Howzat for retribution?**

Burds are usually predictable; but not this one - ending a relationship can be uncomfortable for both parties and generally played out over a period of weeks, trying not to hurt each other's feelings; *that's assuming there are any feelings left*. Not this time, No! Not with Jodie who was an exciting, independent unpredictable girl; always full of surprises.

When the circus came to town, Jodie took a fancy to one of the roustabouts and when the circus left town so did Jodie - 'just like that'; she

'dunna runner' with her curly-haired, earring-adorned fairground lad and that was it, she was gone, no messing! She sure as hell gave me the easy way out and even now I remember her with affection. Hold on! - come to think of it, we had a romantic liaison a couple years later, when I was on Easter Leave from 'Fort Blockhouse'. I've forgotten how she got in touch, but was delighted with the tryst, *as it was a lean period.* At the time we planned a summer holiday together on the Norfolk Broads, but it never happened - I can't recall why - and I never saw or heard of the free-spirited Jodie again; *you win some - you lose some,* ***c'est la vie!***

That year summer came early - and I've just got to tell you about the afternoon a crowd from the Mess went to Lossie beach to grab a bit o' bronzy time. On arrival it was obvious that others from the Base had the same idea - *there being pockets of navymen all over the place* - remember, it's not long after tot time! A clutch o' local teenage bimbos appear on the scene; you know the type, 'wee hairys' - aye, yer 'on the ball'; **jailbait!** But, *better two at fifteen than one at thirty!* Anyway, they're provocatively parading around the beach exhibiting themselves in their skimpy bikinis, teasing Jack an' fair lappin' up the attention they 're getting. As they were cheekily strutting past us for the third time, two of our mad Aberdonians chorused "Here girls cop a load o' this" and, pulling their trunks aside, flash the wedding tackle. I'm thinking **'Jumpin'Jehovah;** that's bang oot o' order', and expecting them to run off screaming, but **oh no,** the tallest bold prick teaser blatantly retorts "That's five I've seen today!" Charming! Can't help but wonder what became of that one - probably 'took up the cloth' and joined the 'one day week brigade'.

You know how it is; the lower minions always get wind of scandals last, or, more than often, after the event. Well, about this same period a cracker of a buzz was circulating like wildfire when it emerged that a syndicate of Chiefs and POs had been caught running a brothel in an empty schoolhouse near the Base. Furthermore, it was reputed to be kitted out with Pusser's beds and furniture generally issued to Married Quarters. In addition it was alleged to be staffed - *and I use that word loosely*, by RAs' wives, promiscuous Wrens and local ladies; sort of like 'Footballers' Wives', but without the money. 'Twas said, when the shit hit the fan there were demotions and draft chits aplenty. Looking back and thinking about it;

that was a pretty resourceful enterprise, as in those days most would have settled for a bridge club followed by an indulgent game of strip poker.

Call me paranoid, but being a determined sod with the attitude of 'nothing ventured nothing gained', I periodically kept requesting to join the 'Silent Service' which, shrouded in mystery, held a certain magic that I yearned to be part of. This had become a challenge, if not an obsession, and no way did I want to go back to sea on anything, other than a submarine; being particularly concerned that my next draft could well be to a 'flat top' as a follow-up to an air-station; *seems logical, don't it?* These big ships are far too 'Pusser' for my liking, with their Master at Arms and his RPO thug cronies *(the crushers)*. OK, wee ships jump about in roughers, but have a relaxed matey atmosphere, so who, in their right mind, would want anything else? And let's not forget what big ships did to poor old Darryl! The smaller the ship, the more level the playing field, thus making the Wardroom/Lower Deck, *them and us* divide less obvious.

Wonders'll never cease! - just when convinced I've got ***'The Loozer'*** tattooed on my forehead *for all to see,* I stand corrected; persistence pays off, it's a done deal - my submarine request is recommended, but don't think for a minute that I've finally worn them down and 'them wot be' have capitulated. Oh no - that just doesn't happen! It's not what I want it's what Pusser wants and right now he'll even take the likes o' me, because submariners are back in business, as the Cold War has escalated; so, to address the Soviet threat serious 'coin' is being thrown at the Service and more 'boats' built - in turn, requiring trained submariners to crew them. Now the old rules don't apply - "Hay fever? - ***no problem, pal"!***

However, they still don't take Officers' Cooks, but that's 'nae sweat' when it suits - and, so it came to pass that I was proclaimed a Ships' Cook, issued a star sleeve-badge with C instead of OC and transferred doon the road tae the Ship's Company Galley and a Mess in that modern central heated accommodation block; *already spoken of.* The transition's a doddle and now I'm livin' in luxury wi' new best pals - but what about my old mates up the road you may ask. Well, I've said before, that's the way it is in 'the Mob', so these tosspots'll just have to make do without **me!**

Because this is a bang up-to-date well-appointed Galley, it's a breeze to work in, and we do work; it's not all fun and games, but you're no' here

tae listen tae me chunterin' on aboot how to make puff pastry; so we'll skip past all the technical nonsense - however, I need to tell you three things about that Galley before proceeding. Firstly, it had picture-windows along the back wall overlooking the hangars and airfield beyond, so it was exhilarating to see the Buccaneers take off and land. Secondly, RAF Vulcan Bombers would often 'stop over'; they were awesome to see taking off, the sheer power was astounding. When looking from the Galley down to the runway they used, there was a huge hangar in the line of vision, so when watching the 'V Bombers' leaving they were just taxiing along before vanishing behind this massive hangar. Then they reappeared, well up in the air, climbing almost vertically at a speed and with a thrust from their Rolls Royce engines that made the ground shake; disappearing before your very eyes, leaving nothing but a smoke-trail - **amazing, just amazing**. The third thing is; they say everyone remembers where they were when they heard President Kennedy had gone an' got himsel' iced; that could very well be true, as I can remember *more or less* the actual spot I was standing on in that Galley when it came over the radio - **honest!**

After a lively tot time, we'd have eating competitions *(Pusser's 'bubbly' creates a healthy appetite)* then, pigged out, repair up to the NAAFI for a 'lunchtime sesh'; finally *gibberin' like monkeys* toddle off 'in pieces' back to our comfort zone, to sleep it off. But, nothing's perfect - because, since our Mess was just one door of many in a long corridor and next to the 'heads', it was commonplace for a cook *(Aberdonian)* who lived in the next Mess along, to confuse our Mess with the heads when 'stocious'.

Jock would regularly try our patience by wandering in, bollocky-buff, stagger down our Mess on 'autopilot' and pish all over the radiators against the far wall under the windows *(in the same position as the urinals in the heads)*, then about-turn and weave his way back to his pit. Apart from that small fault, he was a nice quiet lad and always mopped up 'his little puddle' on 'surfacing' before supper. I was eternally grateful to be on a top bunk, two from the door, well away from Jock's indiscretion. Just thinking about it I can hear the chorus "**Oh Christ, here he comes, again!**"

We, butch alpha males, were constantly rakin' around forra 'slice o' tail' that's when the car came into its own, making us well-known to the 'snatch' at the dancehalls and pubs we frequented. As said earlier, the

'Swinging Sixties' had yet to happen and 'the pill' not readily available to the less-informed up north, so the success rate not nearly as high as is told by many *in their dotage* who reminisce. However, 'hope springs eternal', so we were five nights out of seven at the jiggin'; 'on the pull'. But here, listen up! It's not all bad news, so read on and weep. In the 'good old days' tights weren't in vogue so 'the enemy' wore stockings and 'sussies'. Oh my! That portion of velvet soft flesh between the stocking tops and the 'keckies'. ***Jings, dis it no gie ye a wee tremor jist thinkin' aboot it?***

'Twas an art making the 'chicken feed' spin out; on pay weeks when 'brassed up' we'd put petrol money in the kitty and treat ourselves to the occasional BLS - 'Figgy' Duff's creation and abbreviation for brandy, lime and soda. So, some o' that and a pair o' Carlsberg 'Speshuls' gave us the gift o' the gab and we could dance deep into the night. Remember, we generally slept like contented babies 'til the sun slipped o'er the yardarm - a great routine, which I highly recommend to all. Yeah me ole mate, Service life has many virtues; so get yersel' right in there!

'Blank weeks' we *the diehards* were 'potless', shufflin' along on the bones o' oor erses and had to improvise, so instead of Figgy's BLSs we substituted 'bennies' *(Benzedrine)* procured from Spike *'The Candyman'* Williams - a chipper two-badge Killick SBA with a craving for Pusser's 'bubbly'. I presume the intended use for these pills was to keep the pilots alert when night-flying; jet fighters being rather expensive to replace.

So, here's the game plan; Sunday - a rave-up in the NAAFI Club, with busloads of home-grown hootenanny ferried in from surrounding gene pools - *there were never enough Wrens to go round.* The ratio was always in Jenny's favour - I suppose, now that it's de rigueur for them to roost on ships they must be getting up to all sorts o' nonsense *bringing a whole new meaning to 'hot bunking'*- thus causing unrest and jealousy amongst the crew, as no matter what obstacles are put in place, human ingenuity will always win through an' they'll be 'friggin' in the riggin'. It's ludicrous, how in recent times centuries of Naval tradition have vanished - *I presume that Wrens on ships has led to the demise of* ***'the Barrel'.***

Monday nights it was Buckie dancehall, always good, especially so, when the "fishin' fleet wis oot" - *making it 'open season'*. One night it was televised, wotta hoot, seeing all the luvrats who weren't supposed to

be out to play, trying to dodge the cameras. Another night, Sergeant Plod, a constable and their talking dog flagged me down and 'fitted me up' by swearing blind, that I didn't stop the car at a Halt sign; which was absolute tosh, as they were round the corner and about thirty yards down the main road at the time. My point being, that if I couldn't see them there was **no way** they could see me. Shitehouses!

I expected the worst, as my juiced-up passengers were shouting "Tell thum tae fuck off!" and "Tell thum tae git tae fuck!" What did they care? Not a jot! Crikey, wot 'appened? Minutes ago I was everyone's pal ***'The Driver'*** now I'm the sacrificial lamb. Having stirred up a hornets' nest, the Polis gave me a ticket and took-off after gesturing dismissal while saying I'd probably hear no more about the matter; of course 'twas no surprise when I duly received a letter informing me the Banff court had fined me a pound in my absence. **Bugger thum!** On second thoughts; belay that- since I've heard tell, **Scotch arse is poisonous!**

Tuesdays and Wednesdays there was nuthin' doin', so the movers 'n' groovers caught up wi' the washin', ironin' an' pressin' - *brek oot the Rinso; must keep lookin' sharp!* Thursdays were, as already said, The Two Red Shoes in Elgin, Fridays - the Huntly Hop; with the highlight of the week being a wild hooley at the Craigellachie Saturday Night Sword Dance, where everyone sneaked in half-bottles, to consume in the 'kludgies'. Yes, quite a night *(the sort that makes yer sporran birl)*, going on until three a.m. - should've mentioned that the pubs 'last orders' had now been extended to a more civilized ten o'clock, causing the Church of Scotland's Bible-thumpers to excommunicate each and every one of us.

A group of local lads, **'Johnny and the Copycats'** played on the circuit**;** to give them credit, as good as any big names from the South, and excellent at mimicking 'The Fab Four'. When listening to Radio Scotland recently, my ears pricked up on hearing their name mentioned; and there was Johnny *the lead singer* being interviewed. He established that they are still on the go and were professional in the mid-60s with *to quote him* "fair success". It was strange, almost like the past coming back to haunt me from all these years ago, when the world was young, exciting ***and ours.***

We got up to all the tricks to give ourselves an edge; like 'Pearl Drops' toothpaste, and once tried a hair lotion called 'Light and Bright' which

claimed to tint your hair just enough to make it appear "bleached by the sun". Great, that's for us, we're havin' some o' that - so, inspired by the advert, slap it on, unconvinced that it would work. That night, it's Friday so we've hit Huntly, and there I am enthusiastically flappin' ma arms, doin' 'the Turkey Trot', imagining myself as smooth as a prom queen's thighs, when 'Randy Rita', the wild *rough as the heather* bi-curious kooky beatnik rock chick, strugglin' to contain her mirth, yells across the dance floor, throbbin' wi' punters twistin' the night away, "Hey Shiner, huv you bin dyein' yir hair?" Jist ma luck, 'Dame Footlights' had made my crowning glory appear as a glowing henna red - **what a clown!** Every move a coconut - yes we were a fine band of troupers; and sitting here now, oh, how I yearn for those halcyon days and smell of the greasepaint.

There were obviously plenty one night stands, all down to the law of averages or numbers game when you're out on the hunt five nights a week. Most of the Morayshire barbarians we met, knew and sometimes pulled, are long forgotten to me; as I'll be to them - *ah'll never forget wots'r name* - although, there are exceptions - **the special ones.**

One night at 'The Shoes', I was extremely lucky to huckle Gillian. Wotta topper - a drop-dead gorgeous bit o' tackle - face and figure, she had it all; this one really got ma kettle steamin', but, sadly, deaf and dumb; so it looked like 'the Big Felly' had tried to make it up to her. My mates were green with envy - *that's a first, since I usually cop the freaks,* so they were kidding me, no end, saying things like "Yer laffin' there Shiner, she'll no' be able tae scream". After the dance I've got her pinned against some crates in a dark close desperate to 'plight ma troth', so as to get my sweaty mitts on her again, but I haven't got paper or pen and just ain't gettin' through. I'm so frustrated that I even try to write on a wall with a soft red half-brick - all too soon her bus comes, and she's off... ***to wherever.***

Next evening, when dittering around, readying ourselves for supper one of the McManus brothers *knowing I was smitten* bursts into the Mess shouting "Hey Shiner, that burd ye trapped last night is on the 'dog 'n' bone'." Dead chuffed, 'Mr Muggins' didnae tipple and without thinking, like a tit in a trance, dashed down the Mess *grinning from ear to ear* to answer it. Daft bastard, they got me a beauty! I looked in vain for that girl for weeks - ever noticed you rarely get the things you want in this life, but

those you'd rather give a pass are sittin' right there on yer doorstep?

Bill Peak, a PO Cook in the Ship's Company Galley took a notion for my Standard Vanguard, so, fancying a change, I seized the opportunity, and 'took his hand off', then bought a Vauxhall Velox I liked the look of from a dealership in Elgin. Should've kept the Vanguard *which had been totally reliable* as the day I bought the Velox the handbrake and wipers decided to pack in, making me think, 'here we go - I've bought a pup'. However, with these fixed it repaid me with trouble-free motoring until I unloaded it to a Canadian Submariner in Gosport, replacing it by 'blawin' ma brains oot' on the worst car I've ever owned - a two-tone Ford Zephyr Six, rammed up me by a dealer in Pompey; an ex-Rep's car - 'well clocked', burning as much oil as petrol. ***The chancin' git saw me coming!***

Sorry, I rambled on a bit there and lost the plot; so, getting back to Bill Peak, there was a beat-up piano in the dining hall; when the mood took him our Bill could fairly knock a tune out that ole 'joanna' *(play that funky music, white boy!)*. He was absolutely brilliant at honky-tonk, which gets me twitchin' *(must hae a touch o' the tar brush in me)*. Every time I hear ragtime played on the piano I wish I had learned to 'tickle the ivories' in my early years; when we all thought music lessons were for 'cissies' - **how wrong we were** *just watch these guys pull the burds*.

Just had a memory flash - there was a roster, tasking the chefs, in turn, to work a back shift, this entailed providing 'night-flying suppers', as Fulmar was operating its Buccaneer fighter/bomber squadrons on a twenty-four hour rota - so the Galley never closed. It was a cushy number, with nothing much to do after ten; to pass the time the dutyman would get things prepped for the next day, then 'set up' breakfast for his reliefs before 'knocking off' 'early doors'. I especially didn't mind covering a Tuesday or Wednesday - having no wish to upset my busy social life.

You'll always find an angle if you're switched on - that said *after dark* it was the done thing to have a reciprocal deal going with the Duty Fire Crew who had a cooker in their bothy down on the airfield. So, in exchange for a box o' rations 'oot the back windae' we'd get something we wanted: you can't beat the old barter system, when everyone gets a result and no one parts wi' a penny - **yae cannae argue wi' that, can yae!**

'Night-flying suppers' were also available from the Wardroom Galley

for the 'sky jockeys' - most were OK guys; but, there's one born every day who thinks he's clever; but hasn't the savvy to know it's unwise to upset the person cooking the food he will eat. I'm remembering the night a smart-arse 'subby' got right up ma nose by sending his steak back three times complaining it was underdone, so after the final insult I sent the smirking steward back to the tosser with the offering sat centred in the silver entrée dish; ***smouldering.*** That shut the twat up - I've seen the soup stirred with a dirty mop, but; believe me, that's childsplay these days; so beware, don't upset the catering staff, as you never know what they might get up to, and if you are a marked man, be warned - **you may cop an unexpected complimentary side-order** *(adding insult to injury - you're not only eating it, you are also paying for the privilege)*. ***Bon Appétit!***

One evening, when having a bit of a blether about Pompey, the conversation got round to scrumpy *(then, unavailable up there)*. Talking about it gave us a galloping thirst for the unique taste of fermented apples, so much so that we were in mind forra 'guid swally'; resulting in us getting a kitty together to have some sent up from the South. I can't recall how we organized it, possibly someone was going down there for a course. Anyway, it must've been delivered to one of the RAs in Married Quarters outside the Base, because I do remember two small barrels arrived, which were dead easy to smuggle into camp in the car boot - *it's always assumed articles will be taken out, not brought in*. We set them up in the cooks' rest room, so as to get a 'buzz' on for the Sunday night hop - it goes without saying everyone was making sure they got their fair share, ***and then some.***

Wotta hullabaloo! You'll be familiar with the NAAFI being labelled the 'Ranch house' - **well;** this was more like the 'OK Corral'. I hadn't anticipated the outcome, and have no idea who started it - all hell broke loose; dearie me, I've never seen a bare-knuckle brawl to equal this; the inmates became feral thugs, hitting whoever was in front of them and I guess a lot of old scores were settled by opportunists. 'Twas mayhem, tables and chairs were flying, the club was a shambles *completely trashed* a 'hairy fairy' kicked 'Dixie' Dean in the nuts, causing him to spew out his false teeth *which Perry promptly stood on with his size tens,* the dance never happened and doses o' 'defaulters' got themselves locked up.

As nervous as a virgin in a brothel and having no wish to be implicated,

I 'took to my toes' - ye couldnae see me for stoor; but thankfully, observing the unwritten code of closing ranks and keeping schtum, no one mentioned scrumpy. A dose o' 'Number Nines' was later dished out and eventually the fracas was just something to talk about - however, will be well remembered by all who starred in the lively ding-dong at Her Britannic Majesty's Royal Naval Air Station in the northern reaches of the kingdom.

The gadabout troupe of cool dancehall dandies could change; what with duty-watches, draft chits and dosh problems, but I always had two diehards with me. One was 'Figgy' Duff, a philanderer from Renfrew with a winning smile and devil-may-care attitude *(he of the BLS fame)*, the other; a wild colonial boy who'd 'kissed the Blarney Stone', and so, could charm the birds out the trees - although I remember his surname we'll stick with just 'Mick' for obvious reasons. Mick was an unmitigated scoundrel, livin' the 'life o' Riley'; couldn't give a monkey's for anything on or off the Base. The Irishman was married with two sprogs and housed in Married Quarters. He never ran out of excuses - I don't know how he got away with it, come to think of it, we never ever saw 'the little woman'. Can't help wondering where he is now - maybe not a good idea, as it's probably best we don't know; but he'd better get his story straight before trying to talk his way past St Peter come Judgement Day.

Weeks before being drafted 'sowf' I snared a chirpy nurse I'd been stalking, ever since she 'tickled ma fancy' at a Fulmar camp dance. Nicely equipped - best described as salacious and earthy, with those irresistible sultry-brown eyes, shoulder-length dark hair and, oh, yes - ***she's a fox!*** I reckon there was some Italian blood in her, but, try as I may, can't get her surname, however recall she came from Huntly. Angela was a little raver, who liked to remove her skirt "in case it got creased" and more than generous with her favours ***- Nurse! Nurse! I'm feeling worse!***

Our first date was at her favourite pub in Elgin, where Angela must've been captivated by my rakish charm, as within minutes she had my mother-of-pearl shirt buttons undone and her hand inside. Mmm - so Nursie's into touchy-feely, is she! Naturally I'm shocked and delighted at the same time with this transformation from mouse to slut; talk about forward - *I wonder if she'd pretend to be a streetwalker for me* - can't remember how far I got that night, but the following Sunday we went to some reservoir she was just

fair itchin' to show me. Now, she'd said "Bring the swimming cossie", so I *fertile imagination in hyper-mode* replied "You too!", thinking, 'gadzooks, this sounds like an invitation to 'slip'r one'.

We park the car and scramble all the way up a steep overgrown track to this reservoir; there's not a soul to be seen, as it's in the middle o' nowhere. The sexpot's brought a hospital blanket for us to lie on - **but, *crikey... why the spurs???*** The blanket's down - within seconds she's pounced and her tongue's halfway doon ma throat, here this is it; talk dirty, an' show me what yiv got Baby! Jings, ***is nothing sacred,*** the eager nymph has my polished cotton chinky-tailored slacks unzipped within seconds. Aw, here, be gentle wi' me; but dinnae stop now - pretty soon it's gonna be

move yir ass ma bonnie lass
ma baws are in the bracken (BURNS)

Intent on defiling me, she's rummaging around but gettin' nowhere, because I've got my cossie on and unable to control myself, foolishly break into hysterical laughter. 'Nurse Naughty' takes the job seriously; so, not amused, gubbs me a beauty round the coupon - talk about a woman scorned. Trust me - I've blown it! She's choked, wotta temper! Sulking? **- oh no**, she's fuming, won't even talk to me. Little realizing that I've made a colossal faux pas in humiliating the poor girl, I whisk her back to town and, in an awkward embarrassing silence, dump her at the Elgin Hospital Nurses' Quarters then vamoose, thinking it wasn't supposed to be like that, I had plans for this radgepacket *(who was 'a cert')* and now I've screwed up - ***so much for dreams of seduction under a hunter's moon.***

However, days later Angie's Ward Sister phones *on her behalf* to patch up the regrettable misunderstanding - next time we're together I'm 'onna promise'; so, being a quick learner, the cossie's left in my locker *and ah'm wearing ma lucky socks*. Looking sweet and still in her nurses' uniform *(at my request)*, squealing like a demented vampire, she attacks my neck, then makes the peace by 'taking me in hand' for a guid thrashin' while listening to Radio Luxembourg in the back of the Vauxhall at Lossie Beach. Perhaps it's in their manual, but ah wus shattered when my adept companion wiped her nimble fingers on the back of my new charcoal grey herring-bone Harris Tweed sports jacket - *the things we do for love!* This little lady, who took a lot for granted, was going to be a challenge.

In spite of the fact that a volatile relationship is the last thing I need, the thrill of the hunt is getting to me. But, at the same time I know this randy nurse is trouble, not to be trusted; and must admit made me nervous. Programmed to procreate, she's just the type who'd let herself be put 'up the stick' and have a ring on her finger before you were even aware you'd 'been there' - *the plan was to bed her, not wed her.* I'm concerned; I realize this is one dangerous liaison, but what a temptation and although the alarm bells have rung *blinded by love* I want a pop at this feisty bitch and the more I fantasize about it the more I'm sure she'll be a demon in the sack.

Well now, like I said earlier, the things you want most you never get - possibly in that case it was just as well, because what I got wusnae 'ma nookie', but my long and eagerly awaited draft chit. I didn't even see Angela before I left; *her being on night-duty that week* - so much for my anticipation of a torrid afair. Who knows, maybe I had the luckiest escape of my life - there again, maybe **she** did! The Lord moves in mysterious ways. **So there we have it, *the eternal story of love lost.***

At last I've cracked it, my draft is to HMS Dolphin in Gosport *known as 'Fort Blockhouse'* the Submarine School and homebase of the 1ST Submarine Squadron. Well, it's not before time as I've been up here duckin' an' divin' for two and a half mental years; it's little wonder I feel like a local - I thought I'd be here a year, tops; so to coin the phrase once more - **doesn't time fly when you're enjoying yourself!**

Experience is a valuable asset, so this time, you'll be pleased to hear, I *being an old hand* have friends in high places - no more lugging a heavy kitbag all the way to Pompey for me, I've packed, or should I say crammed, it tight with all the non-essentials *which is almost everything I own* making it weigh a ton. A few days before 'slingin' ma hook' I take it to my mate, 'Pincher' Martin, a Leading Stores Assistant in the Baggage Store; he assures me it'll be waiting for me in Dolphin's Baggage Store when I get there - ***brilliant!*** They say, its not what you know, but who you know *in this life* that matters so all I'll have to carry is my holdall and the wee broon attaché case. Here - this man's Navy's no' three bad efter all!

So guess what I do next? Well done! You got it! My leaving routine, then I'm for 'the off' - by now I've got it well sussed - the plan is to drop the car off in Edinburgh en route, so I get my armed forces British Rail

travel warrant made out from Edinburgh to Portsmouth - it would've been foolhardy to take the car to Dolphin as I had no idea of what was to happen on arrival. So, I nicked down to 'the Capital', left the Vauxhall in the driveway of our new gaff at 38 Silverknowes Grove and caught the 'overnight express' from the Waverley Station to King's Cross.

The journey wasn't entirely uneventful, as south of Edinburgh a Jenny Wren parked herself in the compartment I was already sharing with a couple o' strange auld duffers accompanied by a parrot that kept on cursin; and screechin' **"Don't eat me, please don't eat me!"** They'd got on the train before me; who knows where, as when I tried to strike up a conversation it was a waste of breath, the old gits were only interested in chirpin' to the foul-mouthed parrot - *which probably had a higher IQ*.

Although in civvies, it was obvious to 'Jenny' that I was one of 'the nation's finest', since my Pusser's grip, sporting name, number and cap tied to a handle, was sitting on the rack overhead. We exchanged pleasantries and newspapers; which was a good start and welcome diversion - if you've done it, you'll know it's a boring journey at the best of times and overnight it's 'the pits'. The old fogeys opposite us have nodded off, just like 'wee Joey' in his now covered cage. It's probably about half' two in the morning, meaning we could also do with a kip - so stretch out and try to get comfortable on the bench seat we're sharing. That's it - we're sorted, her head at one end and mine at the other, shoes off and feet up.

Let's say right now; having had a good look, I couldn't fancy the girl; *even in a lucky bag* truth being, she's a ringer for Olive in 'On the Buses'; however she's in uniform; which always raises a wee twinge - *is this a fetish?*. I must say she had tidy legs, and I don't mean because of the black stockings. No, you must've noticed that the shoes service and policewomen wear do absolutely fuck all for their legs; so if you ever see one in 'uni' whose 'pins' look OK, she's blessed. Anyway, I get a wee flash o' moist gusset as she settles down; it's not intentional - ***just luck!***

With being knackered, and lulled by the train's monotonous drumming and swaying, I doze off. After my nap I gradually become aware that my left foot is lovely and warm; pondering this, it slowly dawns on me that it's right up between her thighs. So, I'm lying there scared to move while wondering if she's engineered this tantalizing predicament and at the same

time getting frisky thinking about it; jeepers - **what should ah do?**

Well, you know the score, 'it' takes control, so ah've got to make ma pitch or ah'll never know; *and spend the rest o' ma life wonderin'*. I cautiously worm my foot up to the honeytrap - and now this rough bit o' kit's lookin' better than a poke in the eye wae a sharp stick. I'm positive she'll give a wee sigh and press down on to my foot - but no, **nothing;** she must be out like a light. I suddenly recognize the danger signals on *fortunately* remembering what happened to poor old Geordie on this very same journey when returning from Christmas Leave to Mercury a few years ago. Yikes - ah don't want ma name in the 'News o' the World'! What goes up, must come down, so, I gingerly withdraw my foot and 'the game's up the pole' *probably a blessing, because -*

You can bet your bottom dollar
It's like a horse's collar

Bitch!
'We come unclean'
Bastard!

Submariners were renowned for the pride they took in their appearance.

19: HMS Dolphin

Ah've dunnit, ah'm in Dolphin - *this is what it's all about.* I've had a walk round to the windswept jetty for a shufti at the cutting-edge P & O Class 'attack submarines' *(known as 'boats')*, I'm ecstatic, yes, I'm about to fulfil the dream, or as those two ravin' poofters, Gerald FitzHenry and Henry FitzGerald, would put it "**Oh! Heaven on a stick!**" Like I said, I'm here, so *as always* doing my joining routine, I've drawn bedding and yes, my kitbag was waiting, like my long-lost child, in the Baggage Store exactly as good old 'Pincher' promised - *just love this man's Navy!*

I'm finding my way around and reintegratin' wi' the 'southern softies' while getting my card stamped. So, I'm sauntering down the main road towards the Fort and approaching the old accommodation block *bottom left* which incorporates the Ship's Company Galley and Mess Hall on the ground floor, when I see this guy about fifty yards away coming towards me, weighed down like a packhorse with kitbag and worldly possessions. His head is down, but there's something familiar about the determined way he walks. The gap closes - well ah'll be blowed, it's Scouse O'Reilly; this is magic, I haven't seen him for 'yonks' and here he is joining Dolphin on the same day as me; also for submarine training, **wotta brammer!**

The months since we've seen each other vanish in a trice, when cool as a cucumber he says "Wotcha Shiner, howzit hangin' mate?" and "You can give me a hand with this lot, Mush!" Nae sweat, me ole tusker, cos ah ken whair the barras are stashed. So, blethering non-stop we do our joining routine together, then find our Mess in the Part 1 Training Area, *named Dolphin 2* round by Haslar Jetty, an' wouldn't you know - we're back where we started, **it's a wooden hut.** The Submarine School turns out to be a cluster of huts and brick utilities tucked away, separate from the Base, up by the Main Gate, and on the opposite side from the boundary sea wall which runs all the way down on the right hand side, as does the road, from the Main Gate, to Fort Blockhouse at the bottom.

So, our self-contained camp with its own Galley, schoolrooms and accommodation is hidden away in to the left on entering the Base. Next

down, heading towards 'the Fort', is the smart modern Senior Rates accommodation blocks; then halfway down the road, the Submarine Escape Training Tank *(SETT)* followed by torpedo workshops, maintenance buildings and an open *then* undeveloped space looking onto a little harbour in a sheltered basin containing yachts and small pleasure craft. Beyond that, the Ship's Company accommodation blocks with the, already mentioned, Galley and Mess Hall - these Junior and Senior Rates accommodation blocks were given over as shoreside living space for the crews of submarines operating from Dolphin.

The men only live on the boats when at sea, leaving all non-essential kit and belongings behind in the locked Shoreside Mess, taking only 'steaming gear' to sea. Everyone has their own locker on the boat, but this is small - making it quite an art packing for a long trip. Beyond these shoreside accommodation blocks is the roadway going round to the jetty where the boats of the 1ST Submarine Squadron are moored when not on patrol; then Fort Blockhouse itself with the Wardroom, plus logistics and admin offices etc. required to run 'the show'; also situated there, is a small NAAFI shop and canteen for our immediate needs.

There's no hanging around for the latest intake of wannabes; the comprehensive course starts as soon as we've unpacked, lasting about three months - with twenty or so keen young guys *some of whose heads were wasted* split into two classes. The first few weeks are bewildering, as we know nothing about submarines, other than they go underwater - by the end of the course, the submariners' secrets will have been revealed, and us expected to know **everything;** a daunting task to say the least.

The stokers and sparks have mechanical knowledge, so have an edge on most of us - however, the 'eager beavers' are soon enlightened, as to elaborate mainline systems, telemotor operated devices, centrifugal pumps, ballast tanks, 'Q' tank, trimming the boat, negative buoyancy, batteries; you name it, we learn it and are required to draw diagrams.

There's little time for runs ashore, because - guess wot? **We get homework and we get tests.** So, it's 'noses to the grindstone'- forget the attitude generally attributed to Jack, like "Bollocks to this" and "Sod that!" No, for us it's a 'labour of love' - all being dedicated volunteers, hell-bent on becoming submariners, *recognized, by outsiders as an elite*

entity, something **we** see as special. Giving credence to this belief, so must 'Their Lordships' as, when qualified, we'll trouser a more than generous extra five shillings (25p) per day as a sweetener.

What an incentive! **We're in the money!** 

The camaraderie took a bit o' beatin'; if any student was having difficulty understanding or grasping a particular subject, a classmate would, when later back in the Mess, explain it differently, possibly in layman's terms, and 'the penny dropped'. I've yet to see people help their comrades more, *other than for personal gain*; and here's you been thinking all the while we were no more than arrogant self-centred pricks. But let's not get all sentimental - we had plenty laughs with the many witty characters and 'basket cases' the Senior Service manages to attract.

There were a couple of classes of Indians or Pakis; I don't know which, because they all looked the same to us. Well, whatever they were, their religion didn't allow them to eat the 'sacred cow', so when in the dinner queue at the Mess Hall they'd point to the various stews and meats asking us if they contained the taboo scran. Of course you're way ahead again, that's right we lied good-style, shaking our heads while saying "Oh no, no, no, Baa!" or "Oink! Oink!" So, assured by the nice Brits, they'd get stuck into a plate heaped full of the sacred moo, licking their lips while greedily throwing it down their necks. ***Praise Allah*** - *they believed us*; I doubt if anyone ever told them the truth; in fact, if it was roast pork or lamb we said it was beef, a cryin' shame; but you've got the picture - **white man, him speak with forked tongue!** Let's face it, these guys were only here being trained because the real snakes, **our** political masters, were selling **their** political masters tarted-up obsolete British submarines.

Cripes, was that course ever a rude awakening - many were having misgivings, thinking ourselves 'Haigs Dimple' and doomed to failure, but not wanting to admit defeat *or afforded an option* plodded on. The Navy have been at this forever - training 'thickoes' is an art they have weighed off to a T, so as the schooling progresses the mist lifts and, it all falls into place. You've got to applaud them; OK it's begrudged, but credit where it is due! It costs thousands to put each man through this rigorous procedure, so 'the powers that be' want their money's worth, and the only way to get

the best is to give the best. A philosophy worth heeding by all you Civvy Street bodgers and hungry swindling rip-off merchants hard at the hey diddle diddle; remember, God's got a big notebook and he knows what you're up to! It's too fuckin' late to say "Sorry!" when you is standin' at dem Pearly Gates man! *(one can't fail to notice how in recent years we've nurtured a culture motivated by selfishness and greed).*

We underwent a two-day course at the Fire Training School near Portsea, covering every eventuality and all kinds of blazes - *fire being the submariners' worst nightmare*. We were black at the end of each day, and well aware that we preferred the Submarine Service to the Fire Brigade; even though so many over-sexed women are said to lust after firemen with their big hoses ***- a myth, no doubt, dreamed up by one of their own.***

I recall taking part in a classic 'Cold War' exercise, and to this day wonder, why? What was the point??? The plot was - there was supposed to have been a nuclear attack which had devastated the south of Britain. So us wannabes and our instructors, were issued rations and piled into huge army lorries with canvas tops - *could've been twenty-tonners*.

All that happened was we got ferried around the Southern Counties for two days, spending the first night in a disused army camp; already prepared and opened for our arrival - makes you wonder: the MoD have properties everywhere. Anyway, as I said, what was the point, as we did absolutely sod all but sit in the convoy of lorries for two days. I guess the planners had decided it was 'NEED TO KNOW' - *and 'the plebs' didn't need to know*. Afterwards, when back at Dolphin the exercise was claimed as an unsurpassed success - there again; weren't they all? Stay with me, because now I'm going to let you in on why I've mentioned the little jaunt.

On the second afternoon we travelled on a long stretch of straight monotonous dual carriageway, for what seemed hours. I've no idea where, as we had no maps, and even on completion didn't know where we'd been - *not that we cared*. Come to think of it, that may have been a criterion of the exercise. Anyway, we had been on this road forever; followed for some time by this cheeky cunt driving a 'rag-top' MGB and obviously showing - off to the bit o' skirt at his side. Now, while he wasn't blatantly taking the piss, he was definitely suggesting something to the dollface, since they were looking up at us and sniggering. A stroppy cockney stoker

in our squad wasn't amused, and possibly just a tad jealous when he stood up at the lorry's tailgate saying, "If they wanna take the piss, they can take this!", whips out the 'old todger' and starts pishin' out the back. We're doubled up, while 'Knocker' White is holding on to the 'greaser's' Pusser's money-belt to make sure he doesn't fall out while his 'golden shower' is spraying in our wake. Smarty-pants has to switch his windscreen wipers on and drops back, soon out of sight; and probably out of luck with the gold-digger he was trying to impress ***- pride comes before a fall!***

Towards the end of each course the students get treated to a day at sea in a submarine. We're all in favour of and looking forward to this experience, but first must qualify by having a crash course at 'the tower' *(Submarine Escape Training Tank)* - anyone going to sea on a boat must initially pass this course. That's what AFOs *(Admiralty Fleet Orders)* say - so that's the way it is. There are mixed feelings about this, with some just a touch apprehensive, but none scared enough to chicken out; *after all it's been tested on 'animals' for years, so if it was to be feared we'd've heard long ago.* Anyway, the Royal Navy is one hundred and one per cent safety conscious; and the many instructors unparalleled.

For starters we get lectures and films about 'free ascent', pressures and atmospheres are explained; all 'velly intelesting' - in theory, this method of escape is possible from great depths, I've, by now, forgotten all the nitty-gritty, but back then the RN held the record for this, *and maybe still do.* Now well clued-up "We know it all, pal!" so, it's time for a wee shot in the decompression chamber - *probably to check us out, to see if we could hack it in the claustrophobia department before the real thing.* All I can remember, was it made our voices squeaky encouraging the clowns in our midst to spout very realistic Donald Duck impressions.

That done, the brainwashed wannabes are mustered at the top of 'the Tank', to see what it's all about and dispel any lingering doubts. Crowded round the guard rail we had a squint into this superb piece of engineering; from memory, about fifteen feet in diameter and a hundred feet deep. On gazing down, the water was clean and clear, with depth markings all the way up *(imperial measurements)* - I refuse to recognize the metric system; ***what are these chancers on the 'Gravy Train' doing to us?***

There are four instructors at various depths; it's long forgotten, but

they possibly had niches with air pockets at stages on the way up. So, we're assured it'll be a doddle and herded down a metal stairway *lookin' hot in our skimpy Speedos* to the foot of the Tank. Now, with this being one hundred feet below the surface, it means we are *or will be* at four atmospheres once through a couple of pressure chambers. It has already been explained that each thirty feet we go down is one atmosphere; therefore the pressure increases. It follows *(as far as I can remember - so this may be off the mark, but you'll get the gist)* that when we are at the bottom, the pressure will have increased threefold, so a deep breath will actually put multiples of air in one's lungs - more than enough to make a free ascent to the surface, but we mustn't forget to exhale all the way up, so as to equalise the pressure as we ascend, otherwise the lungs will explode. This point is made repeatedly; being very important and the only real danger.

Bawling "Comin' through!" I elbow my way into the first batch; as I believe if you've got to do something like that, don't hang about, **do it!** I'm not so quick at partin' wi' the readies, as many will vouch - *every penny a prisoner.* Anyway, we're offered goggles so I grab a pair, as I want to experience the whole bit. We're ushered into a chamber, which is then flooded to chest level. All I have to do now is take a DEEEEP breath, duck under the twill trunk and I'm in the Tank on my way to the surface, blowing out gently as I go. It was great, but of course the hastily snatched goggles were useless and filled with water - *bloody typical!* About halfway up I thought I had blown out all my air, but as I rose the pressure decreased letting what was left in my lungs expand, so, right enough, it just kept coming and I blew bubbles all the way to the top where I was helped out by a nice man who called me 'Sunshine' - and that was it.

I must say, an exhilarating experience, certainly no ordeal, and if they'd said, go again, I wouldn't have argued, but requested better goggles. Now, don't get me wrong, I'm no hero and, for instance, wouldn't dream of attempting a bungee jump. Also, if some clever bugger with a better memory is claiming my description of the SETT and ascent to be a 'loada clap', I say in my defence - **up yer pipe, pal; it wusnae yesterday!**

That accomplished, we get our eagerly anticipated day at sea in a submarine, an' you know, for the life of me I can't remember which one it was, but it makes sense that she would've been one of the 'P' Class boats

belonging to the 1ST Submarine Squadron based at Dolphin. Although intriguing it was an anticlimax, as with boats being cramped at the best of times, taking our class onboard aggravated the situation. So feeling in the way, we hung around, huddled in corners - not wishing to hamper the crew as they went about their tasks in a relaxed professional manner.

I'm sure we must've been on a one-day exercise with 'target ships' in the English Channel; *since Pusser doesn't organize pleasure trips*. The boat was on the surface *known as 'passage routine'* for a couple of hours then on reaching the designated area went to 'Diving stations' - the klaxon blared, the Bridge was cleared; then we slid silently beneath the waves. I've been asked many times "What's it like?" and "Don't you feel claustrophobic?" Well, I've always thought and said it's just like being on any other ship; only with no portholes - when on the surface 'subs' roll and jump about a bit if the sea is other than flat calm and you are always aware of the diesel engines thump thump thumping. However, when dived it's stable and quiet, as you are away from the 'roughers' and running on electric motors - actually rather tranquil; just the way submariners like it.

I had some good mates on that course, but can't now remember names, however, there was, as you know, Scouse O'Reilly and another chap, who I christened Hirum Holiday, a dapper bespectacled fellow who reminded me of a TV character, so named. I think he and 'Knuckles' Newman were drafted to the Rorqual; which may well've been the boat assigned for our introduction to the 'Silent Service'. Another, was a tall Irish radar plotter with an infectious smile, and, would you believe, his name was Paddy. He was drafted to one of the 'nukes'; today my befuddled memory bluntly refuses to recall the boat's name; but obviously one of the early ones - probably one of the seven now lying decommissioned, and under wraps at Rosyth. It's a crying shame to see these rusting, once proud, monarchs of the sea lying abandoned, looking as if hiding shamefully in a far corner of Rosyth Dockyard. **See page 338*.

I didn't fancy nukes - thinking, that being large with big crews they'd be too 'Pusser' for my liking; therefore strict and less matey. I've an inkling that, on becoming serious players, we had to fill in a preference form, on which I gave a negative to nukes - something I now regret, as, after all, nuclear propulsion was the future. I also have misgivings, concerning

when I had the opportunity, I never even bothered to go aboard one for a mooch around to get the feel; it didn't seem important at the time, but, like so many things, would now be high on my list of priorities.

I've purposely left the best 'til last, because no one who ever met him could forget the one and only 'Bisto Kid' - and yes, I do well remember his name, but you'll see from his exploits it's best that I stick with that nickname, as today he **may** be a reformed character. I first became aware of 'Ginge'; I've decided that I also have to use 'Ginge' - as I can hardly keep saying the Bisto Kid since he will be mentioned many times from here on in. I realize I've given the game away to a degree - but that's all yer gettin'. Now then, where was I? Oh yeah! I was saying, I first became aware of Ginge *(another wideboy Londoner; from Paddington)* one night while still in training and returning from one of our few runs ashore. Two small groups of us were making our way back to Dolphin 2 after a night out 'on the sauce' in the homely Gosport hostelries when we met up on 'Pneumonia Bridge' while wolfing our way through sausage wedges; with the bread cut doorstep-style *the way it should be* from Sam 'n' Ella's 'greasy spoon'; a real 'tightner' after swillin' down a few jars o' Red Barrel.

sung to 'It's the Same the Whole World Over'
She stood on the Bridge at midnight,
Throwing snowballs at the moon,
She said, "Jack I've never had it"
But she spoke too fuckin' soon.

We're all in high spirits, larking around having a laugh, when 'Sugar' Kane says "For Christ's sake, what's he up to?" pointing at Ginge who has this big black and white cat, and holding it up with his face buried between its back legs. Scouse says, "What in the name o' fuck are you doing, man?" A barely audible Ginge replies, "I'm practising muff diving!" This answer in turn encouraging many amusing remarks from our merry bunch of revellers. Now the centre of attention and in the limelight, so to speak, Ginge is dancing on the middle of the bridge with the poor submissive cat held on top of his head like a Russian hat. It seemed hilarious at the time, an' d'you know wot - I can still picture the episode, but now depict the moggy *being a teetotaller* as none too happy.

Although I already knew him *(Ginge was also a slosh - but because 'too many cooks spoil the broth', in a different class and Mess)*, this was the first time I'd been ashore in his company, and it seemed to me that under that angelic persona lurked a bit of a lad, definitely one of life's extroverts, who would be trouble, but good for a laugh if kept under control.

On 'passing out' of Dolphin 2, we were both drafted as 'Spare Crew' to work in the Ship's Company Galley, while awaiting our first submarine appointments; so became fellow conspirators, and the things we got up to when gallivanting in Pompey and Southsea was nobody's business - *these mental times ashore bring a smile to my face, when daydreaming*. Yes, I realize it was another unholy alliance with us both running at the same speed back in those heady days; with me the brains and he the 'eye candy'.

This guy was a maverick, it was obvious he believed he was still in 'Civvy Street', so somehow managed to project this impression - it's weird that whenever I've thought of the monster over the years I've always pictured him as a civvy. Perhaps, because I have kept this photo of the two of us sitting on the casing of a submarine in the middle of the South Atlantic - him wearing jeans, sandals and a black T-shirt and myself similarly attired, hardly looking as one might expect of Royal Naval Ratings; more like a pair o' brickies' labourers - at sea, on boats *upholding the pirate image* we wore whatever we wanted; therefore, uniforms were obviously out of the question.

Shiner and 'the Bisto Kid' reminiscing on the casing of Odin in the South Atlantic, when returning from South America

When I tagged him as 'a bit of a lad' that was an understatement, there was no stopping him. **Wotta beast!** He'd tackle anything, it didn't matter how rough *some ugly as sin* as long as it was breathing he'd nail it - I often thought he homed in on proper gronks just for the hell of it, and it sure made a change for me not to cop the runt o' the litter.

'Early doors' *before I knew him well* he returned from a weekend at home, 'up the Smoke', happy as a dog wi' two cocks, sporting a very expensive leather jacket and offhandedly saying "Go on, ask me where I got it!" So, since he was just aching to tell me, I did and he boastfully admits from his friend Ray Martine; who *allegedly* 'took it up the jaxie' and hosted 'Stars and Garters'; a major TV song and dance extravaganza in the 'Swinging Sixties'. Then my pal 'spills it' that he regularly went with Ray to showbiz parties, and for the rest of the day took delight in relating tales of tampering, and the goings-on at 'the luvvies' colourful orgies.

One of his saucy tales claimed that a seductive songstress, whom we all drooled buckets over and fantasized about 'sweepin' her chimney', wasn't the 'butter wouldn't melt' girl we had 'the hots' for. Apparently, she had a wee problem wi' the bevvy and as if that wasn't enough, her 'party piece', *when tipsy,* was to 'jack off' her German Shepherd, while he lay on his back, four paws pointing at the ceiling and long slobbering tongue hanging out. Well, it takes all types; *they say anyone who loves animals can't be all bad* - pity about the alcohol problem though! You know, I've often considered that when the time comes to fill in my reincarnation request form, I'd like to return as a film starlet's poodle! - *think about it!!!*

Easter Leave that year was the last time Joe, Benny, Doogie and myself were all home at the same time - 'twas also the last time I saw Benny, who soon after was drafted to Woomera Rocket Range, which, I believe, was some three hundred miles from Adelaide in Australia. I thought **even he** couldn't get into bother there, but on asking Joe about Benny some time later *(as they kept in touch)*, he told me the waster had managed to crash a Land Rover into the only rock for miles, in the middle of a desert. Sure sounded true to form for the feckless lunatic, who that Leave, with typical aplomb, treated himself to Joe's mother's early evening bath.

This came about, because we had all met up at the McGlinchey Mansion to get revved up in readiness for a night on the town. The Lady of the

House was running a bath, prior to getting 'dolled up' to hit the Old Tyme Dancing, which you'll remember was her great passion. Benny gets to his feet, saying "Excuse me, I'm just nipping into the bog" and is away for ages. Growing concerned, Joe knocks on the door enquiring if he's alright - *ask a silly question*; is he ever! **Benny's having a bath** which only he thought funny, but that was Benny with his twisted sense of humour; a quality rarely *if ever* appreciated by the recipients.

Big Doogie, the one we used to call 'big daft Doogie', he's showing us all the way it's done. He really found his niche when he took an interest in diving - it turned out he was a natural and already has his 'Killick's hook up', Doogie's a star in Pusser's eyes, and has excelled on every specialist course the Navy offer. He is now a qualified Clearance Diver and been everywhere, there's nothing daft about Doogie and from some of his stories, he's 'huvin' the time o' his life'. We're not exactly green with envy but it would be nice to get a slice o' Doogie's action. In fact, one night, thinking about Doogie's luck and life, I asked God for "a wee kick at the ball" - unfortunately he thought I said **"a wee kick in the balls!"**

Speaking of Doogie's enthusiasm for diving reminds me that Joe had also been around since his days on the destroyer HMS Dainty. One of the many things he had done was a Shallow Water Divers' Course - *which used to be termed a frogman*. I fancied a pop at that, as it would entitle me to another half-crown a day and a prestigious gold-sleeve badge to enhance the Number Ones - so thought, given the chance, I'd go for it. Joe was now with the minesweeper squadron based in HMS Lochinvar at Port Edgar by South Queensferry - *a stone's throw from Edinburgh*. He was on one of the small 'Ton' Class minesweepers; which wouldn't have been my choice, preferring something larger and the more temperate 'sowf' - but there again, you don't get a choice, and 'hometurf' suited Joe; then in a meaningful relationship with a student, who came from Dollar.

That was a particularly memorable Leave, as we widened our horizons by discovering two 'swinging boozers', in Newhaven. Sounds familiar! yes, it should, because that's where this story started. Friday and Saturday nights, Newhaven was the place to be, as both the Stone Pier Inn and the Peacock Hotel had 'singsongs'; with punters gettin' up to 'give it laldy', many of whom were 'rer wee chanters'. It goes without saying, we also

had to suffer some serious shite, with half-pished burds *convinced they could sing* beltin' oot 'Honky-Tonk Angel' and 'Nobody's Child'

Both places were busy, as the drink was cheap compared with uptown, so it was best to meet there early, in order to get a decent seat and a head start before party time. The music and entertainment went down a storm; this, as you'll know, is a magnet for pulling in the dragons - they being the main attraction for us. What a selection, we were spoilt for choice as, apart from the regulars, groups of willing maidens *who'd been round the block more than once* came from the numerous whisky bonds along the shore at nearby Leith and, take it from me, a game bunch they were. "*Get it up me, nivir mind ma skinny legs!*"

There was a young lady from Leith
Who circumcised men with her teeth
(if you want the rest, phone my chatline)

Uptown girls who'd heard about the Newhaven weekends, would pitch up for a look, or possibly a 'bit o' rough'. Sometimes students appeared; they were, or so we thought, a touch out our league, but that's where Joe *(our intellectual)* came into his own - when push came to shove, he could talk their language and handle them 'nae bother'. With impeccable timing he'd let it slip that we were in the Royal Navy - that often clinched the deal, so if the curious ones wanted to see our tattoos they had to take us home - the wonderful thing there, was they shared rented flats, whereas we still lived at our family abodes. There was many a hilarious piss-up with the students after closing time; one such night up at Bruntsfield so many of us were piled cavorting on this big old double bed that one of its legs snapped, making it collapse, causing its lecherous occupants to tumble out and land giggling, amidst empty bottles, in a tangled heap on the floor.

Because the pubs and hotels still closed at ten **yes ten!** it was the done thing to get a 'cairy oot' and go 'firra a cairy oan' *(carry out and carry on)*, so there would often be a party in someone's house after closing time. The word 'party' could be translated to drunken orgy if the truth be later told, and many of the resulting stories well worth a listen!

The other fleshpot we started to frequent was Fairley's in Leith Street, which for the uninformed was not, as one might conclude, in Leith, but about a hundred yards down from the east end of Princes Street in the city

centre. Fairley's had, you'll understand, until now been oot o' bounds tae us- being popular with the Yanks stationed at Kirknewton, so, more's the pity that it was pointless trying to cop a burd there. We couldn't begin to compete with their bulging cowhide wallets, cars or clothes, and to cap it all, the tarts who went there were after nailin' a smilin' GI not a 'common or garden' local lout - punchin' above his weight. But, times change; Kirknewton is closed and the Yanks have gone off to bomb Vietnam, but Fairley's is still here, so now it's our turn to patronize the temple of desire, and this time we've hit the jackpot - this **is** the Holy Grail.

Wotta place; *not for the faint-hearted, an' awash wi' hot snatch* - obviously built and kitted out to catch the trade it had enjoyed for years. The building brazenly boasted that 'come on in' glitter with its big red neon Fairley's sign on the roof and eye-catching luminous blue neon displays in the windows advertising the Oyster Bar and Dancehall. Americanised outside and in, with a large public bar and behind this *down beyond some wide curved stairs* a huge sunken cocktail lounge. There was an entrance to the right of the main doors *the side nearest to the Black Bull and Princes Street* on being admitted through this, one had to negotiate a narrow steep stairway *while dodging half-pished gladiators being ejected by tartan-coated bouncers* to reach the pulsating dancehall.

This magical Utopia for the discerning few, had the atmosphere and draw of the bars in Hong Kong and Manila - certainly unique for Edinburgh - the architect responsible for this *thought by some, 'seedy dive'* had done his homework. Thursday nights were favourite - full o' cut-throats, rejects, pimps and whores, so whenever home, never happier than when *amongst my own* mingling with the dregs of society, I made a beeline for the pleasures on offer. As said earlier, 'twas there I encountered my old Leith Academy classmate Alex 'happy' Howden. We spied each other when queuing on the stairs, waiting to file up to the dancehall in the hope of copping a lumber. "Great minds think alike" - *and yes; I know the other bit!*

One such night when in the sunken cocktail bar 'scoopin' up' with some 'lounge lizard' friends, while sharing a banquet-sized table with four fit burds from Dunfermline, I was busy weaving my web of deceit round an astounding, wispy, ash blonde - *the real thing, not a bleached job*. Now, at the risk of having you think I have some kind of kinky obsession, I say it

was purely by chance that, like the girl in Elgin some two years previously, she was deaf and dumb; although not such a profound case, so we were managing to converse. I'm convinced that 'the Big Guy' gave these girls something special in recompense - there's a line in a song, '*You smile and the angels sing*' - well, anyway, once again I was doomed to failure. I assumed that they, like us, would be going upstairs to the dancehall at closing time an' ah wus 'in wae a shout', but that wasn't to be as they had to catch the last SMT coach at St Andrew's Square bus station *(just up the road)* before eleven in order to get back to 'the sticks', so that's it, ma bubble's burst again and yet another little cracker escapes into the night.

However, maybe there is a God as even I score sometimes - so, got ma share o' one-night stands from the place; which is why I kept returning - and here comes a such a night, that is hard, no not hard, **impossible** to forget. I'd seen this voluptuous specimen in the lounge bar earlier in the evening, and when our eyes met briefly there was a spark of recognition between us. Later, when I clocked her in the dancehall I took my chance and moved in smartish - up there it was a case of he who hesitates is lost - the competition being fierce; talk about dog-eat-dog! We are up dancing and chatting, both sure we've met previously, but agree that's impossible, because she's from Inverness, only resided in the 'Festival city' a matter o' weeks and never been to Fairley's before. She's fair-haired with lovely skin, slightly plump, or dare I say a sturdy wench with huge knockers; you know the kind - after removing her double D industrial strength bra, you could play with them all night and not touch the same bit twice.

We've clicked, and before I know it I've 'bagged off' *(pulled)* and am taking her home to her tiny rented flat in Stockbridge - like I said, even I get lucky sometimes. Well, ***I've still got it!*** I've scored, and there are no maybes about it, I'm staying the night; it's just taken for granted and she ain't hanging about because, like she says, "Tomorrow's Friday, another working day". So, no beating about the bush or cups o' tea, I'm in the kip - 'just like that!' The lights are out apart from a Minnie Mouse table lamp, which must've had a fifteen-watt bulb to be so dim - as if shy, she's taking her time getting the kit off, and I'm thinking 'it's a bit late for that now, hen'. After what seems ages she sidles over to the bed and coyly whispers, "Do you mind if I take this off?" Now, I can't see what she's on

about, as, with the lamp behind her, she's casting a shadow, so naturally I *happily* say something affirmative like, "No, not at all". **She does**, then I realize what it is, when - **off come 'the stays'**, revealing her ample charms - a mountain o' flesh and no' a pound hingin' the right way.

Well, feeling 'sporty' (and to coin a phrase used earlier - *'never look a gift horse in the mouth')* I was the personal trainer who strengthened her pelvic floor that night. However, it didn't go down big bundles when she caught me doin' the 'soft-shoe shuffle' in the wee small hours; thinking she was still recovering in a dream-filled sleep.

It's okay to lie to women - they're not real people, like wot we are!

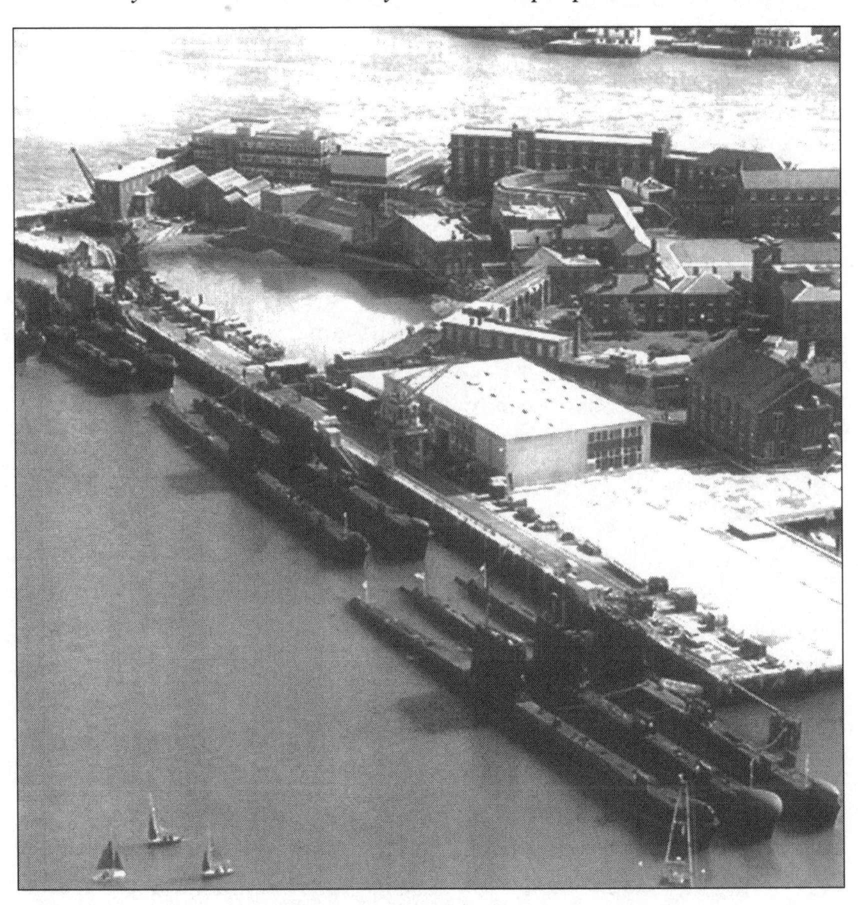

HMS Dolphin (Gosport) - 1ST Submarine Squadron Base

20: HM Submarine Odin

On returning to Dolphin after my Easter Leave, guess what's waiting for me? **A draft chit!** To HMS/M Odin - this baby's a purpose-built state-of-the-art Oberon Class diesel electric submarine. So, dead chuffed, I move my kit into their shoreside Mess and *pretending to be normal* nip down to the boat smartish before they find out about me and change their minds. I report to the Coxswain, 'Spud' Murphy, a quiet spoken easy-going Irishman with a droll sense of humour, who is 'top banana' on the boat. There's no joining routine on submarines, he just shakes his head and, gesturing, says "There's yer bunk and there's the Galley, get on with it!"

My bunk, *it's already speakin' to me* - my very own private haven for the next ten months, was situated on the port side of the main passage just for'ard of the control room, and opposite the steward's little pantry; shoe-horned in at the side of the Wardroom and Captain's mini-cabin. They say submarines are cramped, but to me this was the real deal, luxury itself, as I had considerably more personal space on Odin than I ever had on the good ship Tenby. *Och, aye - ah wus as snug as bug inna rug!*

I meet my new boss, Leading Cook John Slater - John, who 'showed me the ropes' *and taught me the dodges,* was an old hand on boats; knew his job, a good egg, easy to work with and easier still to get along with. Thank fuck! - imagine coppin' another 'steamer' like **the Mole!**

Because we live and work in close proximity, in no time at all I've met the rest of the crew I'm being inflicted upon and am delighted, as they strike me as a shower o' vagabonds with a sprinkling of real cards and not a rotten apple amongst them. This makes for one happy boat and that is, like the best thing that can possibly happen in the Submarine Service; *or on any ship for that matter.* This bunch o' nutters smile, joke, taunt and take the piss non-stop, always probing for a chink in each other's armour - *looking back, I now consider myself fortunate to have been one of them.*

So, as I say, Odin was a happy and therefore efficient boat, for which the credit goes to the whole crew; but in particular the three gems at the top: the Captain, Lt-Cdr R. H. Mann RN - a real toff! with the dashingly

HM Submarine Odin

handsome appearance one would expect of a Submarine Commander. The Jimmy, Lt-Cdr N.R. Boivin RCN, a top man with an uncanny resemblance to Clark Gable; and, of course, the already mentioned Coxswain, CPO Murphy who had an innate talent for handling men. These three guys, who didn't suffer fools, were naturals, instinctively knowing how to treat Jack, consequently getting his respect and best efforts - something few Officers could grasp; which was a great pity for both them and the Service.

Try as I may, I can't remember my first weeks as a submariner, therefore will hazard a guess that we must've been on fleet exercises, stalking prey, in Home Waters; since anything special would jog 'the leetle grey cells'.

While, at last 'livin' the dream' I passed my Part Two Submarine Exam, then was promoted to Acting Leading Cook (S), so now I could 'walk the walk, an' talk the talk'. Sometime later my Rate was confirmed, elevating me to the dizzy heights of Killick, which at the time fired me with enthusiasm; *little knowing that was as good as it would get*.

During the Cold War all 'combat capable' boats were sent on clandestine two-month patrols, *known as 'sneakies'*. Now, although every whore in Pompey could tell all, we, the crew, signed the Official Secrets Act and *I kid you not* made our wills, so, although sorely tempted, I can divulge

nothing concerning these 'classified' war status missions. We *(the skivvies)* never knew our exact whereabouts, so what's to tell, other than bristling with hush-hush espionage gizmos, we would glide inconspicuously from Dolphin then proceed on 'passage routine' *hugging the coast* to an uncharted position, *well away from the shipping lanes* off the Shetlands.

Stealth now being the name of the game; ghostlike and obscured from prying eyes by an early morning haar, the boat's pennant number was painted out, then *ceasing to exist* we dived, remaining submerged until returning to the same location weeks later; having, each night, put up the Snort Mast to run the 'donks' *(engines)* so as to charge the batteries and drag fresh air through the boat. Apart from a few 'hairy' moments 'twas tedious, but we all had our part to play and a cache of films to relieve the boredom. That's when a good chain of command and a happy crew is valued, life's never dull when shared with seventy *plus* witty high-spirited guys.

The 'Commies' were aware of our presence, so there was a 'cat-and-mouse' element of danger attached to these covert spying missions in hostile Russian Waters: it wasn't unknown for returning boats to discreetly put into Campbeltown or Invergordon to have minor external damage patched up before continuing south. However, these stalwart 'front line' crews harboured no fear; having complete faith in each other's abilities, their boat and above all the CO, since Royal Navy submarine commanders are considered the best money can buy. Nevertheless, having laughed in the face of death, towards the end of the patrol we *(the hash-slingers)* were becoming increasingly concerned about the dwindling stores situation; so much so, that on the last day the crew were hungry enough to devour a newborn baby; so I took a bone from my arm to make a pot of soup.

That's it, the patrol's history, Odin has slipped quietly and unheralded back into Dolphin and tied up alongside two other boats of our squadron. It's a super midsummer morning, the for'ard and after hatches are opened for the first time since we left all these weeks ago; so, 'full o' the joys', we, the stir-crazy crew, are merrily scrambling up the for'ard ladder to the casing and first daylight we've seen in donkey's; and let me tell you it's ultra bright to our unaccustomed eyes. Everyone is elated - the jokes and comments are flying with gay abandon when Ordinary Seaman Tokarz pops his head out the hatch and, on looking across at the boat parked next

to us, sees three of the Paki *or Indian* trainees on its casing; pointing over, he says, "It must've been some summer; just look at the colour o' these cunts!" A classic, a true classic! His timing was spot on.

It's a busy morning, as we have to clear the boat of all bedding, perishables and incinerate a host of disposables *both the boat and ourselves are chuckin' up*. 'Conventional' boats don't have the home comforts of the big nukes, with laundries and the like, we just have small washbasins; no such luxuries as showers. When on risky patrols, the crew had to be constantly prepared to race to their 'action stations', so we slept fully-clothed in our sleeping bags - I think AFOs included shoes, but few *if any* heeded that one. As said, a busy morning; everyone gets stuck in and by 'Up Spirits' *which is on the boat,* the whiffy accommodation is stripped and we've earned ourselves a 'make and mend' *(afternoon off)*.

Tot time's over, the bubbly gone and the merry throng off to Dolphin's canteen for lunch; *we are now back victualled in the Base*. As always, there's a queue all the way out the door of the dining hall, with plenty banter and jostling. Most *being veterans of 'top secret' undisclosed missions* know where we've been, so it's a ritual when the pheromones work and everyone, to a man, stands aside letting 'the great unwashed' through to the front of the queue while holding their noses, condemning us ripe and passing coarse remarks. Make no mistake - **we are honkin'**, but hardly notice it, having become used to the pong. Anyway, what's another half hour, we've had our rum and want some scran before going upstairs to our Mess, showers and clean Number Eights. Not only do we get to the front of the queue and first choice at the servery; we also, understandably, get a corner of the dining hall all to ourselves. ***Fame, at last!***

D'you know, I actually came over all emotional, whilst imagining myself, there, back then - *must be getting soft!* Well anyway, we spend our free afternoon getting scrubbed up, organized and having a kip in our clean comfortable 'pits'; because, tonight 'the vultures are circlin'. Just watch us Baby; we've got loadsamoney - accrued in Pusser's safe while we've been spying in the Barents Sea and 'the beanbags' are swollen so after supper the Old Spice will be uncorked and we're off to 'Sugartown' to do our civic duty ***- yeah man; we're gonna jump some bones tonight!***

It's ideal for John and myself when the boat is alongside the wall,

because we shut down the Galley; since the crew is always victualled in the Base. This doesn't mean we have nothing to do, but with a change being as good as a rest, we clear out and thoroughly clean our workplace, making sure any repairs deemed necessary are up to scratch. We destore and restore the boat, emptying and replenishing the large tightly packed freezers helping 'Tankey' *(the storeman on boats)* return unused stock in big dark blue canvas-topped Bedford five tonners to the huge Naval Victualling Yard in Gosport. We are now having a much-needed maintenance period during which the Coxswain *who is our immediate boss* will find all sorts of jobs to keep us busy and so, make his own 'lot' easier.

After we slid unobtrusively back into Dolphin our Captain and the Jimmy reported to FOSM *(Flag Officer Submarines)* for debriefing and top-secret analysis. Now then, **here comes the good bit!** It's customary in the Submarine Service that after having endured a long, and occasionally hazardous patrol you are rewarded with a 'Jolly' for your next trip - *that's the deal*. So, as can be imagined, on the day after our return the air is euphoric when the Captain musters the entire ship's company in the fore-ends, to address the troops and bring us up to speed - yes, the Jolly is uppermost in everyone's minds and the buzzes are flying with growing absurdity; but no one is prepared for the treat in store.

An expectant hush falls over the assembled men - after 'singing our praises' we are informed the intelligence gathering mission was a triumph, apparently making FOSM a happy chappie. *We already know it was a success - since, undetected, we got back without as much as a scratch on the paintwork*. Our Commander, savouring the moment; is dragging it out with witty remarks, so as to keep us in suspense. The crew, crammed in the fore-ends, is heeding his every word while excitedly whispering "the Jolly, the Jolly", and 'the Boss' *perched on the ladder, so that everyone can both see and hear him* is basking in it; knowing exactly what everyone is desperate to hear - after a pregnant pause *while striving to maintain a straight face* he announces Odin is to join a flotilla 'showing the flag' on a four-month cruise round South America. "**South America - *awesome!!!*"** even in our wildest dreams we wouldn't have wished for better ***- yes sir, all ma birthdays have come at once - LET'S DANCE!***

The maintenance gets done with enthusiasm and both watches have

their Summer Leave, soon it's mid-August with the 'Jolly' breathing down our necks, and little else talked about. A few days before we are due to sail, the Coxswain sends for John and myself. Aw, shit! what the fuck is it this time? Things are lookin' shaky - we're in a cold sweat as we head for the Chiefs' Mess *(which doubles as the 'Swain's' office)* each thinking we are somehow going to miss out on South America - well, that's life, innit? We're both ready to expect the worst - let's face it, when did **you** last hear good news? - that's me, forever the pessimist.

We needn't have worried; this time it's **good! good! good!** and totally unexpected when 'Spud', hiding a sly grin, tells us the last thing we expect to hear - **we've been allocated a third cook for the trip**. At first we think he's winding us up, because this just doesn't happen, two cooks being adequate for the seventy *or so* complement carried by P & O Class boats. Goodness knows who wangled that one, but let me tell you; he 'played a blinder'. Wotta wheeze, this really is going to be a cruise for us - remember the old saying, ***'Many hands make light work'.***

As if that isn't enough - here's 'the icing'; we're told that when in South American ports Odin will berth alongside a big County Class destroyer *which I think was HMS Devonshire* allowing our crew to be both victualled aboard her and afforded 'free gangway' to lather-up in her showers. So, on entering harbour we will secure the Galley and have no duties for the duration. You'll be thinking - it doesn't get any better than that - *but don't be too sure!* The Swain's parting shot as we left was, "Shiner, your new cook joins in the morning, so you meet him when he turns up, get him sorted out with that empty bunk in the main passage and see he gets a billet in the inboard Mess!" At that I smartly jump to attention while replying loudly "Ah hear you Boss - ah'm onnit, you can rely on me!"

Next morning the new joker arrives - well; **yabba dabba do!** there's the Bisto Kid standing grinning like the cat wot got the cream, this is phenomenal; life's never been so sweet, is this **ever** going to be the trip of a lifetime! I hadn't encountered Ginge since joining Odin - with not seeing him in Dolphin I assumed he'd been drafted to a boat in another squadron. How wrong can you get? He'd been in Haslar Naval Hospital, and fair burstin' for me to ask why; so, to make his day, I did, saying "OK! OK! tell me!" He proudly says, "I've been circumcised! D'you want to see

it?" Although fascinated, I'm thinking **no thanks,** but before I can give an appropriate answer he's got 'the pecker' out, and it's still looking wicked after its ordeal in the *none too steady* hands of the Haslar surgeons.

I'd long since pegged this guy as crackers, and he seems determined to prove me right. So what's it all about? I've got to know and feel stupid on asking, **why:** it wasn't a religious thing **- oh no,** someone told'm it would give'm an extra two inches; sure looked as if it had, but there was a lot o' scar tissue and bruising on his 'mutton dagger', and the swelling yet to disappear. There again ***maybe he was just 'happy to see me!'***

Anyway, I get him organized before 'Up Spirits', when he meets the crew; only too willing to tell anyone who'll listen, where he's been - what for and, **of course**, do they want to see it? - this guy doesn't know what the word 'shy' means. 'Smudge Smiff' chirps in, "Let's hope you wash yer hands regularly, you're supposed to be a fuckin' cook". The only response he gets is the 'one finger salute' - 'shot down' and, employing discretion while pursing his lips, Smudge capitulates. You've got to hand it to the Bisto Kid; he's been on the boat five minutes and they've all got the message - *aye, gon yersel pal, that's what ah call an entrance!*

The 'big day' arrives an' we're 'good to go' - the order 'Casing Party muster and Special Sea Dutymen close-up for leaving harbour routine' is given, and we're off - **this is what it's all about - *Game on!***

We've left a week before the other ships - *Odin lacking the grunt of the surface vessels;* so we're alone, plodding along 'passage routine' on the surface crossing the 'big blue yonder', while at the same time heading south for Bequia; one of the small islands making up the Windward Islands in the South Caribbean. Sounds magic, throw more coal in the boiler, Stokes! - funny, you know, I never thought it at the time, but the idea of a lone vessel ploughing through a restless mist-blanketed moonlit ocean, now seems romantic - *must be the Prozac kickin' in!*

Halfway across the Atlantic thar's a storm a brewin' - *might even've been a hurricane*. John says it's the sword of Damocles, which encourages some typical gallows humour - submarines aren't too handy when surfaced in roughers, so we're goin' everywhere - **it's getting dangerous.** The Captain signals FOSM for permission to dive the boat ***- request granted -*** so it's 'diving stations' and we descend to the calm depths; *cheers, pal!* But our

troubles ain't over yet 'China' - the Grim Reaper is still in the vicinity - we suddenly have a telemotor failure; so lose control of the rudder and hydroplanes. You'd think that would result in panic stations, maybe it was a close call; who knows - I guess this is where solidarity, brute strength and ignorance comes into its own. It wasn't a question of will the 'Outside Wrecker' be able to fix it? Just, how soon? A bit 'hairy'; yes, but no one appeared alarmed - now that's training and professionalism for you! Or possibly *as in my case* **just the ignorance!**

Mercifully, the storm has abated and the 'white horses' have vanished: we're back on the surface making good time; and although still in the Atlantic now well south, so the weather is clement and consequently, the sea becoming warm. The 'Main Mann' decides his crew are in need of a bath, so stops the boat in the middle of the ocean and pipes 'Hands to bathe'! **Wotta treat** and totally unexpected, everyone not required is 'up top' and within minutes bodies can be seen flying in all directions. They are diving off the pointy bit at the front *(**bows?**... OK! - so ama **cook,** pal);* they're jumping off the casing and sliding down the ballast tanks into the sea.

The water temperature was just right, something I would never have expected of the Atlantic. It may have been just imagination, but the 'oggin' seemed more buoyant than anywhere I'd swam before, making me wonder if this was due to depth, because it would certainly be a long way down - *best not to think about things like that!* I did a bit of treading water while watching all the shenanigans and became aware of a slight current. I, being no hero or Olympic class swimmer, therefore stayed close to the boat; cos it's said the unforgiving sea can be a fickle mistress.

A couple of hours would've been enough to give everyone the opportunity of a swim, but, one of the 'baby stokers', unaware of the current, had been doing the crawl, head down, going ten to the dozen away from the boat. When he looked round, Stokes discovered he'd gone much further than anticipated - the treacherous current, having helped him along, was now hindering his return, so he was drifting further from safety by the minute. The Officer of the Watch and lookouts on the Bridge; well aware of the greaser's predicament, had been shouting to warn young Stokes, who, not having heard, sped towards the horizon. After a coin was tossed, it was decided the lad deserved another chance, so our Gemini was launched

and the *now floundering* whippersnapper plucked from a potential watery grave - that'll be one of many tales the grandchildren never get told - ***and, being the soul of discretion, my lips are sealed.***

So that's it - cleanliness being next to godliness, we're now ready to 'steam' further south. The non-swimmers had to rely on having an 'atomic bath' - *throw a tin o' talc in the air and walk through the fallout.*

It was of course hot onboard, but not uncomfortably so; as on Tenby. This, being a newer vessel probably had an upgraded ventilation system, though not, as I recall, air-conditioning. When slogging along at a steady ten knots on the surface - the 'donks' were running, thus dragging air down from the Bridge and through the boat to the engine room creating a very welcome draught. Better still, when in 'harbour routine', an engine was run at low revs to charge the batteries and generate power. At such times the for'ard hatch would be open, so cool air wafted all the way through the boat to the engine room in the after-ends, making the temperature quite pleasant. So life on boats was pretty good by comparison - the only downside being a suntan was hard to come by!

The curtain's up; *let the show begin* - yes we've arrived at Bequia and lying at anchor in a beautiful bay. This devine sun-kissed Caribbean playground of the aristocracy is *we are told* where Princess Margaret and Lord Snowdon spent their honeymoon at a bungalow owned by Sir Anthony Eden; so if it's good enough for them, it's good enough for us. No sharks, barracuda or other nasties wi' big sharp wallies, so anytime we feel the urge it's over the side for a dip, but, better safe than sorry; there's always a 'triggerman' with a big 'shooter' looking out for us from the Bridge.

Odin had made good time, reaching the West Indies well ahead of 'the skimmers', which have been ordered to rendezvous here with us, so thanks to a prevailing wind, the noble efforts of the greasers and expertise of our Navigating Officer we have 'Fantasy Island' to ourselves. Well, not quite, as it's inhabited by a friendly and very happy small population of native people who live in a village that looks like a film set - golly - no wonder 'dem black fellas' is happy; dae must be permanently 'wasted'; as, with the local dark rum being so cheap it's almost buckshee.

We'd anchored at our destination two days ahead of the Flotilla, so had 'first dibs' at this 'bit of alright' millionaires' retreat, which was totally

undeveloped, no hotels, nuthin' - probably the same as a hundred years ago. The majority of our crew had been around, so few were strangers to the powers of the 'demon drink', and the trouble it could land them in if not handled with respect; however, many *who should've known better* threw caution to the wind - ending up on report. Fortunately, I wasn't one of the numpties who got into bovver, as although I, like most, had developed a palate for Pusser's rum, I didn't care for shoreside brands.

That said, I did sample their rum in a picturesque beachside bar that looked the part with its straw-thatched roof shaded by a canopy of palm fronds. Now, we all know that there's rum and there is RUM; this 'firewater', I thought ghastly, so, that was me on the cold 'San Migs' and Vino Colapso for the foreseeable future - if I'm paying for something I want to enjoy it - this turned out to be a wise decision. *(You'll be well aware by now that all these wise decisions were more by accident than design).*

That first run ashore is worth a mention both, to describe the island, and the start of the drink-related hooliganism; *although we didn't realize this at the time.* Ginge and myself were on the first Liberty Boat ashore - which was a small native ferryboat hired by Pusser. We had commandeered the beachside bar, where we were having a drink with some of our exuberant happy-go-lucky crew, while quizzing the locals as to where the action was to be found - and can't believe what we're hearing when *taking the wind from our sails* they tell us, **this is it!** What's the score? Surely they've misunderstood. No! This is as good as it gets man; there **is** nothing else - hard to believe, but there you are; if there was more we never found it.

Well, if there was ever a recipe for disaster; the only thing to do was drink, and that was ultracheap. Naa, they're at it - we're gettin' the old mumbo-jumbo here, they must be hiding somethin' - *perhaps they haven't forgiven us for the slave trade.* So, suspicions aroused, we ask this tame native barman where the shops are; he tells us there's only one store, which is on top of a mountain at the other end of the island, owned and run by a Yank. Nothing seems real, it's bewildering - am I awake, or is it all a silly dream? Let's call this daft cunt's bluff! "We want to go to the store! How can we get there?" Rastus calls over to one of his mates, telling him "Dem white boys, dae wanna go to di stowah onna toppa da mountain!"

After givin' it the "Hey Winston, ma man, whe' is you at!" and gettin'

the "Assa comin' Boss, assa comin!", it turns out this heavy-set giant *black as the Earl o' Hell's waistcoat* has a beat-up ex-WD long wheelbase open-top Land Rover, that's seen a bit action over the years, and can take "the young massas", on the "excursion" for a small consideration. So we 'give the brother five', 'weigh'm in', climb up and off we jolly well go, not thinking or even caring that he, the driver, had been canin' the rum and coke since who knows when - **so big Winston was reekin'**.

No kiddin', that was one hairy run up this mountain road, which had sheer drops most of the way *(kiss yoa sweet white ass goodbye)*; Bequia being another of those volcanic islands, spewed from the ocean before time began, but that's not why I remember the trip so vividly. At a particularly nasty bend, where there was just nothing on the right-hand side, one of our ODs suddenly tried to push his best mate out the Land Rover, and let me tell you, if the rest of us hadn't been so quick in holding on to them both, they'd've plunged to their deaths. We couldn't figure out why it had happened, since it was so out of character for this young fellow, and them being such good pals. After a few anxious moments it all calmed down; 'twas a weird experience - the guilty party appeared confused, saying he didn't know what he'd done; minutes later he seemed OK, although visibly shaken; needless to say our inebriated driver chappie hadn't, slowed down *or even missed a beat, while singing 'Ole Man Ribbah'*.

On getting there, we were amazed; this shop was incredible - in the middle of nowhere and like the man said, "onna toppa da mountain". The Yank *who lived there* was mid-thirties, a rangy, laid-back type with a very 'healthy' young mulatto 'trophy wife'. The shop was well-stocked, you name it - he had it. God, only, knows who he sold the stuff to; 'Zeke' was obviously living out some kind of dream or *thinking about it now* may well've been a Vietnam draft-dodger. I purchased a pair of clippers and hairdressing scissors from him, as I had long needed replacements for those bought from Burnett's, the cutlers in Leith Street at home some years past - well, I said he had everything, **didn't I!**

Where was ah? Oh yeah; many got 'dropped innit' at Bequia through guzzlin' the cheap hooch - none more memorable than the Captain's Steward 'Pedlar' Palmer. Pedlar was built like the proverbial brick shithouse; generally a placid chap, but no one took the piss oot o' Pedlar.

He commanded a deserved respect from the crew, not because of his job, **oh no!** The fact being he was one 'stormy' guy, so everyone, to a man, knew it was foolhardy to rile the 'punchy Captain's flunkey'.

There's something about stewards in 'the Andrew', they're nearly all 'knuckle bosuns'; it's almost as if they have something to prove. This was especially noticeable at Lossiemouth, where some of these shady *hard as nails* Glasgow boys would have a go with anyone - certainly a far cry from their counterparts on ocean-going liners - *they, we're told, are a collection of limp-wristed 'knob jockeys' and 'old queens'*.

Anyway, on the second night, Pedlar, being a bit stressed, is off ashore for a well-earned break. At about nine-thirty the Duty Shore Patrol *looking suspiciously harassed* return to the boat, to have words with the Officer of the Watch and the Coxswain. The plebs don't miss much, we can see something's wrong but they're keeping a lid on it, so we get told nothing. Well, we know our place, soon finding out from one of the patrol that someone upset Pedlar who, off his face, screamin' drunk has 'thrown a wobbler' gone berserk, wrecked a bar and 'filled in' a couple o' 'Sambos'. The two patrolmen can't handle the situation, so have come back for reinforcements - *with both requesting bigger truncheons*.

To address the problem, a squad, armed with a Neil Robertson stretcher *(likened to a full body-length straightjacket made from stiff bamboo and canvas)*, is mustered on the casing to be ferried ashore, sort out our 'well-guttered' steward and drag him back to face the music. An hour or so later the squad return *barely disguising their taste of victory* with their 'prize' securely trussed up in the Neil Robertson stretcher, some sporting black eyes and swollen lips, proving a mighty battle had ensued.

Now, Jack isn't known to hold a grudge - no; not much! so with Pedlar restrained and helpless, it's 'the law of the jungle'. Best I don't detail the extent of the victors' wrath; however, the *by now paralytic* steward is dropped, unceremoniously, from the native ferryboat onto our ballast tanks, then manhandled up to the casing. Next, in good seaman-like fashion, Pedlar's despatched down the for'ard torpedo-loading-hatch, carried *none too carefully* aft to the control room then lowered like a sack o' spuds, down the main periscope-well, where he remained, semi-conscious, to be released in the morning sober, subdued and lookin' rough - yes, when it

comes to discipline, Pusser has the answer every time.

On arrival, the surface ships also experienced unseemly behaviour from Shore Leave Parties. Naval personnel are well-known for being boisterous and getting legless ashore - all put down to high spirits, but rarely fight or cause bovver, **knowing the consequences**. However in Bequia it was getting out of hand, so the management's suspicions were aroused resulting in a meeting being held on the Command-Ship, at which it was decided that the Squadron Doctor should analyse the rotgut being enthusiastically consumed by the masses. The 'medicine man's' findings detected a considerable content of meths; well, ***'tally dae banana'***, it appeared that 'dem black fellas' *(who didn't have much earning potential)* had decided to make a killing when presented with this unique opportunity.

Let's face it, rarely will the impact of a thousand thirsty matelots be felt converging on that little island, so as is human nature, and thanks to greed, they spoiled what could 've been a 'nice little earner'. We were to be there another two days, which would've had the Kaffir's pockets bulging, but instead Shore Leave was cancelled, plans changed, the 'donks' 'flashed up', anchors weighed and the 'candy' disappeared over the horizon.

Forget Bequia; that was then and this is now. Odin has just docked in La Guaira, the port for Caracas, Venezuela's capital. We've been told this is the most expensive city in the world; so surely they must have everything we're looking for. *That Barrel's OK, but it makes yer erse sair!* Ginge and myself have got the Galley 'squared off' and like many others, fair burstin' to step ashore after tot time. I don't know about him, but I'm dying to 'get back in the saddle'; since the Far East playground, as you know, was a long time ago; so we're going looking for a good 'Tufty Club' and let's not forget Ginge hasn't, as yet, tried out his 'new cock'.

That reminds me; he has a little bottle of pills in his locker, acquired from a bent SBA when in Haslar Hospital, these, according to my accomplice, are some sort of antibiotic that *supposedly* prevent the user from catchin' a 'dose' if taken before goin' on the razzle. Most probably a right load o' old tosh, and likely to be aspirins. However, they say the power of suggestion can work wonders, so "**Lordy Lordy, ah is a believer!**" and we religiously take them every time we go ashore. Now, let's face it Sport - we 'ragged, bagged and shagged' our way round hedonistic South America, call it luck,

call it what you will, neither of us 'caught a packet', but many, who weren't so demanding or adventurous *as you will find out* **did**.

It's showtime! - under 'starter's orders' and, rarin' to go, the jockeys race down the gangplank like creatures possessed, with Able Seaman Barnet *hot to trot* taking the lead at a fast gallop, closely followed, with a thunder of hoofs, by 'Orrible 'Arry. Like always, there are plenty 'Joe Baxis' on the jetty, big Yank jobs, so we share one with three rampant ABs in the same frame of mind as ourselves. Ginge tells the driver we want to go to Caracas and need girls, **pronto,** while giving elaborate theatrical action shots to demonstrate what we're after. He needn't have bothered, taxi drivers the world o'er know the score - they're no' daft. Quick as a flash, he says "Ah! Fucky! Fucky! Sucky! Sucky!" **Caramba,** ***we're educated!*** If you can remember that and say "San Miguel" you've cracked it!

Near explodin' wi' energy, the five amigos are larkin' about in this taxi, all in high spirits hastening to our first South American brothel telling 'Pancho' we want a good place heavin' wi' Hispanic beauties, not some shoddy rip-off dive where he gets bunged packets. He gives us the yeah! yeah! - he knows what we want, and driving like a bat oot o' hell, swerves off the dual carriageway and pelts up a private road through well-tended grounds with neatly manicured lawns and slams on the anchors in front of an impressive pile with an imposing entrance, and line of flash motors parked outside. We're thinking 'What the fuck's this', as it looks like a country club, and saying "No! No! It's a brothel we want, ya daft twat", while he's giving us the "Si! Si! Señor, thees good bordello!", and cramming us through the huge wide open Spanish mahogany doors.

It takes two shakes o' a lamb's tail and we're in, all completely taken aback, as it's an open-air dancehall - real weird; there's a stage with one of these South American bands *(blaring trumpets, big daft hats, cummerbunds and sashes),* giving it their best. There are tables and chairs dotted round the perimeter of the dance floor, there's a bar across from the stage and an 'old fox'; wearing a sombrero several sizes too large, in charge of a booth with a counter that appears to be for checking in coats and hats; a few couples up dancing and ***praise be!*** - the place is littered wi 'spare' patiently drumming their fingers on the tabletops. Wot ama gettin', this 'ere's crackers; it's early afternoon and these soft gits are dancing; stupid

bastard taxi driver gave us a bum steer - oh well, we're here now, so may as well have a bevvy, an' maybe even a dance. Someone slides over to the bar and gets them in, while we establish ourselves at a table which is a good vantage point for ogling the fud and sussing the situation.

Oh, my giddy aunt - ***it is a brothel!*** and a class joint at that - hence the flash wheels outside. These must be 'big noises' from the city who've nipped out for a 'bit o' the other' - and here's the drill. They get the bint they fancy up to dance and if chokin' for some slap an' tickle, drag her over to what I thought to be a cloakroom, pass over 'a wedge' in exchange for a key to one of the 'leetal cabanas' tucked around the grounds, motel-style; **neat!** So, d'you know wot - **we're havin' some o' this**!

At first they seemed wary of our presence - ***no problemo,*** we had Ginge 'in our corner', who *on form* with his captivating panache soon put them at ease. I've clocked this striking willowy 'stoater' wae legs right up tae her erkie, well-brushed glossy black hair, big dark eyes, tits like rocks and the expression of a startled fawn. She's wearing a simple red dress, which hangs well on her slender body, and looks every inch the pretty Señorita - wait till she gets a loada me, ah'm gonna ride this like a fairground attraction; so I swoop in for the kill, before someone else grabs her.

Whilst coppin' a feel on the floor I teach her the Lambada, she moves suggestively, making this punter feel ten feet tall - definitely one class burd; although, not exactly the girl one would introduce to one's family.

Well, this'll do for me - wastin' no time, I rush my prize to the desk and part with the bolivars to 'Mexican Pete the Bandit' in exchange for a key with a gold tag. 'Juanita' of course knows where to go *and what to do* so we go, *and do it* - **cor blimey** I'm quick, that's me, Speedy Gonzalez - Ariba! Ariba! ***Ah'm rubbish, but they don't know till ah'm finished***.

'Another one bites the dust' - *one shoot an' yer oot*; this is made abundantly clear when she puts me in the 'recovery position' then dismisses me saying I'm **magnifico** - the best she's ever had, squats on the bidet and douches her 'maiden's secret'. Sod it! Seen off again; she wasn't that good anyway - just have to get more practise in. So, in next to no time ah'm back at the table; an' ah'm no' first, **honest!** Minutes later Ginge returns with a smug self-satisfied smile on his coupon, gives a sweeping mock cavalier-style bow to all and sundry while shouting **"Olé",** then informs

us the 'new cock' works a treat - **and** "d'we want to see it?"

On entering Caracas we found it to be 'full-on' - wide motorways leading into the city, with *what appears to be marble* pillars holding up the flyovers. Now that's opulence for you! There was an airfield called La Carlota in the centre of the city with a mountain range behind, creating a scenic backdrop. Although Caracas just reeked of excess, like all such places there are the 'have nots'; beautiful big buildings - here ***'bling is king'***, everything appears wonderful, but cast an eye up the desolate hillside and there's shantytown - a stark contrast; where the peones live in a quagmire of degradation - ramshackle huts made from cardboard boxes and corrugated iron. Talk about from the sublime to the ridiculous; these pitiful, disadvantaged no-hopers and street urchins didn't have diddly-squat.

Crosses my mind that amongst the squalor there must be some real cheap 'nookie' to be had up there, but as you know the beanbag wus emptied less than an hour ago; *must get a grip* - perhaps later tonight.

We soon discover we are out of sync with the lifestyle. Here early afternoon is 'siesta time'; *a practice Jack was well acquainted with, as an after Tot ritual* - in the evenings the revellers *being nighthawks* don't hit the town until gone ten, with the bars staying open until the last customer leaves - *sounds like a good routine*. Being quick learners, we now have it sussed - knowing what time they come out to play, and having already mastered the language, South America should be '**the bollocks**'. It seems that 'the Mighty One' really has smiled on his faithful servants, and restored their beliefs this time ***- Lordy Lordy, yoa d'man!***

We were treated to some wicked 'runs' in Venezuela, accompanied by brassed-up expats working in the oil industry who made a sterling job of showing us around; with the single ones 'marking our card', which always proves useful when in an unfamiliar land on a 'whistle-stop' visit.

They did us proud in Caracas, holding many events in our honour. I was one of the freeloaders regaled at a reception hosted by an oil company in the lavish hall of a magnificent building; **wotta pitch** - acres of cream veined marble, chandeliers, statues in niches and diamonds the size o' peacocks' eggs, everything gleaming and ostentatious; looking like Hollywood to us cheapskates. We could all get used to this unashamed conspicuous display of wealth - the caviar and 'fizz' just kept coming *could well've*

been 'Champers' being 'juiced-up' I couldn't tell, but no way it was from the same bin as our affordable tipple of cheap Cape Red 'plonk'!

The return trip from that reception to the port of La Guaira will ever be remembered by all sharing our private bus, as before leaving the city we were stopped at a road-block. The bus was boarded by soldiers, wearing crisp neat uniforms, white American-style helmets and tooled up with sub-machine guns; they checked our IDs before allowing us to proceed, with no explanation given - *surely, in 'the Queen's uniform', we couldn't have been mistaken for radical subversives.* One trigger-happy twat and we'd've been history, that's how easy it would've been to 'take half our crew out' in a oner as, we, the lackadaisical trusting Brits, don't know the meaning of the word; - **security** - ***just ask any illegal immigrant!***

Who knows whether these guys were soldiers, or police wearing military uniforms in the evenings, but we became aware that they patrolled the streets after dark - coups and revolutions being commonplace in these wonderful, yet volatile, extremist Latin-American countries.

On departing Venezuela *having done our bit* the 'hotshots' headed for Cartagena, in Colombia, a country which we all *now* know as a major drug producer and exporter, with shitloads o' cash pouring in from international 'crims' - it wasn't evident then; probably because in its infancy, but that's another story - and what would we know about it? In these days we were innocents when it came to drugs - bevvy and slutz did it for us *(but far be it for me to criticize the 'space cadets' who like to 'skin up a spliff' and 'toke a big daddy').* If dosh was flooding into the ruthless Colombian drug cartels' coffers back then, it certainly wasn't conspicuous in Cartagena - a rundown and shoddy relation to vibrant Caracas.

I don't recall the place that well, as it strikes me, Ginge and myself only took ourselves ashore there the once and that was a quick, though memorable, afternoon jaunt. Casting my mind back, I can picture a large pedestrianized square with Spanish-type churches and buildings; just like we've all seen on the big screen when the baddies make it over the border on escaping into Mexico, or, say, the sets in Clint Eastwood's Dollar films.

It was probably good old siesta-time, with three-quarters of the population 'festerin' in thur scratchers'. But, not everyone I'm pleased to say, as after raking around and deciding it wasn't for us; dry as sticks we

nicked into a boozer, not looking for action, just a couple o' wets to slake our thirst before returning to Odin. ***Well - root toot, toot...*** there's a bunch of young tinted maidens hovering round the jukebox, swingin' their hips while it's bashing out some Rolling Stones stuff. Well wha'diya know, things are lookin' up! We cop a pair of cold San Migs and astutely settle at a table, close to the music, so as to get a better squint at the scrubbers, who are obviously 'peddlin' the flesh', but there ain't no punters, only us, making Ginge and myself the two most interesting 'marks' in the place - talk about luck; **it's Happy Hour!**

Need I say, it's the old routine; they're giggling, whispering and sneaking coy glances at us. ***Who are they kiddin'!*** Anyway, we like them to wiggle, not giggle - hang about; these harlots aren't Señoritas, they look like Navajo Indians. Then we notice Mama sitting on a stool behind them and that settles it; she's got a damp unlit stogy stuck in her gob and wearing Indian peasant clobber - *shawl, long beaded smock and the pointy beat-up squashed black hat adorned with an eagle feather.* Because she's a wizened auld hag, the wrinkles are prominent **and man, she's one ugly woman!** I wonder if they're her daughters? As expected, two of the damsels shimmy over and delicately park their pert tushes - ***talk about forward!***

We know the lingo, but *playing hard to get* we're keepin' schtum - let's just see where it goes. They could hardly be described as gorgeous, but there again after deekin' Mama they're 'no' three bad'. Now, we - *having no wish to encourage such sordid behaviour*, aren't paying to dally with the likes o' this depraved duo; however the prankster reckons "The early worm catches the burd", so, since this is a matinee, we decide to get the drinks in and have a laugh wae this pair o' crows!

I don't know how it happened - well, OK... I do! *Ye ken how it is when sometimes ye huv the best o' intentions and one thing leads tae another, impairin' yer judgement.* So, we're having a bit o' fun with the pidgin English and hand signals an' *all systems go* we've got their blouses undone an' the jugs oot. Let me tell you, these bints are lookin' nicer by the minute and we, stupified after a few wets, convince ourselves we've copped a pair o' vestal virgins; but they ken whit thir daein' - up to all sorts, arousing us with both hands and bare feet beneath the table.

Their timing's perfect, when down they squirm to play a tune on the

'one-eyed piccolo'. This is magic; and believe me, although they now have **our** undivided attention, none of the 'barflies' as much as glance our way. Well, they know when they have us at the point of no return, so with reservations forgotten and blindfolds no longer required, 'the greengos' were led by the proverbial into the back shop, where, in a moment of weakness, we swapped bodily fluids with 'mama's gals' whilst engaged in their tribal mating ritual; there was no 'air con' and this encounter a mere 10° north of the Equator, so you can imagine the sweaty flesh slap-slap-slapping - ***forgive us Lord, for we have sinned!***

Not only was it the noisiest, it was also the cheapest, being the equivalent of a couple o' 'sovs' - and that was for both o' us, so all I can say is, "it was worth every penny"! If there was ever a time we should've caught a 'snottery nose' that was it; but no - nothing, zilch, *not even the scabies*. Of course we were still poppin' the pills; anyway you can't catch a dose from a virgin, *can you?* - easy now, don't all answer at once!

Can't say how long we were in Cartagena, probably only two or three days, I'm **almost** sure we didn't go ashore again; it just wasn't the place - short on zing and no enticing bright lights. However, I acquired a stuffed alligator from Rico, a down 'n' out trader drinking in Rosa's Cantina on the jetty - *swapped him forra a tin o' peaches an' a few pesos* - when I got home Mother quickly binned my treasured momento, claiming it to be no more than a "rancid health hazard". So, 'hasta la vista' Colombia - South America is turning out just incredible, it's 'snatch heaven' just like the Far East, Ho! Ho! **Fuckin**' Ho! Remember 'Banjo' - the PO 'hairy fairy'? I wonder if he's out 'the slammer' by now! (*mind yer fingers* - **clang**).

Next came the shortest leg of our voyage - to the Panama Canal, where, while waiting our turn to traverse the waterway it was decided to take advantage of the fact that, since we were lying in 'freshers', this would be an ideal opportunity to scrub and hose the grime and salt from what was *and would again be* a black submarine. By midday the boat was looking a treat, thus making the Jimmy a proud and happy man, so to reward and show his appreciation for the noble efforts of the, by now, sweating casing party, he pipes "Well done chaps - hands to bathe!" - but, **no takers.** What he didn't know *and we did* was, the banks of the lake were lined with hungry alligators and on hearing the Jimmy's announcement, the chief

gator , ***'Big Al',*** immediately piped "Hands to dinner!"

That's it, we're through the Canal and now 'steaming' south through the sparkling blue Pacific Ocean. **Isn't life just great!** Our next port of call will be Callao, the seaport for Lima in awe-inspiring Peru; a land that, though steeped in the past, had us dreaming of future promise.

Well now, that same week ah wus mortified to discover I had a secret admirer onboard this sleek silent submarine packed with macho sailors. Get this - one morning my best chiffon Sunspel Black Watch tartan boxer shorts had vanished from the 'smalls'; left drying overnight on my dhobi line in the Galley. Fair makes you think; and they say there's no love left in the world, **hooey!** Pondering it now I wonder, was this petty crime down to necessity, infatuation, jealousy or just pure devilment? Anyway, at this late date, if the perpetrator perchance still has them under his pillow, it's high time I had them back. **Although the deed is consigned to the annals of history, the question remains* - whae nicked cookie's knickers?

Some people would steal the saddle off a nightmare!

So here we are in Peru, where it's always summer. "How time flies". The Bisto Kid and myself aren't intent on breaking any records on our official crusade, but, nevertheless, have resolved to go on the 'randan' together and 'fill our boots' in every port, so as to have something to look back on in years to come and able to say "We humped our way round South America!" 'Twas indeed good fortune to be in cahoots with a soulmate like Ginge, because without his influence it would, no way, have been such fun - *there's a lot to be said for being easily led when keeping the company of them wot 'ave questionable pursuits.*

In saying that, this cruise was reminiscent of my Far East tour with Lew on the good ship Tenby - **remember him?** - that demon 'king of the undieworld', who, you'll recall, wangled a compassionate discharge from the Royal Navy some three-plus years back; intending to relocate to this very city - I hope he's still here; and if that's the case, will make every effort to contact him. Jings, wotta unique opportunity this is; to be able to visit an old mate living on the other side of the world - and *'foh flee'* at that. I think I stand a good chance, as again expats have laid on 'grippos' galore *(freebie runs ashore)* for us and whatismore, the ships will be 'open to visitors', so it's a fair bet old 'luv'm and leave'm' will come aboard for

a 'shufti'. Thinking about it now, I realize my approach was bollocks - I'd have had more luck trawlin' round the many houses of ill-repute.

One of the 'freebies' I put my name down for was to Lima's posh English college; on the presumption that a member of the large staff may know of, and have an address for Señor Lew, but no such luck. However, I remember the Principal was anxious to record our voices; as a tool, to aid him in a planned lecture covering 'the Brits' accents and dialects.

In the week or so we were there I asked every expat I met if they knew Lew and made sure the QMs on the gangway looked out for him, but all to no avail, so I guessed *but mentally refused to believe* he'd 'gone native' or moved on. This was frustrating when I was sure I'd be able to give him a surprise visit; and even more so when he got in touch years later, through my mother's address in Edinburgh, from Lima; where he still lives to this day. We remain in contact - *and* ***they*** *said it wouldn't last.*

He, however, astonished **me** by arriving in Edinburgh back in the nineties, on a 'freebie' with Newton College, where he teaches - *and probably indulges in a bit of extra-curricular activity in the broom cupboard.* We didn't exactly 'do the town'; but on his last night went to a fortieth birthday-bash, which the 'babe magnet' *(still mustard)* obviously enjoyed, especially when oozing rakish charm whilst holding court, chatting up the doting half-pished wives hanging on to his every word.

Ginge and myself stepped ashore forra stab at this wonderful place everyday, as it was vibrant, interesting, and easy to get to Lima, just a short bus ride up the main road from the Port of Callao, in fact, so close the two places were more or less joined - *and probably are by now*. The first day we nicked ashore 'early doors'; which will have you thinking, 'some people never learn'. The reason for this was threefold: one, we had dosh; two, we wanted to have a sniff around, so as to suss the place out *regarding after dark pleasure palaces;* and three, it was a 'rabbit run' because the shops, although inexpensive, were upmarket, particularly the jewellers with their intriguing Aztec/Inca curios, of which I bought some bits and pieces - a good investment when later used back in the UK as an exchange medium for favours from 'the enemy' ***- all's fair in love and war!***

Just remembered an amusing sequence related to this devious scheme, so I'll tell it to you now, before I forget. Along with some cheap trinkets I'd

bought a dose o' key rings, which were cleverly faked to look like silver - nonetheless, they were attractive and unusual with these strange little Inca Gods and symbols *to ward off evil spirits* embossed on their fobs.

Years later I still had two or three left, lying forgotten in a drawer, when one night I'd invited an associate and his wife round for some scran; after a few wets they blabbed that they'd been trying awhile for a sprog, but without success. For some reason I thought of the key rings, and confidently said "I've got the very thing for **you**". Then *leaving them wondering* hastened to the davenport and selected one that looked the part; then presented it to them along with a truly inspired story of how this ugly wee joker on the key ring's medallion was the Inca God of fertility. Well, I'll be blowed if she didn't have 'a bun in the oven' within weeks. Coincidence or the power of suggestion? **You tell me!** - by the way, they went on to have another *and another* before binning my 'mystic rune'.

Getting back to that first daylight run to Lima - at a part of the city appearing to be the vibrant financial district, it was very noticeable that the prosperous portly businessmen all had mistresses - **lucky devils!** It must have been a bye-law, *because, so obvious* - there they were, strutting their stuff in smartly-tailored suits boasting astounding young creatures, hanging like trophies from their arms. Now, don't tell me they were all merely taking the secretary to lunch *(maybe this explains why Mr Lewis emigrated to, and stayed in Peru)*. Most of the people appeared small and neat - possibly of Portuguese descent. Their women were alluring sophisticated, immaculately attired and proudly carried themselves with the poise of models - *just got tae hae wan o' thaim afore ah go hame!*

Another unique grippo was a train trip up the Andes to examine the Inca ruins and hear the story of a lost pagan empire. I can't remember the name of the place, but can tell you that, although we went 'the easy way', it was a fair trek, as we left early morning and were away all day. Our destination was a remarkable twelve thousand feet above sea level *quite a novelty for submariners* which is why it took hours to get there; with the two engines, one pushing and the other pulling, having to shunt back and forward zig-zagging up through steep mountain passes. The rugged scenery, as I'm sure you can imagine, was mind-blowing. When we finally reached the summit, and disembarked for a scout around, we were quite

breathless *the air being so thin* but it didn't seem to affect the little native sprogs indigenous to the altitude, as there they were running around as normal. That said, when I now hear reports that our athletes who go to such places are disadvantaged I can sympathize with them.

Staying 'on target', that night the predators splashed on the Old Spice and went on the prowl - common sense suggesting we return to that fashionable district and cop a better class of whore than had 'serviced' us in the less than salubrious Cartagena the previous week. So, with that accomplished; after a wee rake around we chanced upon the El Lobo Club, a throbbin' carioca gaff - all neon and mirrors with good live music, and, of course, the wee dance floor. Well wouldn't ye know, we are no sooner through the door than onna winner, scorin' a pair o' crackers - *believe me, most of these hot-blooded Latin ladies were* ***sex, personified.***

* Note to self - Nine times out of ten in such places it's so easy it's not true, which is great as long as you don't become complacent and delude yourself into forgetting **they are all 'working girls'.**

Can't remember precisely what Ginge's bint was like, but tidy and slim wi' guid sookers *(the type that would bend like a reed in the wind)* comes to mind; however, it's a doddle to visualize the one I fell deeply in love with that night; ***a Page Three shot!*** Check this out - she must've been a 'half chat', as although every bit the elegant sensual Señorita, there was just a hint of the high-cheekboned Slavic Oriental, along with these limpid almond eyes that stared straight into one's soul; **this was quality!** Yeah, this creature, who moved like a cat, looked as if she'd blow yer bollocks off! And guess what? - I was fair gaspin' to give her the opportunity!

We spent a wild night drinking and dancing with them, then when it finally came to the crunch and time to haggle the price - **wotta a bargain!** In fact, so much so we thought that we must be up for a 'knee-trembler' in some rat-infested back alley; since there's no way we're getting hotel rooms at the price this pair are quoting. Although they speak good English, we're not sure they're getting the message, or what they're on about when we follow them to this small office block - but, **wait a minute!** They've got the keys; Jings - ***the señoritas are secretaries.*** Turns out they're a pair o' amateurs bolstering the wages by engaging in a bit o' illicit overtime. So, we have an office apiece - hear now, this **is** the way to go, ***hallelujah!***

It's amusing when havin' a wee bit o' difficulty conversing and no bed; but, when dem ole hormones is in the driving seat luv will find a way. After the initial burst of enthusiasm had waned, we were getting a tad uncomfortable on this remarkable swivelling office chair, so Miss Peru says "Woof! Woof!" Well, every dog has his day, so after a brief intermission *with my will to live restored* I've got my slave spreadeagled face down forra guid auld-fashioned rogering on the Boss's massive antique desk; ***crivvens!*** - this *'willing for a shilling'* nymph could make a happy man old!

Wotta night! So good that there was no point in looking for better, so, standing on ceremony, the next two were repeat performances, with the finale being 'on the hoose' followed by a tearful adios from our saucy Latin lovers - *after a confession that the company had surpassed the sex.*

Old Mother Hubbard
Went to the cupboard
To fetch her poor doggy a bone.
When she bent over
Rover took over
And gave her a bone of his own.

Bad boy!

Swing them lamps me 'earty; it's a case o' gettin' some sea-time in again. The Flotilla of British Ambassadors are now heading further south, bound for Concepción in Chile - whilst on passage Odin participated in war games with the Chilean Navy, which meant being at sea for a week or more, Cor! 'Shiver me timbers' - enough tae brek yer 'eart!

During this visit our Wardroom played host to the Chilean Admiral *(like, thee top man),* and his team of grandees - cripes, I've never seen that many medals and so much scrambled egg *(gold braid!).* We, the caterers, laid on a cocktail party and conjured up a banquet for the gathering, which could only have been a noble effort, as after the event our Captain thanked, and informed us that El Supremo *much impressed with the tinned aragonis and gourmet salmon spread sarnies* asked if we could be transferred to his personal staff. Praise indeed - but there again, let's not get carried away; 'twas probably no more than good diplomacy. A great deal of our success was due to the dedication and expertise of 'Punchy Pedlar', who had been very low-profile, and *doing penance* worked relentlessly to make amends

since ‘blotting his copybook’ in Bequia. So, just this once, I’ll stand aside, ‘play the white man’ and wing ’m the credit.

The next day should go down in Naval history as **‘the day of the exploding shunkey’**; our officers *having resumed their penchant for the good life* hosted a buffet-lunch and cocktails for some local gentry and poppets they’d trapped at the Embassy. An unforgettable occasion for many, especially one prim young courtesan - mid-afternoon the Duty Stoker piped “Blowing the heads!” Before proceeding, it’s best that for the uninitiated I explain what this entails. On P & O Class submarines the heads were a bank of four cubicles situated on the port side of the passage just aft of the Control Room; the waste being flushed down to a sewage-tank below. Each WC had a non-return flap valve which closed after flushing. Daily, Stokes would play with his valves, so as to pressurize the sewage-tank then open the external hull-valve, thus blowing the waste materials to sea - hence ‘blowing the heads’. Also at this point *(to save doing so later)* I will add that older boats *(T Class etc)* did not have the luxury of a sewage-tank, so the heads were ‘blown’ each time by the user.

Now that you’ve mastered the operation of submarine heads, let’s get back to the ‘Buffet and Bevvy’: so, as I was saying, Stokes has just piped “Blowing the heads” to let the crew know what he’s up to; as they mustn’t be flushed until the operation *(taking minutes)* is complete. Anyway, this daft burd *tipsy from the cocktails she’d been plied with* goes to ‘powder her nose’, unaware of what’s happening, or for that matter, what the pipe means. Well now, when she flushes the toilet she of course opens the WC’s non-return valve, the tank below is by now under pressure, so up it whooshes with a vengeance. She gets covered, it’s splattered everywhere, she’s screaming and the reek is revolting. I tell you it’s at times like that I was glad not to be a seaman as, let’s face it, someone had to clean up the filth; and it for sure wasn’t the burd - *who had to be hosed down.*

I’ve no memory whatsoever of Concepción itself, so ah’ll stick ma neck oot an’ say it was a short visit. Thinking about it, here and now, I’m sure I let the side down and never went ashore, so assume crewmates had said it wasn’t worthwhile making the effort; being a fair old hike into town, and therefore, prudent to save the dosh for better times. *Believe me, if that was the case, they didn’t know how right they were.*

Before moving on, it crosses my mind that the Chilean Admiral, who thought we were cordon bleu material, may not have been overimpressed with the Bisto Kid, who by this time had been christened 'Broken Eggs Bristo' by Ginge Heulet - a 'townie' of the Bisto Kid, although from a different manor. Ginge Heulet, an AB Badgeman *who harboured notions about the Dagenham Girl Pipers* was a 'number one geezer', very popular with the crew, a typical London wit who would've slotted nicely into the cast of 'Fools and Horses'. The reason for the 'Broken Eggs' title being; when the Bisto Kid was Duty Breakfast Chef and frying 'cackleberries' for the entire crew of seventy-four men, every single egg would have a burst yolk, *no favouritism whatsoever.* This was some guy, a born clown who couldn't give a tinker's cuss, but with such a wonderful manner that everyone put up with his contrived failings. I was forever telling Comrade Bristow I thought he was a Russian spy who had infiltrated our Submarine Service to then, do the bidding of his Soviet paymasters, whose orders came straight from the Kremlin - ****spot the deliberate mistake!***

The next stretch of our voyage took us to Punta Arenas, at the foot of the vast South American continent - still in Chile, a huge country, although smaller than its neighbour, Argentina. We are now down at a latitude of fifty-three degrees, so it's cooler - belay that; '**brass monkeys**' after wot we've become acclimatized to. Consequently, we've stowed the white sailor suits and reverted to our blue uniforms, which is a blessing as these 'whites' are a bastard to keep clean. There may've been a 'chinky laundry' on the Devonshire; yeah, there must've, as there's no way we could've managed otherwise. Having made that statement there's sure to be hordes o' know-alls fair burstin' to correct me; so either piss off or form an orderly queue, but listen up; I'm not accepting 'drip chits' today!

So, 'Daily Orders' state 'Cold Weather Routine' *(two in a bunk)* and the 'Pusser's Burbs' has been pulled back into service - *I'm so glad I brought it*. This is a bleak American-style dockyard; not unlike the one in Manila. As said, it's **'baltic';** making the place seem hostile and certainly doesn't look like offering a good run ashore. Someone says it must be the arsehole of the world, *but we know different, don't we?* **Cos that's where we live!** It's got that "fuck you, pal - don't bother" look, so we aren't rushing ashore, but after supper and watchin' a 'shitkicker' *(cowboy film)* in the fore-ends

we're bored. Ginge, and some others *who no doubt would prefer to remain nameless* think 'what the hell, let's check it out!' Having nothing better to do, I decide to tag along.

There's always a 'fast black' to be had at dockyards, so we pile into one spouting the usual instructions, and in no time at all; because it's within spittin' distance o' the jetty, we're at a big cheesy *straight out of Babylon* whorehouse which reminds me of Fairley's back home.

Cor, this bawdy cathouse should be named 'the Crazy Horse Saloon' - it's like a vision I once had - doses o' manic action an' awash' wi slutz; whose features remind me of Eskimos, so I can easily imagine I'm in a bar in Alaska during the gold rush and it's party time, cos some ole 'forty-niner' has just struck the 'mother lode'. **Talk about coming up trumps**, this is priceless; it just goes to show, that true enough, you can't judge a book by its cover. There we were, huddled together *for warmth* in the fore-ends, watching a crap film, completely unaware of this throbbin' 'sin bin' up the road - so, we'd got it wrong. Now in our element, *so to speak,* we're eager to join the 'action' and 'stake our claim'.

But, not everyone had got it wrong; half our crew were already there makin' a meal o' it - collars askew, lanyards out, caps perched at jaunty angles, half-bevvied and havin' a whale o' a time. Some of the maidens are quickly over to us, ***the new arrivals***, and like flies round shite *with the courtesy of a bygone age* chorusing "You wan' fucky, fucky, sucky, sucky?" which seemed a tad presumptuous; *but ah liked the sound of it.*

'Supersonic' Sam, one of our ODs who looked the worse for wear; having obviously been there for hours, loudly says, to no one in particular, "Forget the fucky fucky, I tried to shag that skinny cow over there!" pointing at a real pig. "It wus like throwin' a chipolata up the Mersey Tunnel; it's got a fanny like a billposter's bucket, but she knows what to do wi' the laffin gear!" "So get her gums round yer plums!" Well, while I don't condone lewd behaviour, such a recommendation is hard to ignore, so ah'm for some o' that. Let's get the San Migs in and see what happens.

Wotta a turn-up, more like a private party than a 'knees-up' in the boozer. Rounded off nicely wi' the speciality o' the hoose, "Here hen, sook the poison oot o' this!" - *if anything, better than anticipated, as long as you weren't shy* - these brazen hussies didn't bother taking punters to the

back shop, no, **not them**, just pushed their victims into booths, wriggled under the tables and 'blew their tools'. They were certainly well-versed in their profession, so it was a jovial and gratified ragtag and bobtail gaggle that returned to Odin in the wee small hours. When safely back onboard and 'turned in' I had a flashback to Mercury and dropped off with Jock McNutter's voice ringing in my ears - yes indeed; he was spot on!

Like the Indian Chief said to his new squaw,
"No stroke um, smoke um!"

Linda Lovelace eat yer heart out! Come on, don't give me that shit - you've seen 'Deep Throat'. **Oh here!** Get this, I recently heard *on the radio* that old 'suck it 'n' see' is 'potted head'; seemingly she'd been in a car crash some time back and, later, 'snuffed it' from the injuries sustained. Poor cow! she always maintained she neither enjoyed nor wanted to make that film, but was forced by an ex-husband, or lover. Aye, it's a cruel old world! Or, as they say **"life's a bitch; *and then you die!"***

Crikey! I almost got trampled in the rush when we stormed back the next night for 'seconds' *as 'one swallow doth not a summer make'*. By now the word had circulated and everyone knew the score, so the bulk of the Chiefs' and POs' Mess turned up to see the show and join the cast.

Here's a little nugget - a dozen or so, arrived around midnight, making us think the duty 'chew bosun' must be 'off-watch'. The party is by now chaotic and in full swing, this stoker *(who shall also remain nameless)* standing near the door with his arm draped over a pretty little thing, spies them, so totters over, with her in tow, to meet the late arrivals, and says to one of the Senior Rates "Hi Chief, this 'ere's my girlfriend d'you wanna to give'r a kiss?" No messin', Chiefy's right in there and just about sucks the face off her, after which Stokes, with an innocent look on his coupon, confesses "She blew ma stones five minutes ago!" ***Woops!***

We never found out if there were similar bars, or *for that matter* what the rest of Punta Arenas was like, as with that on your doorstep, why bother going further afield - *what more could one want?* Hey! here's a perk I should've been crowin' about way back. Submarine catering staff were privileged to be victualled for rum in the Senior Rates' Mess; so we got 'neaters' *(the Junior Ratings' rum was watered down)* - life just keeps getting better! How could I have forgotten that? ***Must be losin' it!***

So we've left Punta Arenas behind - our next stop will be Montevideo in Uruguay, which entails a long voyage round Cape Horn - I'm sure you'll know that old Cape to be notorious for giving generations of poor mariners a hard time and rough passage through wild seas. We're not exactly relishing this leg of the trip, furthermore, I may be wrong here, but I'm sure I remember we were told that Odin would be the first submarine *"known"* to have made this passage, making us wonder **why**. Anyway, they say God smiles and the sun shines on the righteous - well now, the fact that it was sunny and flat calm all the way must tell you something.

I've already spoken highly of the Captain, *one of a kind* - always concerned and friendly to his crew; in fact, one of the boys. It pains me to say this, but few Officers were that praiseworthy - many of the witless fops assuming it their devine right to treat Junior Rates as they would their 'fags' at boarding school. *That observation is down to them and their attitude towards the Lower Deck, as, unfortunately, it was generally a case of 'them and us'. A pity, yes, but they made the rules - **or did they?** Deep down everyone resents authority, but you must have a chain of command, so maybe it was down to us - in their defence, these strutting tosspots had been totally indoctrinated during years spent learning their profession coupled with the 'social graces' at Dartmouth Naval College.

Just after 'Up Spirits', on the day Odin rounded the Horn, we, the cooks, were busy serving up lunch to the ever-hungry crew when the Captain poked his head round the Galley door, and on catching my attention said "Chef, have you got a minute?" He's the boss, so the answer is obviously "Affirmative Sir!"*accompanied by a smile*. He says, "Come to the Control Room." Quite concerned, I follow him thinking - 'What the fuck! - don't tell me I've poisoned someone.' He seems friendly; so it can't be that bad, perhaps the phantom knicker thief's been caught, whatever, my mind's working overtime. I'm put out of my misery when he says "Have a look through the periscope, it should remind you of home". This was a quality gesture, since most of the 'exalted ones' thought we were androids.

I guess he'd never been to Edinburgh, because what I saw through the 'scope'; being bleak and mountainous, reminded me of Greenland. **Well, ah'll be a monkey's uncle!** - on zooming in, I spy something remarkable. There they are; three mermaids glistenin' in the spray, preenin' themselves

on the nearest seaweed-covered rock, tits hingin' oot, combing their long golden tresses, cooeeing and singing seductive songs whilst beckoning us to join them. Jings, they're enchanting - I'm almost under their spell when I realize that while two are 'essence', the third's an old crone, **the granny** - an' you know which one ah'll cop; **don't you?** Worse still, what if the boat gets dashed onto the rocks, forcing our return to Punta Arenas - holy moly, ah couldnae handle any more o' that just yet; they burds back thair didnae take any prisoners an' wid sook the baws oaf yae; so I blow the 'sea vixens' a kiss, keep what I've seen to myself, thank the Captain and saunter back aft, wondering just how many unwary sailor boys had been lured to their doom through the centuries by that trio of aquatic sirens.

OK, enough o' that, we've 'dropped anchor' at Montevideo in Uruguay. Argentina's been given a pass, although it would indeed have been a bonus to stop in at Buenos Aires, but even then diplomatic relations were shaky between our two countries - nothing to do with the people; but once again down to the 'puppet-masters' and liars. **God help us** - it's a cardinal sin, that the few can assert their will on so many, generally, against their wishes and to realize how, carte blanche, the short-sighted weasels have squandered our identity and screwed our heritage over the last five decades.

Cor! Just when we thought things couldn't get worse, along came George and Tony. D'you no' get pig sick o' hearin' these two untouchable egomaniacs mouthin' off about Saddam Hussein. How can we take their likes seriously? - actually, we don't *as most are convinced that they and their cronies, are demented.* If you're going to do something, **do it!** That said, if they ever get the finger out, they'll cock it up just like the last fiasco, when old man Bush and John Major *(the clown who was pumpin' Edwina Currie)* blew billions getting right up to Saddam's front door and never even rang the bell - his type should be 'taken out' **long before** becoming a threat to the world. We've no gripe with the <u>ordinary</u> Iraqi people - like ourselves, merely pawns with no say. However, the lunatics running the asylum certainly do, which is ludicrous, as although well-versed in the art of deception, they haven't an iota of 'common dog fuck' between them - **it's impossible for our troops to defeat faceless Muslim fanatics,** brainwashed into believing the fable that they'll go to Paradise, ***and*** be rewarded with seventy two virgins apiece - *high time someone told them*

the truth. What is more, every bodybag that returns to our shores is down to the sleepwalkin' lickspittles who sanctioned the futile blunder ***- och, c'mon, get real, I'm just sayin' what everyone's thinkin'!***

Where are we this time? Oh yeah! Montevideo, great city; that's the place where I went ashore and scored two rides; so when I got back I gave my mate one! Super place for buying leather goods, well made and so cheap you wouldn't believe. After a bit o' hagglin' and diggin' deep, I 'parted' for a doeskin waistcoat, a heavy reefer-style black hide three-quarter length coat *(great for 'flashing', but made me look like a high-ranking Gestapo Officer)* and then 'done my tank in', purchasing a navy blue soft leather suitcase in which to transport all my shrewdly acquired bounty up the line come Christmas Leave, which was by now nearing reality.

Laid on was a super 'up-country' grippo, so ah wacked ma name down, smartish - glad to have done so when we finally arrived; following an amusing journey, traversing bumpy unmetalled roads, trailing swirling dust clouds in our wake. Jarring aside, 'twas interesting, as by going to and through the hinterland we saw what Uruguay was really like - the haciendas and roadside stalls just as shown in films *such as 'The Magnificent Seven'*, but this was for real. The strange thing is, that having viewed similar scenery so regulary on both big and small screens, it appears familiar - as if you've always been there. Well it did to me! - *but you've, no doubt, long since formed an opinion, as to my overactive imagination*.

Well, anyway, we went to a huge cattle ranch *and, I do mean* ***huge;*** way up on the Pampas. I've no idea who owned it, but wait for this; you'll be aware that South American cowboys are called gauchos, but, get this - the foreman and his mate were Scotsmen, a pair of confident guys in their early thirties; so evidently in charge. Absolutely amazing! You've got to take your hat off to them, there can't be anywhere on Earth that you won't find Jocks and Jews. The Jocks running the show and the 'four by twos' controlling the money - the world would fall flat on its erse withoot thum - ***don't argue, you know it's true!***

Holy cow! - talk about 'kill the fatted calf', these gaucho guys laid on a barbeque like you've never imagined *even in your wildest dreams*. They'd dug pits in which glowing embers were barbecuing sizzling joints of seasoned beef; so heavy it was taking two to lift them out - their ravenous

guests watching every move with greedy eyes and watering mouths. The caballeros used their wicked-looking machetes to hack off lumps so big 'twas a challenge troughin' them, but, juices dribbling down chins, we managed. Cases of San Migs were stacked high on the grass, 'get stuck in and fill yer boots' was 'the order of the day'. There was enough beef an' bevvy to satisfy the whole fleet, so the 'animals' were getting tore into this feast, like newly arrived vagrants let loose in Valhalla.

Our benevolent hosts intended putting on a wee show for us - probably fancy horse-riding and 'roping' steers with these bolas things they use instead of lassoos; but even there it rains, and all of a sudden the heavens opened, cancelling the programme. It ain't gonna stop, **no chance,** you can see the sky for miles - it's black; and there it is, thunder and jagged lightning - *so much for alfresco!* We are hurriedly ushered back onto the buses, and while exchanging farewells I say to one of the Jocks "What about the beer?" Getting a "Help yersel, pal!" **- crikey! I hate waste!** So, displaying considerable pluck and exuding confidence, hastily salvage six cases before our bus pulls out; strangely no one followed suit - although everyone has snaffled a few cans to down on the return journey.

The boys reckon ah'll be busy smugglin' the beer onboard, and I'm a bit more than dubious, but I'll have to give it a shot, since I've committed myself; so don't want to back down and take a ribbing. Anyway, when we get back to the jetty it's a doddle as the Quartermaster says there are no Officers or Senior Rates around, so everyone, including the QM, mucks in, and we've disappeared 'the goods' over the gangway and down into the boat 'quicker than that'; I stash them under my mattress, which means I'll have to sleep on top of them in the already confined space of my bunk. However, after my moment of glory I, ***'The Kingpin'*** *letting success impair my judgement* distributed them to the poor and needy. A welcome supplement to our beer ration - two cans per man, per day, PERHAPS!

The grande finale was Rio De Janeiro. **Stroll on, wotta gaff!** Straight off, you know this **is** the end of the rainbow; the weather ace, the harbour stuffed with cruise ships, Jesus, arms outstretched, blessing everything from atop the spectacular Sugar Loaf Mountain ***- it's all happening here!***

As usual we are tidying up and closing the Galley, so I'm on the jetty to ditch the gash - while havin' a gander and taking all this in, I get "Psst!"

from a sleazy looking hawker *living in a heavily pockmarked face* who suggests I need some cheap Bacardi. Now, I shouldn't have bought it, but we know how greed can get the better of us, so in a flash I'm thinking we've got Coca-Cola, I could be pretty smart here, I'll sneak the hooch back onboard concealed in the gash bucket, so we can have a nice wee 'sesh' before hitting the town. Decision made, ah'm putty in this cunt's hands, **ah've 'parted'**, I've got the rum and I'm back on the boat, feeling quite pleased with myself - *hero of the hour and all that.*

After 'Up Spirits' we give this bottle a trouncing in the for'ard Mess, with Pedlar and myself polishing off the dregs in our bunks; and let me tell you, he had a fair blast at the stuff. I can't remember where Ginge was, but guess he got his share; rest assured, he never missed out, so was more than likely lying happy as a sandboy 'wasted' in his 'pit'. I woke about two hours later feeling rough and that afternoon 'spewed ma ring' so many times my throat was raw. The fore-ends rumrats who'd partaken, were all fine, as was Pedlar *who'd guzzled the most* no adverse effects whatsoever, but that was me 'down the Suwannee' - bang goes ma first night of racy indulgence in Rio - ***Stupid bastard!*** I've never *to this day* been able to look at Bacardi again, talk about a night to remember - I'm sure you'll know how it is; when you have a throat like that you keep needing to swallow, knowing full well it's going to be agony - misery! ***Silly git!***

When in our prime, we heal quickly, so next day there's no stopping me - I'm off ashore to savour the delights with Ginge, two ABs and a stoker. We, when in 'sin cities' are well-warned to steer clear of certain places - *supposedly bad news;* so we always know exactly where to make a beeline for the minute we step ashore, and in this case it's Mangi *(at least, that's how I remember it was pronounced).* This is mind-boggling - it's a square miracle mile rife wi' brothels, sex shops and debauchery, so we're over the moon, cruisin' around like little boys spoilt for choice in a sweetie shop and don't forget, **you can't beat a chocolate brazil!**

Ginge makes the choice for us, he wants to see a 'lesbo show'; and he wants to see this one! The rest of us aren't keen, as we'd prefer to 'probe thum', but the maestro, who has the morals of a sewer rat and knows no shame, employing his considerable charm, seduces us and we relent, so before we've had time to change our minds he's pushed us through the

door of this poky, stale smelling ground-floor apartment.

So, minutes later, there's the five of us crowded round this grotty bed, furthering our education by ogling two brown-skinned bints interlocked, enthusiastically strumming each other while gasping, writhing and grinding in performing their distasteful *but fascinating* act. Given the opportunity, we'd have opted to see 'the donkey' but Ginge - *who couldn't keep his hands off them,* was fair lappin' it up. Sometimes you have to go with the flow - so, what the hell; whatever floats yer boat ducky!

Now, remember this was yonks ago, when there were no big black 'rubber hubbies' or sophisticated battery-powered sex toys *so gettable today.* The dildo this pair o' wanton bitches were straddling was a stick with a bandage wrapped round it and a 'French letter' on each end. We thought we'd been 'seen off', but not so ***'The Perv'*** *whose motor was pumpin'*, he was both enthralled and flushed with excitement. When the burds were supposedly spent and their risqué show over, he cops the 'dildo'; an' ***hey presto*** - it's straight in his gob *(nice touch)!* We are disgusted and wonder, does he do these things to shock? Who knows! But one thing's for sure, if we have a neckin' sesh later it's **'nae tongues, pal!'**

Next day I had my final run ashore in South America, as after my big spend and a quick 'rattle' in Montevideo I was near skint, so had decided on a cheap 'rabbit run' to use up the pesetas left from the previous night, and that would do me until Pompey; now less than two weeks away. So, I'm in the foyer of a trendy tourist shop looking through the big plate-glass window trying to decide what I could afford, when this jumpy nervous young Brazilian hustler asks if I want to change some English money, saying he gives top deals for sterling. I've got next to fuck all, but 'Pedro' just won't take **"No"** for an answer, so I'm getting pissed off with this beady-eyed, persistent bastard, who is all but harassing me. To get rid of the blighter I show him I've only got a ten bob note (50p). He's delighted and I'm confused when he quickly wings me the equivalent of ten quid and promptly does the vanishing act - I just can't follow it, as these guys are generally as wide as the day is long. He's either high on 'Sweet Lady H' or it's his first afternoon on the job, I can't believe my luck and thank fuck the tube's gone ***- talk about takin' candy off a bairn.***

Thinking of that encounter reminds me of a bit o' light-hearted jiggery-

pokery, when *'at the old flannel'* we tried to pass off Embassy cigarette coupons as money to the young novice whores in the Far East; saying they could cash them in at the Embassy ***- of course it never worked!***

Then I start to think 'that was too easy, ah've had ma erse felt and been slipped snide money' - with that doubt in mind I'm hesitant about trying to spend it. But - the shop accept it, ***no problemo,*** when I buy a set of bongo drums and a big pink sombrero ah've had ma eye on. However, as always, pride comes before a fall, and I'm on my way back to the boat, dead chuffed with my booty, but trying to get shot o' this well-used wizened auld skank, probably half the age she looks, tagging along prattlin' on about some carnival thing. I finally got rid o' her near the jetty, and now back onboard, am crowing *to everyone willing to listen* about my good fortune. I make a meal of putting a hand in my pocket to proudly reveal how much dosh I have left - **nothing**! Not a bolt; the whore's dipped me - *the Lord giveth and the Lord taketh away* - ***So much for Rio!***

Si Señor; the show, she ees finito! But how about this, I *and probably most of the crew* never saw or even knew Copacabana existed until I heard Barry Manilow singing about it years later - ***typical;*** poor old Jack! So that was South America; absolutely fantastic - but, all good things come to an end, aye; 'the baws burst' an' we're goin' back to reality. ***Game over!***

After an uneventful ten-day voyage back across the Atlantic we made a well-publicized arrival at Fort Blockhouse. **Now then**, the ironic thing was that *most* married men behaved impeccably, not succumbing to the pleasures of the flesh all the way round South America, but many fell off the perch in Rio - *I suspect,* after having thought, 'Fuck it, this is my last chance!' This was the very place where we abstained, thanks to remembering Lew's wise *but unheeded* words at Mombasa and Ginge's lesbo show; so on returning to the UK, the chickens came home to roost and an unhealthy percentage of the ship's company were 'squeezin' up'.

There we were, tying up alongside at Dolphin with the RAs' welcoming party of wives and sprogs waving from the jetty to many returning spouses who were quarantined under stoppage of Leave, ♫ ***"Blame it on the Bossa Nova"*** ♫. But it doesn't pay to gloat, cos they say what goes around, comes around - ***that's karma,*** and now it's time to 'pay the piper', ***so wait for it;*** and let me tell you - you'll never guess what's coming my way!

Crank up the volume, the boyz are back in town and easy as pie, slip into the old routine as if we've never been away. Revisiting favourite haunts, scoopin' up 'scrumpy tops' and slopin' down to The Mecca, sniffin' out the spare, puttin' on the patter and lying our fuckin' heads off to impress the gullible ones. However, never the shyster, I was always frank and earnest with women. In Pompey I was Frank, in Sou'sea I was Ernest!

I've trapped this Junoesque ash blonde dipstick - you're right, I've got a fetish about big women (*do you think it's perhaps a dark latent desire to be disciplined, abused and dominated, triggered in childhood by the large nurse on nit patrol with her steel comb?).* Her father is German, she's 'a looker'; not the brightest, but got me taped; ***ama that obvious?***

Anyway, I'd been out with her a few times; but getting zilch - *perhaps I should've disguised myself as a tampon, hid in her handbag and played the waiting game*. Trying to get the 'leg over' was hard work because she lived in the back of beyond at Waterlooville - a marathon, as I didn't have the car, which might have helped me charm my way into her kecks, but I'd intentionally left it in Edinburgh because of the South American cruise.

It's a couple o' nights after my last date with the big 'Jerry': The Druids are celebrating their winter solstice, and I'm sprawled in the Mess in the traditional casual attire *boxers, T-shirt and flip-flops* watching 'Bootsie and Snudge' on the 'goggle-box', when... oh! Oh! Ah feel a wee itch around the privates. So I investigate, an' would you believe - **ah've got CRABS!** Aw, for cryin' out loud! An' ah'm goin' on Leave in two days time - that's choice, ah'll look real clever takin' thae wee fellies hame wi' me, well ah'll be jiggered - ***it never rains, but it pours!*** I'm sure my face was as red as a parson's nose when 'Swampy' Marsh said "What the fuck's wrong wi' you?" I blurted out "**ah've got the 'sherbet dabs'!**" Sympathy? *Yeah, that'll be right* - laughed their tits off. I'm stumped as to how I copped them; cos they say yae cannae catch thum oaf the lavvy seat and *as far as I knew,* none of my so-called messmates were infested; so the jury's still out on that one!

No good standing on the seat
The crabs in here can jump six feet.

Aye, go on, knock yersel out - ***but, get this;*** **I know where you live!**

I immediately jumped into a steaming hot bath, hoping to scald and

drown the wee bastards, but that was wishful thinkin' - *as I'm sure you already know.* Anyway, after spending that long *solstice* night fretting and clawin' masel'; I'm first in the Sickbay queue next morning. Of course, to the sniggering SBA it was no big deal, he dished out some delousing powder, which I liberally applied 'down there', as instructed, and they were gone within twenty four hours, letting me breathe a huge sigh of relief - reprieved, clean and once more pure as new driven snow.

Just been havin' a 'sketch' at my Certificate of Service (S459) - the 'rap sheet' kept on each individual and given to the Rating on leaving 'the Andrew'. I see amongst other comments *(which I don't intend to divulge)* Awarded Submarine Badge 10TH December 1964; were they joking? **What sodding badge?** Back then, there was no such thing as a Submarine Badge *(there is now, check it out!)* - the penny-pinchin' Brits couldn't even get a little thing like that right. We were so proud of being submariners *(members of the world's most exclusive club)* that we'd have paid for the status symbol ourselves *(do I sound annoyed?)*. Awarded Submarine Badge - ***what a load o' tosh!*** Shallow Water Divers and qualified Marksmen had gold sleeve badges - so why not us? Far be it for me to lampoon, but it was such oversights wot really spoiled the service! '

Anyway, badges - now there's a thing. By this time I had my first Good Conduct stripe up, so, sporting that and now the respected 'Killick's Hook', my Number Ones were looking more the part. Later, when awarded my second Good Conduct stripe; *signifying eight years of undetected crime*, I never bothered sewing it on - as although we all contrived to look like a 'been there, seen it an' dunnit' old hand, I had no wish to look that old, and, *like many,* preferred the one-badge 'Jack the Lad' image.

Now contracted to 'Rentagent' I'm so glad I kept that old uniform, which has come in **very useful** over the years. On looking at the clock I see it's high time ah 'put ma face oan' and nipped along to my dressing room to slip into my non-issue Hugo Boss jewelled posing pouch, black 'fishnets' and 'sussies', get the *now tight-fitting* trusty Number Ones from the wardrobe, struggle into them ***(Hello Sailor!)*** snort a line, straddle the 'Harley Fat Boy' and collar flappin' in the breeze, hightail it to tonight's hen party gig. Apologies to 'Their Lordships' and sorry to let the side down boys, but old habits die hard; 'a girl's got to eat an' it beats walkin'

the streets!' *By the way, my case comes up next week.*

I'm fair sick o' the comments, but being an 'old trouper', have heard them all before - *haven't we all?* Yes, you'll be familiar with the likes of "You sailors are all the same - big dicks, crabby knicks and nae fuckin' money!" and "Let's go hijacking - Hi Jack!", sayings frequently tossed our way by 'brownhatters' cruisin' Southsea Front, droolin' forra slice o' 'Navy cake'. So you think that's funny - well cop this. I've been booked by a gay lap dancing club, situated in the Broughton district of Edinburgh known as the 'Pink Triangle' ***- better keep ma haund oan ma haipny!***

Christmas Leave came and went. I don't remember much about it other than when out 'on the pull' I used one of my Peruvian trinkets as bait to acquire the favours of a supple young hottie, snared in Fairley's; she was a willing accomplice - strangely I can't picture her face, only her perky breasts which kept on saying "Touch me! Touch me!" Since she was well-connected and her presence in such a place *especially with a sailor* would've been frowned upon; I won't expand on the encounter, although thinking back, I'm sure I had mind to bade her "Unhand me" but the wench was so big and so strong that I was still saying **"No"** when she finished.

Following a short maintenance period we were back at sea on various Home Fleet exercises and getting in some 'two-bit' Jollies; but after our blast in South America, any of the usual little continental trips pale to insignificance and are now long forgotten.

As with all boats, we had to take our turn as COQC's training boat, at both Portland and Rothesay. This was the most loathed duty in the Submarine Service and, if my memory serves me well, the drudgery had a duration of three weeks. COQC stands for Commanding Officer's Qualifying Course, *known in the Service as 'The Perisher' - because so many of the candidates did just that.* With the fail rate averaging 25% this obviously is a gruelling course, which exceptional First Lieutenants, so recommended, must pass, before gaining their own coveted Command.

The stakes are high, with only the crème de la crème, who have to be real cool dudes, finally qualifying to join the ranks of the élite. So, for the candidates it was a traumatic, nerve-racking experience, but for the crew, it was a drag. Monday through to Friday sailing 'first light' each morning, 'closing up' for 'Diving Stations' within the hour, then on patrol

for the rest of the day, with the hopefuls being put through their paces doing precise manoeuvres and taking turns at the attack periscope to fire dummy 'fish' *(torpedoes)* at ever increasing and more demanding targets, while being appraised by an alert team of gold-braided instructors with exacting standards, led by a skilled taskmaster ***known as 'Teacher'***; a long day, returning to harbour for midnight *(if we were lucky)*. But that wasn't 'lousin' time' for 'the plebs', as torpedoes had to be taken on for the following day, which started and finished at the same times. So, 'twas a mercy that most of the crew, who were off-watch, got some 'kippo-time' in, after 'Up Spirits' and a crackin' three course lunch.

Portland! Sweet Mother o' Jesus - I've sailed from there many times at different seasons of the year, but can't recall it ever blowing less than a Force 8; which hardly seems possible - thankfully it was policy to dive soon after putting to sea. At Rothesay the routine was the same, but the bad news this time was that we were 'anchored off', wallowing in the *all too often* choppy bay - not so easy getting back from the weekend runs ashore - *hardly worthwhile, unless there were holidaymakers to prey upon*.

I recently caught a brilliant television documentary featuring places of great architectural interest, one being the public toilets on the seafront at Rothesay where the tiling is exquisite, and well worth a look - just like Copacabana, **another one I missed!**

We finally 'paid off' Odin at Rosyth, where she went for a major refit towards the end of March '65, whilst there I treated Ginge to many a good run ashore around the unsavoury drinking dens and fleshpots in 'Auld Reekie', which I guarantee he'll remember to this day. On saying that, it occurs to me that the good people of Edinburgh will still talk of days when ***'The Beast'*** walked amongst us.

After preliminary stripping and destoring the submarine, which took two or three weeks, we all returned as 'Spare Crew' to 'Mother Dolphin' - each of us filled with high hopes of being assigned to another such boat, preferably bound, once more, for the *highly-prized* Spanish Main.

Many's the time I've thought - I'd have done a deal with the Devil to do that commission again. (Minstrels will write songs about us).

21: HM Submarine Thermopylae

Since there's no rest for the wicked, it wasn't long before my Draft Chit arrived - ah'd only 'had ma feet up' a matter o' days, when ordered to report to Thermopylae; a 'T' Class boat close to completing a two-year life-extending refit in Pompey Dockyard. So off I went to join her; absolutely delighted on arrival to find Coxswain Murphy and many old mates from Odin already onboard. There wasn't as yet an assistant cook, so I did my utmost to collar Ginge, as having a good rapport, and being kindred spirits we worked well together - it was a long shot but worth a try, however I failed miserably; can't say where he went, as I never saw my alter ego again. It's devastating to lose touch with such good mates - I oft-times wonder what became of all these very special people. But let's not get all sentimental, as it doesn't fit the image, could cramp my style and undeservedly destroy what's left of the hitherto untarnished reputation.

So I meet my new Captain, an arrogant wee pasty-faced guy, not unlike John Mills, the actor. Can't remember his name, but do recall he rubbed me up the wrong way, so we got off to a less than amicable start during that first encounter; when the tool told me he expected good results from the Galley, with the fayre including cakes and suchlike. ***Cakes! fuckin' cakes!*** *Was this joker for real?* What possessed the man, was he delusional? Gies a brek, **pal,** this isnae the QE2, it's an auld knacker, built during WWII; about to begin her 8TH, and final commission before becoming razor blades, so let's not get carried away here - **humour me, Baby!**

Cakes indeed, this snooty clown needed his card marked - respect works two ways; if I knuckle under now I'm forever fucked, so, may as well go for the jugular an' get ma tuppence worth in - he's got me confused wi' someone who gives a toss, little realizing ah don't give a flying wotsit.

Jaisus H. Christ, 'shudder the thought', imagine dishing up fairy cakes to sweaty submariners; next they'd be wanting icing - only to end up fighting over and throwing them at each other. Worse still; it's a cert some smart twat would dream up a nickname derived from fairy cakes; well, I know we all have our little crosses to bear, but I could live without that! So forget

diplomacy, there was **no chance!** Anyway, havin' sniffed around, I was already scunnered at the thought of having to produce so many piping hot meals from such a small poorly equipped Galley.

While not 'Michelin rated' the scran was pretty good on boats, at least we thought so - our generation having been deprived 'war babies', brought up scrimping on a Spartan diet. Nothing resembling the pampered bloated mutant Neanderthal crackheads, with the savvy and behavioural patterns of warring baboons, we encounter roaming the urban ghettoes today.

The provisions supplied by Royal Clarence Victualling Yard were of excellent quality, so when you start off with nice grub you have to be a pretty crap cook to make a dog's breakfast of it. There was no choice *other than take it or leave it* due to lack of space and facilities; however *spoilt rotten* the crew had their taste buds tickled daily with a freshly cooked breakfast, dinner and supper *with the Wardroom sharing the same menu* - if the Toffs dreamed up an excuse for 'puttin' on the ritz', the Jimmy had to go 'cap in hand' and plead his case to the Coxswain and Tankey, who *as if misers* jealously guarded and allocated their stores.

Jack, like most, enjoys yafflin' chips with his snorkers, an' d'you know wot - my domain on this old tub didn't have a deep-fat fryer, so, since I was in the firing line, valued my life *and have always been a whore for applause*, this problem had to be rectified. Being in refit gave me the opportunity to have one designed, fabricated and fitted in a corner; in place of the unnecessary Hobart mixer already there. This meant the extraction canopy needed extending to cover the new fryer - everything has a price, and nothing ever comes cheap, so I shudder to think of how this little move cost me more 'bubbly', to bend the chief ERA, than I care to remember. I also had to bribe the bloodsuckin' dockyard mateys *possibly with 'duty-free ciggies'* this noble sacrifice proved worthwhile, letting Jack get wired into lashings of crisp golden brown chips two or three times a week, which in turn helped manipulate the crew's goodwill; as come tot time they were literally 'eating out of the palm of my hand'.

Navy cooks cop a fair bit o' flak; which goes wi' the territory *especially on an unhappy boat* so, if there's any discontent the Galley is generally 'piggy in the middle' for taking the brunt; therefore, if not thick-skinned when joining 'the Mob' you most certainly acquire one before your next

birthday - ***come to think of it, the larger than life Ginge Heulet was forever telling me he'd rather be shot than poisoned.***

We got plenty ribbing but few real complaints - the only two I recall are; a stoker 'mouthin' off' about his meal being too salty - the whinin' dipstick was swiftly put in his place when told "If you think that's salty, **pal,** wait 'til tomorrow!" The other confrontation was with an OD in the lunch queue bitchin' about something 'Twas just after 'Up Spirits' when everyone should be happy and relaxed - he wasn't, and kept on 'beatin' his gums', offering to 'punch ma lights oot' - talk about bite the hand that feeds yae. I'd also downed my Tot, so, feeling as bold as he, warned him it wouldn't be wise as we slept in the same Mess, and the minute he shut his eyes I'd fit **that** round his bonce, indicating a substantial cast iron frying pan swinging from a butchers' hook behind the stove. That put his gas at a peep - all of a sudden it was just a joke, and he my best pal - *it's worth noting that making *idle* threats can so often gain respect. *Of course, Pusser's nasty old rum was responsible for our bravado that day.*

I guess Captain Pugwash had been less than impressed with me and reported our contretemps to his hatchet man ***the Jimmy,*** since he was hostile from day one - this prick was misery itself with a personality disorder. Keep this tae yersel - *they were two of a kind, an' both got on ma tits* - can't remember his name either; which I suppose is par for the course for those of no consequence. I often thought that pair had a chip on their shoulders, imagining themselves destined for better than an obsolete 'T' Class, possibly thinking they should be 'driving' nukes, so this was like being 'passed over'; but why take it out on the crew? - these prats reminded us daily, that life isn't all just 'beer and skittles'. They were never pleased with anything; so praising the crew was 'not on' - during my twenty-six months spent on that 'old nail', I can't remember a smile or joke from either of these two Naval Officers *(neither of whom, in my 'umble opinion, had the aptitude, or charisma required for the job).*

Oh here! hang about; you'll love this - one weekend halfway into the 'commish', the Jimmy, who, being a 'control freak' got his rocks off 'pulling rank' - running true to form, he's in the Wardroom throwing his weight around about something trivial; upsetting two of his Junior Officers *(Lt.s Rutherford and Tall)* to such an extent that the forthright Rutherford *(a*

future vice admiral) lost his rag; asked Tall to shut the door then promptly 'decked' his superior. The incident was hushed up; otherwise, *if castigated,* that trio's Naval careers would have been finito, or at the very least, put on hold; but there are no secrets on subs - **how cool was that!**

Let's spare a thought for Sub Lt. Gadsby, who, being the Subby in the Wardroom, must've taken some shit from the demigod and his enforcer. Subby Gadsby was a cleancut keen officer, more than often a pain in the butt, nonetheless, without knowing it, favoured by the crew. It was a love-hate relationship, as he still had that 'Little Lord Fauntleroy' aristocratic appearance, and obviously unaware that his rash enthusiasm could be annoying - such as when racing along the narrow passage giving it "Gangway, gangway for a Naval Officer!" This infuriated the EMs when kneeling down leaning into the battery compartments taking readings and him charging over their heads, so they'd squirt battery acid from their hydrometers at his trouser legs. He was young then, with many faults, but the crew definitely had a soft spot for him and most would've moved heaven and earth to help him out of a sticky situation. I like to think that with such zeal, he made it up the tree and, if he stayed in boats, may well have aspired to commanding a big nuke. ***So, 'Gadders', if you ever read this; the very fact that I've remembered your name says it all!***

My understudy, when he arrived, was a young slim OD called Scouse Roberts: Scouse - a solemn woebegone lad who spoke with a pronounced nasal Liverpool accent; 'no ball of fire' but, to his credit, clever enough to know when to act stupid. My new 'winger' was a loner with a drouth for scrumpy; most of us liked to visit more than one boozer and maybe end up at The Mecca, but not him. He would go straight to his preferred scrumpyhouse - the Golden Fleece, and that was our Scouse for the night, he'd get a 'gibber on' after two pints, miraculously staying the same for the rest of the sesh, no matter how much he poured down his throat. 'Robbie' was an amiable lad, but with no special mates amongst the crew and seemed a lost soul; he'd had an unhappy childhood and been *(for some reason long-since forgotten to me)* brought up by his granny.

The first person I clapped eyes on when negotiating my way down the gangway to board the 'auld plug' - *which was lying in dry dock when I joined her,* was my old mate from Odin, Ginge Heulet, the big happy-go-

lucky Londoner. That was a good start, I remember him introducing me as 'Slosh' to Subby Gadsby who was the OOW *(Officer of the Watch)* and on the casing at the time. 'Gadders', looking dapper, came bounding across, swashbuckling-style and just about shook my hand off, while saying loudly "Welcome aboard, I'm Gadsby, but **you** can call me **Sir!**"

As always there were plenty amusing characters in the crew, so, to keep you happy, I'll try to recall some names as I go along. It's a pity that I don't have a Rogue's Gallery of photographs, but at the time such a thing didn't seem important, though, today, would obviously be a bonus.

Because we were refitting in Pompey Dockyard and Dolphin, our Base, was across the Solent in Gosport we were put on RA *(ration allowance),* which I can only guess made it easier for Pusser. This meant we were given dosh *not a lot* and had to fend for ourselves in the way of grub and accommodation, which was, in my and others' cases, a tiny cubicle with a chicken-wire ceiling in Aggie Weston's. Unsurprisingly the 'midnight cowboys' had cozy 'up homers' arrangements with 'local ladies'. It seemed odd to me that Pusser didn't billet us in the near empty 'Vicky' Barracks; these being close to the dockyard - *but what would I know!*

Two of my neighbours in Aggie's, were also crewmates on Thermopylae, the sharp-witted 'Bruvver' Streames and his buddy Pat were a pair o' whackos. Haven't a clue as to Bruvver's Christian name - because he called everyone 'Bruvver' or 'Bruv' he was known as Bruvver *(just as 'Parky' Hannant on Tenby had called everyone 'Parky').* I 'fink' *the very proper* Bruv was a 'radio ham' and his constant shadow, Pat, a 'dabtoe'.

The hands down favourite, on returning to Aggie's after a night 'on the sauce', had to be 'babies' heads' *(individual 'snake and Sydney' puddings)* with chips, beans, or mushy peas, a buttered roll and a pint o' milk. This 'feast fit for a king' being a steal, priced at a knock-down 3/- (15p) a shot. There was always a swaying queue for this meal at closing time, so they must have sold thousands of 'babies' heads' over the years to hordes of hungry noisy gannets - all 'merry from the drink'. The thought occurs that I could handle a plateful right now, cos I'm 'Hank Marvin!'

I've completely forgotten how many weeks we were 'shacked-up' in Aggie's, so *off the top o' ma head* I'll say probably six or seven. As already said, we did get extra money to pay for our lavish lifestyle outwith - *albeit*

a meagre amount. However, if frugal we could run at a profit, which meant Pusser stood for a modest amount of scrumpy.

'Twent something like this - the daily allowance was a pound, Aggies charged around 5/- (25p) for the room and a modest 2/- (10p) for a cooked breakfast. We'd spend *let's say* a further 4/- (20p) on pies and chip butties in the course of the day, then the 'baby's head' etc, late on, took care of another 3/- (15p) making a daily grand total of about 15/- (75p) leaving say 5/- (25p) to blow on beer or whatever. Doesn't sound much; does it? But, here we go - I can't tell you the price of beer then, but will hazard a guess of 1/- (5p) a pint, however, well remember scrumpy being 10^{d} *(about 4p)* a pint. Look at it this way, it was half a crown ($12^{1}/_{2}$p) to get into The Mecca, so, if prudent, we could have a couple o' pints o' rocketfuel and get into the dancing *on Pusser* twice a week.

That was fun for a while, but too much excitement can tip one over the edge and it's soul-destroying living out a suitcase for long periods, so *most* were pleased when Thermop left the dockyard and took her place in the 1ST Submarine Squadron over at Dolphin. I know it felt comfortable to be back in a proper Mess with its facilities, and dining hall downstairs; *and, of course, to be reunited with the rum tub* **"God bless you Mam!"**

Tot time, For'ard Seamen's Mess, HM Submarine Thermopylae 1966
Shiner 2ND left, the 'Rum Bosun' is 'Buck' Ryan, with 'Jonno' to his right

Well, the start of a commission means 'sea trials' and hard work, as routines must be established, and the crew learn to work as a team. Then, *prayers said*, it's time for the first dive; when each piece of equipment must be tried, tested, approved and often mended or replaced. The boat requires degaussing and sound trials, this entails going to Arrochar and Lochgoilhead on the west coast of Scotland; and there sure ain't much up there in the way of a run ashore - *I'd seen more life on a tramp's vest*.

Now operational, it transpired the crew *to a man* suffered seasickness *(the long spit)* on this boat, making life grim in bad weather. Since all craft have their own peculiarities, sailors generally get used to the motion of their ships after a few days - but no; not this one. It may have been due to the alterations Thermop had undergone since her initial design and build twenty years earlier, and most likely the addition of fifteen feet to her overall length during this final refit. Whatever the cause, 'you can't polish a turd' and this abortion didn't just roll and bounce in heavy seas - oh no! she would 'corkscrew' at the arse-end and no one gets used to that. I felt sorry for the stokers and 'lamp tramps' in the After Mess, who were most affected, but, as already said, 'we all have our little crosses to bear'!

I've found the commissioning pamphlet for Her Majesty's submarine Thermopylae so I'll copy a few details, to put you in the picture.

> Dimensions: length 285 feet, beam 26 feet, draught 15 feet, displacement surfaced 1500 tons, dived 1700 tons, propulsion 2 diesel engines and 4 electric motors, speed surfaced 10 knots, dived 15 knots, armament 6 bow torpedo tubes, complement 65 Officers and Ratings.
> Short history: HMS Thermopylae was built at the end of the war, but saw no active service. Since then she has been extensively modernised, which has included cutting her in half and inserting a new 15 foot section to make room for extra batteries and generators. In addition all guns and external torpedo tubes have been removed, improved radar, sonar and periscopes fitted and the whole vessel streamlined.

So there you have it, she's a tarted up relic that ain't goin' nowhere, and I very much doubt we'll cop many stowaways!

Well, now we know, there'll be no foreign cruises to look forward to; just exercises and the likes in Home Waters. This, I suppose, can only be expected from such an old non 'combat capable' boat, which, let's face it,

is a dinosaur in this new age of nuclear submarines; certainly not something to proudly 'show the flag' to Johnny Foreigner - truth is, she should've been scrapped years ago. However, her redeeming factor was her crew, a terrific gang of lads, with, as always, some real stars; and it's as well, since I'm to be stuck with them for the next two and a bit years; just as they are with me - *said by many, to be the worst cook in the Royal Navy.*

On thinking about Lochgoilhead it comes to mind, that when there having a few wets and 'spinnin' the shit' in the Arrochar Hotel snug, our young assistant wardroom flunkey let it slip that joining the Navy was a mistake, as his ambition was to be a cabin-crew steward with British Airways. This immediately aroused our suspicions, so he took a fair bit o' stick that day - *probably wishing he'd kept his trap shut.* I now wonder if Terry, in years to come, ever realized his dream; since few ever do.

Well, that's Terry rubbished, who's next? Oh yeah, we had a 'Janner' Killick called 'Brigham' Young, a fore-endsman with an unusual hobby and earner. Jan was on RA when we were at Dolphin, so lived in Married Quarters, and, when home, had a passion for buying old cars, breaking them for scrap and selling the spare parts. I can't recall whether he rented a yard, but suppose that must have been the case, as he could hardly have used his married quarters garden *(although, as we know, stranger things have come to light).* It's quite out of the ordinary for a matelot to be running a business when off duty but Brigham did, and, because of his enthusiasm, had 'a nice little earner' - no doubt he would, in later life, make use of his boundless energy to go on and do wonders in the business world.

Another two inseparable guys on the fore-ends team were 'Jonno', a sparky blonde-haired kid and his pal, Pete; both great at acting 'camp' and spouting *off the cuff* smutty innuendoes. I had a lot of time for these smart witty lads with wisdom beyond their years; both car daft, who at one point bought a tidy old Triumph Mayflower between them, on which they lavished money and attention. Come to think of it, I'm not too sure if either of this 'class act' possessed a driving licence.

There were, as ever, a shower o' tickets in the engine room, which was immediately aft of the Galley; so Scouse and myself were regularly entertained by their antics. Picture this; having just left harbour we couldn't believe our eyes and were aboot 'fillin' oor breeks', when this scrawny

'Brummie' stoker came on watch wearing his girlfriend's floral-print summer frock and well-snagged 15 denier honey-toned tights, which looked quite classy with the big greasy, down at the heel, 'steaming boots'.

Well, I know I said earlier that we could wear whatever we wanted at sea, but cross-dressing was pushing it a touch. When the 'Killick of the Watch' LME Coutts confronted him, Brummie feebly explained he was missing the girlfriend and this made him feel close to her - fair makes the mind boggle as to what that pair got up to when alone behind closed doors; but we all have our little secrets - **don't we!** The Chief Stoker was an open-minded man, however, Brummie was pushin' his luck with that one, so was sent *amid jeers* back aft, to the Stokers' Mess to change into something more suitable; *after he had taken his shot in* ***'the Barrel'***. Oh yes! It's no myth, and there's you been thinkin' it was just a joke amongst sailor boys. Think again - many a true word is spoken in jest! Remember what they say, *"Women are OK, but you can't beat the real thing!"*

It's as well we had a good and humorous crew, since all we ever seemed to do were exercises in Home Waters, or take trainees to sea. Thermopylae spent a period running daily, as luck would have it, **from Portland** being target boat *('clockwork mouse')* on which more sophisticated craft honed their skills - and, of course we did more than our fair share of the hated COQCs *(mumble, mumble, discontent)*. By performing these menial, but necessary, tasks Thermopylae freed 'combat capable' boats to accomplish their covert operations behind 'The Iron Curtain'. In recompense, we were privileged to have had some great and interesting guys from the Canadian, Australian and Israeli navies as members of our crew for a few months at a time *(all of whom were much better paid than ourselves)*.

I think the Canadians *(labelled, as Yanks with breeding)* were the first batch we took. They were all married, so had their wives and families over here - which reminds me, they hosted some riotous evenings, with lashings of booze and scran, in their smart upmarket rented homes - oh yes, we had some fabulous nights with these party animals. I've already told you I sold my trusty Vauxhall Velox to one of them - a Leading Seaman, who, as they say, 'could talk the hind legs off a donkey'. I guess he must have liked the American styling that model had, he in turn introduced me to 'Old Port Cigars' which, it's no secret that I quickly acquired a taste for - being

"wine-soaked and rum dipped" they left a pleasant lingering aftertaste on one's lips long after having been smoked and discarded.

Then came the Aussies *(crude 'n' rude)*. Mostly young guys in their late teens and early twenties who took some stick, as we used to kid them on no end, jesting they were convicts from billabongs in the outback; but they handled it well, soon learning to give as good as they got. We were amused that so many were called Bruce, but I do remember two exceptions.

One was 'Skippy', a short-sighted 'spark', he was dead easy to wind-up, which encouraged everyone to have a go - ***"What's that Skippy?"*** The other, I of all people should remember *(now, now, don't be hasty)* - he was a young chap of about nineteen, a sturdy lad, square-jawed with blue eyes and blonde hair, nicknamed Taff. He, and most of the Aussies *like the Canadians* was married and had his 'Sheila' *(a real case)*, over here with him. While here they 'dropped a sprog' and for some strange reason wanted me to be godfather to the wee guy. ***Strewth!*** I was horrified and attempted to squirm out of this obligation by explaining they would all go back to Aussieland; therefore I'd never see them *or sprog* again. So, to me, ever the logical thinker, this wasn't too clever, but Taff and his bonkers wife were adamant. Possibly missing something and not wanting to hurt their feelings I bowed to their wishes, and so, have a godchild 'down-under', whose name *I'm ashamed to admit* I don't even remember.

Well, that takes care of the Canadians and the Aussies, now it's the Israelis' turn; and this is so so sad. All these guys were with us for months, so we obviously got friendly with them, since they were accepted as part of the crew. We found the Israelis to be particularly well-mannered, clever, properly educated, very clean and tidy and if anything overqualified. One of their Chiefs was a great favourite with all - this guy had badges for everything; he was a commando, a paratrooper, a diver *talk about versatile* yet to look at him you'd never have guessed - small, slim, neat, unassuming and quiet; nevertheless with time to talk to everyone ***- a prince.*** OK, no doubt you'll be thinking, 'what's so sad about that then'? - well, sometime later, when delivering their submarine, the Dakur (ex-RN Totem), from Britain to Israel, it 'went down' with all sixty-nine hands in the Mediterranean, a mere 400 miles from home on 26TH January 1968, **allegedly** after colliding with a merchant ship. **Oh yeah?** What a waste!

What a loss and wotta a load o' shite! **that was never an accident!**

Talking about badges brings me back to the subject of the Shallow Water Divers' Course - still one of my pet ambitions, so, being a stubborn optimist, just as for submarines, at regular intervals I would get up the Jimmy's nose by tendering a request-form for this course, each time getting a knock-back, on the tosser's insistence that **"This Rating cannot be spared"**. Persistence usually pays off and we **will** come to that later, so, do us all a favour, be patient, try not to interrupt and we'll get there.

Can't recollect many runs ashore, other than Pompey, since Thermop didn't venture far from home. However, we often called into Londonderry, when exercising in the temperamental 'Oirish' Sea area. 'Derry' was, then, a stonking run ashore, with ninety per cent of the ship's company suppin' poteen in Paddy's Bar, then ending up *with a good gibber on* at the dancing, having a whale of a time trying to do 'the Hucklebuck'. I remember trapping a little startler there, whose dad was some kind of RAF officer, but her name is lost to me, since it was a one-night-stand - *us sailing 'on the tide', refuelled, re-energized and hungry for more war games.*

There was a weekend visit to the Naval Base at Brest *(you'll recall I'd been there before, and remarked I wouldn't rush back).* I remember being particularly impressed with the French warships, which looked 'the business' - very streamlined and modern. The battleship Richelieu was lying at anchor in the middle of the harbour; although formidable, she lacked the visual impact of our Vanguard, but still a topper, appearing massive in relation to Thermopylae; having a displacement of 35,000 tons compared to our 1500 tons. So Pusser's 'auld reconditioned scrapper' must have looked like an insignificant wee black 'toli' being flushed out to sea when passing this enormous battlewagon. Nonetheless, it occurs to me that, comparing the sizes, it's hard to believe that our jaded boat could destroy a mighty leviathan such as 'Powerful Pierre' with a brace of well-placed 'fish'. ***Mon Dieu*** **- spread the word; size doesn't matter after all!**

While there we were fair chuffed when allocated a comfortable 'shoreside' Mess by our French sailor chums, *an unexpected perk;* however, weren't best pleased with the 'shunkeys', which had no 'porcelain throne' - merely a floorlevel enamelled device with a hole in the centre, which squatting over required no end of concentration from us unskilled Brits,

who managed to soak our feet every time we flushed the contraption. I'm sure you'd prefer I don't bother to embellish - so let's move swiftly on.

That run ashore was rubbish; however on our return we stopped in at a terrific patisserie, where we bought a load of baguettes, paté, cheese and **a big trifle;** so had a right old 'nosh-up' when back in our 'squat'. *So much for the pundits who'd have you believe sailors do nothing other than sing about 'a life on the ocean wave' and screw their nuts off in every port!*

Contrary to the opinions of rival crews in the squadron; *who all too often bandied insults,* we did our fair share of 'sea-time'; even allowing for the fact that we never strayed too far from 'Mother Dolphin'. One night an AB from the Olympus *pointing the finger of scorn* remarked that the Gosport Ferry got in more sea-time than wot we did. There could well've been some truth in the jibe but what did we care? Not a jot! - since, as they say, 'all work and no play makes Jack a dull boy'. The fact is that all Pusser's vessels spend more time 'against the wall' than at sea; this is because the country today is run by accountants and basic economics say it's cheaper that way - what with the price of fuel and many other factors. Don't forget, ships *just like cars* need regular maintenance, so the sooner the miles are knocked up the sooner a very costly service is required.

Controversially, it's across the board these days; we all know speed cameras ain't in place to slow the traffic **- oh no!** Those responsible for them are absolutely delighted with motorists who race along; wallet open. **It's all about the folding stuff** - how stupid do them wot walk the corridors of power think 'Joe Public' is? Don't they realize *or even care* that we see through the moves they make to save dosh, *or relieve us of ours!* Ever thought about why prison sentences are fewer or more lenient than deserved? Time off for good behaviour - **bollocks**, it's always down to money. But we know the answer to that one - don't we? It's high time the Chancellor propositioned 'Sky', offering a licence to televise neck stretchin' parties. Cor! Imagine being The Public Executioner, *wotta number that'd be for job satisfaction!* And, as for that Congestion Charge - aw, fer fuck's sake stop me! ***It's not just the roads that are polluted wae eejits,*** *like yourself,* ***it's the whole effin' world!*** ***Wake up!***

It's understandable that with Pompey being our homeport we spent most of our time there - this was home as far as we were concerned, so, we, like

locals anywhere, had established set patterns and favourite boozers in the city's underbelly for our frequent runs ashore. The three we paid homage to on Commercial Road were the Albany, the Lennox and the Golden Fleece, just a few staggers from each other and all full o' characters, none better known than 'Geordie Joyce' and 'Peter the Bat'.

Geordie Joyce was a 'good-time girl'; the undisputed reigning queen of Pompey *who must, in her time, have met every matelot in the fleet* was generally to be found in the Albany or the Lennox. Many presumed her a 'Lady of the Night' but I can't recall anyone admitting to having 'parted' for her favours. Joyce *who had a right pair o' hooters* was always good for a story and a laugh. Rumour had it she'd come down for a weekend, way back in 1948, met and married her consort, a stroppy hopeless seaman who spent most of his time in DQs. Never the prude, her party-piece was to bend over, whip up her skirt, revealing the eyes tattooed on the cheeks of her ample derrière and shout a suggestive comment - all good fun, well appreciated by an audience; ever happy to encourage her.

Peter the Bat was to be seen in the same two pubs, posing by the jukebox, wearing a manky submariners' off-white polo neck sweater and greasy skintight jeans. The story was, he had *in his day* been a ballet dancer - if looks were anything to go by there was a lot of truth in that - he being tall, lean and wiry-framed with broad shoulders. It was said that three rash baby 'Bootnecks' *(marines)* had been taking the piss one night, resulting in him clearing the floor with them. Although possibly folklore, I think most o' the punters had heard that story, as Peter was afforded the respect due to someone known to be able to handle himself in such a fashion. We presumed him to be a 'horse's hoof' but wouldn't put money on it, since he was generally surrounded by an entourage of racey young scrubbers; so perhaps he was their pimp who, no matter what, was given his space, and passed as no more than a nodding aquaintance to most.

A huddled gathering of 'Nancy Boys' was a permanent fixture in the Albany posing astride high stools up at the far end of the bar, presided over by a treasured glam photo of Danny La Rue in drag. Being 'together', never a nuisance, but fun to pass time with, whilst disappearing into a pint of Red Barrel and contemplating the arrival of one's aquaintances. The deluded old queens *(who saw themselves as princesses)* were ever in high spirits

perhaps why called gay never tiring of their 'guessing game'; as to which toilet one of 'the Sisterhood' would favour; after provocatively mincing across the parquet floor with short quick steps and wiggling hips. This OTT effeminate display encouraging the fairies to squeal with pleasure, while shrieking catcalls and squirming with fiendish delight.

Yes, the infamous Albany was a pantomime well worth visiting!

Across the road, and down a bit stood the already mentioned Golden Fleece - our favourite scrumpyhouse. I liked it there *(probably because of the prices)* frequently enjoying a couple o' pints o' 'apples' as a quick fix before making tracks for The Mecca or Southsea. Every pub has its 'principal player' and 'the Fleece' boasted 'Big Sylv'; a muckle bleached blonde; the very epitome of Scrumpyland. Yeah, that was a good boozer, but it had two drawbacks - the deck was always sticky from spilt scrumps, and the *outside* bog - like those of all scrumpyhouses - **reekin'!**

We also used the Balmoral *(known as the Immoral)* - although I often met the team there, for some reason I can't picture it or recall where it was. I suspect it must've been close to the others *and near Aggie's* as we tended to meet around that area, 'our patch' - handy for The Mecca dancehall, after the amber tongue-loosening liquid had worked its magic.

Come the summer, we'd boogie on down to 'the Front' at Sou'sea - great fun when 'fair hoachin' wi' holidaymakers from the Midlands and London. So, scouring for 'gullible snatch' was 'the order of the day' and it has to be said, we generally scored quite easily there. "Can I touch your collar for luck, Jack?" "Touch anythin' ye want, hen!"

sung to 'All the Nice Girls love a Sailor'

All the nice girls luv a candle
All the nice girls luv a wick
All the nice girls luv a candle
Cos it resembles a sailor's prick
Nice and greasy, slips in easy
It's the joy of every sailor boy
So when you're strolling down the Front
With a candle up yer cunt
Ship ahoy! Sailor Boy!

Everyone loved the 'grab a granny' nights in The Seahorse down by the South Parade Pier, where hordes o' unchaperoned 'matrons' arrived by the busload - we had some epic nights with these crazy old mares! The Seahorse was a swingin' lounge bar catering for a fun night out, Blackpool style, with entertainment laid on by, the already spoken-of, Reg at the Hammond organ; the auld tart revelled in all the showbiz glitz - a poor man's Liberace with his mighty organ, lurex suits that shrieked 'gay boy', and bouffant blue-rinsed swept-back silver hair *could've been 'a syrup'* the very picture of what you'd expect in such a place. However, he could fairly belt out the many requests, so, after a few wets, by Jove it was party time. What a spectacle; us makin' complete cunts o' oorsels, cuffs turned up *dragons on display* caps perched on the backs of our heads, and the half-sozzled old boilers lappin' it up, eggin' us on, while up dancin' themselves, hitchin' up summer dresses to exhibit fat erses encased in outsize bloomers fashioned from Union Jacks. **Yeah, them were good times!**

There was a dancehall next to The Seahorse, but for the life of me I can't remember its name and rarely afforded the place my custom, which probably accounts for the fact that I only 'bagged off' there the once. Pat *a squealer* was a vigorous and amusing piece o' top drawer totty, and **yes**, I do remember **her** name, also that Acker Bilk was on the menu that night; but it was always hard work there - *I could never figure out why.*

Not like The Mecca, which was good to me - yes, The Mecca in Portsmouth will forever have a place in my heart. It was newer, but akin to the Edinburgh Mecca Palais - similar in design, also with a revolving stage, balcony, and two bars -a great hunting ground after a gargle, and by the 'Lord Harry' some 'porkies' were told in that place. Most nights I masqueraded as a hovercraft pilot on the Isle of Wight run; that was a good line! - *they loved it.* Down Sou'sea you were a sailor; however, in Pompey, anything but. Usually they gave it the - **oh yeah!** but never say die; it's said practise makes perfect and often was the time I could carry off the deceit nae bother! *(at least, in my half-pished state, that's what I imagined).* However, one night there was an amusing consequence, which we **will** come to shortly, so, pay attention, but if you're gettin' sleepy I'll tell you the rest tomorrow; because there could very well be a test at the end.

But first, let me crow about the be-all/end-all evening at The Mecca

when I copped a 'winning hand'. 'Twas yet another night when my 'dance card' was empty, but it must've been my turn, because, **lo and behold,** 'the Good Lord' smiled down on yours truly, while saying "Cop a squint at that, Sunshine" suggestively pointing a well-manicured finger at this *'really something'* posh burd standing on her lonesome, looking lost and fragile. You'll be aware that there hadn't been any serious contenders for yonks and here was a chance meeting that was to change my lifestyle.

I recognized quality the minute I set eyes on K and was doubly delighted when *luckily not using the standard introduction* - **"I suppose a shag's completely out of the question!"** she accepted my invitation to dance. I'd've happily settled for just a dance with her; but you know how it is, occasionally you connect with a stranger. Well now, that's exactly what happened - the vibes were there, ah couldnae believe ma luck; as she was well oot o' ma league, so ah must've been on top o' ma game that night. Reluctant to part, we lingered on the floor blethering and dancing, even staying up to the Mick Jagger number *(or was it the Troggs?)* 'Wild Thing' *to which us 'Jolly Tars', sang - "Wild thing, you make my ring sting".*

Wotta stunner; poise, attractive features, neatly styled short raven-black hair, the deepest blue eyes you ever saw, a sun-kissed complexion that didn't need 'warpaint' and an elegant hourglass figure which did justice to her haute couture wardrobe. One of these serene beguiling creatures who *without realizing* had it all - so perfect that I now wonder if she was a figment of my imagination; well educated and very intelligent, working as an accountant's PA - aw that an' a guid pedigree; her father *I gathered* discreetly fronted some obscure Admiralty 'technical warfare' department. I thought 'this can't get any better', **but it did** when, fortuitously, she said the family home was in Gosport and yes, since it's on my way, I can see her home. ***Result!*** I'm walking on air thinking 'this could be the best thing that's ever happened to me' - *and it probably was.*

Thankfully I wasn't in 'lying mode' that night, as she'd have seen right through me - so far in this life I've made more mistakes than you could shake a stick at - ***it's a gift!*** 'Twas indeed fortunate that I'd recently brought the car down the road, otherwise it would never've happened, and therefore the same old story - getting wrecked and missing the last Liberty Boat across to Dolphin - paying a shilling to 'crash out' on a camp bed, while sharing

the rancid basement of the Home Fleet Club with fifty snoring matelots droppin' their guts in sweet harmony throughout the night *'thar she blows'*, to be woken 'early doors' by an old lag offering a cup of well mashed tea, laced with ash from the dowt danglin' frae the corner o' his lower lip, and then *the worse for wear* make my way back to Fort Blockhouse with ma gob tasting like the inside o' a Sumo wrestler's jockstrap.

So, as I was saying, at the end of the best Mecca night **ever,** I drove her home; when we wrenched ourselves apart she didn't just dash off into the house *like so many do*, and **yes**, I could see her again - possibly the next evening, if our enthusiasm was anything to go by. Thereafter we saw each other at every opportunity - it seemed K and I were meant for each other; more or less inseparable, going everywhere together; cinema, dancing, pubs, peaceful picnics at a little-known beach. Before I knew it, this eloquent girl, who had the ability to make a pauper feel like a prince, had become my best friend, my world *and eventually 'mon amour'*. No doubt the inevitable could've happened sooner, but I had the greatest respect for her - I'll bet you never expected to hear that after recent exploits; could be a case of, act like a lady, get treated like a lady - *although, I remember the old adage* - **'Treat a lady like a whore and treat a whore like a lady!'**

There was only one hiccup, and that was early in the relationship; really all very innocent, but it's so easy in affairs of the heart to blow things way out of proportion. K and the family *(she had two brothers, one older and the other, a decent sort, younger than herself)* were going to a wedding; which may well've been the marriage of her older brother; but can't be sure, as not being present I've forgotten. Anyway, when K mentioned the wedding I naturally assumed she'd ask me to be her partner; but this wasn't the case and she was a tad evasive about the topic. So I didn't pursue the subject, guessing she had a long-standing arrangement to honour, from before I arrived on the scene and we became an item. Perhaps even with her last boyfriend; as I always suspected, this, *almost,* too good to be true, girl had relished being tried and tested in the hands of an experienced tutor before we met; so, had been 'off the circuit' prior to that night at The Mecca; possibly I'd caught her, when vulnerable - ***'The Rebound Guy';*** which didn't bother me, as opportunists are rarely proud - let's face it, they've all got a track record - yes, ***there's always a jockey!***

Anyway, we had been seeing each other constantly for a number of weeks by this time, in fact, rarely apart, so with the liaison now paramount I was made to feel like one of the family by her parents and brother Mick *an asute capable fellow, who still lived at home*. Naturally the tender canoodling had become steamier, and I didn't have the heart to stop my enthusiastic companion and confidante teasing me by performing some tantalizing moves. I had the impression she was keen to keep me sweet, lest I took to my toes - **fat chance!** - so *without conviction* I'd say "You don't have to do that, you know", only to be delighted by her answer, which she put so simply, replying "I like to give you pleasure!" Oh my, if mummy could see you now - *certainly no shrinking violet this one!*

You'll know what I'm on about, and *unless extremely unlucky* agree that, living takes on a new meaning and the world becomes a much nicer place when you stumble on and trap that very special girl. Strangely, because she's so perfect some of it rubs off, making you feel rather special *and important* yourself; particularly when with her. Yes, together you are complete and can take any aggro life cares to throw your way.

The day of the wedding arrives and by now I'm so used to seeing my femme fatale that I'm at a loose-end, bored, brooding and just a touch jealous. The hours drag by with me thinking about her whilst knowing this is not a healthy reaction, as tomorrow the event will be history. After supper the gang are getting dickied-up for the Saturday night spree in Pompey; with the agents provocateurs goading soorpuss me, saying even when on a diet one is allowed to look at the menu - after concluding that makes sense I've succumbed to their prompting; they've reeled me in for a night on the sauce, *yeah Papa's goin' fishin'* - ten minutes later *foot to the boards* we're heading for the old haunts in Portsmouth. ***Game on!***

First stop the Albany; on stepping through the door we spy Ginge Heulet holding court with Geordie Joyce and some floozies - we know them all, so over we go to join in and have a laugh. 'Loopy Lou' *clearly toying with my affections* sniffs my neck while saying, "What's that nice smell, Shiner?" I look her in the eye and innocently answer"Soap!" - it must've been the tone of my voice, as she takes exception and skelps me one right on the kisser; wotta start to the evening. Some hotshot me - do I **ever** know how to put the dampers on a party! It just goes to show how

a little misunderstanding can result in disaster; I'd taken to using Wright's Coal Tar soap, which has an unusual carbolic fragrance and that's what Loopy had got a whiff of - perhaps I'd unintentionally slighted her in the past - *sometimes it's all too easy to fall out with 'the enemy'!*

I wasn't going to tell you this bit - but what the hell; we're two of a kind! After drowning my sorrows, following my instincts, I *somehow* ended up in The Mecca and 'copped off' with this slinky sexpot I'd had the pleasure of being involved with, some time back.

Now well astray, I've separated Julie from her pals and am *by habit* spinnin' the shit, trying to worm my way back into her favour, when 'the bint wi' the squint' catches me out by asking, "What did you say you do then?" I smartly tell her I'm an undertaker. This makes her laugh, so I say, "What's so funny, someone has to do it!" Nice as ninepence, she replies, "Last time you were a hovercraft pilot, and anyway, it's a bit of a coincidence!" "What is?" "Never mind, you'll see when you take me home!" Well, wha'd'ya know, at least I've not blown myself out; just goes to show that when lying you should stick with the same story. So, as promised, I end up seeing her home, and guess what? This **is** ridiculous, she now rents a flat above a funeral parlour, which we have to go through to get upstairs. ***Well, - bugger me bandy, isn't life a hoot -*** **top that!**

We've 'arsed' the coffee, polished off the gypsy creams and now sounding each other out by jousting with suggestive doubletalk - this, causing the pixielike Julie to squirm around on my knee. I'm thinking, 'it's not beyond the realms of possibility that we'll be playing Truth or Dare shortly', when she whispers in my 'shell like', "I've got a confession!" "What's that then?" "My husband is a Royal Marine!" **What? *- the tramp!*** That's rich - didn't see that coming; **married** - *nice one, hen, and cheating on the poor bloke!* When this registers I conclude I'm no better, as here am I doing the same, so, far from true to form, prise ma body from her clutches; make a flimsy excuse and vanish into the night. ***Game over!***

Who said a hard-oan disnae hae a conscience? Even so, I'll bet you're thinking '**mug**' but put it this way, I'm no hero and don't fancy the chance o' havin' a big mental 'Bootneck' on ma case - when I met the lovely K next day I was so glad I hadn't been a rotter betraying her trust; strange indeed, and well oot o' character; but I felt quite noble, whilst at the same

time fully aware that I could do without the strain of complications - *and there lies the case for the defence - so, make of it what you will!*

I still hated crewing the 'Black Pig', so kept slappin' in forra transfer; months felt like years, what a drag with no jollies or foreign service to look forward to. But we did go somewhere out of the ordinary - **Middlesbrough**. Wotta joke! I won't bore the arse off you with the naff details of a very ordinary run ashore; most likely down to the fact that we ourselves made little effort, getting no further than our natural habitat - the first boozer outside the docks. Ah ha! Hold it, I've just remembered - they had an excellently appointed Municipal Turkish Baths, to which we had 'free gangway'; *well worth a visit!* I've dug out a photo which shows Thermop and another submarine, berthed inboard of us while there - our pennant number was S55 and I see the other was S20 - don't recall her name, *(possibly Opportune)* however, note she was a P & O Class boat.

Can't speak for other old hands, but I've got a touch of arthritis these days - which I presume my service in submarines contributed to; since they could be cold and damp at the best of times, especially so when on 'passage routine' in 'roughers' or 'snorting' in cold heavy seas. *Hip - hip for paracetamol!* What if it were the Middle Ages and I had to visit the

HM submarine Thermopylae, visiting Middlesbrough

local witch *clad in a revealing cheeky little black off the shoulder number* at her dingy hut, with its dangling lopsided sign reading 'Mrs Trotter's Apothecary' deep in an enchanted forest, then cross her palm with silver for some foul 'magic' potion. If she was young, or not exactly an auld hag, and worth a dangle I'm also paying for a 'wee shot', which takes my mind off the pain for three or four minutes - that's right, nuthin' changes, I was ***'Speedy Gonzalez'*** way back then as well *(maybe that's why they call it a 'short time')*. Anyway, I've got a good thing going there, when the pitchfork-waving village loons, incited and whipped into a frenzy of evil dancing by the *paedo* parish priest, burn the sorceress at the stake - *aye thank the Good Lord for Paracetamol!* Wha'd'ya mean CRACKERS? Remember Mystic Meg! Of course you would ya sly git - you'd be pushin' the rest o' us aside. ***Don't give me that 'holier than thou' shit, pal!***

K introduced me to a new way of life, showing me places I would never have guessed existed - country pubs, jazz evenings at Botley, a theatre in Southampton playing the excellent Lionel Bart musical 'Oliver', trips to quiet beaches with novel picnic lunches. Yes, a thoroughly enjoyable time to look back on, in fact, never better. This remarkable fun-loving girl made life sparkle and in my eyes could do no wrong; so unlike those boring females who never knew where to go or what to do - you know, the lazy grunters who always say "Oh, anywhere, you choose", therefore, you never suss if your efforts were appreciated, or even worthwhile. When you finally find one that's got a brain it makes such a difference, allowing a fifty-fifty relationship, yes, a proper friendship, as opposed to towing some indifferent slag around trying to make her enjoy the date; so as not to feel too guilty when later tryin' tae get the leg over. What's that? You don't feel a bit o' guilt! Mm... OK, sorry! What's that yer sayin'? You don't know what I'm talking about - fair enough; maybe it's just me!

I enjoyed the Sunday routine, when at midday we all ambled along to the homely local pub on Elson Road, where the clientele were fortunate to be well-entertained by the landlady; what a character! - very theatrical. It was a sociable relaxing hour, after which we retired to a slap-up Sunday lunch, beautifully presented on the meticulously laid-out dining table - K's mother took great pride in this typically English and very civilized weekly event; *at which I felt honoured to be included.*

Months passed before she 'had her way' with me, sadistically we'd enjoyed denying ourselves, so as to savour the precious moment - I'm not romanticizing, in calling 'our secret' a unique experience; certainly no disappointment and well worth waiting for. This may sound ridiculous, but to add to the occasion, I swear at that very moment I saw a shooting star fall from the heavens, which I thought amazing and must indicate this was meant to be - **an omen!** Sounds soppy, I know, but it happened. I now wonder if I told my confidante about that star - ***I sure hope I did!***

Now that we had got our act together, so to speak, we weren't gettin' tore in about each other like rabbits on Viagra; but suffice to *again* say, practise makes perfect, and, also, K was more than comfortable about her healthy appetite for indulgence. To my eternal delight she had a natural talent for keeping it interesting *without making me feel used* never looking away, and whilst in the throes of passion uttering appropriate sounds while gazing straight into my eyes - ***now; that's special!***

We had a calamity, the time she missed out on Mother Nature's monthly gift - I admit to being more than just a little worried, and, while praying for a crop failure, kept going over in my mind what I would say to her parents, whose trust I felt I'd exploited. However, one evening she announced our troubles were over, letting me breathe a huge sigh of relief while promising myself to be more careful in future - *far from easy with such a zealous partner.* Nonetheless, it shouldn't've happened in the first place, as I always jumped off the train at Haymarket *(an Edinburgh quip)* - who knows, maybe it was a test; no, surely not; not K - **but you never can tell!**

During the commission we had two big maintenance periods in Pompey Dockyard, and again put on RA. The first time I took advantage of Taff the Aussie's bonzer offer, so 'cased-up' with him, his missus and sprog; 'fair dinkum', if compared to 'Aggie's'. On the second occasion I stayed snuggled up with K *(whose parents were in Wales at the time)* - sheer bliss, to say the least. Yes, the stolen moments are always the best!

It wasn't the Almighty
Who put his hand up her nightie
It was Roger the lodger
The randy old codger!

WHO! ME SIR?

I keep complaining about 'Thermop' never going anywhere, but here's one for you. We must've done something right, because we won a trip to Kiel in Germany - Oh my; **that was wunderbar,** leaving often recalled memories, which remain stamped on what's left of my brain.

We were tied up alongside the German frigate, Braunschweig. So there I was 'up top', on the casing, coppin' a look at the place, when it struck me that U-218, the U-boat responsible for my father's premature demise, was built here some twenty six years ago, and now here we are visiting 'the Fatherland' as a friendly nation. *'Tis indeed a sick old world!*

For you Tommy, ze vaur - she is ofer;
You vill haf a fair trial, and be shot in ze morning!

Wow! Our night out in Kiel was the highlight of the commission - at first it didn't seem to be going anywhere and very much like Rotterdam; where I'd been a couple of times previously - the bars we visited near the shipyards, dead, with little or no atmosphere; although this time we were swiggin' schnapps - *just because it seemed like a good idea.* All bored rigid, we agree that there must be better; so decide to go further afield in search of some action. We hit the street, hail a 'fast black', pile in and, fingers crossed, give the driver our usual instructions. After joking that being sailors, it's a gay bar we'll be wanting he 'wellies it' all the way to the bustling town centre, where he slaps on the anchors, grinding to a halt outside the glass canopied entrance of what appears to be a swanky hotel telling us this is a good place, which we **will** enjoy. So we pay the cabbie, thank him and full of drink-fuelled enthusiasm burst into the foyer.

It's all faux marble, glass and chrome, modern, plush and very sharp. I'm impressed when Herman, the liveried concierge, ushers us up a wide sweeping stairway with satin brass handrails, to the Kama Sutra Klub; a luxuriously appointed cocktail lounge on the first floor. Getting 'the red carpet treatment', we're escorted to a table on the perimeter of a small half-round dance floor, which has a little stage set behind it, and this, in front of big picture windows affording a panoramic view over the brightly-lit city centre. There's a quartet, in evening dress, playing the kind of music one expects of such a place, but no one up dancing - even though most tables are taken by smartly-dressed couples and foursomes.

This doesn't, although erotically named, seem like the kind of nightspot we had in mind, but since now here may as well give it a shot - so, hoping we haven't been hoodwinked, order a round of drinks from an attentive waiter who looks Latin and, like other staff members, resplendent in his uniform with its tailored waistcoat and long snow-white apron.

I've by now decided schnapps isn't for me, so, not fancying beer, swapped to whisky - *never a good move;* but I'd no intention of having a skinful and couldn't *there and then* decide on a safe alternative, however, I was, as always, making it a 'long one' by topping up with 'skoosh'.

Well, as luck would have it, we seem to have arrived at an interval; as there's entertainment laid on. After the break various decadent acts *(one with transvestites)* come on and do their thing; there's the usual comedian doubling as compère and although it's in German he takes pity and throws in quite a bit of English for our benefit - so we're getting the gist of things and with the colourful acts being visual the language barrier was unimportant. It was pretty weird stuff, but possibly that's the way it is in Germany - with hindsight, it seemed reminiscent of scenes in the film 'Cabaret'; come to think of it, the place we were in must have been a nightclub *within* the hotel. After a couple of drinks, we're settled in and while enjoying being made a fuss of; told we must see the main act, and so *feeling real welcome* decide this'll do for us, we'll stay put; there's no spare, but, so what! Let me tell you that ***yet again*** was one wise decision - and I'm sure you'll - agree when I paint you a picture.

At somewhere around eleven-thirty the tempo increased, heralding the star attraction's spectacular entrance - now, listen to me; if you don't just love this, you may as well call it a day. This tall raven-haired beauty appears - she looks real mean, like a gypsy dancer; but wearing a scanty revealing leopardskin number like Jane in 'Tarzan of the Jungle' films. She's striding confidently behind two snarling cheetahs straining on chains; we wonder, **'what are we gettin' here!'** as she parades the graceful animals round the dance floor. We understand the big cats are tame, but even with a few wets in us we're no heroes - so, sitting well back in our seats giggling nervously at each other: don't forget we're right out front. A wee guy, who is a dwarf decked-out as 'Sabu' with jewelled turban, dagger and pointy slippers shuffles on and leads the cheetahs off-stage, leaving 'Jane' posed

there before us, looking like Satan's bitch.

The lights dim - coloured 'spots' come on, then the jungle is projected onto a large screen, now dropping in front of the picture windows, simultaneously background jungle noises *with drums and the like* blast from the impressive sound system. There's a blinding flash as this massive roaring hairy gorilla leaps from nowhere and hurtles into the limelight screeching and beating his chest. It happened so quick that we almost jumped out our skin. What an entrance! It was **nuclear!**

Quicker than greased lightning, he pounces on the alarmed creature, now squealing, and struggling to preserve her virtue as the rampant brute wrestles his quarry to the floor - hoots maun; this could be construed as rape. Crumbs! He's got the jugs oot; *a fine upstanding pair*, he immediately grabs one and starts biting and slobbering over it. **She's smokin'**, *the erect nipples say it all* - now hang about, I'm not finished ***and neither is he***. All of a sudden 'King Kong' *intent on violating her* whips the bottom of her velcroed costume aside, and Christ Almighty! **He's got the 'tadger' out;** which must be angry, because it's roused - *waving at us like a baby's arm,* and hey, check the goolies swingin'; ***gee whizz, the boyz're oot the Barracks!*** There's a further *well-rehearsed* staged struggle to get 'Jane' in position - she's got the ankles tucked behind the ears and **'he's in like Flynn'** - bloody hell, this is shocking, he's actually 'givin' her one' right there in front of us.

"It's surprising what's in me ole ditty box"

This isn't simulated; no way - they are less than six feet from our table, and seeing is believing; he's rammin' it home - *arse goin' like a fiddler's elbow.* This randy pair are amazing, sliding round the floor making sure everyone 'cops an eyeful', while beltin' away at each other like there's no tomorrow. He's beastin' at it for ages - by now, so engrossed, we, the audience, don't exist - howlin' like a wounded banshee, he finally galloped to the 'money-shot'; causing Jane's lust-filled eyes to roll in their sockets; as in a spiritual moment the Fräulein stared towards the heavens. ***Jings,*** *wotta climax* - now, ***'that's show business'!!!***

'Gerry' Attrick was so turned on, he was up on his feet wanting to join in this outrageous behaviour, and so, had to be restrained by the waiters. Holy shit, that was some performance - he must've been 'sweatin' neaters' in that gorilla suit. I wonder where the management dug that pair up *and what they were on*, I've never to this day seen the likes and should've enquired as to whether they were in need of an agent.

Blimey, **never** mix schnapps and whisky! The next morning wasn't too clever, talk about death warmed up - ma heid wus nippin'; at the slightest noise it erupted, just like you see in cartoons; barely touched my Tot, couldn't face it - and that's saying something. I was duty-watch and that was one long day, but **what a phenomenal night** - *aye, yae cannae beat a wee bit o' culture!* A show like that is never forgotten and makes one feel just a touch inadequate - naa, that's a load o' cobblers; green with envy is nearer the truth. I guess that lucky old 'gorilla' must've shoved his way to the front o' the weddin' tackle queue - ***cos he copped the lion's share!***

There was a long weekend *(a 'Friday while')* well worth a mention. Bruvver Streames *(who was qualified so to do)* had requested the use of Dolphin's yacht 'Cyclops', on which we had fun in the English Channel, where a stiff summer breeze filled the sails. Cyclops was around thirty feet O.A.L., extremely well built and appointed *(if my memory serves me well, she, like many things, was 'liberated' from the 'Third Reich Treasure Trove' as booty at the end of WWII).* It was the first time I'd crewed on such a craft, but can't speak for the others; who seemed to know what they were doing. The weather was brilliant, so I was all for nipping over to 'La belle France', but strangely no one else was the slightest bit keen, so instead we 'lorded it' at Cowes - *cheers Bruv, you were a star!*

As the 'commish' wore on so did my nine-year stretch in Her Majesty's Navy, so I was at the crossroads, in a quandary as to which path to take; yes, this predicament required careful consideration. Although just a small cog, I enjoyed life whirling round on Pusser's carousel, so, should I pledge allegiance to the throne for a further thirteen years and go for the full twenty-two; with a pension to look forward to at the end of my service? I was still only a Killick, but had already passed my Trade and Educational tests to take me to Chief, so was 'on track'; however, it was a roster-system for advancement, therefore, a case of 'wait in the queue, pal', and that sodding roster was a bone of contention for those with ambition.

On the other hand if the next thirteen years whizzed by as quick as the last nine, I'd be through in no time. But, there again, did I really fancy hitting Civvy Street so late in life; who'd want me? What would I be able to do *of interest* to keep myself out 'the grubber'? I also had to take K into the equation, as by now she was the 'one and only'; in fact *discounting myself* the most important person in my own little private world - *we had never said we loved each other;* ***because, we didn't need to!***

So there you have it, if I signed on, then volunteered for nukes, which would be the next step *and the only way to go* I'd probably be promoted to PO in the next couple of years - that is, if I could keep my nose clean, work hard, grovel tae ma betters an' back-stab them wot were below me. But the other side of the coin was; I would then be stationed at Faslane - the nukes' Base. After a fair bit of soul-searching, the problem I foresaw was losing K; her being a complex creature, with needs and an appetite that would not take kindly to long separations. Furthermore, a girl from a background such as hers, deserved better than to be marooned in Married Quarters at Faslane ***- 'twas indeed a dilemma.***

In retrospect I've thought many times over the years, that had it been the other way round; if the 'Thermop' commission came first and I had been on **Odin** at decision time, it would then have been no contest - I'd've happily signed on the dotted line. I'd like to say I enjoyed my time on Thermopylae - but, not so; it really got to me, making myself, and others believe we hated 'the Andrew' - even then, I wasn't so blind that I couldn't, see that wasn't the case. Furthermore, we were by now more than two years into the commission, which had to end sometime soon.

I'd mused over this so many times, weighing up the pros and cons; when it came to pass that the Jimmy *(long since crucified as worse than useless)* unwittingly made my mind up for me. As I recall, we were submerged in the Channel *shadowing a Russian 'trawler'* when the klutz strode along from the Control Room, with a sheet of signal pad in his hand, and the usual sneering haughty look on his coupon. After bellowing "Make way" while elbowing the scum in his passage aside, he barks, in front of the duty messmen waiting in line for the lunches to be plated up, "Chef, this signal has come through; your nine year contract expires on 25TH August: do you wish to sign on again?" then, tactlessly adds, "By the way your Shallow Water Diver's request can now be recommended; but here's the rub, you'll obviously have to re-enlist!" - *subtle or wot?*

Yes Sir, sing an' ah'll dance! - that's rich; did he think I was stupid and he was being smart *or did he really hate me that much?* This, was the same snidey cunt who'd been jerkin' me around for the past two years and now, all of a sudden, I **can** be spared. Come off it, pal, if you're attempting to be devious, at least try not to be so transparent! ***So what happened to courtesy?*** He didn't even have the decency to call me to the Wardroom; this was supposedly an Officer and a gentleman. There again, the truth was, this clown of the first order didn't give a fish's fart whether I signed on or not; as far as he was concerned, a serf in Dolphin would open a box marked 'Chefs' and send a replacement android.

I hasten to add, a deciding factor causing myself, and many valued others to relinquish our service was the scandalously poor pay structure suffered by armed forces personnel during the fifties and sixties. Back then I was paid the paltry sum of £22 per fortnight - *including submarine pay*. There was of course no overtime to keep the wolf from the door, and *as already stated,* advancement slow. So, we 'lived for the moment' as it was impossible to save, therefore a masterpiece of understatement to say the financial future looked bleak *(we weren't to know substantial increases were soon to be granted; making the Royal Navy a lucrative career).*

I will also mention that on my service files, my Trade Efficiency Assessment for the previous five years had been recorded as 'VG Superior', whereas my worth from Thermopylae, on which I worked my tits off in poor conditions and **never once** let the side down, was dropped to 'VG

Satisfactory' which would've effectively slowed my advancement to PO. You'll, no doubt, remember I said at the start of the 'commish' that the Captain and the Jimmy were a pair o' ratbags - **confirmed**; not an ounce of gratitude between them! Well, c'est la fuckin' vie, shithouses in control of our destinies, we don't like it, but *being of 'the lower orders'* must accept it. I suppose, after hearing that, it's a foregone conclusion that, hoping I wouldn't live to rue the day, I terminated my distinguished career in the Submarine Service by politely telling the ignoramus to 'shove it', knowing full well that, because of my attitude, he'd be glad to see the back of me *(by the way, I'm still stickin' needles in the dolls)*.

Aye, 'twas a tough auld life!

22: "Roll On My Nine"

Let's not brood, as *being overqualified* I was never likely to become First Sea Lord - actually, I thought I was 'in wae a shout', but some joker who claimed his handle was Varyl Cargill Begg pipped me at the post. So anyway, in a matter of weeks I got the elbow and was drafted into Dolphin as 'Spare Crew' and *(to my regret)* never asked if I wished to reconsider my decision - I thought that was coming, because I had it so easy for about six weeks, but in the immortal words of Leading Steward Packer, *(who, like so many others, I fondly remember)* ***even* I *can get it wrong!***

I was billeted at Pactolus Block in a Mess that I never knew existed; and appointed Killick of the Mess ***(top dog)***, which really meant, no duties - so, left to my own devices *suiting me just fine*. There were only two other guys in the Mess, both qualified submariners from 'the Big Smoke' *who referred to everyone as 'throbbers',* a quiet pair, thick as thieves and not long out of DQs - each 'wif previous' having been 'inside' more than once; a pair of scoundrels, if judged by the scars on their faces. To me it appeared that Pusser was at a loss as to what to do with these two reprobates who, like myself, weren't in a duty watch *(Blue Card men),* so during the working day they formed part of the 'skirmishing party' that wandered round Dolphin picking up litter and keeping the Base 'tickety-boo'.

My job was to see the gaff was kept tip-top; which was a doddle as nobody ever came to inspect it - I don't think many realized its location, ensconced as it was behind the NAAFI and some offices. Another bonus, was; being at the sea wall the shuttered storm windows at the far end of the Mess looked out over the Solent towards Southsea, and outside these windows there lay a narrow strip of pebble beach, *hidden from prying eyes*. Being early June, I took advantage of this and would climb out to loaf there worshipping the sun god all day, only breaking for my Tot and the midday feeding frenzy. Each evening I'd hand in my station card and shoot-off ashore to meet my svelte princess, so life was 'a bowl o' cherries' - *they say 'home is where the heart is' and I'd be there yet, with not a care in the world,* ***if*** *it was down to me*.

So what about my two messmates, with whom I got on famously; and why not, since we were all 'on a good thing'. You'll remember 'Brigham' Young's scrap car business; well now, this enterprising pair also had a sideline. At 'secure the hands' they leapt on the first Liberty Boat at four on the dot, steamed across the water and raced each other round to Billy Manning's Funfair by Clarence Pier at Southsea, where they were 'barkers' on the waltzer and dodgems. Who knows how long they spun that little caper out, as they were at it before I arrived and still had it going when I was drafted, once again, to RNB Portsmouth, this time for a course *(known as rehab)* to deactivate and prepare me to fend for myself in the ***real*** world. There were a number of trades on offer - bricklaying, mechanic, steeplejack, etc. I chose electrician's mate; not planning this as a career, merely thinking it would be handy for household jobs in the future.

'Vicky' Barracks hadn't changed a bit, as far as I could see, still a big seemingly empty place *as quiet as Aberdeen on a flag day.* Six other guys were on this particular course, all RAs, so, did the disappearing act at four, with just about everyone else in the Barracks. Me; well, I'm back up in one of the big old Victorian Messes with three other old hands, who having 'finished their time' are, now, of no interest to Pusser.

In the next Mess is a legend, who I *like most of the fleet* have heard of, but never met, and had wondered if he *(she?)* was just another fable. Like, for instance, the 'Cream Cookie Man', who *folklore has it* would buy a big box of cream cookies then entice bored young matelots up Portsdown Hill where he'd get the kit off and pay the 'sprogs' to throw the cookies at him, while he pranced around in the scud indulging in a bit of 'hand relief' - *well, who knows!* - but, many's the time I heard versions of this tale repeated on the messdecks. So anyway, next door we had none other than 'Tokyo Rose', who was also 'demobbing'. It's lost to me in the mists of time, but I believe he was a three-badge Killick Steward whose favoured mode of dress *when off duty* was a kimono and bamboo-framed spectacles. I never had the brass neck to go through for a proper gander, but more than once caught a glimpse of the 'tranny' in all 'her' splendour through the *half glass-paned* Mess door. Oh yes, it takes all types; and wouldn't life be such a bore without the likes of Tokyo Rose?

The instructor, a quiet-spoken easy-going POEM, didn't overwork or

push us on the course, if we didn't listen *or even turn up* what did he care; it made no difference to him. As expected, it was really a bit of a skive and all pretty basic stuff, but it's amazing how much we should, and don't know about such an important *relied upon* commodity - so, yes, it was worthwhile. Something that proved valuable, when, in years to come, I quietly followed the stampeding herd and profited from a *lucrative* wee dabble in the *then buoyant* property market.

The peace and harmony generally enjoyed throughout the Barracks was shattered at this time of the year, by the Pompey Field Gun Crew practising endlessly at the far end of the Parade Ground. A demanding physical challenge *(much more arduous than the watered-down version of today)* endured by a team of desperadoes, picked for their brute strength, daring and agility, training to compete against the Guzz and Fleet Air Arm crews in the Royal Tournament at Earls Court.

Now, there's a thing, the Royal Tournament was a popular inter-services annual event; now most probably *like 'Navy Days' at Rosyth* - had the plug pulled; disappeared, along with so many other things due once again to financial cutbacks. What **do** the overpaid Ministers, heads of department, fat cats, freeloaders and spongers *'hard at the lash' on the Whitehall merry-go-round* do with the dross left in the bottom of the kitty after they've raped the system and blantantly fiddled their expenses? **And we let it happen!** *Are we happy?* ***That'll be right!*** *—* **Is it me?**

HMS Dolphin's crest

23: Honourable Discharge

Well, that's it, 'how time flies', I've done my leaving routine, handed in my AGR *(gas mask)* and everything else Pusser wanted returned. I've got my discharge papers ***(Honourable Discharge),*** Pusser and I have said a tearful adieu and 'auld scattercash' is off up the road - a self-made failure with a suitcase full o' memories - but, no medals, no pension, *not even a 'luckpenny'* in my oil-guzzling Zephyr Six; possessing considerably less dosh than when I joined up in a previous existence nine carefree years ago. I'm not elated, or sure I've done the right thing and more than just a little concerned about K, who hasn't tried to influence me in any way, although she, like myself, must 've been in a turmoil over her and our future.

I couldn't understand why Doogie, by now a PO and one of the Navy's specialized divers, wasn't in Pompey Barracks, as having joined 'the Mob' on the same day, it went without saying we should be discharged together; making me wonder if the big bugger had become institutionalized and 'signed on' - in turn making me doubt my own decision moreso. However, he appeared a few weeks later; explaining he'd been on a hush-hush recovery assignment in the Med, where Pusser required him to stay put to complete the job, rewarding him handsomely for his co-operation.

Doogie, *despite having been cast as a ne'er-do-well in his formative years, has turned out to be a man of vision* - being a star in the diving world, knew exactly what was going on in the 'big bucks' North Sea Oil Exploration game, so had taken every course necessary to secure a top appointment diving there for a multinational consortium. Oor Doogie had his future sorted, having, on his last Leave, had an interview in Aberdeen and been snapped up by one of the global giants; who thought they'd 'won a watch' on seeing his track record. Yes, oor Doogie was indeed a prize as Royal Navy training is *as I keep repeating* second to none. Also, at that time the North Sea Oil Industry hadn't been up and running long, so professional Saturation Divers were as rare as hens' teeth.

Well, there we have it, I had joined the wrong branch, but wasn't to know at the time - just like at the supermarket checkout; after making a logical decision, **I inevitably choose the morons' queue!**

24: Back to Reality!

Shedloads were made in the North Sea, especially by Deep Saturation Divers, *who were the cream;* big Doogie's salary was astounding, he was paid more per month than he'd got in a year from Pusser. In next to no time he was established in an elegant New Town flat and changing his flash cars more often than he did his socks back in **'the happy days'**. He and his diver pals threw riotous parties, where they raised more than just a few eyebrows and did some 'damage' as there was always 'entertainment' laid on - yeah, no half measures - these guys could afford style; in fact so much so that their wild rave-ups fast became an urban legend. None moreso than Doogie's stag party - the most memorable; ***but a complete farce.***

What had happened, was - Doogie and his whacko mate Cootzie, also a 'Sat. Diver', had both been going out with *(and slipping a length to)* this pretty little hippie-chick and 'quicker than that' she was 'up the stick' - *by who knows?* Doogie, being the big softie we all knew and loved, decided to marry her because she was "a nice wee burd" and "it was only fair!" Knowing him and Cootzie they probably tossed a coin and Doogie lost.

Anyway, this party was the mother of all stag nights - *never outdone*; he'd hired a function hall, decked out with streamers and white 'balloons', in the prestigious Minto Hotel uptown. The buffet was superb, with free bevvy and so much scran that the long trestle-table, postioned against the far wall, was dipped down groaning in the centre. But Doogie's **'The Man'** and this ain't about nosh. He's engaged seven strippers, and they've brought an extra one along, as the 'bonus ball'.

'Twas a hoot from the start; when the snake dancer's python pished on her as she held it up; we were endin' oorsels, but being a professional the clarty bitch carried on as if nothing happened. Another *artist,* who, dressed as, and doing a saucy Charlie Chaplin act *in an ill-fitting suit,* performed 'strip the willow' to whoops of glee. Brace yersel for **'The Freebie'** a rough bit o' kit wi' spots 'n' specs, who fancied herself as a go-go dancer. This we did not want to see *especially in the buff* so there was an uproar, with the alpha males shouting "Gies a brek an' dinnae bother, hen", while throwing sausage rolls at the poor girl; who 'wusnae the full shillin''.

The rowdy audience had to be encouraged by Doogie, and the rented skirt, to give her a chance. Well, we were in stitches and just about 'fillin' oor breeks' laffin' as she went to it accompanied by a tape of Miss Bassey singing 'Big Spender'. The wee nutter was 'oot'r box' doing what she thought was dancing, while peeling off - something I try to forget, and would've preferred not to have seen - rolls o' dimpled fat an' paps like spaniels' lugs. Here's the worst bit *(or the best, depending on your preferences)*, Doogie, 'in fine fettle' *troosers roond ankles* brushing the sarnies aside, went for an Oscar and 'gave'r one' on the table; well... if anyone was entitled! - *it was his party, wasn't it?* ***Wotta hero!***

Then came a trim creature dressed as a ballet dancer - judging by her antics she must've actually been one - we were certainly ready for her, after watching the poisoned dwarf's nauseating display. The next treat; twins dressed as pupil and teacher ***with cane,*** theirs was a unique well-rehearsed act - I did so enjoy the finale, which was a **good sound spanking**, with the overexcited crowd baying for blood *(everyone loves a whip-round)*.

The best, as always, was saved for last. **The policewoman and the traffic warden**; a pair o' startlers. One blonde, the other dark, both with long hair - can't remember which was which, as they got their kit off so quick and stuck right into their lesbo act with such enthusiasm that we'd've taken bets, as to them actually being gay - *it's surprising the fun two consenting adults can have!* But Doogie *who, on reflection, looked pretty slick in his beautifully tailored tartan tuxedo* said it was just an act, as he and Cootzie had engaged their services on many an occasion and "screwed thum senseless" in the privacy of the impressive Georgian flat.

Well, Doogie did the deed *in the nick o' time* making an 'honest woman' of the 'damaged' hippie-chick and giving the mystery-child a name - as was on the cards from the start, the union ended in divorce, costing our easy-going pal a packet. But, to give the generous bugger credit, he gave the snapper a head start in life by providing a first-class education at Edinburgh's finest young ladies' college. Our old mate *(far from a reformed man)* is now living 'down under' where *I'm told* he cohabits with a Thai girl and runs his own successful diving and salvage company.

I thought it stood to reason, that Joe and Benny, having been 'New Entrants' some weeks ahead of me, nine years previously, would therefore

be discharged first. However, in Joe's case, I hadn't taken into account that, on joining, he was under age for 'the Andrew's' definition of 'man's time', therefore classed as a Junior for his first few months, so his nine years service actually started later than mine and likewise his 'demob'.

I hadn't seen Joe for ages, as our recent Leaves didn't coincide, so it came as a surprise when I found that, not only was he not home, but, in the Persian Gulf, on the frigate HMS Minerva. He finally arrived home just before Christmas, and after a few weeks R&R, joined Ferranti's at Crewe Toll in Edinburgh; who, at the time, were big in defence contracts. Joe *being an intelligent chap* quickly became one of their boffins - often sent abroad, as far as South Korea, to sort out problems in the nose cones of Harrier Jump Jets. He stayed with Ferranti for the rest of his career, eventually taking early retirement - *for health reasons*. My good friend Joe has, I regret, sailed his last voyage - I suppose, we all often think of those we have known: **if** there's a heaven... ***well... whae kens!***

No doubt you'll be wondering about Benny - **me too**, as I'd like to say a few words about him, but I'm afraid I can't - Benny disappeared. After his posting to Woomera I never saw or heard of him again; he may've 'signed on', stayed 'dahn sowf' or even changed his spots and got religion - *don't laugh, stranger things have happened to less complex guys*.

K - well, I've been putting off telling you this depressing bit, because I ***still*** feel remorse; so thinking about it is like going through the sad episode again. K will be forever on a pedestal; never asked where she stood, made demands, or even as much as mentioned marriage. I could be looking back through them good old rose-tinted glasses, but can only remember her smile, never an argument, harsh word or disagreement.

I cherish vivid memories of an emotional reunion, when the girl I should have shared my life with, came up to Edinburgh a couple of months or so after my demob. The morning I met her off the overnight express, she looked better than ever and it sure felt good when we embraced *- jings, I'd missed her.* We made the most of an unforgettable week; *screwing's like dancing* - ***a good partner makes all the difference.*** Talk about 'going for gold' -let me tell you, because my soulmate was on her 'best behaviour' the week passed so quick 'twas like a dream. I've a vague idea that she may've hinted about getting a job and taking a flat in the City, but it's so

long ago that, today, ah could be givin' ma mind a treat.

Being unsettled was par for the course, following close on a decade in the 'Imperial Navy', so after years of fun and adventure I was restless and determined to 'make good', but *ever cautious* knowing if I made commitments I'd never *for financial reasons* be able to take any chances careerwise. We exchanged frequent letters, and *after considering re-enlistment,* I was back 'chefing it'; having already had a pop at a Rep job selling a cold welding process, but the company *(Molecular Metals)* refused to extend the crap territory they'd allocated me in the sparsely populated Borders. Being keen, I canvassed the area 'dawn till dusk', so soon ran out of potential customers and had to call it a day; then the snidey gits sickened me by neglecting to forward my final commission cheque; *promised on return of sales aids and briefcase*. Mumble mumble, mustn't grumble - as you know, I'm not the type to hold a grudge - **not much** - so, pray the rotten slimeballs went down the tubes **bigtime.**

Since I'm unable to accept failure, K suffered; with me having nothing positive or interesting to say the letters became less frequent - only because I took longer and longer to answer hers. It got so bad, that she must've thought I'd strayed into the arms of another; consequently *dropping a bombshell* she wrote me a 'stinker', facetiously asking what had happened to her "inky-fingered lover". I'd never seen this side of her; so the verbal lashing came as a shock, burdened by gloom, I put off and put off responding and the longer I dithered, the harder it became ***- to my eternal regret, I took the coward's way out and never did.***

I blew it, and, to this day wearing my 'hair shirt'; far from proud of my lack of obligation to that selfless girl; but, when musing, like to tell myself it just wasn't meant to be, and she went on to exonerate me by finding happiness with a worthy *and deserving* suitor. Without wishing to put myself down, I oft-times wonder if I missed out on a dowry - and what K saw in the likes of me. Flippancy aside, I take little solace in the assumption that being callous is a human frailty; ***and that eventually I got my just rewards.*** So, although I had the best intentions and no wish to trifle with the affections of such a fabulous person, there's no excuse for what I did *or rather didn't do* - and since it's a bit late in the day to make amends, the guilt remains. ***Oh to have had a crystal ball!***

**She gave me a pearl tie tack, an'd'you know wot; every time I see it her words haunt me "Pearls are for tears" - probably the two biggest mistakes of my life were letting K escape and leaving the Imperial Navy.*

I'll bring my tale to conclusion, by telling you - I still had 'a thing' about cars, so was forever fucking about with them and, although nowhere near Doogie's league, had a 3.4 Mk II British racing green Jaguar with chrome wire wheels, a nice 'honest example' which looked 'a million dollars'. This would be a year or so after my apprehensive return to Civvy Street; in which time I'd got to know a number of proprietors of small garages and coachworks. Because of this pursuit, I met and became friendly with Lionel Hook, an ex-schoolteacher with a similar passion for prestige cars. So much so, that he'd left the teaching profession, jumped in with both feet and bought a twee mews garage, trading as Christie and Price at Circus Lane near Stockbridge in the city centre, from where he dealt in interesting pre-owned cars. Since it was a one-man business, Lionel was hard-pushed to run it on his own, therefore always grateful when I turned up in my spare time, to lend a hand and trade my expertise forra bit o' 'bunce'.

Before long the business was doing so well that we were often still there wheelin' an' dealin' at midnight. This meant I was finding it a bit heavy going to my chefs' job next day, especially when on early shift *requiring me to be up an' out by five-thirty* so I put it to Lionel that I should jack in the old catering lark - learn to 'cook the books' instead and work with him full-time. Anyway, that's what happened - and so it came to be that I joined the ranks of the self-employed, finally finding a niche I enjoyed in an industry full o' characters, rife wi' gossip an' a barrel o' laffs. So, Lionel provided the stepping stone I needed to reinvent myself as a motor trader and retailer; but that's another story, in which I quickly found out how to make a small fortune in the car trade ***- start with a large one!***

Bollocks! Can't believe ah've gone an' shared all that wi' you. I suppose I ought to say "Your company's been a pleasure" - ***but I'd be lying!*** Must dash, as Nurse will be arriving shortly to give me my daily bath, shave and medication - *an' if ma luck's in, she might scold me;* **toodle-pip!**

Yeah, them certainly were

Due to nothing other than the ravages of time, the author, currently sectioned, languishes sedated in the security of a small state-run institution on the outskirts of Edinburgh, and when not denying everything in therapy relishes the company of visitors who help while away the lonely hours; generally spent in a dreamlike stupor drooling over videos of topless Brazilian Ladies' Beach Volleyball teams. Any correspondence should include a current copy of 'Hot Asian Babes' in good condition.

Many names have been changed to protect the guilty, but I've no doubt some of you 'old campaigners' had a 'sweat on', knowing which of the characters were you. Try not to worry, yer secrets are safe wi' me!

Any koffindodgers missed out who feel they deserved a mention for their indiscretions, please accept my humblest 'ajopilies' an' keep takin' the ugly pills!

D'you see that silly old fool in the tatty Afghan coat, string vest and saggy long johns dozing in front of the telly? Who is he; yer dad? OK, look at him closely - can you catch the trace of a smile on his weathered face? D'you really know what he was like before you came along? He wasn't always the stupid ole git you see stretched out, gently snoring on the couch. Oh no! When mummy met him he was different to all the others, exciting, even dangerous - that was the attraction. But this 'ere's wot 'appened. The little woman changed'm and now spends her days torturing herself, wonderin' why she married the 'borin' auld fart'.

Here endeth the Lesson!

Glossary

Andrew - Navy
Banyan - Alcoholic picnic
Bootneck - Royal Marine
Bowser - Airfield tanker
Boat - Submarine
Buffer - PO Seaman
Chief - Chief Petty Officer
Chippy - Carpenter
Casing - Submarine's deck
Cap Tallies - Ribbon with ship's name
Cackleberries - Eggs
Coxswain - Senior Petty Officer
Crushers - Regulating branch thugs
DQs - Detention quarters
Divisions - Parade
EM - Electrical mechanic
ERA - Engine room artificer
Fast black - Taxi
Grippo - Freebie
GI - Gunnery Instructor
Goffers - Cold drinks
Gregorys - Spectacles
Guzz - Plymouth
Heads - Toilets
Hairy Fairy - Fleet air arm bod
'Haigs Dimple' - Simple
Jimmy - 1ST Lieutenant
Killick - Leading Hand
Long spit - throw up
Line ahead - Single file
Master at Arms - Regulating Chief
ME - Mechanical engineer
MoD - Ministry of Defence
Number Ones - Best uniform
Number Threes - Duty uniform
Number Eights - Working rig
Number Nines - Punishment
NAAFI - Navy Army & Air Force Institute
OD - Ordinary Seaman
OOD - Officer of the Day
OOW - Officer of the Watch
Outside Wrecker - Chief ERA
Pompey - Portsmouth
Pongoes - Soldiers
Poor oot - Pour out
PO - Petty Officer
PO Tel - Petty Officer Telegraphist
Politician - Parasite
Pigs - Officers
QM - Quartermaster
RPO - Regulating Petty Officer
RNAS - Royal Naval Air Station
Seaman - Slave
Stoker - Mechanical engineer
SBA - Sickbay Attendant
Slops - Naval Store
Subby - Sub Lieutenant
Shitehawks - Seagulls
SEATO - South-east Asia Treaty Organisation
SLR - Single lens reflex camera
Senior Rates - Chiefs and POs
Scrumpy - Rocketfuel
TOT - Rum issue
Wardroom - Pigsty

The author was not alone in reporting that submarines were 'dark, cold, damp, oily, and crammed full of intricate machinery'. These cartoons from *Thumper*, the magazine of the SSN *Churchill*, well summarise both the physical discomforts that submariners endure and the sense of fraternity that this inspires. James Perowne, a distinguished Cold War submariner and Flag Officer Submarines in its aftermath, remarks, 'It's not the men who make the machines, but the machines who make the men'.

*Afterthought - as reported on page 249 - at present there are seven decommissioned nuclear submarines *with ultra-safe MoD approved reactors,* lying redundant in Rosyth Dockyard - one wonders as to the feasibility of reactivating their plants, in order to provide *soon to be sorely needed* power, which could then be fed into the national grid.

'Snappers' are an expensive fashion accessory, ***The Party's over!*** *There are too many people - there are too many*

people - there are too many people - there are too

many people - there are too many people - there are

too many people - there are too many people - there

*are too many people - there are too many people - there are too many
people - there are too many people - there are too many people - there are
too many people - there are too many people - there are too many people
- there are too many people - there are too many people - there are too
many people - there are too many people - there are too many people - there
are too many people - there are too many people - there are too many
people - there are too many people - there are too many people - there are
too many people - there are too many people - there are too many people
- there are too many people - there are too many people - there are too
many people - there are too many people - there are too many people - there
are too many people - there are too many people - there are too many
people - there are too many people - there are too many people - there are
too many people - there are too many people - there are too many people
- there are too many people - there are too many people - there are too
many people - there are too many people - there are too many people - there
are too many people - there are too many people - there are too many
people - there are too many people - there are too many people - there are
too many people - there are too many people - there are too many people
- there are too many people - there are too many people - there are too
many people - there are too many people - there are too many people - there
are too many people - there are too many people - there are too many
people - there are too many people - there are too many people - there are
too many people - there are too many people - there are too many people
- there are too many people - there are too many people - there are too
many people - there are too many people - there are too many people - there
are too many people - there are too many people - there are too many
people - there are too many people - there are too many people - there are
too many people - there are too many people - there are too many people
- there are too many people - there are too many people - there are too
many people - there are too many people - there are too many people - there
are too many people - there are too many people - there are too many
people - there are too many people - there are too many people - there are
too many people - there are too many people - there are too many people
- there are too many people - there are too many people - there are too
many people - there are too many people - there are too many people - there
are too many people - there are too many people - there are too many there
are too many people - there are too many people - there are too many
people - there are too many people - there are too many people - there are*

*too many people - there are too many people - there are too many people
- there are too many people - there are too many people - there are too
many people - there are too many people - there are too many people - there
are too many people - there are too many people - there are too many
people - there are too many people - there are too many people - there are
too many people - there are too many people - there are too many people
- there are too many people - there are too many people - there are too
many people - there are too many people - there are too many people - there
are too many people - there are too many people - there are too many
people - there are too many people - there are too many people - there are
too many people - there are too many people - there are too many people
- there are too many people - there are too many people - there are too
many people - there are too many people - there are too many people - there
are too many people - there are too many people - there are too many
people - there are too many people - there are too many people - there are
too many people - there are too many people - there are too many people
- there are too many people - there are too many people - there are too
many people - there are too many people - there are too many people - there
are too many people - there are too many people - there are too many
people - there are too many people - there are too many people - there are
too many people - there are too many people - there are too many people
- there are too many people - there are too many people - there are too
many people - there are too many people - there are too many people - there
are too many people - there are too many people - there are too many
people - there are too many people - there are too many people - there are
too many people - there are too many people - there are too many people
- there are too many people - there are too many people - there are too
many people - there are too many people - there are too many people - there
are too many people - there are too many people - there are too many
people - there are too many people - people - there are too many people
- there are too many people - there are too many people - there are too
many people - there are too many people - there are too many people - there
are too many people - there are too many people - there are too many
people - there are too many people - there are too many people - there are
too many people - there are too many people - there are too many people
- there are too many people - there are too many people - there are too*

It's not just the roads that are overcrowded; it's the whole effin' world!

Wake up!